THE PATRIOTISM OF DESPAIR

A VOLUME IN THE SERIES

Culture and Society after Socialism

edited by Bruce Grant and Nancy Ries

A list of titles in this series is available at www.cornellpress.cornell.edu

The Patriotism of Despair

Nation, War, and Loss in Russia

Serguei Alex. Oushakine

Cornell University Press *Ithaca and London*

Repeated efforts were made to obtain permission to include previously published materials. If acknowledgment has been omitted, rights holders are encouraged to notify the publisher.

First published 2009 by Cornell University Press
First printing, Cornell Paperbacks, 2009

Printed in the United States of America

Library of Congress Cataloging-in-Publication Data

Ushakin, S. (Sergei), 1966–
    The patriotism of despair : nation, war, and loss in Russia / Serguei Alex. Oushakine.
        p. cm. — (Culture and society after socialism)
    Includes bibliographical references and index.
    ISBN 978-0-8014-4679-5 (cloth : alk. paper)—ISBN 978-0-8014-7557-3 (pbk. : alk. paper)
    1. Post-communism—Social aspects—Russia (Federation)—Barnaul (Altaiskii krai)   2. Political culture—Russia (Federation)—Barnaul (Altaiskii krai)   3. Patriotism—Russia (Federation)—Barnaul (Altaiskii krai)   4. Social change—Russia (Federation)—Barnaul (Altaiskii krai)   5. Ethnology—Russia (Federation)—Barnaul (Altaiskii krai)   6. Barnaul (Altaiskii krai, Russia)—Civilization.   I. Title.   II. Series: Culture and society after socialism.
    DK781.B3.U76 2009
    957'.3—dc22
2008049114

Cornell University Press strives to use environmentally responsible suppliers and materials to the fullest extent possible in the publishing of its books. Such materials include vegetable-based, low-VOC inks and acid-free papers that are recycled, totally chlorine-free, or partly composed of nonwood fibers. For further information, visit our website at www.cornellpress.cornell.edu.

Cloth printing   10 9 8 7 6 5 4 3 2 1

Paperback printing   10 9 8 7 6 5 4 3 2 1

For Kim Lane Scheppele

Contents

Acknowledgments

As any research, this book is a product of multiple social interactions, both planned and accidental. I am greatly indebted to all those people and institutions who gave me a chance to pursue the questions that interested me for years.

Preliminary research for the book was supported by Columbia University Dissertation Traveling grant and by a grant from the Global Supplementary Grant Program, Open Society Institute (New York). The fieldwork in Barnaul was funded by the International Dissertation Research Fellowship of the Social Science Research Council and the American Council of Learned Societies, and by the Special Program Grant of Open Society Institute and Civic Education Project (New York). During the writing, I was supported by fellowships from the Social Science Research Council and The Josephine De Kármán Fellowship Trust. A year-long fellowship at the Harriman Institute at Columbia University in 2005–2006 was extremely helpful for finalizing my research.

Work on this book started at Columbia University. I am grateful to my colleagues, Narges Erami, Krista Hegburg, Sofian Merabet, Nauman Naqvi, Maya Nadkarni, and Juan Obario, for their willingness to listen even when my facts were still unclear and my interpretations were only half baked. Nicholas Dirks, Bruce Grant, Mark von Hagen, Marilyn Ivy, and Rosalind Morris provided much needed advice when I was in doubt, and I thank them for their trust in my work. I have been lucky to work with my supervisor, Rosalind Carmel Morris, whose theoretical breadth and discursive virtuosity at times would leave me speechless. Over the years, Roz has been pushing me to recognize (and expand) my own limits, and I thank her for this truly exceptional intellectual experience. I thank three more people whose conversations, lectures, and seminars have changed my intellectual makeup forever. Alan Bass showed me that psychoanalysis and deconstruction do not have to be esoteric (or weird). Partha Chatterjee taught me how to read Foucault through Gramsci. Boris Gasparov opened up for me the world of Russian formalists; without him, my passion for Shklovsky and Jakobson would not be the same.

I learned immensely from frank and intense discussions of post-socialist ethnography during the meetings of the informal anthropological colloquium at the Harriman Institute in 2005–2006. Katherine Verdery, Alexei Yurchak, Eugene Raikhel, Tanya Richardson, Adriana Helbig, Larisa Honey, and Pamela Ballinger shared their critique and offered generous comments on my work in progress. I thank Jack Snyder who made these meetings possible.

Beth Mitchneck has witnessed different stages of this book, and I am grateful for her extensive comments on various drafts and for her persistent encouragement to explore more. Helena Goscilo's insightful suggestions, as well as repeated appeals for clarity, were invaluable. Natalia Danilova, Evgeny Moroz, and Elena Trubina shared with me their knowledge and their materials about contemporary Russia, for which I am particularly thankful.

Different parts of this book were presented at various colloquiums, seminars, and conferences. For their invitations and criticism, I am thankful to the Harriman Institute, Columbia University, Institut für Geschichte und Biographie in Berlin, the School of Modern Languages and Translation Studies at University of Tampere, The Havighurst Center for Russian and Post-Soviet Studies, Miami University; the Centre for European, Russian, and Eurasian Studies, University of Toronto; Department of History, University of Illinois, Urbana-Champaign; the Center for Slavic, Eurasian, and Eastern European Studies, Duke University; and the anthropology departments at University of Pennsylvania, Princeton University, University of Chicago, and the University of Cambridge.

I am particularly indebted to people who have read and commented on different parts of this book: Elena Baraban, Timothy Colton, Nina Eliasoph, Michele Rivkin-Fish, Susan Gal, Sergei Glebov, John M. Janzen, Beth Holmgren, Caroline Humphrey, Lilya Kaganovsky, Anthony Koliha, Susan Larsen, Alaina Lemon, Maria Litovskaia, Harriet Murav, Dmitry Musolin, Benjamin Nathans, Catharine Nepomnyashchy, Kevin M. F. Platt, Madeleine Reeves, Irina Savkina, Tim Scholl, Andrey Shcherbenok, Seteney Shami, Olga Shevchenko, Mark Steinberg, and Tony Wood. Since my arrival at Princeton University in 2006, I have benefited from its rich intellectual environment. I am thankful to my colleagues in the Slavic department for their expertise and their insights, but, above all, for their unceasing support of my attempts to bring literature and anthropology closer.

I thank Bruce Grant and Nancy Ries for inviting me to submit my manuscript to their series. They were immensely important for transforming my project into a book. Ever since the idea of this book emerged as a grant proposal for conducting my fieldwork in Siberia, Bruce Grant has been extremely enthusiastic about the project. Over the years, he has read multiple drafts of my articles and chapters, and I am especially grateful for his numerous comments, suggestions, and corrections, as well as for guiding me through the world of American anthropology. Nancy Ries convinced me to turn the structure of this project inside out and to revise frameworks that needed clarification. I am thankful for her patience and ability to persist, despite all my litanies and laments.

Peter Wissoker, Emily Zoss, Jamie Fuller, and Karen M. Laun from Cornell University Press made the publication process as smooth as possible, and I thank them for their expertise and professionalism. I also want to thank an anonymous reviewer for the Cornell University Press, whose objections to this project inadvertently taught me about the importance of being generous, even in disagreement.

My fieldwork in Siberia was made much easier because of the help of my friends, Dmitry Bychkov, Svetlana Bobrova, Tatiana Garshina, and Elena Sokolova; my parents, Alexander and Nadezhda, and my sister, Natalia. During all these years of researching and writing, Kim Lane Scheppele has been a part of my life, trying to understand what this Soviet Motherland was about and why it matters now. Her love and interest has sustained this project and kept me going. I dedicate this book to her.

Introduction

"We Have No Motherland"

On December 25th 1991, the headline in *Komsomolskaia Pravda,* a major Soviet daily newspaper, reflected the nation's shock at the just-announced dissolution of the USSR: "I woke up, and I am stunned—Soviet power is gone" (*Ia prosnulsia—zdras'te! Net sovetskoi vlasti!*). In a week, the system of state-controlled prices in Russia would be gone too, and very soon inflation would reach 2,000 percent per year. Within next few years, the Communist Party would be banned (but legalized later), and many other traditional institutions associated with state socialism would fade away.

The collapse of state ideology and the attendant dismantling of the elaborate system of state domination were a significant part of the story of the dissolution of the Soviet Union. But they were not the whole story. Amplified by the corrupt privatization of national assets and a massive transformation of existing norms and conventions, this collapse produced a lasting impact on individual and collective identities, modes of social exchange, and forms of symbolization. Usually framed as a "period of transition," the 1990s were quickly dubbed by Russians as the time of *bespredel,* a word that means a lack of any visible obstacles or limits but also an absence of any shared rules or laws.

Apart from this institutional dimension, for many ex-Soviets the collapse of the USSR had a more personal meaning, too. For several generations, the Soviet past and personal biographies had become indistinguishable, and the disappearance of the Soviet country often implied the obliteration of individual and collective achievements, shared norms of interaction, established bonds of belonging, or familiar daily routines. The abandoning of old institutions and the erasing of the most obvious traces of Communist ideology did not automatically produce an alternative unifying cultural, political, or social framework. As a result, the trope of loss turned out to be the most effective symbolic device, one capable of translating people's Soviet experience into the post-Soviet context. In the summer of 1992, when I visited Barnaul, the administrative center of the Altai region that became the main field site for this book, I encountered a striking example of these attempts to articulate a new life in terms of absence. Along a main road that runs from downtown to a suburb there was a huge link of a metal pipe, left behind by gas workers some years earlier. A dozen meters long, the pipe was also very high, and local kids used to hide inside it. During that summer, someone used the pipe for a graffiti display. Facing the road, large white-washed letters announced simply: "We have no Motherland" (*Nyet u nas Rodiny*). I could not tell whether the statement was an ironic comment, an outcry, or a line from a famous Russian poem. Perhaps the sign, addressed to no one in particular and to anyone who passed, combined all of these.

This book grew out of those pipe graffiti—as an attempt to understand how people in Russia explained their sudden "loss" of motherland, how they reconciled their personal lives with dramatic social and political changes. The project was originally aimed at documenting the local practices through which people tried to restore their feeling of belonging once Soviet power and the Soviet motherland were "gone." The book traces how Russians in a Siberian province filled up the vacant place left behind by the collapsed socialist order and how they reconfigured, reimagined, and objectified their connections with the new nation and the new country.

When I returned to Barnaul in 2001 to do fieldwork, the pipe was gone, and the city had also changed. Yet, in contrast to some of the more prominent Russian cities, there was no radical erasure of the important cultural objects of the past. No revolutionary memorials had been destroyed, no streets renamed. The main city boulevard, fittingly named after the Bolshevik leader, is still punctuated by three old statues of Lenin (one every two miles). The Soviet background persisted, or rather, it silently offset the emerging signs and symbols of new post-Soviet reality.

In 2003, during my fieldwork, another striking juxtaposition of these two culturally distinct periods caught my eye: a clumsy local billboard in a Barnaul neighborhood invited people to celebrate Independence Day on June 12.[1] Its surroundings, however, added an ironic twist. Behind the billboard an old Soviet building bore a reminder of a very different political

---

1. The day was introduced in 1994 to mark the Declaration of Sovereignty adopted by the Russian parliament on June 12, 1990. It was the first new official holiday in post-Soviet Russia.

Fig. I.1. "With love to Russia": a poster for Independence Day with nonfunctioning neon signs celebrating the seventy-third anniversary of the October Revolution in the background. Barnaul, 2003. Photo by author.

event. On the roof of the building, nonfunctioning neon combinations of the number 73 and red carnations referred to the Bolshevik Revolution of 1917 (Figure I.1). Originally erected in 1990 for the last widely celebrated anniversary of the October Revolution, the sign had been neither removed nor replaced, freezing in time and space the power that had been gone for more than a decade.

In his study of liminality, Victor Turner reminded us that a temporary suspension of semiotic and discursive activity of the "liminal personae" is one of the typical features of a liminal stage (Turner 1969, 103). Nonfunctioning revolutionary signs were indeed an example of this temporarily halted semiotics. Ignored yet not removed, they continued their tacit life as a part of the symbolic landscape. Having lost their primary meaning, these "suspended" signs nonetheless retained their ability to demarcate the line between the present and the past, to remind about a past that had become irretrievable yet not erased.

Despite their implicit and even explicitly nostalgic undertones, these remnants of the disappeared Soviet state were far from being just an indicator of a conservative clinging to the totalitarian past or another reflection of "path dependence," blocking the steady movement toward a bright neoliberal future. If the post-Soviet period can teach us anything, it is, perhaps, that during times of comprehensive social and political transformation culture matters more than ever. In this book, I show how such traces of loss, the remains of objects and histories that had disappeared, helped sustain continuity in people's lives during a time of personal or collective transition. By analyzing narratives collected in Barnaul, I identify symbolic anchors— "transitional objects" as Winnicott (1971) called them—that provided the liminal subject with a minimal set of navigation tools in the fragmented and disorienting post-Soviet landscape.

With no predictable beginning and no expected end, Russia's post-Soviet transition came with no clear set of rules or paths to follow. Individual and group liminality of the 1990s coincided with the liminality of the society at large: communities had to be created, new systems of values had to emerge, and traditions of discursive interactions and social exchange had to be invented. Unlike Turner's study of liminality, this book emphasizes not the structurally conditioned "suspension" of the symbolic activities of post-Soviet "liminars," but the new languages and skills through which people–in-passage endowed the period of radical changes with some graspable meaning. In short, the book examines popular forms of symbolization that were used to frame the perceived liminality of the Russian state and the Russian nation in the 1990s and the beginning of the twenty-first century.

As I discovered during my fieldwork, these new languages were often profoundly pessimistic; loss was their beginning, their driving force, and their destination. Veterans of the Chechen wars and mothers whose sons died while performing their mandatory military service were my first informants in Barnaul. While talking to these people, reading the mothers' letters and veterans' memoirs, watching videotapes of their public events, and listening to the soldiers' songs, I became more and more aware of the link that my informants built between their personal exposure to violence and the general condition of the post-Soviet state. As a result, I transformed the project into an attempt to outline the prominence of the traumatic in the process of national reconstruction. In some cases, literal violence caused deaths, suffering, and pain. In others, the sharp disruption of once stable institutions resulted in poverty, a loss of status, or professional disorientation. Extensive depictions of misery coupled with practices of suspicion saturated mundane daily conversation and sophisticated intellectual debate. What remained similar in all these cases was the feeling that state institutions had profoundly altered people's lives. Yet, as my materials demonstrate, while provoking or in some cases even organizing violent experience, these institutions proved to be consistently incapable of dealing with the traumatic consequences of their own actions. In the absence of a developed network of civic institutions, it was the logic of connectedness that was used as a mechanism through which trauma and violence were depoliticized, domesticated, and integrated into one's daily life. Questions of political responsibility were eventually displaced by collective practices of grief and discourses of bereavement, as if no positive content could function as a basis for a sense of belonging, and a community must envision a shared experience of loss in order to establish its own borders.

This post-Soviet tendency to achieve a sense of belonging by framing the nation's history as one of experienced, imagined, or anticipated traumatic events remains at the center of this book. The chapters trace how "the work of the negative" (Green 1999) was used in creating new forms of collectivity and demonstrate that the sharing of actually experienced suffering among soldiers' mothers, the unceasing circulation of traumatic memories of war among veterans, the academic production of intellectualized narratives about the Russian tragedy, and the persistent striving to discover in new economic practices a hidden source of imaginary or real danger all brought a new focus to people's relations with the state and the nation.

Telling personal stories about dramatic changes, losses, or violence in one's own life involved the construction of both a general framework within which these stories could make sense and a potential audience for these narratives. Frequently, the individual and group narration of these trauma stories produced communities of loss, which simultaneously acted as the primary author and as the main target of narratives about suffering.

The patriotism of despair, as I call it, emerged as an emotionally charged set of symbolic practices called upon to mediate relations among individuals, nation, and state and thus to provide communities of loss with socially meaningful subject positions. In 1933, disillusioned with the unfulfilled promises of the Bolshevik Revolution, Nikolai Punin, a scholar and a critic, wrote to Anna Akhmatova, his wife at the time, "do not lose your despair... —there is nothing else to lose." Despair, he explained a decade later, was a way of keeping a distance from the unbearable reality; it was a way of preventing oneself from being totally consumed by things that could not be controlled otherwise (Punin 2000, 323, 375). This book explores the patriotism of despair that is also rooted in disillusionment and aimed at providing distance from painful reality. There is an important difference, though. What is crucial in the cases described here is that the feeling of loss, the emotional memory of experienced or imagined injury, was not a result of withdrawal into one's private life but was translated into ideas of national belonging. Stories about the nation and the country were used as a major organizing plot for *individual* accounts: these personal feelings acquired a socially recognizable narrative structure. Triggering an immediate emotional response, the ritualized descriptions of the wounded past provided their authors a crucial entry point into the public discourse at the time when other mechanisms of interaction and recognition ceased to function. After all, *otchaianie,* the Russian-language equivalent for "despair," means lost hope and dejection but also decisiveness and courage without any constraints.

This analysis of such narratives and practices does not aim to pursue them through the lens of contemporary studies of melancholia and mourning, which tend to emphasize the "internal" and "projective" aspects of the identity preoccupied with loss. Rather, it seeks to both document and understand the relations, things, and discourses through which people's traumatic experience became materialized. This interest results in a somewhat different framing of trauma as well. Instead of focusing on the limits and constraints that trauma imposes on one's symbolic capacity—instead of exploring the unclaimed, the unsaid, and the unrepresentable—this book examines mechanisms and forms that capture the individual or collective experience of the traumatic.[2] At the collective level it discusses the fragmentation of the social fabric in two forms. The first is the intense search for missing links and hidden connections that many felt would reveal the concealed logic of seemingly random post-Soviet changes associated with the second coming of capitalism to Russia. Equally important are the ways that narratives of "Russian tragedy" and studies of "vital forces" were taken up by Russian scholars in order to decouple the nation from the state and ethnicity from the nation. These were marked by persistent attempts to reformulate the Russian past along lines of ethnic distinction—as a history of hostile nations who were made to live together. Among individuals much can be learned about the role of trauma in creating post-Soviet society by understanding how the veterans of the Chechen and Afghan wars gradually transformed their individual narratives of self-sacrifice and patriotic duty into rituals of public recognition. Each "exchange of sacrifices," in which the premise of mutual loss functioned as a common starting point, helped ex-soldiers evoke the respect of a larger public, leading what had

2. For a discussion see Caruth (1995); Bar-on (1999); Friedlander (1992).

been considered a questionable military activity to be rewritten as a story ~~USiho~~? of individual perseverance. Likewise, the mothers of the soldiers who died in these wars developed a set of rituals that allowed them to somehow objectify their loss and their own community: these domesticated metonymies of death became a way of preserving a continuing link with the past. Their practices of memorialization not only made clear the mothers' bereavement but also produced a series of material artifacts that transformed grief and loss into a physical as well as an emotionally inseparable part of mothers' everyday order of things.

In Barnaul and throughout much of Russia these stories of the hidden structure of capitalism, ethnic vulnerability, devalued military sacrifices, and unacknowledged deaths merged into an extensive memorial service for relatives who had been lost, for a country that had vanished, and for achievements and expectations that no longer mattered. Different in their scope and scale, each post-Soviet obituary is also a sign of a gradual, postmortem disengagement from the past: an attempt to recognize what has been lost by focusing on the accessible that remains.

This book relies on field materials I collected during extended stays in Barnaul, the administrative center of Altai *krai* (region), located in southwest Siberia on the borders with Mongolia and Kazakhstan. However, for all its specificity, the site of my research was hardly an exception in post-Soviet Russia. In most respect, Altai was a typical province searching for its way in a market economy without the influx of investment that radically changed a small number of mineral-rich Russian regions. The ethnographic materials that I draw upon in this book provide a close-up view of tendencies that could be generalized to many other Russian regions.

In fact, various forms of the patriotism of despair outlined in this book provided a key base of support for the resurgence of Russia's national assertiveness that became so vivid during Vladimir Putin's presidency. While high oil prices in the first decade of the twenty-first century were certainly instrumental in making the new Russian nationalism heard, it was the shared memory of loss, along with the firsthand experience of living through the *bespredel* of the 1990s, that ensured the widespread positive reception of this revitalized patriotism in postmillennial Russia. My book uncovers the local roots of this national pride and presents those still fragmented and isolated voices of patriotic despair that would later merge in a chorus of powerful support for Russia's new identity.

When planning my research, I was deliberately interested in studying how post-Soviet changes were perceived in a remote province. This geographical choice was stimulated by my attempt to break away from a dominant trend in post-Soviet ethnography to study Russians in a few major cultural and industrial centers. I thought that an in-depth ethnographic study in a region that did not have immediate access to the global flow of ideas, images, and goods so typical of Russia's two capitals could produce a somewhat different picture of changes and people's responses to them. While focusing on the local knowledge of my informants, I also trace the larger historical and geographical links that situate my ethnographic encounters within broader cultural and political contexts.

My choice of location had a more personal reason, too: I grew up in Barnaul during the late Soviet period. During perestroika, I studied history in a local university there. In December 1991, right before the unexpected end of the USSR, I moved to St. Petersburg (then still Leningrad), returning to Barnaul throughout the 1990s, albeit less and less frequently. I watched from a distance how life in this provincial Soviet city was slowly transformed into a post-Soviet experience. Neither from within nor quite from outside, these observations followed the uneven and confusing process of "the unmaking of Soviet life," as the anthropologist Caroline Humphrey (2002a) aptly phrased the period of postsocialist changes in Russia.

Barnaul is a city with an unusually long history for Siberia. It was established in 1730 as an important eastern outpost of the Romanov dynasty. Most of Russia's silver and copper in the eighteenth century came from the Altai region. By the middle of the nineteenth century these sources were depleted, and until the Second World War Barnaul remained in a state of economic hibernation. The war returned the city to its earlier status as a major provincial industrial and cultural center: in the 1940s, several large military plants were moved from the western regions of the USSR to Barnaul and its neighboring towns. Until the very end of the USSR, this heavily militarized industry served as the backbone of the regional economy, sustaining the city with its eight hundred thousand people, multiple universities, museums, theaters, and symphony orchestras.

Throughout the 1990s, many of the large factories and plants were shut down, following the state's radical reduction of military-related spending.[3] The military-industrial complex that dominated the Altai economy for decades was replaced by labor-intensive "merchant capitalism." Heavily influenced by their Turkish, Greek, and Chinese partners, shuttle-traders (*chelnoki*) and small retailers brought to this Siberian city a new commercial culture. They also changed the power balance in the region. Within the centralized

3. During the privatization campaign in 1992–95, 20 percent of all military plants throughout the country were deemed "bankrupt" and were closed (Analiz 2004), 93.

Soviet economy, the city's industrial plants were traditionally autonomous from the local authorities. CEOs were appointed by the Soviet government. The plants' substantial budget came directly from Moscow, and a large portion of it was used to support the social infrastructure (housing, schools, hospitals) associated with the plants. The economic changes of the early 1990s radically reversed this situation. Plants were privatized, with CEOs elected by their working collectives. In their attempts to survive the quickly changing economic conditions, the new leadership dumped the dilapidated social infrastructure onto borough administrations, which had neither money nor skills to maintain it. Merchant capitalism, still in its infancy, could hardly provide any powerful support in this respect. Financially weak, this form of economic activity tended to be heavily dependent upon privileged relations with local authorities. Moreover, as many post-Soviet ethnographers pointed out, the dominance of small retail business has rather negative social consequences: it usually prevents rather than contributes to the formation of economically and politically independent groups (Burawoy and Krotov 1993).

In addition to these local economic trends, Altai in general and Barnaul in particular had only very limited exposure to many of the favorable economic trends and influences that became associated with post-Soviet reforms throughout the first two decades of changes. The region has no gas or oil; the city is not a major transportation hub. The region's potential economic asset—beautiful mountains, lakes, and rivers—is underdeveloped and requires investment and management that have not been readily available. Along with a majority of Russia's provinces, the region could not sustain itself financially; it was habitually labeled by the local and federal media as "economically depressed."[4] Subsidies from the federal government usually made up more than 50 percent of the region's expenses. For several years in a row, Altai was consistently the second largest recipient of federal funds in the country, following the Caucasus province of Dagestan (*Altai Daily Review* 2003).

Control over state subsidies and an absence of economically independent groups have turned the local government into a major—and often the only—source of financial and political support available for local educational, civic, and political organizations. This confluence of administrative and financial power produced a certain political stability and perhaps stagnation. As in many other regions of the country, sweeping political changes

---

4. In 2003, at least seventy-one Russian provinces (out of eighty-nine) relied on financial subsidies from the federal center (Grozovskii 2003.)

at the national level did not significantly influence the local makeup of major regional institutions. Until 2004, the key administrative positions in Altai were all occupied by members of the Communist Party of the Russian Federation. The same mayor administered the city from 1986 until his sudden death in a car accident in 2003. In turn, the last Communist governor of the region was in charge of the *krai* from 1991 until 2004, when he was unexpectedly defeated in the local elections by a famous stand-up comedian, labeled "Altai's Schwarzenegger" by the media (Mereu 2004).

The economic and political stagnation in the region had a significant impact on its population. Barnaul's post-Soviet history is the history of the city's steady shrinking. Migration, early deaths, and low birth rate significantly changed the city's population. In ten years, Barnaul lost two hundred thousand people, about a quarter of its Soviet-era peak population of eight hundred thousand. By 2005 the city's population was below six hundred thousand.

Traditionally inhabited mostly by ethnic Russians, Barnaul also interested me as a possible place for studying the formation of Russian (*russkoi*) national identity.[5] Throughout the Soviet period, the meaning of "Russianness" and modern practices of "being Russian" remained largely unclear. In the USSR, the Russian dominance in political, social, and cultural areas was widely practiced but rarely acknowledged in any explicit way. The ethnic makeup of leadership positions, university admissions, and party membership was indeed closely monitored. However, practices of this control were not formally institutionalized. The Soviet Russian Federation, for instance, never had its own republican branch of the Communist Party, Komsomol, or KGB (unlike, say, Estonia or Uzbekistan). Hidden by the homogenizing official notion of the "new collectivity, the Soviet people" (*novaia obshchnost' sovetskii narod*), many Russians found their own ethnicity left unspecified. This imperial model of Soviet nation building allowed Russian ethnicity to persist as a blank spot, as an indeterminate source of power, framed by ethnic differences of other Soviet nationalities, which were constantly reproduced by the official Soviet policy of indigenization (Martin 2001; Hirsch 2005).

After the collapse of the USSR, the situation changed dramatically. As a distinctive nation with specific characteristics, Russians did not follow the

5. In the early 1990s, in addition to *russkii* (Russian), the country's officials started actively using the words *rossiianin* and *rossiiskii* to refer to the post-Soviet nation. Unlike *russkii*, *rossiianin* has no clear ethnic connotation and implies a supraethnic collectivity identity (see Tishkov 2007 for a recent attempt to defend this approach). In English, both terms tend to be rendered as "Russian." I follow this tradition, indicating in parentheses the original Russian term.

path of other nationalities from the former Soviet republics (and east European countries) that used various versions of presocialist national identity models as their fresh starting point. Attempts to claim the legacy of the Romanov empire were mostly limited to funeral rituals, associated with the exhumation and reburial of the royal remains. The aborted history of Russian democratic development between the two major revolutions in 1905 and 1917 did not attract a lot of attention either. The initial post-Soviet fascination with Russo-Soviet émigrés and exiles quickly faded away. Several highly publicized attempts by the Yeltsin government to invent a new national idea that would rejuvenate and consolidate the Russian nation ended up as spectacular failures: a fragmented Russian society could reach no consensus about its long-term values, perspectives, and expectations. Such a limited cultural repertoire of identifications, I anticipated, would make it difficult for ex-Soviet Russians to frame their new social and cultural location in positive and/or nonimperial terms (Oushakine 2000a, 2000b). Barnaul provided a good ground for studying this tendency. The city had a large group of local intelligentsia and a network of political groups actively involved in the production of nationalistic narratives. The city's relative isolation made these movements and intellectual trends more salient and, at times, more radical.

As many anthropologists have pointed out, the lack of easily available positive models of social and political development often results in attempts to build social, political, and economic activity around notions and practices of individual- and group-relatedness (Weston 2001, 153). The post-Soviet fragmentation of the social fabric has forced people to similarly revisit or rediscover basic premises of long-term interaction (Dinello 2002; Oushakine 2004b). It is indicative, for instance, that in the absence of an easily available sociopolitical vocabulary, my informants—Russian veterans of the Chechen wars, mothers whose sons were lost in the army, national Bolsheviks, regional politicians, local sociologists, and politically active youth—framed new forms of post-Soviet connectedness through the language of family and kinship ties such as "brotherhood," "soldiers' mothers," or "Slavs."

Studies on kinship have demonstrated that a striving to naturalize social bonds is a common characteristic of groups whose narratives of origin are threatened or challenged (Borneman 1992; Carsten 2000). If references to trauma, violence, and disorientation point toward a possible origin of the discourse on post-Soviet relatedness, then the naturalizing terms of kinship used by my informants, I suggest, reveal a "biopolitical" context in which postsocialist transition takes place. These post-Soviet attempts to naturalize imagined communities reveal the extent to which the emergence and development of new sociopolitical regimes depend on such an intertwining of biological and political categories. Predictably, loyalty to one's familial interests is often counterbalanced by hostility to racial or ethnic outsiders. This book makes clear that the legitimizing of one's individual or collective membership in a marginalized group is not the only function that the naturalizing relations and terminology of social kinship could perform.

In many cases, examples of post-Soviet communities of loss could be read as an attempt to restore—at least to some extent—the sense of collectivity and cohesiveness they felt during the Soviet period. At the same time, communities of loss repeatedly pointed to the untranslatability of the shared substance that bound them together. Thus, in their interviews and writings, veterans of the Chechen war routinely distanced themselves from those who "have not lived through the war." In turn, Russian nationalists persistently highlighted the unique nature of the suffering associated with Russia's recent history, while soldiers' mothers watchfully maintained social distinctions aimed to reflect the types and degrees of their injuries and losses. These examples could be easily multiplied, yet what unites them all is the differential deployment of pain that brings these groups together at the same time as it sets them apart from others.

This tendency to deal with social instability and individual vulnerability through exclusionary, naturalizing bonds was precipitated by Russia's specific external conditions. Unlike that in many eastern European countries, the transition from state socialism to a market economy was not undertaken with clear goals (Burawoy 2002; Lovell 2006). There was no motivating prospect of joining a large multinational alliance with established democratic traditions—for example, the European Union or NATO—which would significantly mediate the shape of the evolving rules and procedures, principles of political activity and civic participation, and patterns of relations between the public and the private (Böröcz 2000; Bruszt and Stark 2003; Kolarska-Bobiriska 2003). Against this background, the rhetoric of exclusion could be seen as a reaction to a perceived geopolitical isolation, often epitomized in Russia by the image of the steady proliferation of NATO's bases along the country's borders.

As my fieldwork shows, the emphasis on group loyalty and closely monitored group boundaries was a direct reaction to the fundamental economic changes that followed the collapse of the USSR. The market economy was accompanied by an immense social polarization of the Russian population, by a quick and unfair transfer of national property to a limited group of appointed oligarchs, and by an increasing role for money in structuring various aspects of public and private life. This post-Soviet capitalization of the country was often interpreted by my informants as an invasion of foreign values, aimed at undermining Russian traditions and ways of life. In turn, the volatility of new economic practices, the unpredictability of economic exchanges, and the nontransparency of market behavior were all associated with notions of falsity, corruption, and mistrust. As a result, the alien character of differentiating capital and a lack of trust in monetary mediation stimulated a search for "real" values able to withstand what was perceived as the corroding and atomizing effect of money. For many of my informants, an image of a self-enclosed national community with in-convertible values and an untranslatable history, framed in a vision of an exceptional Russian path, was the usual outcome of this search. With their clear delineation of spaces of nonbelonging, these newly created configura-tions of relatedness shaped and strengthened communities of loss.

The specifics of Russian nationalism and Russian national self-perception have been studied before, of course. Scholars usually focus on the political implications and political meaning of speeches, published materials, and organized events.[6] This book, by contrast, attempts to explain how the rhet-oric of trauma influenced producers of these texts and organizers of these events. It examines how this regular symbolic reinscribing of violence and suffering in the fabric of daily life was used as a means of self-organization, a way to produce meaningful forms of connectedness in a situation of radi-cal changes. The chapters trace how this solidarity evolved into a patriotism of despair.

Each of the following chapters deals with a particular aspect of post-Soviet transformation: capitalism, ethnicity, state, and memory. Chapters 1 and 2 look at forms of connectedness that were based on the "activation and reactivation of traumas that have not been personally experienced" (Ewing 2000, 249). Each chapter explores a set of politically and intellec-tually driven efforts to produce overarching ideological frameworks, in which national cohesiveness was constructed as a reaction to a potential or concealed catastrophe—be it a threat of invading capitalism or a danger of "competing ethnoses." Chapters 3 and 4 analyze interviews with groups that were directly affected by Russia's recent military politics: Russian vet-erans drafted to participate in the war in Chechnya and soldiers' mothers, whose sons died while performing their army service. The Chechen war in particular (1994–present) and Russia's recent military history in general

6. See Cosgrove (2004); Franklin and Widdis (2004); Hubbs (1988); Kozhinov (2002); Tumarkin (1994).

offered the potential for constructing new state-oriented identities, but the state routinely failed to deliver on its promises.[7] Sharply outlining the relationship between the government and individuals in post-Soviet Russia, these war-related stories highlight the traumatic core around which new communities emerged.

Certainly, it would be wrong to reduce the post-Soviet development in Russia only to stories about trauma, suffering, perceived ethnic extinction, and state-organized violence. Fortunately, communities of loss were not the only form of belonging that emerged in Russia after the collapse of the Soviet Union. Yet by discussing these narratives, this book demonstrates how people were capable of sustaining dramatic personal changes while their country collapsed and their state, their economy, and their culture were all radically transformed—all within less than two decades.

In 1923, describing St. Petersburg after the Russian Revolution, the Russian formalist Viktor Shklovsky compared the city with "a man whose insides have been torn out by an explosion, but he keeps on talking." As the formalist continued, "Imagine a group of such men. They sit and talk. What else are they to do—howl?" (2004, 133–34). This book is an attempt to document similar talks after an explosion, in a situation where cultural and social insides have collapsed or have been torn out. The traumatic symbolic anchors and practices of sharing suffering that I discovered in a Russian province may not be the best solution for dealing with radical dislocations, yet they kept many afloat in the flux of post-Soviet changes.

7. As chapter 3 shows, from the military point of view, the war in Chechnya is divided into two separate campaigns: from 1994 until 1996 and from 1999 to the present. In public discussions and presentations, however, the "Chechen war" tends to be perceived as a continuous process that started with the assault of Grozny, the Chechen capital, in 1994.

1 Repatriating Capitalism

Fragmented Society and Global Connections

It was understood in everyday economic life that many items could not be bought. State trade was institutionally structured in such a way that money was not important....If you had money but no connections, you would not have access to goods in short supply. You were a nobody. Your money just demonstrated your lack of position in society. This was the economic reality not just for a year or two but for decades.

—YEGOR GAIDAR, "Russian Reform."

Only recently, we were all together. During the [Second World] war, our grandfathers together fought Germans. In the 1960s–70s, our parents studied in the same universities. But in the middle of the 1980s, our paths were split apart. Today there are *Them* and *Us*. *They* are the masters of this life; *We* are this life's orphans. One thing is still encouraging, though. *They* make up only 5 percent of the Russian population; *We* are the remaining 95 percent. Those among *Us* who are smart, bright, and active are still dreaming of becoming deputies and businessmen under the current political regime. This is why this regime is being treated with some respect. Soon, *We* all realize that these dreams are utopian. In the world of capital, only *They* could become deputies and businessmen. Then *We* will decide to build a new world for us. And *They* won't stop *Us*.

—VIKTOR, a student at Altai State Agricultural University, Barnaul, 2004.

Conspiracy theory is not an open-ended set of "reading practices" but a particular structure of feeling. It is a nervous system, a split sensitivity, an internally divided cultural space that has force, that generates as well as registers the contradictions of contemporary social transformations.

—SUSAN HARDING and KATHLEEN STEWART, "Anxieties of Influence"

Paths and Patches of Postsocialist Capitalism

For anyone coming to Barnaul, the city's new commercial landscape presents a startling postsocialist palimpsest. Fading signs of the Soviet past are merged in an unlikely combination with new symbols of post-Soviet capitalism (figure 1.1). This palimpsest has a certain consistency: local shops, entertainment centers, and casinos that have been built in the city's downtown are usually marked as destinations with an ostensibly foreign flavor.

Fig. 1.1. Square in front of the Central Universal Store (TsUM). The apartment building to the left of the store carries a symbol of the Order of October Revolution that the city was awarded in 1980; the sign reads "Order-Bearing Barnaul." The striped emblem below is an ad for a mobile phone company. June 2006. Photo by author.

Over several years, a series of upscale establishments with exotic names have appeared on Lenin Prospect, the main city street. The "trading house" Kaligula, built near the dilapidated cinema-theater Rodina (Motherland), was joined by a "trading center," Tsezar' (Caesar). The fur store Ellada (from Hellas) now sits next to El'dorado, a branch of the electronics chain store. Less than half a mile away another shopping mall presents a different but no less foreign-inspired outlook. In this case, the mall's name, Ultra, has not even been transliterated (figure 1.2). The symbolic reshaping of the local landscape is most visible on Red Army Prospect, the city's second major avenue. In this case, the symbolism of ancient decadence was combined with references to less distant examples of Hollywood glamour and bandit chic. Tsentr Vavilon (Babylon Center), the city's main and the most expensive shopping mall, symbolically echoes Kolizei (Coliseum), the most prestigious club and entertainment venue. Next to Vavilon and Kolizei, the casino Oskar mirrors Las Vegas, a gambling machine pavilion across the street (figure 1.3).

Fig. 1.2. Trading House Ultra on Lenin Prospect. Barnaul, 2004. Photo by author.

The tendency to give exotic names to new economic practices and institutions was not limited to this particular city. Throughout the country, this early post-Soviet capitalism was marked by similar corporate and private attempts to reconfigure public space by establishing new historical and geographic connections. To understand the full significance of this process, one needs to remember that for more than seven decades Soviet public space was largely devoid of individualizing features. Generic names were used to indicate the establishments' function, while numbers pointed to their place within the larger system of Soviet institutions. For example, my apartment building in Barnaul was located next to Secondary School Number 22 and Secondary School Number 76. Close to the schools, in a striking contrast between the two traditions of naming, the generic Public Library Number 10 faced Maria-Ra, a new grocery store named after the owner's wife.[1]

1. Dubin (1994, 223–30), Krongauz (2008), and Yurchak (2000) provide useful details of a similar process in other regions.

Fig. 1.3. Barnaul's own Las Vegas: a "gambling club" on Red Army Prospect. June 2006. Photo by author.

The tendency to personalize the public space started in Barnaul in the early 1990s, when a small group of businessmen opened one of the very first private stores in the city. Located on Lenin Prospect, the store was called the Butik Renome (from the French *renommé,* "renowned"). The shortage of available real estate in the city and the high costs of new construction significantly influenced the architectural outline of early postsocialist capitalism. In the beginning, it was newly privatized apartments in buildings located on main city streets that entrepreneurs converted into market space.[2] (The free-standing Kaligula, Vavilon, and Kolizei became a part of Barnaul's landscape several years later, when new construction started.) Epitomizing the trend of the decade, Renome was created in a two-room corner apartment on the ground floor of a residential building: internal walls were demolished, the floor was sunk into the basement (to increase the height of the space), a window was transformed

2. For more discussion of this tendency in Russia's provinces see Ruble (1995).

Fig. 1.4. Carving out an entry to the market: new commercial sites in Barnaul often begin as converted residential space. In this emerging commercial row in an apartment building the store Avtozapchasti (Autoparts) is joined by a yet unnamed establishment. Barnaul, 2004. Photo by author.

into a door, and a separately built staircase provided an autonomous entry (*figure 1.4*). With its foreign-inspired *renomme,* initial commercialization was materialized as a literal intrusion into private living spaces, which had formerly been excluded from the circulation of money.

Carving out their separate domains from what had been domestic territory, new commercial establishments extended their presence into available public space as well. Turning a residential property into a commercial site was normally accompanied by a typical stipulation: the new owners had to maintain the sidewalk in front of their premises. Given the uneven pace of privatization, this often produced a peculiar spatial experience in practice. Each owner of the apartment-turned-into-a-store would pave and decorate the corresponding part of the sidewalk in a particular way. As a result, many sidewalks could tell vivid stories about buildings' gradual commercialization. What had formerly been a sixty-foot-long stretch of ordinary pavement now could be made up of a series of unmatched and uneven patches: several squares of white cinder blocks would be interspersed with pieces of old asphalt, which in turn would be continued by areas of red brick.

Diverse in its shape, depth, texture, and color, this hazardous landscape mapped in stone the uneven path of Russia's post-Soviet development. In an idiosyncratic form, it represented a primary sociosymbolic problem of postsocialist capitalism: no economic, legal, or aesthetic framework was able to homogenize fragmented pieces of semiprivatized public space into a seamless surface. No basic "social contract" or at least no social consensus among newly appearing owners could yet be used for redefining their common ground. The previous pavement might have been drab, but it was coherent. The new sidewalk was established as a chain of adjacent but aesthetically and physically disconnected patches. It is perhaps only fitting that in daily conversations, people often referred to new shops and kiosks as "lumps" (komok, from kommercheskii kiosk) and "commercial dots" (kommercheskaia tochka). New economic formations were perceived as something that broke out of the existing environment (lumps) or as something that only punctuated it (dots).

During my fieldwork, I witnessed how this trope of the fragmentation of social fabric was discussed in different settings and environments. Images that emerged in these conversations were not always commerce-related, nor were they always exotic. Sometimes metaphors of disjuncture were translated into a very literal feeling of personal disconnectedness. In the fall of 2001, soon after my arrival in the city, thieves cut off all the wires that supplied electricity to street lamps in an urban district where I lived during the fieldwork. The wires had copper and aluminum, which could be sold to scrap metal collectors.[3] Local authorities had no money to rewire the lamps, and for more than two years this part of the city—with dozens of apartment buildings, twenty thousand inhabitants, several large schools, kindergartens, stores, and a big hospital—remained totally dark during long Siberian nights. Few people drove cars, especially in winter; the majority just walked around the district or relied on public transportation. Every morning and evening, one could see an improvised light show around neighborhoods: to illuminate the road to stores or nearby schools, neighbors used flashlights. During this time, the bankrupt city government drastically reduced the number of municipal buses and promised to completely replace them

---

3. The so-called aluminum rash started in the 1990s and has not stopped since, despite the authorities' efforts to outlaw the scrap metal business. Probably the most publicized case took place in 2003, right before the highly advertised three hundred-year anniversary of St. Petersburg, when malefactors cut out 1.5 km of electric wires along the railroad from Moscow to St. Petersburg, effectively blocking the traffic of electric trains between the two cities (Popov 2007, 4).

with more expensive *kommercheskii* (privately owned) transportation.[4] The lack of illumination was aggravated by the enforced immobility. Small talk with neighbors and friends was frequently peppered with ritual complaints about being left in the darkness (*ostavili v temnote*) and being cut off from the rest of the world (*otrezali ot mira*). My informants were eager to take the theme of disintegration beyond their daily problems, too, and easily extended their grievances about the failing infrastructure to complaints about the wrecked country (*razvalili stranu*) or to debates about disintegrating minds (*razrukha v golovahk*).[5]

This does not mean that people gave up their attempts to connect the isolated dots and cut-off parts. In fact, if the perceived feeling of disconnectedness resulted in anything, it was the incredible production of popular and theoretical discourses that exposed missing links and discovered hidden structures. The "zero years" (*nulevye gody*), as the first decade of the new century was often called in Russia, were marked by an intense striving to imagine a new environment that could symbolically unite the diverse pieces that had been isolated by quick commercialization. Surprisingly enough, the articulation of loss and dislocation did not result in practices of disengagement. Instead, the mutual recollection of negative experience was often used to shape new forms of solidarity and belonging.

This chapter explores the post-Soviet obsession with missing links exposed by the rapid fragmentation of public and private space. It attempts to reconstruct the dazzling picture of the post-Soviet provincial landscape, with its confusing, contradictory, and often barely compatible patches, pieces, and shards. It also documents how emerging market relations both polarized people and simultaneously activated what Jean and John Comaroff have fittingly called the "will to connect" (2003b, 297). The disintegration of the previously coherent public space and the domestication of foreign-looking enclaves (in the shape of Kaligulas and Vavilons) resulted in increasing attempts to envision and objectify "'traditional' ways of life as cultural wholes" (Harrison 2000, 662). The experience of global circulation of capital was counterbalanced with ideas of an enclosed national community and unmediated values. Increasingly, Russo-Soviet culture was construed as "inalienable wealth," as a particular form of socially meaningful

---

4. In addition, to save money, the city authority wanted to stop removing snow from streets and to cancel buying chalk for public schools (Negreev 2000).

5. For more discussion of the trope of *polnaia razrukha* (complete disintegration) see Ries (1997, 44–49).

property that could be shared among people but that could not enter commercial circulation or exchange (Weiner 1985).

I refer to this sociosymbolic dynamic as the "repatriation of capitalism" in order to highlight both the return of the economic regime that was abolished after the Bolshevik Revolution of 1917 and widespread attempts to filter new market-driven practices through the lens of myths and histories that were perceived by my informants as distinctively Russian. The narratives analyzed here show how people redesigned and regrouped history and geography in order to respond to new politico-economic realities and social identities. In many of these stories, the "invisible hand" that was supposed to guide the free market was made dramatically real in various scenarios of manipulation.[6] The post-Soviet uneasiness about the increasing social role of capital was translated into stories about universal lies and deceptions. After all, despite all its obvious pretense, Butik Renome was selling nothing but imitations and counterfeit versions of expensive French perfume.[7]

In order to understand how the atomizing and deceptive logic of capital was routinely contrasted with an abstracted Truth and an idealized wholeness of the Soviet collective, I examine a set of interviews and materials that I collected in Barnaul. During my fieldwork in 2001–3 and shorter visits in 2004–5, I attended meetings and interviewed individual members of local political and religious groups. Originally, my informants ranged across a wide spectrum, from Western-oriented liberals to hard-core Communists, from neo-hippies to neo-pagans. This chapter, however, focuses only on Communist, National-Bolshevik, antiglobalist, and religious groups that were most active in the city during my fieldwork. In my analysis, I actively supplement transcripts of these conversations with texts written by my informants or widely read by them. Such a combination allows me to trace a wider range of emerging rationalities that were shaped by experienced or imagined threats of Russia's exposure to the global circulation of capital.

Money, Cycles, and Moral Dilemmas

Scholars studying transitions from noncapitalist economic orders to capitalist ones have already pointed out that these moves inevitably involve a comprehensive reorganization of the moral presumptions necessary for

6. See also Verdery (1996, 180–84) and Ries (2002) for different examples of a similar tendency.
7. The store's business did not last long: in 1998, in the aftermath of the major collapse of the country's financial system, the store went bankrupt.

justifying new choices and alternatives. For instance, Michael Taussig observes, "There is a moral holocaust at work in the soul of a society undergoing the transition from a precapitalist to a capitalist order. And in this transition both the moral code and the ways of seeing the world have to be recast" (1980, 101). Readjusting their moral and social optics, Taussig suggests, groups and individuals tend to resort to preexisting cosmogonies, using them either as sites of resistance to the emerging order or as a means of mediation. Rites and myths are the most visible forms of such socio-symbolic reconfiguration (101). Katherine Verdery, in a similar vein, argues that the radical change of the property regime that followed the collapse of socialism "alters the very foundations of what 'persons' are and how they are made" (2000, 176).

Jonathan Parry and Maurice Bloch (1989) in their seminal collection on money and morality suggested a useful model for understanding the relationship between pecuniary exchanges and ethical assumptions. They maintained that it is impossible to grasp the meanings of money if we limit our analysis to the immediate context of short-term transactions. To realize the full social importance of exchanges mediated by money, these transactions must be approached within a larger set of practices through which groups maintain their social and symbolic continuity. Relying on diverse ethnographic material, Parry and Bloch pointed to the fact that individual monetary transactions were indeed prominent in precapitalist societies, but they were usually limited to a separate domain that was "ideologically articulated with, and subordinated to, a sphere of activity concerned with the cycle of long-term reproduction" (26). To put it differently, money and monetary exchanges were viewed as part of a larger, nonmonetized, symbolic system rather than as a form of activity opposed to this system. The balance between the individual and the collective was achieved through maintaining a particular form of relationship between the short-term sphere of politico-economic exchanges and the long-term sphere of morality. Within this framework, then, the "moral holocaust" described by Taussig is not so much a reflection of the detrimental impact of money itself as a product of a situation in which the values and logic of the short-term cycle encompass values of the long-term transactions (Parry and Bloch 1989, 29; see also Maurer 2006).

Russia's socialist legacy adds an interesting theoretical and practical twist to understanding the restructuring of the relationship between existing assumptions and an emerging economic order. The starting point here is both anticapitalist and—at least theoretically—postcapitalist. As early as 1938 the exiled Trotsky pointed out that Soviet money had "ceased to be money." It no longer served as a measure of value, working mostly as a "universal distribution card" in the USSR's planned economy (2004, 54). Reduced to its "accounting role" (Clarke 2000, 178), Soviet money nonetheless performed a significant role in everyday life. As Alaina Lemon rightly points out, the lack of a developed system of individual credits and checking accounts made the daily presence of cash quite salient under state socialism (1998, 24).[8] However, there were several important factors that modified the role of monetized exchanges among institutions and individuals in the Soviet period. The heavily controlled distribution of physical goods and strictly regimented system of salaries and prices created a situation in which one's individual prosperity no longer depended on the amount of accumulated money one had. Moreover, severely policed channels of currency exchange made it almost impossible to use foreign money for saving. By and large, "making money" as an autonomous form of social activity made little sense (Gladarev 2000; Yurchak 2006, 138). What was important within this system of constrained financial circulation was access to actual flows of goods and services, secured through a ramified network of informal social relations usually known as *blat*. Money did change hands in these transactions, acting mostly as "adjustments" to the established process of distribution of goods and services (Verdery 1996, 181). But as Gaidar (1995) indicates, it was neither money itself nor its amount that was socially meaningful. Calculations were structured around potential strategies of nonmonetary exchange, "a kind of barter based on personal relationship," as Alena Ledeneva puts it (1998, 34). The moral assumptions and economic practices—as deformed and informal as they were—complemented each other, providing a relatively stable sociosymbolic framework for late Soviet society.[9]

This particular cultural matrix of the previous period heavily determined the new meanings that became associated with money after the dissolution of state socialism. Perceived through a particular interpretive lens, the traditional economic functions of money (exchange, accounting, accumulation) were incorporated into daily life and discourse. However, the speed and intensity of post-Soviet "shock therapy" left no chance for a gradual integration. When on January 2, 1992, after decades of stable prices, Yegor Gaidar led the Russian government to abandon state control over prices altogether, money suddenly emerged as an independent social institution, almost totally disconnected from previous habitual practices and

---

8. See also Pine (2002) for a similar argument regarding Polish households during the socialist period.

9. I discuss this at length in Oushakine (2003).

assumptions. With some exceptions (bread, milk, alcohol, public services, transportation, electricity, and gas), all prices were "liberalized." Anticipating high inflation, the government even ordered the issuance of ruble notes of higher denomination.[10] The subsequent rapid inflation, financial pyramids, repeated rounds of ruble denomination, increasing monetization of welfare services, widespread salary arrears, privatization of industry and housing, as well as new practices of consumption pushed monetary exchanges to the forefront of social practices and the social imagination.[11] In the early 1990s, trying to deal with the collapse of the national financial system, some provincial governments even issued temporary "surrogate currencies" and "regional money" (Anderson 2000). This fragmentation of the country's financial circulation had its own hierarchy. Along with the ruble economy, a new commercial world emerged around the circulation of the U.S. dollar in Russia. In daily conversations, the inconvertible Russian ruble was routinely labeled "wooden" (*dereviannyi*), in contrast to the "green" (*zelen', zelenye*) U.S. money. Endless jokes referred to U.S. dollars as "Russian bucks" (*russkie baksy*), and many stores began listing their prices in dollars.[12] The Moscow Pizza Hut added to this "currency apartheid" a spatial dimension by creating two separate dining enclaves for its dollar and ruble customers respectively (Lemon 1998, 41).

The situation was all the more striking because only a few years earlier, the circulation of foreign currency in the USSR was extremely limited and the undocumented possession of foreign money was a series criminal offense.[13] The Yeltsin government tried to stop the proliferation of the dual currency regime and in 1993 banned the open use of the dollar sign in advertising and price labels. In response, stores and service providers switched to listing prices in u.e., an abbreviation that stood for a "conditional unit" (*uslovnaia edinitsa*) of measurement, equal to the market value of the dollar.[14]

This reemergence of monetary exchanges as a distinctive yet highly volatile sphere of postsocialist life often met strong resistance. Of course, it was

10. For more details see Gaidar (1999, 130, 95).

11. See Woodruff (1999) for a detailed analysis of monetary changes in the 1990s.

12. Evgenii Popov (1998) in his novel provides many relevant examples from this period.

13. In 1961, Khrushchev succeeded in including capital punishment for violating "the rules of currency transactions" (*valiutnye operatsii*) in the existing Criminal Code (Fedoseev 2005, 154).

14. In 2006, the Russian parliament made yet another attempt to reestablish the ruble as the only currency in the country. Deputies seriously discussed possible measures to punish those state bureaucrats who would attempt to use the u.e., euro, or dollar for measuring values in Russia (*Nevskoe vremia* 2006).

not money or its amount that produced such a negative response. Rather, it was the fragmentation of transactional systems that caused persistent anxiety. The hierarchical relationship between the long-term and short-term spheres of exchange vanished. At best, the profit-driven politico-economic domain and the sphere of moral exchanges emerged as competing areas of social activity and symbolic production in post-Soviet Russia. At worst, the values of the long-term cycle became radically marginalized by new market relations.

The recognized arbitrariness of the conditional units tended to provoke angry responses to the new system of valuation. In January 2005, the Russian government decided to implement its program of *monetizatsiia* and replaced remaining individual welfare benefits such as free (or heavily discounted) medicine and transportation for pensioners, war and labor veterans, decorated citizens, and others with fixed financial allowances. In response to this decision, for several weeks (in spite of frost and snow), angry people marched around the country, blocking roads and administrative buildings and demanding the restoration of social privileges and material benefits. Using the metaphor of the time, some journalists described these protests as waves of a "political tsunami," referring to the earthquakes and tsunamis that killed more than two hundred thousand people in Indonesia in December 2004 (Arkhangelskaia, Rubchenko, and Shokhina 2005).

That the amount of calculated financial compensation for the loss of previous benefits was both insufficient and arbitrary was only part of the problem. Predominantly, protesters reacted against a new form of equivalence that directly linked the amount of money offered with the social recognition of individual achievements, which the previous nonmonetary benefits used to signify. Again, it was not money itself that caused the trouble. Rather—to use Parry and Bloch's terminology—the public discontent was caused by a broken link between a short-term sphere of monetized exchanges (compensation) and the long-term order of social and moral values (social achievements).

In a very different form, a similar tendency of avoiding the monetary equivalent was also demonstrated in Russia's industry. In 1992, barter accounted for only 5 percent of enterprise transactions. By 1998, at least 60 percent of enterprise transactions were done in kind (Marin, Kaufmann, and Gorochowskij 2000, 207). Barter was also used by plants and factories for paying local and federal taxes (Guriev and Ickes 2000, 147). People's salaries were often paid in kind as well, providing a constant supply of goods for local bazaars. While a general lack of liquidity was the primary reason for this mass demonetization, it is important to keep in mind that this postsocialist "economy of debt" emphasized first of all networks of ex-change rather than the substance of exchange (Commander and Seabright 2000, 363; Anderson 2000, 343). At least in Russia's case, the conditions of these transactions, as scholars of barter have stressed, were determined more by personal connections between the parties than by the nature of the exchanged objects (Guriev and Ickes 2000, 173). Speaking about the average Buryat household in 1996, Caroline Humphrey summarizes the prevalent attitude toward money that could be largely applicable to Russia's early capitalism in general: "Money is greatly desired for its instant convert-ibility into many different things, but no one saves money....Money as a substance is regarded with suspicion (there are special machines to check the validity of dollar notes at most banks and stores). The rationale now is more or less immediate transactability" (1998, 459; also Rogers 2005).

Different as they are, all these cases seem to point in a similar direction: people had difficulty accepting monetized social exchanges when those exchanges were not accompanied by the expected symbolic context. The core of this difficulty had to do with a lack of trust, a lack of shared un-derstanding of norms, values, and evaluation. The attractiveness of barter in this respect is telling. Unlike monetary exchanges, barter exchanges and informal personalized networking are built on trust that "has no external moral referent outside the deal itself and the belief generated by partners in the truth of one another's statements" (Humphrey 2000, 83; also Hedlund 2005, 326–31).

There was another important echo of Soviet economic practices in post-Soviet life. Soviet individual and group cosmogonies were closely associated with or even created by the political regime itself. Explicit identifications with Soviet life, the dissident negations of it, and the late-Soviet distanc-ing from anything ostensibly Soviet were all significantly shaped by Soviet practices and institutions.[15] Given this preexisting context, how did people in Barnaul link the parts of their biographies and experience that had been disconnected by radical economic changes?

"Everyone Lies, Everyone Steals"

In post-Soviet studies of Russia, it has become a commonplace to view the existing Communist movement as a hangover of the previous period, a political phantom that persisted rather than developed. This perception

---

15. For more discussion see Kharkhordin (1999); Oushakine (2001b); Yurchak (2006).

has some validity. A majority of supporters of the Communist Party of the Russian Federation (the KPRF, as it is usually called) belong to the generations that developed their political views in the Soviet period. Communist-oriented groups and organizations are most active in areas outside major industrial and cultural centers, usually in rural and newly demilitarized provinces. Given these two factors, scholars of Russia routinely frame Communist-inspired actions as "protest-like" behavior, as a backlash *against* liberalization and reforms, not as an intrinsic and inseparable part of these processes (Shestopal 2004; Sedov 2003; Kiewiet and Myagkov 2002; Wegren 2004).

The situation is not that simple. From 1991 on, the Altai regional parliament was continuously controlled by a pro-Communist coalition. However, the typical "Communist prototype"—"a retired *babushka* with a hearing aid who tries to relive her Communist youth," as a young Barnaul Communist described it to me—had very little in common with people who were actually associated with Communist institutions in the region. In fact, many Communist deputies elected to the Altai parliament in 2004 were thirty or forty years old. People who worked for local leftist organizations were relatively young, too: most of them were born in the 1970s and 1980s. Many studied at local universities, majoring in social sciences; there were quite a few among them who became full-time politicians. To avoid historical and terminological confusion, I refer to this new generation of Communists as "neocommunists," or "neocoms." Increasingly, this group describes itself as the "children of reforms" (*deti reform*), resolutely distancing itself from the generation of "pro-Western and liberally-minded 'children of perestroika'" who came of age in the 1980s and early 1990s (Ekart n.d.) (figure 1.5).

Providing numerous and extensive descriptions of the "detrimental impact of capitalism," my neocommunist informants often started by identifying an unexplainable gap between new economic relations and practices of daily life produced by this economic order. It was precisely this disjuncture of the economic and the quotidian that I was interested in exploring. How did young people in Altai react to the limited applicability of their social knowledge and interpretive skills? What symbolic resources did they draw upon in order to produce meaningful structures in the context of uncertainty?

On December 16, 2002, Aleksei Z., an eighteen-year-old member of the radical National-Bolshevik group (*natz-boly*) and I agreed to meet in front of an old shopping center, the Central Universal Store (*Tsentral'nyi Universal'nyi Magazin, TsUm*), in downtown Barnaul. It was snowy and windy outside; the temperature had dropped to −10°F. In this weather, the *natz-boly's*

Fig. 1.5. Children of reform: a Barnaul neo-communist during a political rally. Barnaul, 2002. Photo by author.

usual place of socializing, the Eternal Flame Square near a local monument to the martyrs of Socialism, did not look very attractive. The TsUM was crowded, and there was nowhere to sit. Finding a place to have a talk with Aleksei was a problem. Actually, it had been a problem throughout my entire fieldwork in Barnaul whenever offices or private apartments were not available for meetings. Apart from flashy, loud restaurants and fast-food stands—the two extremes that defined the public space in the city—there were very few affordable cafés. Nor was there any developed pub culture. Shopping malls, one possible indoor hangout, tended to be cluttered with stalls and kiosks to maximize the real estate's revenues. Public libraries required special passes (or a passport). In a warmer season, things might look different in Barnaul, but from October until early May the shape of public space remained narrow.

I asked Aleksei if we could go to any café nearby. The only plausible choices were a Baskin-Robbins around the corner or a newly opened cafeteria-style Food-line (transliterated in Russian), located half a mile away. Aleksei's reaction to Baskin-Robbins was negative. He explained that as an antiglobalist he found it objectionable. There was a more personal story to tell, too. Earlier in the fall, Aleksei, together with several other National-Bolsheviks, had smashed several big windows of the Baskin-Robbins to protest the invasion of global capital into the region. Police never discovered them, yet revisiting the crime scene did not sound like a very good idea. I respected his choice, but the cold weather was also persuasive. Vacillating, Aleksei picked the Baskin-Robbins in the end because it was closer.

Labeled an "ice-cream store," the Baskin-Robbins franchise (the only one in the city) had, nonetheless, several tables and chairs. Being faithful to its strategically chosen name ("store"), it had no public bathroom, an old and proven Soviet trick to discourage customers from staying inside for too long. As became clear, Aleksei's knowledge of this particular form of global capitalism was rather distant: he had never been inside the Baskin-Robbins. Apparently he had also grossly overestimated its impact on the local economy. During the entire two hours of our conversation, we remained the only customers in the café, a fact that deeply surprised him.

Our interaction with the salesperson, a young girl behind the bar, provided some interesting local information about adopting global trends to "native" tastes. The place was plastered with posters advertising its seasonal special: "genuine hot chocolate for 69 rubles!" (about $2.20). I asked if the chocolate was indeed real. A bit hesitant in the beginning, the girl explained that it was not. The *real* "real hot chocolate" would be "way too expensive," and it would be "too bitter" anyway. Hence, the drink was "diluted by half" with water. Having settled on tea (7 rubles), we started a conversation for which the image of partially "genuine chocolate" seemed to be a perfect metaphor.

From the very beginning Aleksei told me that he had joined the National-Bolshevik Party because his views were "exactly anti-Semitic" and because he saw "nothing good in our state order [stroi]." Despite my inquiries, he did not explain what "exact anti-Semitism" was supposed to mean; instead our discussion was mostly focused on his views of the state and the fate of Russians. The party's active (and at times violent) defense of the Russian nation had led the mass media to associate it strongly with fascism (Likhachev 2002, chap. 2; Job 2001; Mathyl 2002). But Aleksei rejected that view, maintaining that it was completely wrong: the party was not fascist—it was "patriotic." Being "half-German," as Aleksei put it, he did not welcome fascism at all: "Patriotism is good, but fascism is too much." Yes, he agreed, the party's main slogan, "Russia—for the Russians!" was interpreted sometimes as nationalistic; but the party had already modified its ideological policy. Now the slogan was supposed to be inclusive: anyone who "lives in Russia and likes it can claim to be a Russian (*russkii*)." As he summed it up, the party's ideology was nothing but "naked patriotism" (*golyi patriotizm*).

In 2003, Eduard Limonov, the ideological leader of the party and a famous writer-provocateur, defined further the gist of this naked patriotism in his book *The Other Russia: An Outline for the Future:*

> We have to revolt. For ourselves, for our group, for those people whom we consider to be a part of us. We have to think. We have to figure out a different model of life, and we have to impose it. But first of all, we have to create a new nation. Everywhere one can hear today: "Russians," "We—are Russians," "I am a Russian," "For the Russians" (*russkii*) But this label hides all kinds of people. This label applies to Yeltsin, and to an alcoholic, bluish from drinking, and to a dirty bum, and to the active spermatozoon [ex-prime minister] Kirienko. If all of them are Russian, then I am not a Russian. What should we do? We should select people for the new nation. We could call it differently; say, "Eurasians" or "Scythians." Names don't matter; the new nation should be based on different principles. The color of one's hair or eyes isn't important. What counts is the courage and faithfulness to our commune." (2003, 8)[16]

Scythians or not, the communal emphasis of Limonov's National-Bolshevism certainly appealed to the younger generation. Perhaps even more important was the fact that the party was the only organization that remained "honest," as Alexei Z. emphasized during our conversation. It "says what it thinks," and the party's members "don't lie, they tell nothing but the truth." This description sharply contrasted with Aleksei's account of the situation in Russia: "Today everyone lies; everyone steals. The whole country steals because of our [leadership's] politics....In short, some people are good at stealing, while others work for those who steal." Then followed his brief summary of the period of changes:

> People were used to building socialism, and they had this goal [*stimul*] to build communism. Gorbachev destroyed all that overnight. People rushed

16. In 2006, the title of Limonov's book was appropriated by a group of politicians who formed a loose opposition to Putin's government. Together with the name, this political movement, The Other Russia, also eagerly embraced Limonov himself (as well as his National Bolshevik Party), the former prime minister Mikhail Kasianov, and representatives of the neoliberal Union of Rightist Forces. Led by the former world chess champion Garry Kasparov, this political motley crew presented itself as a new democratic force.

about, fussed about, and ended up with nothing. Those who managed to steal a lot, they rose above others [*podnialis'*]; they opened their firms; they became oligarchs. The majority initially hoped that all these changes were for the better, but they missed the turn. Now some of these people drink themselves to death; some toil for their masters.

With some adjustments, it is possible to read this narrative, in which the universal deceit and corruption among strangers are opposed by truth shared only among close friends, as yet another edition of the theme of cynicism, imposture, or dissimulation that has been firmly linked with the Soviet period.[17] One can also read this story of lying and stealing as an inverted trope of dispossession, as an attempt to explain and justify the process through which people "missed the turn" and "ended up with nothing." Firmly linking immorality ("stealing skills") and property, the story shaped the perception of the new capitalist order and its moral economy as a system of lies and thefts. In turn, a connection between the truth and naked patriotism was used to overcome morally the state of post-Soviet material dispossession.

The interplay of these two lines of narration—lying/stealing vs. truth/patriotism—significantly determined the development of Altai leftists' discourse in general. Not only did it emphasize the structural intertwining of the economic and the symbolic, but it also drew attention to distinct logics that each narrative suggested. The interrupted circulation that stealing introduced and the flawed communication exchange that lying indicated were counterbalanced by uncoined values of truth/patriotism that resisted any exchange or circulation.

"It Just Can't Be This Way"

A self-described Trotskyite and "*alter*-globalist," Nikolai T. was a full-time leader of a Barnaul political organization that defended "alternative ways" of political and economic development. In our conversation in September 2002, Nikolai explained his political evolution. Born in 1973, he grew up during perestroika. But the extreme politicization of the time barely influenced him. He paid no attention to the changes, nor was he a political activist during the first years of his student life. As Nikolai put it, "In [October] 1993, when there was a live TV broadcast of tanks shelling the White

---

17. For different versions of this approach see Kharkhordin (1999, 270–71), and Fitzpatrick (2005).

House in the very center of Moscow, I watched all that without the slightest understanding as to who was right and who was not. It was just so shockingly interesting that in the middle of the country's capital there were tanks shelling the parliament. It was an aesthetic experience of sorts."

The White House that Nikolai described was a big administrative complex in downtown Moscow, where the Russian parliament resided in the early 1990s. In September 1993, after a series of disputes with deputies, President Yeltsin issued a decree that disbanded the parliament and called for new elections and a new constitution. The Constitutional Court found the decree unconstitutional, and the parliament began appointing new ministers. Negotiations between Yeltsin's team and the leadership of the parliament were unsuccessful. On October 3, armed supporters of the parliament tried to storm the headquarters of the Russian TV center in Moscow. In response, on October 4, the army troops began shooting at the White House, following Yeltsin's decree. Deputies refused to leave the building, and the troops started bombarding the White House from tanks. By the late afternoon on October 4, the deputies surrendered and the White House was in flames. The shooting continued in Moscow for several more days and, according to the state prosecutor's Office, 148 people were killed. The parliament's supporters cited 1,500 casualties as a more realistic number. Yegor Gaidar (1999) in his memoirs calls these events "a brief civil war," while the post-Soviet media routinely perceive Yeltsin's decision to shell the parliament in October 1993 as the origin of his later decree to use heavy weaponry to storm Grozny in December 1994.[18]

Nikolai's ambivalent reaction to this event was not entirely unusual for the first post-Soviet generation. The changes of the early 1990s did not immediately produce a political framing that could present the transitional period in a graspable manner (Rimskii 2003; Solov'ev 2004; Ryklin 2003). For many, the aesthetic gloss over political reality remained the dominant mode of symbolization, with its strong (and carefully sanitized) nostalgic appeal for all things Soviet.[19] In Nikolai's case, however, the "aesthetic experience" ended in 1995. Graduating with a master's degree in history from a local university, he started a teaching career in Barnaul's semiurban suburb. "It was exactly the time when salaries were not paid at all. And in general, the school was a distressing sight [*udruchaiushchee zrelishche*]....When

---

18. For a discussion see Gaidar (1999) and Pikhoia (2002). For the constitutionality of the October crises see Scheppele (2006).

19. On post-Soviet nostalgia in Russia see Boym (2001); Ivanova (2002a); Oushakine (2007). For a similar tendency in other postsocialist countries see Nadkarni and Shevchenko (2004).

I saw all that, somehow I got a clear idea that it just can't be this way [*tak byt' ne mozhet*]: a teacher who is hungry, barefoot and so on."

In the first half of the 1990s, the miserable material conditions noted by Nikolai were not a small factor. With galloping inflation and salaries unpaid for months, teachers—along with doctors and other professionals who were employed by the state and paid from the drastically shrinking state budget—perhaps suffered the most from economic reforms. The following statistics give a rough picture of the level of inflation. According to the official data, within a year, from 1991 to 1992, the consumer price index in the country increased 26.1 times (Analiz 2004, 79).[20] In 1992–94, wholesale prices for commodities produced in Russian industry went up 1,115 percent. In Altai, between 1994 and 1998, prices for products of daily consumption increased by 7,530.1 percent. The subsistence wage in the region in 1998 was 378 rubles; the average income was 439 rubles. For comparison, in Moscow the same correlation between the subsistence wage and average income was 552 rubles vs. 3,164 rubles; in the neighboring Novosibirsk province—478 rubles vs. 735.[21]

Important as these miserable conditions were, they rarely acted as a politicizing factor in my informants' explanations. As in the previous example, it was the theme of deception that channeled the motivation for political engagement. In Nikolai's case, the trope of universal falsehood was framed as a felt nonpresence in the flow of publicly available images, as a form of discursive disfranchisement that marginalized politically those who were unwilling or incapable to join in symbolically. As he put it, apart from his personal experience, there was "another important thing" that influenced the formation of his political view during the Yeltsin era: "It was the impression that 'They' constantly lie on TV. That is to say, there was a huge discrepancy between official propaganda and the reality that surrounded us."

The lack of correspondence between personal experience and public representation was often generalized further. *Their* lie on TV would mutate into an overwhelming general distrust of "liberal values" promoted by Yeltsin's reformers in the 1990s. In daily usage, liberal values would become associated not so much with individual liberties as with a total absence of any constraints. It is somewhat not surprising, that in the 1990s among

20. For an extensive collection of data related to economic changes caused by the liberalization of prices and privatization in the 1990s see the report of the Russian Audit Chamber (Analiz 2004).

21. Before the financial collapse in August 1998, $1 was about 6 rubles; after August 17, one U.S. dollar cost between 18 and 20 rubles. For details see Raiskaia, Sergienko, and Frenkel (2001, 111, 97–99).

younger generations the abbreviated form of "liberal values" (*La-Ve* in Russian) became a slang word for "cash."[22]

The distrust produced a double effect. The dismissal of liberal values, democracy, and private property was accompanied by a parallel move in regard to dominant post-Soviet interpretations of Russian and Soviet history. Irina L., an eighteen-year-old student at the local university and a very active member of the KPRF, said: "If I know that I am being lied to right now, right here, I start asking myself, 'What else did they lie to me about? Maybe socialism was not that bad?'" Perestroika-driven attempts to open up suppressed or censored moments in the past in order to disclose the true history of socialism in Soviet Russia seemed to have come full circle. The Soviet past and socialist legacy had become once again a major source of inspiration for political activism. The trope of the Soviet tragedy was supplemented by the trope of Soviet grandeur. It was, however, the presumed falseness of the present that made the post-Soviet reappropriation of Soviet cosmogonies possible.

"History Already Loves You!"

In 2001, a group of young Altai neocommunists and the antiglobalist organization Alternativa started publishing their own newspaper, *Pokolenie* (Generation), using their age as their main organizing category. In the first issue, the newspaper's authors presented themselves as a "young opposition to the [ruling] regime," and compared *Pokolenie* to "a breath of fresh air in the smoky Motherland, which has been burned down by reformers" (*Pokolenie* 2002). The slogan of the newspaper, "History already loves you!" (*Istoriia uzhe liubit vas!*), emphasized *Pokolenie*'s clear attempt to suggest a positive alternative to the dominant tendency of turning Soviet history into a grim list of political crimes and persecutions, into a "black book of Communism," as one publication had it (Courtois et al. 1999).

Pokolenie became a major outlet for organizing political events and campaigns. For instance, in December 2002 Altai leftists conducted an essay competition among the region's schools in order to stimulate students' interest in the eightieth anniversary of the Soviet Union's creation (December 31, 1922). The theme of the competition, "The Soviet Union Is My Address," was borrowed from a Soviet-era hit song written in the mid-1970s. The song's chorus line is often quoted in mass media or used as the headline for multiple

22. For an extensive exploration of this transformation see Pelevin (1999); for an etymological review see Erkhov (2007). On liberalism and distrust in Russia see Veselov (2004, 135–85); Eremicheva and Simpura (1999); Guzeva and Rona-Tas (2001).

nostalgia shows on TV.[23] This choice brought with it a historical reference that perhaps was not entirely intended. Back in the 1970s, the song was originally meant to weaken one's attachment to one's place of birth ("a small mother-land") and to provide some romantic flavor to the organized migration of workers to construction sites in the Far East. Regardless of its initial context, however, it is striking that just as in the past, a search for a sociopolitical "ad-dress" was preceded by a sense of dislocation, whether this dislocation was caused by a move to a remote construction site or by a vanished country.[24]

Among seventy entries in the competition, a majority were about the Great Patriotic War, "the only remaining sacrality," as Aleksei Ekart (2003), the leader of *Pokolenie,* called it.[25] Many participants also tried to draw comparisons between Soviet and post-Soviet periods. One student, for instance, wrote:

> I realized that the Soviet people were several steps higher in their moral at-titudes than myself or my generation....I think individualism is not typi-cal for the Russian national consciousness, even though a lot of people in my generation welcome it. They will be disappointed later, for individualism leads to alienation, loneliness, and self-isolation; it destroys links between generations. We should be developing according to our traditions; that is to say, we should follow the Russian path. (Quoted in Ekart 2003)

Together with the trope of universal falsehood, the anxiety about indi-vidualism that opposes the traditional "Russian path" was a major theme in my discussions with Altai neocoms. Emerging in different contexts and articulated in different metaphors, this threat of "alienating individualism" (and the private property that reifies it) contrasted with the idealized col-lectivity that was allegedly so typical for the Soviet people.

23. "I am with smart guys / I am next to the sign "Forward!" / I am among working people / I sing working songs with everyone in the country! / My heart is concerned / My heart is anx-ious / My cargo is ready to go / My mailing address is not a building / Nor is it a street / The Soviet Union is my address!" (Lyrics by V. Kharitonov, music by D. Tukhmanov.)

24. In 2005, a somewhat similar attempt was undertaken by pop singer Oleg Gazmanov. One of the most popular songs of the year was his clumsy ballad "Made in the U.S.S.R." Known for his patriotic bent, in his new song Gazmanov strung together a long list of Russo-Soviet names and objects (the Riuriks, the Romanovs, Lenin and Stalin / This is my country) inter-rupted by a chorus line: "I was born in the Soviet Union. / Made in the U.S.S.R."). As the singer explained it: "[In the song] I decided not to debate what is good and what is bad; these are our symbols....We grew up with them. Why should we erase them from our memory?" (Chernykh 2005, 8; see also Arvedlund 2005).

25. The Great Patriotic War refers to the Soviet participation in the Second World War—from June 22, 1941, when Germany entered Ukraine, to May 9, 1945, when Germany capitulated.

This romanticizing view of the generalized "people" (*narod*) is important. Like many other key cultural concepts, narod provides a stable conceptual container, a familiar symbolic form for new experiences and meanings. Usually understood as inclusive and all-embracing, the term often refers to "populace," "folk," or "nation."[26] Frequently, it references something traditional, earthy, and provincial: a fundamental social layer that can withstand the extravagancies of fickle urbanites. Russian populists (*narodniki*) of the 1870s famously turned narod into a cultural and moral icon, into a repository of knowledge and skills that were to epitomize the Russian way of life. Of course, bonds of solidarity that my informants retrospectively associated with the "Soviet people" were no more real than the "innate communism" that the populist movement of the 1870s discovered in the Russian peasantry. For my discussion here it is crucial that in both cases appeals to narod were used primarily to frame a reaction against capitalism in Russia. In both cases, appeals to popular knowledge and the narod's daily experience were supposed to undermine the "abstract intellectualism" of yet another generation of bookish Westernizers. In his analysis of populist ideology, Andrzej Walicki reveals the core of this attitude: "[T]he Russian democrats [of the 1860–70s] were so much impressed by [Marx's] *Capital*, especially by the description of the atrocities of primitive accumulation, that they decided to do everything to avoid capitalist development in Russia, thus becoming full-fledged, "classical" Populists" (1979, 225).

More than a century later, Altai neocoms were inspired by a similar process. Evgenii M., a twenty-year-old antiglobalist and a big fan of William Burroughs and Gabriel García Márquez, framed his reaction to the second coming of capitalism in Russia in the following way:

> In the Soviet period, there was this communion [*prichastnost'*] with something big. People felt that they were part of a certain whole, a part of a certain totality. And now everything is completely atomized. Maybe this is the way Americans want to think about themselves. But if we recall Aristotle's idea that man is a social animal, we would see that his idea was realized pretty well in the Soviet period. Today, in the post-Soviet person the level of this sociality [*sotsialnost'*] is next to zero. Everyone is as isolated as a grain of sand.

It is precisely this experience of being socially marginalized and pushed beyond meaningful networks and relations in the present that brought back the desire for the connectedness of the past. The historical component of

---

26. See Ries (1997, 27–30) for a detailed discussion.

this "meaningful totality" often remained unarticulated. It was not the actual Soviet experience that my informants were trying to rediscover. Rather, it was the "sociality" missing in the present that the reclaimed Soviet backdrop helped to reveal.[27]

In some cases, the juxtaposition of capitalist individuality and the empowering encasement of Soviet belonging led to unusual metaphors. In my discussions with Margarita Nurmatova, an active member of the KPRF (and a student of political science at a local university), she compared the Soviet people with "a person who lives in a golden cage with a blister on his toe." In her view, predominantly positive features of the Soviet period—stability and social cohesiveness (*splochennost'*)—were somewhat offset ("blistered") by economic shortages and a constrained freedom of movement and speech. Unlike the contained-yet-content life in the Soviet Union, the post-Soviet situation produced very different associations. As Nurmatova said, people now are "scared, intimidated, and worn out" (*zapugannoe, zatiukannoe, zadergannoe*). Projecting the dichotomy onto herself, she brought up the issue of belonging: "Soviet people did realize that they were elements of a whole; the whole that was cohesive and very strong.... Today I do not feel that I am an element of something big at all. I have a feeling that I am totally on my own in Russia today, and Russia hardly needs me."

It is easy to dismiss these desires for a meaningful wholeness as a post-totalitarian throwback, caused by the inability to properly work through the nation's traumatic history. Yet, as Étienne Balibar reminds us, the individual emerges as "a *responsible*, or an *accountable*, subject" only through subjecting himself or herself to a higher moral authority, a superior power, or a lofty ideal (Balibar 1994, 9; emphasis in the original). Regardless of its actual content, the process of subjectivation highlights the "transindividual" character of norms to which the individual submits himself or herself (Foucault 1997, 264).[28] Or, to use a slightly different framework, the formation of the subject can be understood as a process of recognition of values of the long-term cycle of exchange, discussed earlier. It is by realizing his or her own location within a larger symbolic order that the subject could address and be addressed by others.

27. In her study of postsocialist Poland, Elizabeth Dunn traces a similar reluctance of people to easily see themselves as "anonymous providers of abstract labor." In their symbolic struggle, employees often appeal to "alternate interpretations of socialism," evoking such forms of organic collectivity as kin and family as their main organizing metaphors (2004, 82, 158).

28. For a detailed discussion see also Foucault (2005, 365–66).

Such longing for an address, for a subject position within a field of long-term values, was clearly reflected by my informants. Again and again, in their interpretations, sociality and social relations were seen metonymically: the individual was perceived first of all as an element of the whole, as a part of the totality. My informants, however, tended to reject the other side of the equation: the status of the *part* of the totality was rarely specified. The content of the part's own distinctive quality often remained unspecified. As a result, the idealized totality of the past not only provided an important feeling of belonging to something big but also helped one to deny (or ignore) the individuating principles that underlay the present. Within this frame of reference, the collectivity was perceived not as a group of distinctive individuals but as a ramified yet integral national body.

Several weeks after my conversation with Nurmatova, I observed how the elemental desire for the whole was realized in practice. On November 1, 2002, I attended a meeting organized by local Communists and labor unions. The event took place in front of the building of the regional administration in downtown Barnaul. Throughout the rally city workers, pensioners, and peasants from the region criticized the federal government's agricultural policy and welfare cuts (figure 1.6).

The demonstration did not last long. After half an hour, the electric power that the regional administration provided for microphones and loudspeakers was mysteriously turned off, effectively forcing the group to leave. Nurmatova, with another young woman, participated in the meeting in an unusual form: with two big banners, they posed in front of the big sculpture of Lenin throughout the whole event. As she described the scene to me, "People tend to think that Communists are nothing but senile elders. So, imagine what happened to all these passersby when they saw us....I paid attention to their reactions on purpose. Nobody who saw us turned their eyes away. People would stop and look at us. For a long, long time. Their entire mocking attitude disappeared when they saw us, our armbands, and our banners. It was really powerful" (figure 1.7).

Expressionist motivations aside, the quotation shows how subjection to the gaze of others is realized through constructing a meeting point: armbands and banners act as "the locus of mediation" between the gazers and the gazed upon (Lacan 1978, 107; 1997, 267–69). The symbolic details (armbands and banners) differentiated Nurmatova and her colleague and simultaneously channeled the outsider's gaze toward the source of the detail's origin (the whole).[29]

29. See Barthes (1981, 55) on the role of metonymic *punctum* in structuring the gaze.

Fig. 1.6. An antigovernment meeting in Barnaul. The banner reads: "Patriots, Unite in the Name of the Motherland and the People!" November 2002. Photo by author.

In his work on language, Valentin Voloshinov, a Russian linguist, emphasized a similar dialectics of belonging (element/part, detail/picture, metonymy/whole) and dialogical exchange. As Voloshinov put it, if experience "is susceptible of being understood and interpreted, then it must have its existence in the material of actual, real signs" ([1929] 1998, 28). This material sedimentation of experience has its own spatial dimension. The "medium of signs," as Voloshinov insisted, "can arise only on *interindividual territory*," between socially organized individuals (12; emphasis in the original). Nurmatova's case demonstrates a somewhat reverse tendency, where the interindividual territory was claimed as dialogical through the will to connect, through constructing a material meeting point. A metonymic sign (an armband) not only created a bundle of social relations among responsible subjects ("people would stop and look") but also reconfigured the character of these social exchanges (the "mocking attitude disappeared").

The importance of such exchanges and meeting points—as imaginary as this importance might be—was widely shared by Altai neocommunists. But successful performance of subjection or deliberate self-inscribing in already existing settings occurred infrequently. More often, neocoms failed to establish an effective locus of mediation for expressing their position, as the following quotation indicates. In January 2003, summarizing the results of the

Fig. 1.7. Connecting with "something big." The Square of Soviets with a sculpture of Lenin (and a Baskin-Robbins ice-cream store behind it). Barnaul, November 2002. Photo by author.

essay competition mentioned earlier, twenty-nine-year-old Aleksei Ekart, a former teacher of history, the main leader of Altai's neocoms, and a recently elected member of the regional legislative assembly, wrote in *Pokolenie:*

> Only ten years ago, from each and every corner one could hear a lot of scorn and contempt addressed to the totalitarian Soviet Union, to the cursed CPSU, and to the bloodthirsty tyrannical Soviet leadership. You can still hear all that even now, especially if you spend a lot of time in front of the TV. But if you take a break and look back, if you think just for a moment, then in your consciousness... there would emerge the Great Country; the country where life was a thousand times better and more honest than the loathsome reality of today.... There is a new generation that is seeking the truth, even though this generation's thoughts are still shaped by stereotypes imposed by the regime. With time, these stereotypes will peel off, although the regime's ideologues and owners of the television-screen would try to impose new clichés again. But one cannot hide the Truth.... Looking back at the Soviet Union from a destroyed and poverty-stricken Russia, contemporary school students see the

Mighty Giant whose birthday is a true holiday.... These students are young communists; they just don't know it. They speak the same language as the KPRF's members do! And one day they will realize that things should be named accordingly.... very soon, like a thunder [they'd say to current politicians]: 'Pygmies, get off the stage of History; a new red generation is here!'" (Ekart 2003)

Ekart's statement touches upon major issues raised earlier. Today's "loathsome reality" is counterbalanced by the honest past and a search for the truth. In turn, the (Soviet) Mighty Giant reappears in the foreseeable future as a powerful (and consolidated) "new red generation" that displaces (atomized) pygmies of the present. The present is negatively charged and then rhetorically bypassed altogether by affirming the past and by projecting it into the future. The here and the now are constructed as a virtual territory of stereotypes, as a faceless and timeless space (*bezvremen'e*) colonized by the industry of ideological clichés. Characteristically, various leaflets frequently pasted by neocoms and *Pokolenie* around the city demonstrated the same tendency. The slogan "History already loves you!" was usually accompanied there by "The future belongs to us!"

The language of imposed stereotypes highlighted an important development of the trope of universal falsehood so typical of Altai leftists. Soviet-style deception as a tactic, as a flawed form of social exchange and distancing ("They pretend to pay us, and we pretend to work"), became devoid of its implied malfunctioning reciprocity. Instead, it was elevated to the status of strategy for the manipulation of consciousness. By describing hidden or violent technologies through which stereotypes were imposed, my informants explained away the collapse of the Soviet Union and the current state of affairs in Russia.

These politically charged attempts to unmask the lies and falsities of capitalism have developed historical roots. After all, for more than seventy years the newspaper titled *Pravda* (Truth) was the official outlet of the Communist Party of the Soviet Union. Today, the Soviet *Pravda* is close to nonexistent, and a "new red" *Pokolenie* replaced the old Marxist idea of alienation with the notion of an illusionary subjectivity produced by the media.

Uncoined Values versus Conditional Units

Pravda-seeking neocoms in Altai often started their intellectual search with a basic historical question: "How did the collapse of the Soviet Union become possible?" The neocoms' answer was straightforward. Andrei Andreev, a frequent writer for *Pokolenie*, observed, "There must have been a radical change in the minds of the Soviet citizens, and it was undertaken very cunningly. Forces interested in destroying Soviet civilization carried out a brilliant operation. Yet people neither stopped it, nor did they even notice it. Some of them even thought that this was the only possible course of development during the last fifteen years of our history" (2002, 5).

The brilliant operation in question is what neocoms termed a "technology of domination," realized through the "manipulation of social consciousness." The purpose of this manipulation, *Pokolenie*'s authors insisted, was to "preprogram" the masses' opinions, desires, and even psychological conditions in order to ensure a type of behavior suitable to the interests of those who owned the means of manipulation. Unlike Soviet propaganda, manipulation is a hidden process. As Andreev explained, "Manipulators work tacitly (like thieves) on the subconscious level," convincing people to act in a way they never would act otherwise (2002, 5).

Igor K., a twenty-six-year-old member of the Altai Slavonic Society and an active member of the Communist Party, explained in an interview how this manipulation works. Drawing my attention to the (seemingly) widespread "American films about psychos [*man'iaki*]," he contrasted them with the Russian detective genre. The difference, as Igor's argument went, was crucial. Detective plots require a "work of mind." To be able to narrow a circle of potential suspects down, one has to think and to analyze. By contrast, in American films about maniacs, everything is irrational and meaningless. Anyone can do anything to you at any time. One has to be on a constant alert, expecting to discover a maniac in every social encounter. As a result, Igor concluded, this culture of suspicion encouraged "hatred of others" and promoted "individualism and mutual distrust."

Using very different material, Andreev reached a similar conclusion in his article on manipulation. Combining old schemes of Soviet Marxism, conspiracy theory metaphors, and the post-Soviet fascination with "neuro-linguistic programming," a special set of linguistic techniques that allegedly could influence one's behavior and attitudes,[30] he wrote: "Programming works successfully when people are transformed into an 'atomized crowd.' One way to achieve such an atomized state is by promulgating the 'myth'

30. Almost any big bookstore in Russia now has a special section on "neuro-linguistic programming" (NLP), a special set of linguistic techniques that allegedly can influence one's behavior and attitudes. Sometimes this section is a subdivision of a larger section of books on PR; in other cases books on NLP are categorized as a subfield of psychology. Supporters of this approach like to refer to the "effect of the twenty-fifth frame" as the most typical example of the programming on the subconscious level. See Kovalev (2004).

of civil society, which makes everyone believe that civil society is an absolute good, and that it is impossible to achieve without private property, competition, individual freedom (egotistic individualism), the law-based-state, etc.... This is exactly how the 'atomized' crowd is created" (Andreev 2002, 5).

We have already seen how property and immorality became intrinsically linked in the Altai neocoms' imagination. Andreev's writing logically completed the narrative of dispossession by adding to it the theme of victimhood. As a result, for the Altai neocoms, the post-Soviet redistribution of property—with oligarchs on the one pole and those who "ended up with nothing" on the other—appeared to have two sources of origin. Not only were people deprived of "stealing skills" necessary for participating in the redistribution of property, but they were effectively blocked from taking any significant part in this process by being subjected to heavy psychological manipulations and programming.

One of the neocoms' favorite examples of this manipulative and atomizing programming was the privatization campaign in Russia. In 1992–94, the Yeltsin government conducted large-scale privatization by quickly transferring most national assets into private hands. Within a decade, a state-dominated economy became an economy with mixed forms of property ownership: by 2002 the number of state-owned enterprises was only 3.78 percent of all officially registered companies (Analiz 2004, 87). The campaign is usually associated with Anatolii Chubais, the head of the State Committee on Management of State Property at the time.[31] Under Chubais's leadership, in the fall of 1992, about 150 million privatization checks were distributed in Russia. Each citizen got one check, regardless of his or her age. Usually known as *vautchery* (vouchers), these conditional units could be sold for cash or invested in a piece of public property.

By the end of the campaign on July 1, 1994, more than 240,000 enterprises became private; over 40 million citizens—30 percent of those who received privatization checks—chose to own shares of privatized enterprises (Kokh 1998, 31, 39). The majority sold their checks for money. During the twenty-month campaign, market value fluctuated between four and twenty dollars (Boycko, Shleifer, and Vishny 1996, 101). Meanwhile, by late 1996 seven prominent bankers controlled over 50 percent of the nation's assets and 80 percent of national TV outlets (Goldman 2003, 2). Popularly considered the largest scam in Russian history, this privatization is often

31. On Chubais's career see Goldman (2003, 141–43).

labeled "grabitization" (*prikhvatizatsiia*), and many hold it responsible for the immense economic polarization of contemporary Russian society. Stories about insider deals and fake auctions are numerous. Their plots, though, usually unfold within the same basic matrix. For instance, when VAZ, Russia's major carmaker and the country's largest enterprise with five hundred thousand workers and a 7 percent share of the GDP, was singled out for privatization, the plant's managers designed an elaborate mechanism for restricting any unwelcome bidding. As a result, the market value of the plant established during the action was around $45 million. In 1991, Fiat, interested in buying the company, apparently offered the Russian government $2 billion (Boycko, Shleifer, and Vishny 1996, 108).[32]

When questioning privatization, Altai neocoms did not focus on its actual economic results. They were more concerned with trying to understand how it was possible to convince a huge number of people to give up their property. Describing their views on privatization in interviews and publications, my informants often referred to the work of the prolific Russian essayist Sergei Kara-Murza (n.d.), a Moscow-based historian of science. Beginning in the 1960s, Kara-Murza (born in 1939) worked within the system of the Academy of Sciences, the highest research institution in the Soviet Union. Throughout the 1990s, he published a series of books that discussed the role of ideology in social life. Kara-Murza's magnum opus, the almost seven hundred-page *Manipulation of Consciousness,* came out in 2000, and it was especially popular among *Pokolenie*'s authors. In the book, citing major Western philosophers—from Antonio Gramsci to Michel Foucault, Guy Debord, and Jurgen Habermas—Kara-Murza depicted how in "so-called democratic society" manipulation alters people's desires and behavior by implanting "idea viruses...that give birth to monsters that disable one's own mental capacities" (2000, 92).[33] The book is heavy on anecdote and theoretical conclusion and contains very little evidence about people's actual responses to the technologies of manipulation. One of his ideas, actively publicized by the Altai neocoms, is summarized below.

In an extended excerpt from *Manipulation of Consciousness* published in *Pokolenie,* Kara-Murza explained the reasons behind the success of privatization. He particularly singled out one symbolic strategy of the substituting

32. For brief reviews of the privatization campaign in English see Kotkin (2001, 129–34) and Goldman (2003). For an extensive analysis see the report of the Russian Audit Chamber (Analiz 2004); for a theoretical discussion of privatization see Verdery (1996, 204–28).

33. Elsewhere, Kara-Murza outlines the logic of manipulation this way: "We won't force you [to do anything] but we'll get into your soul and subconsciousness and turn everything in such a way that you'd want to do it yourself" (2000, 26).

mediation that "reformers" relied upon: "Cunning 'architects' [of privati-zation] launched [*zapustili*] a false metaphor in [people's] consciousness." This "false metaphor" equated "public [*obshchestvennaia*] property" with "nobody's property." In turn, public access to property was restricted by vouchers. Given the state of hyperinflation in the country at that time, vouchers were quickly accumulated by would-be oligarchs (Kara-Murza 2002b, 8).

Kara-Murza's focus on metaphorical substitutions in the process of privatization was not as paranoid as it might sound. In the collection of reviews *Who Owns Russia,* published in 2003 by *Kommersant-Vlast',* Rus-sia's major and most informative weekly, there is a section with the heading "A Short Course on Capitalism in Russia."[34] In an ironic twist, each year of the decade is associated in this section with a particular economic trend typical for that time. For example, to indicate the boom of the chaotic retail trade that started in 1993, the year is named as the "year of the commercial kiosk." Nineteen ninety-six is "the year of seven bankers," a description that referred to the period when Russia's seven major commercial banks alleg-edly managed to establish full control over the Russian president and the government (*seminbankirshchina*). The description of 1992 is illustrative: "1992—The Year of the Voucher. It was exactly in 1992 when every citizen was granted a right to a part of the people's economy [*narodnoe khoziaistvo*] in the shape of the voucher. Even though this right was symbolic, it was precisely the voucher that started privatization and ruined the thesis that everything around belongs to the people, that is to say—to nobody" (*Komu prinadlezhit Rossiia* 2003, 11).

The quick evolution from the people's economy to nobody's belongings is essential here, as is the recognition of the merely *symbolic* importance of the right to property in the shape of the voucher. It is even more strik-ing that both supporters and opponents of privatization recognized the symbolic significance of the voucher. Interpretations of this significance, of course, differed drastically.

When I interviewed Maria K., a local bureaucrat working for the office of cultural affairs, our discussion of the Chechen war took an unexpected turn. Complaining about the grim state of the nation's culture and language, Maria singled out the lack of popular understanding of current changes, aggravated by what she labeled "the expansion of imported words." Not

---

34. The title is a thinly disguised ironic reference to *A Short Course on the History of the All-Union Communist Party (Bolshevik).* Allegedly edited by Stalin, this famous hagiographic volume outlined the canonical version of the party's history in 1938, in the middle of purges.

knowing the actual meaning of imported words, she adamantly insisted, people become hostages to the hidden content that these words bring with them. "Look, we were told about *elektorat* and *vautcher*. But *vautcher* actually means "fake money" [*fal'shivye den'gi*]. See how we were duped from the very beginning?"[35] I protested, trying to explain that "voucher" usually means something else in English. My explanations were firmly rejected: "In America it is a slang word; precisely, in America. And where did Chubais study? At Harvard, that is to say, in America. They brought it over here and implemented it. And today we have this dominant attitude that anything could be done in a false kind of manner because it *might* work this way!"

Chubais did not study in America (let alone at Harvard), but neither this fact nor the actual meaning of "voucher" really mattered in this context.[36] What was important instead was the displacing move through which repatriation of capitalism was imagined. Social injustice was linguistically (and geographically) linked with the West; it was preprogrammed by the West, as the Altai neocoms would have said.

Of course, regarding vouchers as fake money was only a reflection of the anxiety about the lost certainty of social exchanges. Aleksei P., an active member of the Altai Slavonic Society, pointed to the root of this symbolic destabilization in his interview, drastically opposing the short-term monetary exchanges to the long-term moral perspective. As the twenty-four-year-old man put it, Soviet ideology provided meaning for people's lives: "People lived not with a single idea of how to stuff their stomachs, but with an idea of creating something new. Even if it was a utopia, it does not matter now; there *was* a supreme goal. The best accomplishment of the Soviet period was the fact that there was created a society that was *not* based on money."

In this quotation (as well as in many others) money was rarely seen as a vehicle of exchange or as a store of value. Rather, it was conceived as a condensed metaphor of change itself, as a "false value" that replaced previous utopian projects and informal relations. Associated with falsehood and substitution, money was frequently juxtaposed to real values. What appeared to be problematic was the conversion scale that could bring these

35. Yegor Gaidar, the head of the Russian government that started privatization, recalls in his memoirs that Boris Yeltsin supported the privatization plan but was resolutely against the term "voucher," which he considered "almost an indecent word." Yeltsin effectively banned the word, and governmental officials used the expression "privatization check" instead (1999, 169).

36. While Chubais did not study at Harvard, some Harvard scholars did influence the privatization process in Russia in a serious way (Wedel, 1998a, 1998b; McClintick 2006; Yale Connection 2002).

two spheres together. What caused uneasiness was the absence of a mediator able to transform a nonmonetized collectivity into a collectivity created by the circulation of the generally accepted equivalent. What was at stake, in other words, was a question of the price that one was willing to pay for such a transformation. Vasilii Filippov, a vocal professor of philosophy in Barnaul, whose work is discussed in the next chapter, expressed this position in the most succinct way: "Money, as the equivalent of value of things (commodities), in fact substitutes things, lumps them together, and then exchanges everything for anything: faith for disbelief, loyalty for betrayal. Money could turn an honest person into a scoundrel; a brave individual into a coward; one's duty to the Fatherland into a treachery against the Fatherland; worship of the ancestors' graves into desecration of the memory of the elders" (Goncharov and Filippov 1996, 351).[37] To put it simply, within this order of things, money becomes a source and a mechanism of "money-pulation."

Hand in hand with the "oligarchic dictatorship of the wild market" (Buldakov 2002, 14), the all-permeating manipulation of capital finally finds its fullest representation in another crucial substitution, pointed to by Altai neocoms. As Vitalii Buldakov, a leader of the newly organized Altai Communist Union of Youth (Komsomol), put it, the simplest way to manipulate people's consciousness consists in "substituting artificial and virtual-cultural needs of the consumer society for one's real needs." Performed mostly by the mass media, such a substitution produces the "illusion of one's own subjecthood" (*illiuziia sobstvennoi sub"ektnosti*) (2002, 14). How does that happen? Buldakov's main arguments were drawn from his experience in a summer seminar on psychological methods, organized in 2002 by professors of sociology from Altai State University. In his article "A 'Harmless' Psychology," the leader of the Altai Komsomol group explained: "An object is invested with a symbol of a certain need, and it becomes valuable not by itself but as a carrier of a certain culture—and history-specific need." Once invested, such needs are universalized. As a result, "freedom is illusory, since all the alternatives are predetermined. Priorities have been selected; the choice has been made. Society is under total control" (2002, 14).

---

37. There is at least one more substitution taking place here. Filippov's description is basically an unreferenced paraphrase of Marx's lines from *The Power of Money in Bourgeois Society of 1844:* "[M]oney is thus the general overturning of *individualities* which turns them into their contrary....It transforms fidelity into infidelity, love into hate, hate into love, virtue into vice, vice into virtue, servant into master, master into servant, idiocy into intelligence, and intelligence into idiocy" (1972, 82; emphasis in the original).

There is a certain irony in the neocoms' oscillation between nostalgia for the meaningful totality of the Soviet past and the fear of a new totality of illusory freedom, between the lost utopia and the horror of predetermined needs. Buldakov's conclusion indicates a possible way out of this deadlock: the critique seems to be aesthetically driven. What is important is not the need associated with a particular object but rather one's ability to value the object by itself. Exchange value and use value, which normally determine the social life of things, are both completely discarded here. Instead, a new value class is constructed (Parry and Bloch 1989, 15). Aggravated by false and illusory connections among atomized individuals, the lost sense of authenticity is restored through appealing to absolute standards of measurement. The following citation from *Pokolenie* is a good example of this anxious search for a reliable touchstone. Explaining why liberalism cannot be "our own value," eighteen-year-old Margarita Nurmatova wrote in 2002:

> By now we've been trained to get accustomed to the West for quite some time. Turn on any TV channel, and you'd watch an American speech or Americanized ads, Americanized serials or Americanized shows....It is hard to withstand this pressure. Russian reformers have everything they need: mass media, administrative power, money. Today the most important thing is to hold out against all the temptations, to resist various attempts of turning us into "free individuals" of the Western mold, that is to say, into "human material" that could be used for destroying Russia. We should remain the way we are—just as nature and history have created us. Not everything shiny is gold. Gold is us. And the best gold is Russia itself" (2002).

Naïve as it might be, this description nonetheless reflects a strong yearning for standards destabilized by the quick advance of postsocialist capitalism in Russia. It reveals an attempt to secure some meaningful control over the flow of ideas and commodities. Its strong anti-Western language should not hide the underlying concern with the perceived debasement of local cultural values.

It is useful to approach this constellation of false money, manipulated consciousness, and illusory subjectivity on the one hand, and references to truth and the gold standard of Russia on the other through a theoretical framework suggested by Jean-Joseph Goux. In his study, Goux traces a structural homology between money and language, pointing to the "increasing disembodiment of value," which is understood both financially and discursively (1994, 17). For instance, money backed by gold corresponds to the expressive realism of descriptions. In turn, paper currency goes hand in hand with representational capacities of language, able to portray reality with only some degree of precision. Finally, and more relevantly, a "forced currency"—that is to say, conventional or fictive money (conditional units)—manifests "a true crisis of confidence in the value of language" (18). The disembodiment of value, in other words, demonstrates how the amalgam of measurement, exchange, and deposit falls apart: "What used to be a complete general equivalent…now explodes in a generalized counterfeiting effect" (80).

The examples discussed earlier reveal a similar tendency. Persistent portrayals of post-Soviet falsehood, taken together with obsessive fixations on manipulative mediation, indicate a perceived symbolic or material imbalance that has been produced by existing strategies of symbolization (a right to property in the shape of the voucher). In the texts of Altai neocoms, words, objects, and values have lost their authenticity; they are not what they purport to be. Just as in the eighteenth-century political economy and courtship novels studied by James Thompson, Altai neocoms are working through the semiological crisis of the concept of value by trying to restore its proper location either in the signifier, in the referent, or in the process of exchange itself (1996, 17).

To put it differently, the gradual uncoupling of different functions of money (equivalent, token, treasure) resulted in the "regime of noncoverage," a mode of symbolizing and exchange based on inconvertibility (Goux 1994, 121). For Goux, the inconvertibility of values under the regime of noncoverage—and the admission of loss and the unpredictability of gaining that are associated with it—is a starting premise of any contemporary exchange. Value is a product of dialogical interaction rather than a reflection of the inherent quality of objects.

The polemical efforts of Altai leftists were aimed at locating principles of inconvertibility and noncoverage in a very different context. It was not a search for an effective form of mediation in a given circumstance that was at stake here. Instead, the Altai neocoms were mostly concerned with the rhetorical substantiation of the regime of noncoverage. It was an attempt to determine the size and scope of the inalienable wealth that animated their symbolic activity. The context-bound perception of values and meanings of the sign was overshadowed here by a striving to resurrect the ultimate referent, to go back to uncoined values (Goux 1999). As a result, a particular set of symbolic practices and symbolic objects was construed as exclusive cultural possessions that had to be protected from duplication, corruption, or piracy by others, precisely because these possessions were perceived as representing important aspects of collective identity (Harrison 1999, 239, 241).

Significantly, the neocoms' attempt to solve the crises of confidence by evoking abstract categories (truth, the Mighty Giant, or gold) has some structural resemblance to the strategy outlined by Goux. As he pointed out, to be effective, the regime of noncoverage must compensate for the decreasing confidence in value with the increasing faith in the abstract aspects of exchange and representation (1994, 45). But here the resemblance ends. For Goux, "the collapse of referents, the dissolution of exchange standards, and the disassociation of the sign from what it signifies" require the "dictatorship" of law to rationalize and regulate the predictability of forms, stages, and outcomes of social exchange (1999, 115). For neocoms, universality of formal law was hardly a choice. The Russian capitalism of the 1990s was remarkably divorced from legality, with law being "up for definition and appropriation" (Humphrey 2002b, 125). What could function as a new source of legitimacy in this case? In what form were social relations abstracted by neocommunists?

There are two main approaches through which Altai neocoms tried to maintain their confidence in the social order. Both reflect the tendencies explored throughout this book. The first approach produced strong bonds of social attachment by repeatedly articulating a culturally shared traumatic experience. The second approach highlighted the commonality of the place of origin as a crucial component of the sociocultural and political solidarity of Russians.[38] These appeals to the nation's trauma and place of origin could be seen as examples of inalienable cultural symbols.[39] As with many other symbols discussed here, the importance of these two forms is determined negatively: claims to particular cultural forms and practices are rooted in the recognition that loss of these cultural possessions would radically affect both the group's self-perception and its ability to relate to others (Welsh 1997, 17; Rowlands 2004). As a part of what Richard Rorty called the "final vocabulary," these symbolic practices reveal that "beyond them there is only hopeless passivity or a resort to force" (1989, 73). Unlike manipulative rhetoric, these final cultural tools aim at creating a community of speakers and listeners by "stating fully and sincerely" the foundations that should be used as a starting point for a common action (White 1985, 6, 17). The next section demonstrates how such statements and foundations were laid out.

38. More on the place of origin (mesto rozhdenia) and the place of development (mesto razvitia) as key elements of Russian nationalist writing see chapter 2.

39. See Michael Brown (2004); Harrison (1999); Weiner (1985) for more details on inalienable cultural possessions.

"Victory Is Not about Gaining"

In February 2002, the Altai Regional Committee on Public Education organized in Barnaul a "scientific-methodological" conference, "Contemporary Problems of Patriotic Education and Some Ways to Solve Them." The conference brought together a diverse group of people. Among the 150 participants were local politicians, educators, heads of regional museums, and military-patriotic clubs (Pol'shchikova 2002). In his long presentation, the head of the committee listed numerous patriotic song festivals, boot camps, and exhibits that were intended to instill the right patriotic attitude in the new generation. The next plenary speaker, Major-General Vladimir Val'kov, the head of the regional division of the Ministry of Interior, which cosponsored the conference, framed the issue quite differently. Quickly dismissing the existing practices of patriotic education as "good and diverse but lacking the most important things," the general appealed to the experience of the Great Patriotic War. The war, the general insisted, was both a source of patriotic values and a source of veterans who had been able to transmit these values to other generations. Bemoaning the drastic depletion of this source, the general asked:

> Who can implement patriotic education today? And, generally speaking, what does "patriotism" mean in today's Russia? It has not yet found its decoding [*rasshifrovka*], if you will. There is no decoding whatsoever! We don't respect our anthem. We don't want to see our state flag. We call the state emblem of Russia...—how do we call [this double-headed eagle]? That's right! We call it a "chicken" [*kuritsa*]! It all starts with educating people, with making them love their native Russia. But how could you possibly love it when the child does not absorb this pure [feeling]? Instead of absorbing it as the infantile sponge [*gubka detskaia*] and carrying [this feeling] with him throughout his life, the child absorbs something else. He absorbs drugs. Very quickly, he absorbs the idea that one can have a lot of money without working. He absorbs the fact that studying isn't important because one can be the happiest and most important person in the world if one has lots of money. And the main symbol of patriotic education today is precisely this: the close-shaven, pumped up physiognomy [of a mobster]."[40]

This basic binary of "patriotism vs. money" articulated by Val'kov is familiar by now. The increasing autonomy of money, as well as the logic of universal exchangeability that associated with it, constantly raises unsettling

---

40. I quote from the tape recording made during the conference.

questions about the limits of monetization. Moreover, the drastic polarization of post-Soviet society in the process of privatization has painfully revealed the arbitrary character of exchange-value. No longer associated with the labor invested in the object of exchange, exchange-value became solely dependent on the interplay between supply and demand. In this respect, Val'kov's appeal to the symbolically grounding experience of the Great Patriotic War as a contrast to the empty symbolic artifacts of the present (anthem, flag, the state emblem) was essential. Acting as the nation's ultimate cultural property in the post-Soviet era ("the only sacrality left"), the activated memory of the war provided an emotional anchoring point necessary for producing a feeling of solidarity. Exchange was equated with empathy.

In my interviews with Altai neocoms, the theme of war very rarely developed into a special conversation. My questions about the Chechen wars were usually shrugged off, too. Aleksei Z., sitting in Baskin-Robbins, seemed to have a point when explaining to me the cultural distinctiveness of the Russians. "If there is a fight, we won't lend a hand, but if there is a war, we'll win it with God's help," Aleksei said, quoting a line from a song. He elaborated: "We can get all together only when there is a war; then we all act as one person, as a single whole."

This mechanical solidarity provoked by threat adds an important correction to the picture of something big that ensured the cohesiveness of the Soviet people and was so often idealized by my informants. Kara-Murza, in his *Manipulation of Consciousness,* follows a similar logic when drawing a sharp line between the "two types of life-arrangement" (*zhizneustroistvo*). As Kara-Murza insists, the main goal of the Russian civilization has been a "decrease of *suffering,*" not the "increase of *pleasure*" that has become so typical in the West (2000, 177; emphasis in the original). Yet attempts to alleviate the traumatic memory are bound to reproduce representations of misery as their ultimate point of departure. Firmly anchored in the negative ("if there is a war..."), the zero point of this decrease of suffering is often way below zero, so to speak.

It is not the war memory as such that is problematic here. Rather, it is the persistence with which images of overwhelming social trauma are used as the universal equivalent that could symbolically bring people together. In this context, it is indicative that despite their very different social and educational backgrounds, Altai neocoms ended up using the same strategy of consolidation that would be deployed by Chechen war veterans (see chapter 3). Both neocoms and ex-soldiers approached social difficulties and a state of moral uncertainty through the lens of the militarist discourse of besiegement. In turn, the symbolic legacy of the Great Patriotic War was reappropriated and reconfigured for an imaginary overcoming of current crises. It is important that Altai neocoms tried to establish links with a broader community by emphasizing first of all popular memories of war losses rather than war victories. An article published in the October 2002 issue of *Pokolenie* illustrates this tendency.

Designed to celebrate the eighty-fifth anniversary of the October Revolution of 1917, the headline of the issue announced: "Our red October is yet to come!" The issue came out in the midst of the national crisis provoked by a traumatic event in Moscow, when a group of Chechen terrorists took hostage a full Moscow theater during a performance. Instead of the usual editorial, this issue of *Pokolenie* had a short essay called "What Victory Means":

> Some time ago Shakespeare wrote: "Tired with all these, for restful death I cry." We have leaders who don't even bother to hide their treason, their incompetence, and their helplessness. We have a sodomite [*sodomitskaia*] "elite" that has occupied all the TV channels and newspapers, despising the "cattle" [*bydlo*, people] and "that country" [*etu stranu*, Russia]. We have a political opposition that is even incapable of picking a leader who could bring its members together.
>
> And then, there are the people....There are the people who are glued to TV commercials for tampons and condoms. There are the people who are dying out and drinking themselves to death; there are the people who go through two million abortions annually, accompanied by the squealing of [the lesbian duo] Ta-Tu. The only reasonable conclusion for all that is: we are doomed....
>
> Perhaps, a similar feeling of despair dominated the mood in 1941, in Moscow's suburbs [occupied by the enemy]. It was the time when the multilingual army crashed through our land and burned down our villages and cities; when untrained cadets attacked tanks only with rifles in their hands; when the Government conducted its meetings in [the security of] underground galleries of Moscow's subway system; when the sarcophagus with the body of the Leader was being hidden in Siberia. And nonetheless, we won then [*i vse-taki my pobedili togda*]....
>
> To keep one's feeling of Victory alive is already a feat. A feat that is achieved in one's soul, where the devil fights with God, as Dostoevsky put it. The whole world—enemies, friends, relatives, and even your own mind—keeps telling you: "Back off." And they give you thousands of reasons and arguments for this. And then, knowing damn well that you will lose it, you make yourself believe. And you become invincible.
>
> The meaning of Victory cannot be expressed in numbers of conquered cities or killed enemies. The Soviet warriors who raised the banner above

Berlin were invincible. But so was the Sixth Paratrooper Company that did not surrender but faced death from a group of Chechen fighters [*boeviks*], which was ten times bigger.

Victory is not about gaining [*vyigrysh*]. One can gain by cheating, or by chance, or by building a quantitative superiority. Victory is the Truth [*Pravda*]. Victory is Providence. This might be a really tough lot for us; yet the enemy cannot have victory. The victorious are the ones on the side of the Truth. As we are. (Borovikov 2002)[41] (Figure 1.8)

Written by a graduate student at a local university, the text repeats motifs traced throughout this book—namely, post-Soviet practices of solidarity that emerge through the articulation of negation and the recollection of loss. What is quite distinctive about these forms of connectedness is a particular type of fixation on the things being rejected. The compulsion to repair the social fabric, torn in moments of crisis, by appealing to the power of the collective seems to be very limited here (if it is present at all). This solidarity of grief is not about restorative mending, nor is it usually aimed at retribution. It appears that the primary meaning of this type of connectedness is to bring back multiple recollections of the traumatic experience, to reveal the semblance of the current situation with grave historical events that similarly consolidated the nation in the past. Continuity of national history is constructed by tracing the unceasing circulation of pain. "Victory is not about gaining" in this cultural matrix; hence successes are rarely associated with the effective use of force or a productive deployment of cunning. Seemingly accidental, achieved in spite of everything, these victories of despair highlight obstacles and recall ordeals (rifles against tanks). Rather than celebrating achievements, they constantly recall their impossibility: "You know you will lose it."

The trope of truth adds an important dimension to this general cultural narrative about the subjectifying role of the traumatic. Introducing an effective rhetorical opposition, statements of truth remain performative ("We are on the side of the Truth"), not descriptive.[42] Undertaking their negative

---

41. The pop-duo t.A.T.u. mentioned in the essay is a Russian teen group that became extremely popular in 2001–3. It was the first Russian group that was marketed as lesbian (Heller 2007). The Sixth Paratrooper Company mentioned later refers to an event on February 29, 2000, when ninety combatants from the Sixth Company were blocked by a large group of Chechen troops (about two thousand people) near the village of Ulus-Kert, Chechnya. Eighty-three Russian soldiers were killed; all of them were awarded highest military distinctions posthumously (Khairulin 2006, 6).

42. For more on truth as a binding value in provincial Russia see Solovei (2003, 98–101).

Поколение

ОН ЕЩЕ ПРИДЕТ - НАШ КРАСНЫЙ ОКТЯБРЬ!

ИСТОРИЯ УЖЕ ЛЮБИТ ВАС!   № 8 (14), октябрь 2002 г.
Выходит с июня 2001 г.
http://altnet.ru/~pokolen

Молодежная общественно-политическая газета

Леонид КОРНИЛОВ

НОРД-ОСТ

И горы встали в полный рост.
И все ветра упали разом.
И только мстительный норд-ост
Гудит над Северным Кавказом.
Берет ущелья за грудки.
Гремит лавинным беспределом.
Но погодите, мужики.
Да не в Кавказе вовсе дело.
А мир трещит наполовам
По тайной прихоти Сиона.
С чадрою носится ислам
А Голливуд раздел Мадонну.
И содомиты у руля.
И ЦРУ живет с «Моссадом».
И на земной оси Земля.
Как стриптизерша, крутит задом.
И сводит нравственность на нет
Все то, что лишется с натуры.
Подогревая кровью нефть,
Схлестнулись насмерть две культуры.
А Русь глядит по сторонам,
Хрипя в предательской трясине.
С одной – разврат, с другой – ислам.
А православие – в средине.
Олег, сбирайся-ка давай
Отмстить хазарам за обиды.
Но знай, американский рай
Не легче пояса шахида.
И преклони свою главу,
Ты уяси себе в печали,
Что сестры зла не на Москву,
А на Бродвей в Москве напали.
И горы встали в полный рост.
И все ветра упали разом.
И только засланный норд-ост
Нас косит вперемешку с газом.
Венец природы, как конец,
Предстал под знаком Атлантиды.
И подпоясана АЭС
Тяжелым поясом шахида.

ПОЛИТИНФОРМАЦИЯ
Как мы понимаем происходящие события

Принятие Госдумой РФ поправок в Закон «О референдуме».

Они долго орали, что являются демократами. Расстреляли Верховный Совет, состряпали и протащили в 93-м году «демократическую» Конституцию. Тогда же захапали предприятия. И сегодня добрались до нашей земли. У народно-патриотической оппозиции ничего не оставалось, как обратиться к мнению народа... У нас ведь вроде демократия!?

Оказалось, что демократ не мешало бы затянуться годика на полтора. Решили, четыре раза «тупо проголосовали», как выразился Митрофанушка Эпидиозвродкин, жидко поаплодировали. Возможно, вечером выпили – шутка ли, закон-то конституционный, нужно 300 голосов, а набрали 304.

Спасибо, Родина вас наверняка не забудет. А мы-то уж точно, поверьте на слово. Вы верите? Клянемся! ГОТОВЬТЕ СПИСКИ.

(Продолжение на стр. 5, 6)

7 НОЯБРЯ МЫ ЖДЕМ ТЕБЯ НА ДЕМОНСТРАЦИИ! Место встречи – пл. Октября у гастронома «Под шпилем», в 9.30. В 10.00 – начало движения колонн. В 10.30 – митинг на пл. Советов. **ПРИХОДИ, ТЫ НУЖЕН РОССИИ!** *Алтайское отделение СКМ РФ.*

ЧТО ТАКОЕ ПОБЕДА

Как писал Шекспир, «все мерзостно, что вижу я вокруг». Правители, даже не скрывающие своего предательства, своей некомпетентности и беспомощности. Содомитская «элита», оккупировавшая все телеканалы и газеты, презирающая «быдло» и свою страну. Оппозиция, не способная выдвинуть такого лидера, чтобы хотя бы просто объединиться. И народ... Народ, не отрывающий глаз от рекламы прокладок и презервативов. Народ, вымирающий и спивающийся, народ, делающий в год по миллиона абортов в год под визги «Тату». Единственный разумный вывод из всего этого – мы обречены...

Может быть, такое же чувство обреченности было в 41-м под Москвой. Когда армия «двунадесяти языков» топтала русскую землю, сжигая деревни и города, когда необученные курсанты шли с винтовками на танки, когда Правительство заседало в подземных галереях метро, когда саркофаг с телом Вождя прятали в Сибири. Но ведь тогда мы победили.

Победа приходит не в борьбе, не в бою, и уж тем более – смешно сказать – не на выборах. Вожди, партии, страны побеждают благодаря тому чувству Победы, той веры в Победу, которые вспыхивают в сердцах искренних и честных людей. Главное, не дать погаснуть этому огню...

В Великой войне мы победили не тогда, когда последний солдат вермахта поднял руки вверх, а уже тогда, когда Матросов бросался на дот и Гастелло совершал воздушный таран. Когда Сталин отказывался эвакуироваться из прифронтовой Москвы или обменять захваченного в фашистский плен сына Якова на фельдмаршала Паулюса. Когда академики и артисты отказывались от «брони» и шли в ополчение рыть окопы. Когда безногий Маресьев начал учиться танцевать. И все бессмертные и безвестные Герои, оставшиеся на полях сражений, вовсе не были безрассудными смельчаками. Наоборот, они с первых дней войны твердо знали, что победят и совершенно осознанно выбирали смерть. Остальное было лишь делом времени.

Победа не сваливается с неба, не даруется просто так. Надо заслужить право быть победителями. Надо быть достойными стяжать Победу.

Сохранить в себе чувство Победы – это уже подвиг. Подвиг, совершаемый в душе, где, как говорил Достоевский, дьявол борется с Богом. Ведь весь мир – враги, друзья, родные, да и твой собственный разум говорит тебе: отступи. Приводит тысячи очевидных и неоспоримых доводов. И когда ты, понимая умом, что проиграешь, заставляешь себя вновь поверить – ты становишься непобедимым.

Смысл Победы нельзя выразить только во взятых городах и убитых врагах. Непобедимыми были советские воины, поднявшие знамя над Берлином. Но непобедимой осталась и Шестая десантная рота, уничтоженная в Чечне десятикратно превосходящими ее боевиками, но не отступившая ни на шаг.

Победа – это не выигрыш. Выиграть можно благодаря обману, случаю, количественному перевесу. А Победа – это Правда. Победа – это Промысел.

Поэтому, как бы тяжело нам не приходилось, враг никогда не сможет победить. Победить могут только те, за кем Правда. А она за нами. И мы, оппозиция, победим не потому, что выиграем выборы. Логика здесь другая – мы выиграем выборы, потому что мы должны победить.

Дмитрий БОРОВИКОВ.

Fig. 1.8. *Pokolenie* (Generation): "Our Red October is yet to come!" October 2002. Photo by author.

selection, determining sites of negative dependency, these statements mostly reject ("incompetent leaders," "a sodomite elite," or "an incapable opposition") without pointing to plausible alternatives. Stringing together a chain of negations, these sentences nonetheless produce an affirmative effect. You know you will lose. You know that victory is not about gaining. But more importantly, you know that the enemy cannot have victory. By framing social relations within the logic of martyrdom, recourses to past suffering (in the name of truth) delimit the nation's borders. The nation's history is presented as a teleological process: a community of people that was brought together by a shared experience of pain in order to memorialize their losses for future generations (see Ries 1997, 126–60; Pesmen 2000, 54–59).

Viktor Shklovsky in his *Sentimental Journey* had a striking observation that sums up this foundational role of loss in Russians' self-perception. Writing after the Bolshevik Revolution and World War I, he observed, "It is impossible to lead the dead into battle, but you can line them up, cover them with a little sand and use them for a roadbed" (2004, 188). As the metaphor of the roadbed paved by the dead suggests, this "cultural transmission of loss" unfolds in a particular interindividual territory (Rowlands 2004, 219). The mother-land (*rodnaia zemlia*) acts as a perfect totality that simultaneously provides an ultimate moral ground, a dominant national symbol, and a literal physical container for the martyrs of the past and the future.[43] Artem Manakov, a Barnaul student, wrote to the editor of *Pokolenie* in his letter titled "On Russia: With Love and Pain. Fighting for Russia":

> In the world's history, there is no other land, except for Russia, that three times shed the blood of its own people in order to rescue the West, as well as the whole world from enslavement....But every nation has a breed of people who associate their mother-land [*rodnaia zemlia*] only with gas, oil, or metals. This is the only value that it has for them. [Russia's] reformers are trying to assess [the land] through auction, and then to sell it exactly to this breed.
>
> For me, Motherland [*Rodina*] means the graves of my ancestors. It means sweat, blood and the tears of our people. For what cause have millions of people died? Did Russian peasants, merchants, tsars, and secretaries-general carefully pull together my Fatherland so that a peddler could sell it piecemeal? He could spit on my Motherland....The Soviet soldier saw burning

---

43. The English word "motherland" is usually translated as *rodina* in Russian, although the Russian original has no direct correlation with "mother." *Rodnoi* has the same root as *rod*, which means *kin* but also *gender*. The word can be used to describe relatives (*rodnye*) or, for instance, one's mother tongue (*rodnoi iazyk*). I will use "mother-land" to render *rodnaia zemlia*, "the land of the kin," intimate land," and will render Rodina as Motherland.

huts and birch trees, he saw the grief of mothers, children, and elders; he saw motherland [*rodnaia zemlia*] burning down. He also saw the enemy, and he crushed this enemy without pity. Today our land is not on fire, nor is there an enemy at the borders. But one invisible force has already passed our borders; this force destroys everyone and everything. This force imposes norms alien to our peoples: the cult of Golden Calf. Tomorrow, having conquered our land, the enemy won't spare our churches, our culture, or our history. (Manakov 2001, 1)

Used as a screen for projecting traumatic histories of the past and economic anxieties of the present, the mother-land (*rodnaia zemlia*) constantly fluctuates here between the symbolic and the material, between the sign and the referent, resisting any stable localization. The quote also suggests an interesting semantic triangulation within which the meaning of the mother-land emerges. It is a combination of land-death-enemy that brings together the sociotemporal (dead ancestors) and the sociospatial ("enemy at the borders") dimensions and activates the traumatic again and again ("For what have millions of people died?"). I follow this unstable symbolism of the land by looking at an attempt to prove a physical incompatibility of neoliberal capitalism with Russia's terrain.

Why Russia Is Not America

Vladimir O. (born in 1962), a high-profile official in the regional Orthodox diocese in Barnaul, was a secular bureaucrat working for a religious institution. Not constrained by church doctrine, he was quite outspoken and opinionated in conversations with me. Comparing "liberal ideas of unlimited permissiveness and freedom" to a "black veil that descended on Russia at the West's request," Vladimir explained why freedom is detrimental in the Russian climate:

People don't know how to use freedom. In the same way our people don't know how to treat alcohol….You cannot grant freedom to them! Especially in our miserable economic conditions. Our economy is forever geographically determined by the negative [i.e., below freezing] temperatures. These conditions demand that Russia have strong state leadership, an authoritarian one. Otherwise, all these democratic values would result in a simple fact: as soon as Russia opens itself to the world market, all our capital flees….The new Russians [capitalists] have saved lots of money, but where would they invest this money? Here? They would have to build a plant and then to heat it all the time, because it is −20°C outside. Plus they'd have to pay their employees enough money so that they could buy a lot of fatty food and warm clothes to protect themselves from the cold. Of course, they'd rather invest their money somewhere in Malaysia.

During my fieldwork I gradually got used to this geographical determinism. In different cultural and social settings I repeatedly observed the same intellectual attempt to reconnect the national history with the soil in order to restore the original configuration of nature and history and return to the geohistorical context that had shaped up the Russian people in the past. These discussions were usually structured around the argument developed by Andrei Parshev, a Moscow-based economist, who in 1999 published the first edition of his book *Why Russia Is Not America*. Written in a highly accessible manner, the book seemed to provide a final, objective, and ideologically neutral argument against the current course of liberal reforms.

Between 2001 and 2004, the book was reviewed in major academic journals. Its main arguments have been examined by a wide range of experts, from local economists, historians, and literary nationalists to senior fellows from the Brookings Institution (Laktionova 2002; Burganov 2002; Kudrov 2002; Rusakova 2002; Hill and Gaddy 2003). Parshev's suggestion to locate the main cause of Russia's consistent economic failures in its own climate and terrain quickly became "an integral part of the economic and geographic knowledge of any educated Russian [*rossiianin*], a truism that does not have to be verified anymore," as one reviewer of the book put it (Tsirel' 2003, 182). Within a very short time, a previously unknown lecturer from a Moscow military college became a highly sought-after pundit. The Russian Academy of Sciences invited him to present his views to economists, and Russia's major TV programs and radio talk shows asked him to participate in their programs (Parshev 2001a, 102–4; 2001b; 2003). For a while, discussions about the climatic predestination of Russia's political and economic development saturated every conceivable venue. Altai also followed this intellectual fad. In August 2002, Aleksei Ekart, the leader of Altai neocoms, published a long review of the book in *Pokolenie* (2002, 15). As if sharing the same script, in interviews and conversations my informants also repeated the meteorological view of the economy already articulated for me by Vladimir O.

When the second edition of the book came out in 2001, it had a political framing that could not be called subtle. Published in the series *The Grand Confrontation* (*Velikoe protivostoianie*), the book bore the subtitle *For Those Who Stay in Russia*. Parodying a familiar cliché, a blurb recommended the book as "an introductory economics course for ministers of finance, ministers of economics, and directors of institutes for the economy in transition."[44] The book's title is somewhat misleading. *Why Russia Is Not America* has almost nothing to say about America, and given the main message of the book, Russia could be easily compared with any other place.

The starting point of the book was a set of seemingly economic questions. Why, despite all these years of liberal reforms, did foreign companies not invest in Russia? What happened to foreign capital in Russia? Moreover, why was there a persistently unequal economic exchange between Russia and the rest of the world? For years Russian merchants brought commodities into the country and took dollars out of the country, even though Russia does not "produce dollars," as Parshev put it (2001c, 36). Instead of looking at political aspects of Russia's investment climate, Parshev concentrated on the potential competitiveness of commodities produced in the country. The end result was discouraging. According to Parshev, only one-third of Russia's territory could be economically "effective," given the temperature regime, fecundity of soil, and so on. Yet even this third is located in the coldest part of the world: Russia's average annual temperature is −5.5°C; Finland, by comparison, has +1.5°C (2001c, 42, 39). Low temperatures would constantly demand high energy consumption not only for industrial production and agriculture but also for the organization of one's private life. The extremely energy-intensive life in Russia would be forever aggravated by yet another geographic factor: the country's expanse. Given the low density of Russia's population, long distances would always increase transportation costs and make Russia's economy even less competitive. Hence, Parshev's general conclusion: given Russia's geography, industrial production in this country is destined to have minimal surplus value (2001c, 103).

Taken at face value, such geographic observations could hardly provoke any substantial interest. But it was a link between Russia's geography and globalization that turned Parshev's book into a subject of hot debate. Parshev repeatedly stressed that the inefficiency and lack of competitiveness of Russia's economy were not a secret. What had been hidden until then was the very fact that factors determining Russia's economic inefficiency were "inalienable" (*neustranimy*) (2001c, 106). As a result, Russia's entry into the world market had to be detrimental, since the country's economy was "fundamentally incompatible" with the world's economy (2001, 125).

Parshev articulated the incompatibility of two different geo-economies through a particular metaphor of Russia's violated integrity: "a capital

---

44. There is only one Institute for the Economy in Transition in Russia; it is organized and chaired by Yegor Gaidar, the leader and the main intellectual force behind the reforms in the early 1990s (Institute for the Economy in Transition, n.d.).

drain" was the major way through which Russia's "openness" to the world was envisioned. As the main argument went, by creating for itself an entry into the free market, Russia simultaneously provided an exit for the capital that had been accumulated at home. As soon as legal and physical obstacles were lifted, money fled for a location with a more efficient (and warmer) climate. In Parshev's view, this "economic law" alone could explain why "knowledgeable American consultants" stayed away from Russia's affairs in the 1990s and did not help Yeltsin's team of reformers. "Americans knew from the very beginning that Russia's economy would be inoperative after its integration into the world' market.... Sad as it might be, the reformers were to be sacrificed for the just cause of the global economy. Instead of a partner state, Americans found the total disappearance of the Russian state" (2001c, 199).

What kind of economic strategy could work in this situation? What could help to avoid Russia's economic suicide? What were the mechanisms that could ensure a "fair exchange" between Russia and the rest of the world (2001c, 316)? In Parshev's view the most effective way to guarantee a fair exchange would be to significantly limit the scope of this repatriated capitalism. The country should buy only those objects that it could not produce in exchange for objects it did not need. In other words, to stop capital drain, the country must introduce a set of barriers. "Anything and everybody could leave the country, except for Russian capital" (2001c, 161). In political and economic terms, three main measures aimed at institutionalizing a controllable form of the regime of noncoverage: (1) a state monopoly on foreign trade, (2) a state monopoly over the circulation of foreign currency, and (3) the declared inconvertibility of the Russian ruble (2001, 260). Put differently, the solution was a mild form of autarchy, "a reasonable distancing from the world economic system" (2001, 389, 311–15).[45] This geopolitical program had its moral underpinning too. Repeating a similar argument, Margarita Nurmatova told me: "Collectivity is typical for the Russian mentality.... It is all determined by our natural conditions. In America, they

---

45. Apparently inspired by Parshev's book, several American scholars have examined the role of climate in Russia's history and economy. While their arguments strikingly resemble Parshev's, their proposed solutions are quite different. Hill and Gaddy, for instance, suggests that Russia's climate problem could be solved by turning "Russians into Canadians," that is to say, by radically shrinking Russia's involvement beyond the Urals and by moving Russia's population to warmer areas (2003, 205–6). Needless to say, such grandiose plans tend to be totally divorced from any substantial ethnographic or cultural research and, as these authors admit, usually require changing Russia's psychology and mind as the starting point (Hill and Gaddy, 2003, 199; see also Lynch 2005, 195–238).

can get by individually, but to survive in this damn climate we have to do everything together....Historically, this communality is in our blood. We cannot let a neighbor down; otherwise we'll all freeze to death."

As Parshev's critics pointed out, many crucial premises of his book were not exactly correct. Critics disagreed about Russia's average annual temperature (Tsirel' 2003, 183). Some of them drew attention to the fact that Russia's energy consumption per person was much lower than that of the United States, Canada, Singapore, Sweden, Germany, or France (Shishkov 2001, 117). Others questioned Parshev's simplistic understanding of free-floating commodities and totally unconstrained competition. Yet others found his rather physiocratic understanding of capital, still unfamiliar with financial derivatives, somewhat outdated.

These factual errors and (perhaps somewhat deliberate) miscalculations were important, but they did not undermine the book's popularity, which was rooted in its opposition to global practices of circulation that the arrival of capital manifested so vividly in Russia. Not unlike the traumatic trope of the Great Patriotic War, the idea of Russia's doomed geo-economic destiny provided a grounded teleology of the inconvertibility of national values. It emphasized a permanent lack of equivalence and at the same time a permanent state of exception. Notions of historical loss and the vital environment anchored people in time and space and suggested useful "constitutive metaphors" for nationally shared substance.[46] They also helped to render current changes meaningful. Economic failures became located within their "proper category" of the natural, with the corresponding "assignment of blame and guilt" to the cursed Russian climate (Mirowski 1994, 469). The next section shows how people in Altai translated this vision of the enclosed community and inalienable wealth into local politics. The region itself was framed as a part of cultural property that could not enter commercial circulation.

The Region in Danger

In the spring of 2004, the usually quiet Altai region was turned into a political hot spot, attracting much attention from the national and even international media. Aleksandr Surikov, the incumbent governor, decided to run for a third term. In 1996 and 2000 he had already won two gubernatorial elections, actively supported by the local Communists. Strictly speaking, Surikov's third campaign should not have happened. Federal law precludes

---

46. On the role of metaphor in economic analysis see Klamer and Leonard (1994).

anyone from being elected for the same state office more than twice in a row. But the law came into effect only in 1999 and did not specify how to count already served terms. Controlled by Surikov, the regional legislative assembly in 2001 removed the two-term limit from the region's statute and made it clear that nothing in the local regulations or in federal laws could prevent Surikov from running for his *second* second term. Altai legislators were not alone in their preoccupation with figuring out how many terms "two terms" actually were. After the federal law was adopted, the interpretive calculation of terms became a favorite pastime for many regional assemblies.[47]

Surikov's third campaign was important not because it provided one more example of the political longevity of old Soviet cadres nor because it demonstrated once again the lack of new politicians able to effectively challenge the old guard. It was the immense symbolic orchestration of the campaign that attracted so much attention. Heavily relying on the popular anxiety associated with the arrival of capital, the election highlighted tendencies described earlier in this chapter.

Originally planned as a routine confirmation of Surikov's third "mandate," the election was supposed to go smoothly and quickly. Surikov was confident that his victory in the first round was inescapable, and his team ran a low-key campaign under the slogan "Happiness to you, my compatriots!" (*Schast'ia vam, zemliaki!*). The slogan stressed the very local nature of the campaign. In the Russian original, *zemliaki* (compatriots) has the same root as "land" (*zemlia*) and usually emphasizes the commonality determined by the same place of birth.[48]

On March 14, 2004, the results were sobering. The incumbent was 3 percent short of the 50 percent plus one vote required for an outright victory.[49] Surprisingly, the election revealed strong opposition. With 39.3 percent of votes, Mikhail Evdokimov, a nationally famous stand-up comedian and film actor, was elected to run against Surikov in the second round.

Within a week, the general tone of the election campaign drastically changed. Dissatisfied with his team, Surikov hired a leading Moscow PR company to manage the second round. On March 22, 2004, Barnaul was

47. These inventive exercises in political chronology abruptly stopped in the fall of 2004, when President Putin decided to get rid of the direct election of governors altogether.

48. Unlike *sootechestvenniki* (people who have the same fatherland), *zemliaki* (literally soil mates) tend to be more geographically specific.

49. To win in the first round of a local election, a candidate had to collect 50 percent plus one vote of those who registered for the voting; the second round required only a simple majority of votes of those who actually participated in the voting.

plastered with huge billboards. Their white lettering read against red and black backgrounds: "Stop the Invasion" and "Come, Vote, and Defend Altai!" A popular FM station, Russian Radio in Barnaul, came up with a political commercial that epitomized the essence of the election in three slogans: "Hands off Altai! Say no to Moscow oligarchs! Vote and defend Altai!" In addition, people's mailboxes were stuffed with copies of a leaflet published by the "Social Union of Patriots of Altai." The title of the letter conveyed the message bluntly: "The Region is in Danger!" Surikov's own interviews followed the same line, promising to "be on guard for the interests of the native region [*rodnoi krai*]" (Salanin 2004).

Suddenly, Altai emerged as a territory on the verge of being looted and occupied by greedy and cunning Moscow capitalists.[50] The political rhetoric became more and more intense. Three days before the second round, local newspapers, generally favorable to Surikov, published a letter from the governor addressed to staff members of polling stations. Adding more fuel to the already overheated campaign, Surikov expressed his confidence in "people's ability to tell the truth from a lie" and called upon every citizen to be suspicious of any effort that "black [negative PR] technologists" (*chernye tekhnologi*) could undertake in order to rig the election and to violate the law (*Vtorzhenie v Rossiiu* 2004).[51]

The election drama reached its peak less than twenty-four hours before the votes were cast. On April 3, the regional administration announced through the mass media that the regional security service had detained three charter planes from Moscow that had landed in Barnaul's airport early in the morning. As the media reported, the charters were "paid for by commercial institutions," and they brought 463 men and a woman ready to discredit or disrupt the election (*Svobodnyi kurs* 2004a). The next day the planes (and people) were apparently sent back to Moscow, but nobody ever came forward with an explanation. Nobody took responsibility for a failed invasion, and the incident remains one of the murkiest moments of the campaign (*Altai Daily Review* 2004; Chernyshev 2004, 34–36).

Evdokimov, with his cultivated image of a simple countryman," including stories about a country cabin that he built in his native Altai village, with his strong passion for saunas and homemade Siberian dumplings, could not have been further from the picture of a "greedy Moscow oligarch" that Surikov's PR team (from Moscow) tried to paint. Nor was Evdokimov actually foreign

---

50. For a detailed discussion see Chernyshev (2004).

51. On black PR and other dubious post-Soviet political technologies see Ledeneva (2006, 28–57).

to the region. He had been born in Altai, and despite his eventual move to Moscow, he frequently visited the area, bringing his fellow actors to the region to film one of the most popular comedy shows on national TV. Having no political experience whatsoever and constrained by a lack of money, specialists, and (seemingly) ideas, Evdokimov responded to his opponent with a different version of the same region-is-in-danger theme. Denied any visible access to local TV and radio channels, the comedian repeated his party line in his meetings with people: the incumbent administration had already looted the region, and it was time to take it back. Surikov's massive billboards and multiple posters were challenged by small yet omnipresent (and hard to remove) stickers, on which a gloomy globe with a blood-red silhouette of the Altai region bore a stamped sign, "I am selling it. Surikov."

On April 4, 2004, Surikov lost the election by more than 3 percent.[52] Tired by a situation of "stable stagnation," many people voted for change. After all, in different capacities, Surikov had been in charge of the region since 1991, when he was initially elected to preside over the regional assembly.[53] However, popular hopes for radical change, associated with the new administration of "Altai's Schwarzenegger," as Evdokimov was quickly dubbed, proved to be in vain. Attempts to see in Evdokimov yet another American actor-turned-politician failed too. Hopes for a regional version of Reaganomics—"Evdokimonomics," as a local journalist called it—turned out to be groundless (Nikulkov 2004). No invasion of Moscow oligarchs, allegedly hiding behind the governor, was in sight, nor was there any corrupting influx of capital.

The biggest and most bitter surprise was the discovery that the election was just a vanity campaign of a popular star with no political program to realize or any strong ambitions to carry out. Originally considered by many as the "governor of hope," Evdokimov could achieve nothing throughout his first year, apart from appointing a handful of his friends (Goncharenko 2004, 41–48). The governor's frequent and extended trips to Europe only aggravated the situation. At the end of March 2005, less than a year after the election, the local legislative assembly passed a vote of no confidence in the governor. In his comments on the impeachment, the chairman of the Federal Election Committee summed up the general disappointment: "Evdokimov was not Schwarzenegger!" (*RIA Novosti,* 2005). Both sides appealed

---

52. In the second round, M. Evdokimov had 49.53 percent, A. Surikov, 46.29 percent (Oleg Mikurov and Vladimir Tokmakov, "Vybor sdelan," *Altaiskaia pravda,* April 6, 2004).

53. Almost two years later, Surikov was appointed ambassador to Belarus (*Altaiskaia pravda,* September 2, 2006).

to President Putin, with no visible result. The deadlock lasted through the summer, and was resolved unexpectedly: on August 7, 2005, Mikhail Evdokimov died in a car accident, when his Mercedes, exceeding 180 kilometers per hour crashed into an unsuspecting Toyota coming from the opposite direction. Following the new procedure, President Putin nominated a new candidate for governor who was quickly approved by the local assembly. On the day when the new governor was sworn in, a leading national polling company published results of a recent survey, in which 52 percent of respondents viewed Evdokimov's death as an assassination masked as a car crash (Sevriukov 2005, 2).[54]

Two moments in this campaign are worth emphasizing. One is the use of danger and threat as a way to mobilize the audience. It is significant that the danger was persistently construed in economic terms—either as an invasion of capital from the outside or as local, homegrown, corruption. The second moment deals with the way that the mass media and my informants chose to characterize the election. Regardless of their actual political preference, a majority of voters and the media perceived the campaign as an operation that was masterminded behind the scenes, as an event whose true meaning *must* be guessed and deduced from various hints and signs. Half a year after the election, I interviewed a wide range of people in Barnaul, from local political scientists, philosophers, and journalists to young radicals and members of the conservative business community. Most of them still expressed a deep conviction that the mysterious politico-economic force that had brought Evdokimov to power would soon come out of hiding. There was no particular agreement about the geographic origin of these interest groups. Guesses ranged from the neighboring Novosibirsk to Vladivostok in Russia's far east to Krasnodar in Russia's south. This desire to locate the agency of economic and political changes elsewhere is quite important. Ironically, the will to connect with a higher power in another place radically preempted the existing environment. Imagining alternative—or at least nontransparent—webs of meaningful relations, these emerging cosmogonies indicated a certain shift in the mode of questioning political figures, too. The metaphoric inquiry "Who is Mr. Putin?" that was so common during the late 1990s, was replaced in the first decade of the 2000s by the metonymic "Who is behind Mr. Evdokimov?"[55] In other words, a search for

54. The Levada Center, a major independent survey company, polled sixteen hundred respondents throughout Russia; 34 percent of them thought it was an accident, and 14 percent did not have any opinion (Sevriukov 2005, 2).

55. For local discussions and examples see Chernyshev (2004, 34–35).

unfamiliar comparison and unknown codes was marginalized by a search for plausible links and connections.

The search for hidden forces was reflected in yet another way. I was told many times that the election was a product of "dirty technologies," an outcome of "black PR." Or at least it was an expression of "a manipulated quasi-democracy," as a local professor of political history put it (Chernyshev 2005). Again, there seemed to be a general consensus that words and people were not what they purported to be. As this chapter has demonstrated, a similar operation of discursive dissociation of the real object and its visible identity could be discovered in many other settings. Framed through a rhetorical pairing of invasion and manipulation, this patriotism of despair structured various narratives about post-Soviet dislocation, dispossession, and detachment. What the election campaign highlighted very clearly was a strong belief that manipulative invasions (of liberal values or Moscow oligarchs) were not accidental but followed a certain logic, if not a master plan. The general picture would become clear as soon as one found out who was *really* hiding behind Evdokimov.[56]

A Sufficiently General Theory of Governance

Maria K., a woman in her mid-thirties, was one of my main contacts in Barnaul. She spent several years working with local nongovernmental organizations and eventually started working for the regional government. When I interviewed her, she worked for the office of cultural and educational affairs in the Altai region. Actively involved in staging and supervising local public events associated with official holidays (Victory Day, New Year's Eve), Maria was also in charge of programs on patriotic education in the region. One of our meetings happened shortly after she supervised a regional competition among school students for the best performance of patriotic songs. Maria passionately complained about the dazzling political diversity of the performed songs that ranged from military ballads of White Russians who had left the country after the Russian Revolution to late Soviet romantic pop songs about Mother Russia, to post-Soviet patriotic military chansons:

> Imagine a teenager, with no feeling of distinction at all, who sits and listens to all this. He sits there and slowly goes out of his mind. He has no clue what

---

56. A set of materials on the results of the 2004 elections, published by Altai scholars in the summer 2004, is a good example of this interpretative strategy (Chernyshev 2004).

Russia means, where the Motherland is. Some people favor the tsar, some—the Russian Patriarch, some—Trotskyites, some—Communists. We do not train the feeling of distinction at all....But information governs the individual; it is like water: your body gets what you drink. People are information animals. What could happen, if they cannot make distinctions? Well, this is why we get skinheads who grew up in one culture and monarchists who were shaped in a different culture. We get all kinds of groups and groupings today. These groups are all created by those who have access to the levers of governance. In a very accurate fashion, they play these groups against each other, and in the right time and in the right place they get the result they need.

As in many other cases in this chapter, depictions of the rapid fragmentation of the environment that had looked so solid and coherent in the recent past generated here a search for a cultural explanation that could justify the evident disintegration. Cultural polyphony was construed not as a representation of autonomous, independent groups and tendencies but as a deliberate outcome of post-Soviet governmentality. Atomizing diversity was linked with a particular regime of power that diffused any consolidated challenge by purposefully differentiating the field of social relations. What seemed to be unusual here was Maria's emphasis on the feeling of distinction that could be trained and applied to surrounding informational flows. It was Maria who introduced me to a group that took such training seriously: the local seminar on the Concept of Social Security, or "a seminar on the Concept," as she called it.

I attended several sessions of the seminar that took place in an auditorium of the Altai State Pedagogical University, in the wing that hosts the Department of Philosophy. This geographical proximity appeared to be quite accidental; the sessions that I visited had no faculty members from the philosophy department in attendance. The seminar seemed to be open to anyone who wanted to come, but given the fact that even getting in the building required a special pass, the seminar could not be convened on the university premises without an official permit. The sessions that I visited lasted about two hours and were typically structured as a short lecture followed by questions and a group discussion. Judging by their questions and appearances, people who attended the seminar came from diverse educational and economic backgrounds. Most participants were men between twenty and sixty years old; there were also a few women in the audience. Each session covered a particular aspect of the Concept of Social Security, also known as the "Sufficiently General Theory of Governance." After each session, participants could buy books and newsletters on the Concept. As I discovered later, introductory lectures by the organizer of the seminar (a graduate student at a local technical university) and his interpretations of current events were heavily based on materials published in the bi-weekly newsletter *Mera za meru* (*Measure for Measure*), easily available from newspaper stands throughout the city. In what follows, I outline the main ideas of this seminar by using its publications as well as the notes I took during the sessions.

The Concept was apparently developed at the end of the 1980s by a group of officers working in military colleges and academies throughout the country. Later the group was joined by technical intelligentsia from provincial universities. In the 1990s, this group tried to institutionalize it-self as a political movement; it even managed to present its views to the members of the Russian parliament in 1996 during a session on national se-curity. The movement's activity has been mostly concentrated in St. Peters-burg and Novosibirsk, but it has a network of local chapters as well. When in 1997 the movement organized its first congress in Moscow, it managed to attract representatives from fifty-four regions of Russia (Moroz 2005, 68). The party's website claims eleven thousand members in fifty-two regional chapters.[57]

It is hard to estimate the actual political weight of this group. Some Russian newspapers and scholars have traced a close connection between the leadership of the Conceptual movement and high-profile Moscow politicians (Soldatov and Borogan 2004).[58] In 2003, representatives of the movement ran for office in the parliamentary elections; even though their party Edinenie (Unification) failed to cross the 5 percent threshold, it was supported by more than seven hundred thousand people throughout the country (Moroz 2005, 14). In Barnaul, Maria K. was absolutely confident that the leadership of the region was well aware of and quite sympathetic to the ideas of the movement. However, it was impossible to either confirm or deny this assertion. In 2004 the party candidates ran for seats in the regional assembly but managed to get only 1.8 percent of all votes.[59] Apart from its possible political influence, the Concept is an important symbol that connects in a plausible way apparently disjointed facts, processes, and motivations by weaving together issues of new economy, patriotic feelings, and a strong desire for an organizing plot.

Since the middle of the 1990s, the group associated with the Concept has been publishing a string of books and brochures as a part of the series

57. For program documents and statistics see Edinenie (n.d.).
58. See Moroz (2005) for a detailed review of this movement.
59. Communists won, with 26.6 percent of the votes (*Svobodnyi kurs* 2004).

Library of Conceptual Knowledge. Usually the publications are not signed, and the texts are presented as the "common property of Russian culture." There is a certain mystical aura that accompanies these texts, too. The short standard blurb printed in each book of the series warns: "When using these materials for personal purposes either in the form of fragmented citation or as a reference, the reader accepts personal responsibility. If such a usage creates a context that distorts the meaning or the integrity of cited materials, this person might face the chance of being subjected to 'mystical,' extra-juridical retribution" (Dostatochno 2003).

The basic premise of the Conceptual movement is hardly controversial: Russia entered the new millennium while experiencing a condition of "conceptual uncertainty." Administrators and politicians carry out opposing, contradictory, and even mutually incompatible plans (*Rossiia, Rus'!* 2001, 12–13). There is a profound lack of "knowledge and understanding of what kind of state and what kind of society we are building" (*Mera za meru* 2002c, 1). As the movement's publications suggest, this conceptual uncertainty is not a result of an accidental combination of individual ignorance, political factors, and historical circumstances. Rather, it reflects the strong desire of "the world financial mafia of globalists" to get rid of Russia altogether (*Mera za meru* 2002c, 1). However, they suggest, politically driven interpretations of the cold war should not be taken seriously. It was not ideological differences between Russia and the Western world that were important for the mafia of globalists. After all, as the argument goes, the Soviet Union and the United States were not that different in terms of their economic bases. In both countries, it was the "corporate ownership of means of production" that provided the structural backbone for the political system. But the two countries radically differed in the ways their respective corporate ownerships were established. Unlike in the United States, where "corporations of hereditary clans" were created during the last two centuries, in the Soviet Union similar clans were shaped only in the late Soviet period, as a "symbiosis of the Party *nomenklatura* and the directorate of major industrial enterprises" (*Mera za meru* 2003, 3).

It was precisely this ideological-cum-managerial (post-)Soviet elite that became the main target of global influence, the authors of the Concept insisted. The "world masterminds" (*mirovaia zakulisa*) chose the Soviet Union as one of their main objects of influence first of all because they realized that their level of consumption could be sustained only by limiting consumerism throughout the world and by establishing global control over pivotal energy sources (*Mera za meru* 2003, 3). This is why, during the cold war, informational outlets such as Voice of America, Radio Liberty, and the

BBC proclaimed the improvement of living conditions in the Soviet Union as their main concern, while in fact they "tacitly pursued both the seizure of the USSR's natural resources, and the annihilation of the country as such" (*Mera za meru*" 2002b, 3).

This general outline of geopolitical disposition was then followed by another conceptual conclusion. One issue of *Mera za meru* has a diagram that presents the process of governing in general and for Russia in particular. The diagram is simple: the "object of governance" (a car or Russia) is connected with the "subject of governance" (a person or state institutions) in a double way. First, the subject directly influences the object, and then it receives feedback on its own action by analyzing the outcome of its influence (figure 1.9). As the newspaper suggests, given the success of the "informational pressure" that the "globalists" have had on Russia, the same mechanism for "seizing governance" could be used by anyone. Predictably, it was the Conceptual Party Edinenie that was seen as the perfect subject to realize this "remote control over bosses."[60] Just as during the process of destroying the Soviet Union, the subject (elites) and the object (the country) could be subjected to informational pressure, the feedback channel could also be tapped. By exercising informational influence at schools and universities, in companies and enterprises, across cities and the countryside, the successful "correction" of the subject's goals of governance could be ensured on every level. Perhaps even more important, the project of "entering governance" (*vkhozhdenie v upravlenie*) should be realized in regard to members of local and federal parliaments, to the heads of all administrations, and finally to all heads of state (*Mera za meru* 2002b, 3).

These conspiracy narratives and scenarios perfectly fit the type of symbolic production that Frederic Jameson labeled "the poor person's cognitive mapping" (1988, 356). Yet, as recent studies of politics of paranoia in postwar America indicate, such a dismissive attitude usually neglects two important aspects of the conspiratorial mode of "thinking critically" (Dean 2000).[61] One of them is the political gesture that conspiracy narratives produce. As Timothy Melley convincingly suggests, conspiracy theory is closely linked with the profound doubt about the dominant methods of knowledge production and about the claims to authority by those who produce

60. For an extremely detailed explanation of this scheme in different social and historical settings such as ancient Egypt or contemporary society see the main manual of the movement Dostatochno (2003, 193–99).

61. For studies of the role of paranoia in political life see Marcus (1999); Knight (2002); West and Sanders (2003); Pratt (2003); and Waters (1997).

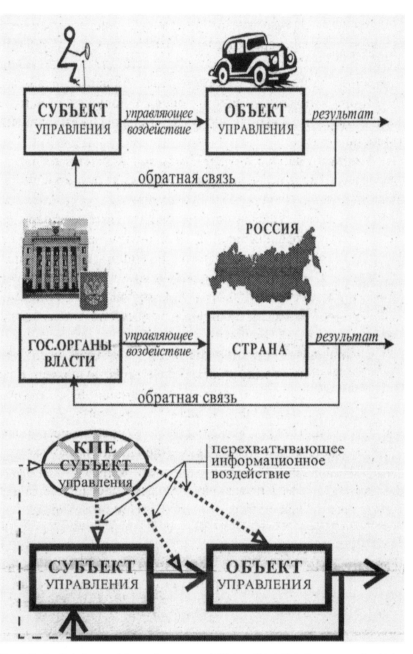

Fig. 1.9. A sufficiently general theory of governance: Subject vs. Object. Each diagram suggests a higher level of generalization of governance: from managing a car (the first diagram) to managing Russia (the second diagram), to managing Russia's managers (the third diagram). Source: *Mera za mery,* September 2002. Courtesy of the newspaper.

this knowledge (2000, 13). The second important feature of conspiracy theory is the particular form in which its will to connect is realized. Providing "an interface between the immediate existential experience…and larger global systems of knowledge," conspiracy theory nonetheless avoids a usual retreat from globalization into marginalized enclaves and fragmented ghettos (Mason 2002, 50).

As has been shown, post-Soviet narratives, brought to life by market irrationality, stemmed from a dual desire to register profound disagreement with the dominant view of Russia's development and, at the same time, to offer a new cosmogony, a new type of connectedness, a new form of totality that could effectively replace fragmented or dysfunctional cultural frameworks of the previous period. Political control of the Soviet regime and consumerist illusions of the market society were replaced by the fantasy of a large-scale presence in convoluted networks of relations. The fear of individual isolation attributed to capital was overcome by a vision of polymorphous embeddedness in the constant flow of information.[62] The main message of this post-Soviet conspiracy, though, was a promise of linking rather than its confirmation. The scenario of seizing governance suggested that everyone and everything *could be* connected, if only through informational pressure.

The publications of the Conceptual movement offer an extensive variety of such potential plots and tacitly realized scenarios. Many treatises in the library are filled with formulas, diagrams, mathematical equations, cybernetic schemes, and extremely close readings of official documents and artistic texts. One example of these exercises in "conceptual power," as it is usually called by its authors, was the interpretation of events that occurred on October 23, 2002, in Moscow when a group of Chechen terrorists and suicide bombers took eight hundred people hostage during the performance of the musical *Nord-Ost*. The October issue of *Mera za meru* published a long letter from the presidium of the Conceptual Party that outlined the hidden logic of the event:

> It is obvious that the main GOALS of *the hostage taking are the following:*
>
> 1. To remove Putin from his position of the head of the country.
> 2. To make the Russian people accept the regime of international fascism [established by the "world masterminds"]…and the return of the Yeltsin

---

62. For less convoluted versions of political conspiracy in post-Soviet Russia see Norka (2004); Prokhanov (2002); Morozov (1999).

clan ("Family") to power, which would manifest the end of fights among
Russia's ruling clans.

3. To start the dismembering of Russia by using the country's regions as the
   basis for a new confederation "Russ-Union" [*Rossoiuz*] under the leadership of Yeltsin. (*Mera za meru* 2002a, 1; emphasis in the original.)

Bizarre as it is, this excerpt nonetheless highlights the basic anxiety about
the actual and imaginary fragmentation of Russian society and points out
the main source of this obsession with disintegration: the institutional collapse of the Soviet Union. The dissolution of the USSR was perceived as a
paradigmatic model for the possible dismembering of Russia itself.

As with many conspiracy theories, what makes them interesting is not
the reasoning behind them but their particular ability to "convert metaphors into metonymies" (Harding and Stewart 2003, 280) and thus to restore the whole picture. The success of conspiracy is rooted in the leaps
of imagination that establish similarity between apparently unconnected
events, objects, and people. In the quoted paragraph, the hostage taking
was viewed as the beginning of a multilevel and multisited operation aimed
at weakening Putin's power in order to clear the way for Yeltsin's return. To
quote from the same letter:

> There were threats to Putin articulated by [Boris] Berezovskii, an old and
> loyal friend of the Yeltsin "family." There was an attempt to create the super-
> state union between Russia and Belarus, so that Yeltsin would become the
> head of it. There was the Ostankino TV-tower fire.[63] There was an explosion
> in a Moscow underpass; there was the submarine *Kursk* disaster; there was
> a terrorist attack in Kaspiisk on May 9, 2002. There were many other events
> that were designed to provoke people's discontent with Putin, to demonstrate
> his inability to establish order in the country, and thus to stimulate his re-
> moval. (*Mera za meru* 2002a, 1)

In Russia, the newspaper insisted, such a removal would be beneficial for all
"clans" interested in preserving the assets accumulated through privatization. Internationally, as the article indicated in October 2002, a politically
feeble Putin would have to give in to the U.S. leadership and to put up with
the U.S. desire to start a war in Iraq. Since Yeltsin and his clans were so
helpful during the time of reforms in "promoting the interests of Europe

---

63. The Ostankino TV center is the main communication hub that hosts Russia's major
radio and TV stations. On August 27, 2000, a fire destroyed the tower's transmitting equipment;
for several days some TV and radio stations could not broadcast in the Moscow region.

and America, not the interests of Russia itself," they could reasonably expect now that "the U.S. leadership would defend them from Putin" (2002a, 1).

It is the Concept's ability to connect "objective multiple qualitative distinctions in an unambiguous fashion" that *A Sufficiently General Theory of Governance,* the manual of the movement, singles out as its main theoretical advantage (Dostatochno 2003, 188). Within this context, governance is associated with one's ability to ensure the "stability of the object from the point of view of the predictability of its behavior" (21). In a situation of change, ability to predict requires a special kind of interpretive skill. For the Conceptual movement, only a "mosaic type of consciousness" could trace the connections among diverse facts and objects, paths and patches. That is to say, fragmented bits and pieces of information could be seen as parts of a meaningful (yet disconnected) mosaic panel only by those who possessed the necessary mental glue.[64] Without such a skill (the will to connect), individuals would be constantly exposed to the manipulative media that treated them as a mere container for disjointed views and impressions. Unable to form their own "world picture" or to predict their own behavior, "object individuals" would be totally dependent on frameworks provided by others, becoming an easy target for external influences or internal impulses (281–82).

Interestingly, Sergei Kara-Murza, whose *Manipulation of Consciousness* was discussed earlier, construes the same idea of disjointed consciousness as the main tool through which a collapse of national statehood can be accomplished. As long as the "cultural core of society" is stable, Kara-Murza maintains, "[t]here is a 'stable collective will' aimed at preserving the existing order, too. The undermining of this 'cultural core' and destruction of this collective will lead to the collapse of the state. Such undermining is carried out through a 'molecular' aggression in the cultural core" (2002a, 168). Unlike the authors of the Conceptual movement, Kara-Murza sees this aggression against cultural values of the nation not as a product of *external* forces. The virus of molecular aggression was conceived and implemented as a conscious "anti-Soviet project" by the Soviet intelligentsia in the 1960s. As Kara-Murza insists, Soviet society might have been sick, but it was alive. It was the bomb of the anti-Soviet project that killed it (10–12). Moreover, the intelligentsia failed to realize the global condition of its own activity. As Kara-Murza points out, liberal capitalism in Russia is a utopia,

---

64. In a less radical form, the same post-Soviet will to connect bits and pieces of information into a coherent plot is reflected in the incredible popularity of the detective novel in Russia since the early 1990s. For an extensive discussion see Olcott (2001).

since no *local* capitalist order could emerge today without being drastically modified by existing global structures: "The West devours the very sprouts of "other" capitalisms, just like bacteria destroy the mucus (*sliz'*) from which life could have sprouted....Accelerated globalization...will inevitably get rid of the majority of Russians. Those who would survive would be subjected to a profound involution so that they could be easily controlled by a tiny enclave of "modernity" that extracts gas and trains ballerinas" (195).

In his essay on "paranoia within reason," George Marcus rightly suggests that at least two important factors help to keep conspiratorial schemes of understanding afloat. The end of the cold war did not automatically remove its epistemological premises, its ways of questioning the unknown, as well as its constitutive metaphors. The symbolic legacy and structuring residues of the cold war, Marcus suggests, made conspiratorial frameworks "an expectable response to certain *social facts*" (1999, 2; emphasis in original). Second, a broader crisis of representation reveals the inadequacy of existing channels of communication, modes of translation, and genres of interpretation. Hence, paranoia within reason is a result of striving for "knowledge in the absence of [a] compass" (5).

There is another important factor that helps us understand the intellectual and emotional attractions of conspiratorial thinking in contemporary Russia. The end of the cold war (with the demise of the Soviet Union that accompanied it) and the contemporary crisis of representation were intensified in Russia by a rapid transition to the market-driven economy and to the unprecedented monetization of social relations. Produced in the course of privatization, the extreme social differentiation activated a variety of discourses rooted in mistrust. Social dislocation and economic dispossession were accompanied by "moral holocausts" (Taussig 1980, 101) that gave rise to various forms of "naked patriotism." Partly capitalizing on the hermeneutic of suspicion honed during the Soviet period, the post-Soviet narratives about universal falsehood, lies, and corruption presented nontransparency and nonfamiliarity of the newly emerging social order as a set of practices and institutions that lack authenticity. Simultaneously, they situated the true origin and usually negative content of these socio-semantic inadequacies outside or behind. Metaphors of spatial and cultural fragmentation that often framed this search for post-Soviet meaning could be read as a form of symbolic cartography. Initial fragments were turned eventually into meaningful clues, unified by the implicitly present organizing system. Providing a map for navigation, this post-Soviet cartographic endeavor defined the available space by outlining the borders of unknown terrains.

THIS chapter began by documenting ways in which Russia's socialist past modified the country's transition to a capital-driven economy. More specifically, it explored local cosmogonies, those emerging hermeneutic practices and forms of rationality that were able to capture the fleeting meaning of post-Soviet changes. As has been shown, the arrival of capital in provincial Russia was often perceived as a culturally alien, geographically and historically distant event. Newly emerging commercial institutions rarely grew out of existing forms of life. More often they appeared as a stylistic invasion, a physical rupture in the established social fabric: Butik Renome in a former apartment on Lenin Prospect. The chapter examined different social and political enclaves and suggested that fragmentations and ruptures precipitated searches for missing links and hidden connections. In turn, the foreign flavor of repatriated capitalism stimulated heated debates about local loyalties, national values, and patriotic feelings. A dizzying array of groups, tendencies, and ideas were eventually brought together by an organizing plot. This organizing plot, no doubt, was far from being a linear and coherent narrative. Like recent sidewalks in front of new commercial establishments in Barnaul, it consisted of disconnected patches of different color, texture, and size. This symbolic dissonance produced by post-Soviet changes revealed a shortage of positive mediating cultural mechanisms in Russian society. This shortage, in turn, has been significantly amplified by a lack of trust in emerging procedures and processes of social exchange. As has been demonstrated, the unpredictability of outcomes that social exchange might produce frequently activated discourses of universal manipulation. These discourses helped to justify failed or unequal exchanges ("We were duped"), but they also usefully located the source of responsibility for these interactions elsewhere. The popularly shared linkage between money and lies or capital and corruption resulted in yet another important strategy: attempts to rediscover real values, uncontaminated by the logic of the market were called upon to overcome the corrupt and false present.

In some cases, this search led to revisiting Russia's recent past in order to recover a lost sense of unifying collectivity ("History already loves you"). In others, a similar striving for an ontological anchor found an outlet in neoromantic interpretations of the economic predestination rooted in the national soil and climate. What was significant about this alternative search for the true Russian path was its overwhelming pessimism. Even a perfectly organized national economy would be forever doomed by its geography, and even major national victories were not about success. This national poetics of despair was not without its own value, however. Used as a lowest common denominator, this conscious resort to suffering often managed to generate communities of loss bound by the solidarity of grief.

2 The Russian Tragedy

From Ethnic Trauma to Ethnic Vitality

We were killed as a nation [*narod*], as a country, as a society, as bearers of communism—this is the truth. We weren't just defeated, we weren't just squashed. We were killed. Killing a nation does not mean killing all its representatives.... Some representatives of the nation can exist; they can even flourish. But socially speaking, a large number of individuals have ceased to be a nation. Having lost its ability to resist the powers that try to destroy them, the nation is disintegrated and atomized.... One can witness today how this is happening to the Russian people in Russia.

—ALEKSANDR ZINOVIEV, *Russkaia tragediia* (*gibel' utopii*)

When we are unable to impose our power on another person, we can always elude the other's power by destroying ourselves. In this way, we control the situation. In this case, positive and negative are both positives of opposite value, each striving for eventual pre-eminence.

—ANDRÉ GREEN, *The Work of the Negative*.

[T]here's no racism without a language.

—JACQUES DERRIDA, "Racism's Last Word."

"Is This Not a Tragedy?"

On April 25, 2005, in his annual address to the Federal Assembly of the Russian Federation, then president Vladimir Putin made an unexpected rhetorical turn. Revisiting Russia's recent history, he offered his own definition for the early 1990s. As Putin framed it,

We should acknowledge that the collapse of the Soviet Union was a major geopolitical disaster of the century. As for the Russian nation, it became a genuine drama.... Many thought or seemed to think at the time that our young democracy was not a continuation of Russian statehood, but its ultimate collapse, the prolonged agony of the Soviet system. But they were mistaken. That was precisely the period when significant developments took place in

Russia. Our society was generating not only the energy of self-preservation, but also the will for a new and free life.[1]

The passage caused a stir in the foreign press; in Russia the comment did not provoke any particular reaction. As in many other cases before, Putin's address did not offer a distinctively new vision but mostly articulated an opinion that was already widespread in the country. Indeed, for many Russians, the perception of the collapse of the USSR was quite different in scale from the view of Putin's foreign critics. In Russia itself, the disintegration of the USSR was linked much more closely with the painful immediacy of everyday survival than with archived horrors of the Great Terror and the cold war. The need to equate the Soviet Union with the Stalinist regime, which was so crucial for many Western commentators, was less obvious in the midst of post-Soviet changes. Yet two weeks after the original speech, Putin defended his choice of words in extensive interviews with foreign correspondents. "Liberation from dictatorship should not necessarily be accompanied by the collapse of the state," he explained. The collapse of the USSR divided the Russian nation, leaving millions of Russians outside the border of the Russian Federation; it severed family ties, it ruined economic networks, and it obliterated people's life savings. "Is this not a tragedy for these people?" asked Putin. He then drew the final line under the discussion. "People in Russia say that those who do not regret the collapse of the Soviet Union have no heart, and those who want to bring it back have no brain" (ARD 2005; CBS 2005).

The following discussion explores this tendency to perceive and narrate the collapse of the Soviet Union as an emotionally charged discourse on political disintegration and traumatic survival. The genre of the Russian tragedy is the main subject of this chapter. From the early 1990s, the Russian tragedy has been defining major interpretive approaches to Russia's recent history. It is articulated differently by people with different social and educational backgrounds and may be framed as sociological journalism, ethnological analysis, demographic forecast, or political essay. Over the years, the traumatic component of this genre has expanded. The Russian tragedy started as a way to emphasize the essence of Russia's socialist experiment. By the end of the 1990s, the term was further applied to the period of the post-Soviet transition.[2] By analyzing a range of nationalist texts, this chapter

---

1. For the Russian original and an authorized English translation see Putin (2005).
2. For different variations on this theme see Govorukhin (1991); Iskhakov (2005); Kara-Murza (2002a); Kozlov (1996); Solzhenitsyn (1998a); Troitskii (1997); Zinoviev (2002).

shows how authors of the Russian tragedy equated the dissolution of the Soviet state with the dissolution of the Russians as a nation. The demographic *decline* and the erosion of national values were to mirror the lost Soviet state. The intense circulation of themes, ideas, and images of the nation's demise reveals the crucial role of traumatic discourse in shaping post-Soviet forms of belonging. The chapter also traces how recognition of the loss eventually resulted in the rediscovery of the Russian nation's new vitality.

Unlike the previous chapter, where the experience of social fragmentation was often linked with intensive searches for unifying narratives, this one emphasizes a different symbolic strategy. It shows that in their obituaries for the vanished country and dying nation, authors of the Russian tragedy exposed the underlying attempt to reshape Russia's recent history in ethnic terms. Ethnic mapping was called upon to reformat a past that had suddenly become incoherent and incomprehensible. Using the notion of *etnos* (defined below) as their main analytic tool, my interlocutors and the authors of the texts discussed here were able to introduce a clear-cut split between the Russian "etnos proper" and institutions of the Soviet and post-Soviet state whose politics was deemed to be non-Russian or even anti-Russian. The ethnic split produced an important effect. It juxtaposed traumatic experience and responsibility for it; rhetorically, narrators and victims of the Russian tragedy were isolated from the real or imagined perpetrators. This chapter explores these post-Soviet strategies of reinscribing ethnic difference into what was previously seen as a homogenous historical space. It relies on two types of sources. Texts written by prominent Moscow scholars are supplemented by interviews and publications of Barnaul informants. This combination demonstrates the symbolic consistency of the post-Soviet discourse on Russian tragedy throughout the country, and at the same time it highlights Altai variations of this genre.

National History as an Ethnic Project

Until perestroika, the term *etnos* was a part of the professional lingo of a small group of Soviet scholars. Originally, the concept of etnos, or ethnical unit (*etnicheskaia edinitsa*), was introduced into Russian ethnography by Sergei Shirokogorov (1887–1939), a Russian ethnographer of the Far East.[3] A scholar from Petrograd, after 1922 Shirokogorov resided in China, where

---

3. For more details and discussion see Kuznetsov (2006) and V. Filippov (2006). Francine Hirsch traces a different genealogy of the term in her book on early Soviet ethnography (2005, 196–97).

he wrote extensively on the ethnography of aboriginal groups of the Far East (Tungus). In his major theoretical work, *Ethnical Unit and Milieu: A Summary of the Ethnos,* published in 1923–24 in Shanghai, Shirokogorov maintained that the "division of mankind into ethnical units" is simultaneously a "natural function" and "an impulse of development of man[kind] as a whole" (1924, 31).[4] Writing in the aftermath of the Russian Revolution and bloody civil war, Shirokogorov was preoccupied with the issue of ethnic survival, emphasizing in his work that the principal purpose for "all biological species"—etnos included—is maintaining their "right of existence" among other etnoses and animal species (1924, 7). A successful ethnic self-maintenance can be traced through the type of relationship that an etnos establishes with its environment. Shirokogorov even invented the notion of the "ethnical equilibrium" to describe the optimal correspondence between the size of the etnos and available resources. To achieve "ethnical equilibrium" each etnos has to properly position itself within the ethnical milieu, exercising resistance "to the pressure of other etnoses." When necessary, etnos must be able to incorporate adequately "the sum of impulses" for changes that it received from the "interethnical environment." In some cases, the demand for adaptability might force the etnos to "utilize" other etnoses in its own interests (1924, 9).

Shirokogorov's ethnic Darwinism was not widely known or even directly available in Russia until the late 1990s.[5] However, in the 1960s a limited circulation of his writings among the intelligentsia significantly inspired the work of several prominent Soviet ethnographers and resulted in a substantial body of academic publications on the topic. Shirokogorov's attempt to link his theory of ethnic survival with his analysis of natural environment and ethnical milieu was used to create an academic version of the late Soviet doublespeak. The revived binary "etnos versus nation" allowed Shirokogorov's followers to keep intact the dominant homogenizing concept of the "Soviet people," which was supposed to mark the formation of a new, ethnically inclusive type of nation and at the same time to draw attention to autonomous etnoses and ethnic environments.[6]

With perestroika, the academic prominence of the Soviet theory of etnos temporarily faded; yet at the turn of the twenty-first century the etnos theory became, once again, a major analytic device for conceptualizing the

4. I slightly adapted the translation using the Russian original (Shirokogorov 1923, 127).
5. For a review of Shirokogorov's work and his influence on Russian ethnography see Revunenkova and Reshetov (2003).
6. On the notion of the "Soviet people" see Hirsch (2005, 314–19).

continuity of post-Soviet nations. As before, renewed discussions about etnos were focused on ethnic stability and the role of the ethnic environment in the nation's history (Kozlov 1999; Tishkov 2003). Reflecting the increased importance and autonomy of Russia's ethnic regions and republics, the term began to be widely used in the academic and popular press to mark something local and essential. Russia's Ministry of Education, usually reluctant to deal with anything that might remotely concern national feelings, in 1993–94 actively encouraged regional educational boards to include in their curricula courses that would introduce high school students to "ethnocultural values" and the "ethnonational" history of their particular region (Shnirelman 2006c). Within a decade, etnos became the subject of a major intellectual industry; new disciplines and fields of studies emerged almost daily—from *etno-pedagogika* and *etno-psikhologiia* to *etno-ekonomika* and *etno-ekologiia*.

There are at least two main reasons that made the concept of etnos especially attractive for the post-Soviet intelligentsia. Methodologically, the concept was useful in providing a plausible substitute for class categories of orthodox Marxism, which were so typical in Soviet humanities and social sciences. The theory of etnos stayed away from such ostensibly Marxist notions as means of productions or basis/superstructure. But just like the Soviet class-based approach, etnos offered a comprehensive system of social classification (ethnic groups) and a certain vision of progress (ethnic development). Theoretically, etnos helped to isolate the constructivist view of ethnicity. "Nation" was exclusively linked with the nation-building process, normally initiated by the state. In turn, etnos itself was used to describe "bio-psycho-social" collectivities that transmit their most prominent features from generation to generation. Not unlike the concept of race, etnos provided an elaborate vocabulary of somatic metaphors for mapping out various social organisms and social bodies.

Indeed, restructuring the nation's history along ethnic lines often amounts to a politics of racism. As alarming as it is, however, it is not the racist content itself that is significant in the ethnocentric, xenophobic, and anti-Semitic texts analyzed below. There is an important difference that distinguishes the post-Soviet emergence of racism from the "privileged moments" of the racist outbreaks in modern societies (Foucault 2003, 255, 257). In post-soviet Russia, racist discourses were no longer a privileged instrument of the sovereign or state. Instead, while still acting as a "technology of normalization" (256), the post-Soviet edition of biopolitics was used first of all by various communities of loss as a "maintenance mechanism" with which they could uphold the borders of their public space (Theweleit

1989, 210). The scapegoating aspect of the Russian tragedy should not be underestimated, yet the main appeal of this genre was in its affective production of the suffering subject. What was created in these literary and historical exercises was a list of injuries that could anchor new networks and sustain new collectivities. What seems to occupy a prominent place in this tragic version of national belonging was the ability to claim a particular injury as one's own.

The link between expressions of suffering and the subjectivity that these expressions produce is crucial for understanding the work of the patriotism of despair. As Ludwig Wittgenstein pointedly indicated in his *Philosophical Investigations,* the purpose of pain behavior is to identify the painful place and to draw attention to the "subject of pain," that is to say, to the agent who gives expression to pain (1958, 101). After all, articulations of pain can hardly describe pain. Hence, the trope of the Russian tragedy is predominantly used as a performative rather than a descriptive device, as a tool with which to "stir the memory of our feelings," as one of my Altai informants wrote in his book (Filippov 1999, 87).

Ironically, by merging memory and perception, the Russian tragedy acted as a peculiar defense mechanism that encapsulated the subject of pain in this tragic genre and compelled its authors to keep revisiting their traumatizing plot. Thus the genre inspired Russia's scholars and intellectuals to examine "instincts that control the mechanisms of the [Russian] ethnos' self-preservation" (Filippov 1999, 59). It pushed some authors to investigate the factors of "ethnic viability" (*zhiznesposobnost'*) of Russians (Kozlov 1995, 6). But perhaps even more important, it allowed these people to assume a critical social position in post-Soviet Russia. Having lost much of its influence after the collapse of the Soviet Union, the Russian intelligentsia recovered at least some of its clout by producing multiple accounts of traumas that had taken place in the past or would take place in the future (Panarin 1998; Kniazevskaia 1999; Iskhakov 2005).

It is not easy to dismiss the narratives of the Russian tragedy as the intelligentsia's pragmatic attempt to accumulate certain political or social capital by utilizing available symbolic tools. Nor can these theoretical constructions be understood (or debunked) by demonstrating their logical flaws, historical inaccuracies, or theoretical dead ends. Neither normative or political critiques nor attempts to dismiss ethnoframeworks as more sophisticated examples of the post-Soviet turn to "archaic" or "mythic" thinking (Gudkov 2005)are helpful in explaining the high degree of intellectual and emotional intensity with which ethnoframeworks are often charged by their producers. Such a critique would have missed the point: namely, the cultural and social effects that these discursive constructions are capable of delivering for their authors and audiences.

Despite their obvious academic vacuity, I want to approach these desperate explanations of Russia's ethnic development as alternative forms of post-Soviet cosmogony that challenge the flattening mechanical functionalism of postcommunist neoliberal ideology. By rationalizing their fears and anxieties, these nationalist texts envision the "organismic ontology" (Cheah 2003, 2) of the Russian nation as a new logic of nation building. These ethnonarratives can be construed as an example of "enactive remembering" (Bass 2000, 118), in which the line between representation of the past and experience in the present is blurred. Put simply, enactive recollections of the Russian tragedy do not just register a lived (or imagined) past; they situate the past content in the present. Hence, the past never loses its emotional grip, repeatedly stirring the feelings of the authors of the Russian tragedy.

Academic approaches examined in this chapter fall into two major categories. Histories of ethnotrauma usually addressed Russia's current problems by rewriting the country's past in order to demonstrate the non-Russian character of its state institutions. Ethnic differentiation was used to restructure national memory and to reshape ways of remembering. The second category, ethnovitalism, while being closely associated with the rhetoric and methods of ethnotraumatic narratives, was less preoccupied with depicting past tragedies. Its main goal was to provide the analytics of ethnic survival, to outline methods that could "compensate for the loss of the cultural genotype" of the Russian nation, as one Altai scholar put it (Maltseva 2004, 240). Ethnovitalists replaced the struggle over constructing and interpreting the nation's memory with a similar struggle over channeling and interpreting perceptions of the nation's current experience.

The construction of these post-Soviet ethnonarratives would have been impossible without a particular ideological groundwork conducted during the last decades of the Soviet Union. The basic split between etnos and nation, on which post-Soviet narratives of the Russian tragedy are based, resulted from the efforts of a group of Soviet ethnographers and historians to carve out their own domain within the ossified and politicized field of nationalities studies. Without an understanding of the logic of the Soviet theory of etnos, current Russian debates over nationalism and ethnicity may appear only as an extravagant mixture of peculiar ideas and strange frameworks. The following discussion outlines the main aspects of the two major Soviet theories of etnos and then explores modifications of this theory in post-Soviet approaches to nationalism.

Etnos as Such

Two of the most prominent contributors to the Soviet theory of etnos were Yulian Bromley (1921–90), a well-established Moscow-based historian of the Balkans, and Lev Gumiliev (1912–92), a nonconformist historian and geographer from Leningrad. Emphasizing different aspects of ethnic development, both scholars demonstrated a desire to break away from the dominant Soviet tradition of perceiving nation formation as a steady linear progression (tribe–nationality–nation) that was to mirror the development of means of production in primitive, feudal, and capitalist/socialist societies. Both scholars significantly influenced the development of Russia's theories of ethnicity. Bromley's framework was the main academic doctrine of national development in the Soviet Union. Gumilev's model was presented as a powerful intellectual alternative to it. Bitter rivals at the time, today these authors appear as a product of the same intellectual endeavor aimed at decoupling the two parts of the nation-state. In both cases, their appeal to the not-quite-social essence of etnos was a key factor in avoiding the stifling schemes of Soviet social sciences.

In 1966 Bromley (a grandson of Konstantin Stanislavskii, a famous Russian theater director, and a son of a university professor) was appointed director of the Institute of Ethnography, the highest disciplinary unit within the Soviet hierarchy of science. The institute was a part of the Soviet Academy of Sciences, a large academic industry that included several regional divisions (for instance, the Siberian division and the Urals division), libraries, a network of laboratories and institutions throughout the country, and a powerful publishing house. In the Soviet period, each disciplinary institute in the academy (for instance, the Institute of the Russian History or the Institute of Laser Physics) heavily defined and policed the standards of its respective discipline in the country. Bromley was in charge of the Institute of Ethnography for almost twenty-five years and became known first of all for his persistent attempts to expand and clarify the analytic vocabulary of Soviet ethnography.[7] In the 1970s–1980s, through his access to administrative resources, publications, and academic appointments, Bromley turned the theory of etnos into a leading research theme of the field (Basilov 1992, 7; Hirsch 2005, 313–15). Despite its certain shortcomings and current critique, this theory remains the most serious and "conceptually grounded" contribution to ethnology in Russia, as some Russian

---

7. For a review of Bromley's work see an article of Viktor Kozlov (2001), his frequent coauthor. For a range of views on Bromley's legacy see S. Kozlov (2003).

ethnographers have recently maintained.[8] This section summarizes the key elements of this theory.

Starting at the end of the 1960s, in a series of articles, Bromley theorized a complex web of relations through which an ethnic group transforms itself into a national or political formation. Etnos became the central category and was used to produce a host of connected notions and neologisms. Defining the fundamental feature of ethnic groups, Bromley repeatedly singled out "self-awareness" as the "essential feature" of tribes, nationalities, and nations (1989, 9). Ethnic self-awareness included the individual's general awareness of his or her "actions, feelings, thoughts and motives of behavior" (9, 38). In turn, on the level of the etnos itself, ethnic self-awareness was manifested in "so-called ethnic auto-stereotypes" and collectively shared opinions about the nature of the ethnic community, its specificity, and its achievements (38). To put it simply, within Bromley's framework, ethnicity became a psychosocial pivot that sustained other individual and collective identities.

Somewhat reluctantly and usually without any further elaboration, Bromley often accompanied his discussion of ethnic self-awareness with a standard statement that would deem as mistaken attempts to "reduce the essence of etnoses" to their self-awareness only. As Bromley insisted, ethnic self-awareness was not a "demiurge" that could create etnos out of nothing (1989, 38); if perceived this way, etnos would be merely "a figment of imagination" (1976, 14). However, Bromley never identified in details those "objective factors," from which an ethnic "form of consciousness" derived (1989, 37–53).[9] Questions about the origin of ethnic division were replaced by discussions of etnos's historical past. Evidence of etnos's existence was enough to undermine any doubt about its place of origin. What became crucial instead were issues of survival of the already existing etnos.

Such an approach to ethnicity allowed the official Soviet ethnography to conceive etnos as a unit that was not firmly rooted in *any* specific social arrangement. As Tamara Dragadze (1980), a British anthropologist, saw it, etnos could be compared to a language that changes over time but cannot be fully located within a particular historical period. Etnos's historical autonomy, then, allowed Soviet ethnography to stay away from the more politically charged studies of national pasts. Instead, the theory of etnos

8. For current approaches to the etnos theory see Tishkov (2003); Zarinov (2003, 18); Rybakov (2001); "Discussing Imperial Legacy" (2005).

9. Bromley's critics were quick to point out that his concept of etnos "ignores the significance of socioeconomic factors and the role of socioeconomic formations in the development of ethnic communities" (Ivanov 1976, 237).

was used to trace the vertical continuity of the ethnic unit that unfolds itself diachronically in radically different epochs, stages, or formations (163).

In Bromley's work, the split between the ethnic and the historic emerged in two main forms. The first form was etnos proper, "etnos in the narrow sense," or "etnos as such," defined as "a stable group of people that has taken shape historically, who have common, relatively stable, specific features of culture (including language) and psychology, as well as an awareness of their unity and distinction from all other similar formations" (1989, 20). Was this narrowly conceived etnos, then, any different from a tribe or nation? For Bromley, the distinction was crucial: while etnos always takes the shape of a particular social institution, it is not equivalent to this institution (1976, 14).

If etnos as such was to emphasize the immutable ethnic component, then the category of the "ethnosocial organism," or "etnos broadly conceived," was introduced by Bromley to highlight the social aspect of ethnicity, despite the obvious biological connotation that the term "organism" suggests. Such ethnosocial organisms as nation or nationality, Bromley indicated, are volatile formations that include territorial, political, economic, and social factors, along with the ethnic component. Emerging within very particular social settings, "tribes," "nationalities," and "bourgeois and socialist nations" inevitably change their "principal topological features" during transition from one socioeconomic order to another (1989, 94). Unlike volatile ethnosocial organisms, etnos as such can sustain itself throughout a sequence of different socioeconomic formations because of the "relative conservatism as well as certain independence of ethnic properties" (1976, 15).[10] For instance, as Bromley liked to point out, the Ukrainian etnos retained its "ethnic factors" while taking the shape of different ethnosocial organisms in various periods (feudalism, capitalism, and socialism) and in various countries, such as the USSR or Canada (1976, 15).

The analytic distinction between the self-conscious etnos and ethnosocial organisms made possible a further split in the process of nation building: etnos and nation-state became autonomous entities, as it were. "Ethnogenesis" (ethnic processes) described how core elements of a distinctive etnos were modified or completely changed through "ethnic division" and "ethnic amalgamation" (Bromley 1989, 92). On the other hand, "national

10. Bromley does offer, however, a taxonomy of etnoses that correlates ethnic origin with a particular stage of social development: "paleogenetic etnoses" ("the peoples of the North") were formed "during the primitive epoch"; "archogenetic" ones arose in "precapitalist class society" (the Russian etnos could be an example); and finally, "neogenetic etnoses" were formed under capitalism (the French) or under socialism (the Altaians) (1989, 29).

development" signified the evolution of the social and political forms of etnoses such as republics, regions, or autonomies.

It is precisely this distinction between the ethnic and the ethnosocial in the nation's history that was reclaimed after the collapse of the Soviet Union by the authors of the Russian tragedy in order to justify splitting off a certain political experience from the natural life of the Russian etnos proper. The framing of the Soviet past as "the seventy years of Holocaust imposed by the Bolsheviks on the Russian nation" (Popov 2000b) became possible first of all as a result of the semantic differentiation between the past of the etnos and the past of the national political institutions. As a result, the nation's history was turned into a history of the Russian etnos's resistance to pseudo-Russian political institutions, eager to impose their anti-Russian agenda. Post-Soviet students of ethnic trauma appropriated yet another important moment from Bromley's construction. In Bromley's own work, the interplay between the continuous ethnic self-awareness and changing ethnosocial organisms was sustained to a large extent by avoiding questions about sources of ethnic self-consciousness: the main apparatus of the basic ethnic distinction (ethnic psychology) was located outside the field of political relations or forces of production. Even though Bromley himself tried to stay away from a direct biological essentializing of ethnic differences, his theory provided enough room for such a move. At the turn of the century his followers logically connected the dots by transforming the extrasocial status of the ethnic, outlined in Bromley's work, into a nonsocial, substantive, or even primordial quality grounded in the "internal content of the individual" (Rybakov 2001, 19; Zarinov 2000).

The Etnosphere

Bromley's theoretical attempts to fundamentally divorce etnos from the social and political forms that it had assumed throughout history were paralleled in the theoretical project of Lev Gumilev. Bromley's emphasis on the importance of biological and psychological processes in maintaining ethnic self-awareness became the central argument in Gumilev's construction. There was an important twist, though: Gumilev firmly linked elusive manifestations of the nation's psychological qualities with the formative environment. In this version, ethnogenesis emerged as a late Soviet version of romantic psycho-geography.

At the time of his writing, Gumilev's ideas lacked any official institutional or political support. With the changes in the late 1980s, the situation became dramatically reversed. Gumilev's work became a source of major inspiration for a wide audience—from radical nationalists and more moderate heads of newly independent states to schoolteachers and university professors. Despite their convoluted prose and heavy dose of clumsy neologisms, hundreds of thousands of Gumilev's books were sold. In the early 1990s, his historical exploration *From Rus' to Russia* was adopted as an official history textbook in Russian secondary schools (Gadlo 1995, 3; Lavrov 2000, 360–62; Shnirelman 2006b). Gumilev's writing was widely used as a major theoretical foundation of the emerging political and philosophical movement of neo-Eurasianism.[11] His ideas seemed to be especially popular in Central Asia. In 1996, Nursultan Nazarbayev, president of Kazakhstan, unveiled a newly established Eurasian university in the newly built capital, Astana. The university was named after Gumilev to memorialize his originality in studying ethnic relations in Eurasia.[12] During his time in office, Askar Akaev, the first president of Kyrgyzstan, actively used Gumilev's ideas as a primary source for his historical ruminations on the nature of Kyrgyz statehood (Akaev 2002). Terms like *passionarnost'* and *etnosfera*, introduced by Gumilev, became a part of the popular vocabulary. Implicitly or explicitly, his concepts shaped many post-Soviet debates on nationalism and ethnicity in Russia in particular and in the former Soviet Union in general.[13]

This incredible public recognition (unparalleled by any other late-Soviet scholar), happened, however, mostly after Gumilev's death in 1992. His life was quite tragic. The son of two major Russian poets, Anna Akhmatova (1889–1966) and Nikolai Gumilev (1886–1921), Gumilev was under the constant surveillance of the Stalinist regime. Accused (falsely) of plotting against the Soviet government, he spent several years in prison and gulag camps. In a break between the two camps, he managed to defend his doctoral dissertation in history. In 1956, three years after Stalin's death, Gumilev was vindicated, but his own dramatic life, intensified by the complicated biography of his mother and the tragic death of his father (killed in 1921 by the Soviet regime), made Gumilev's integration into the Soviet academy extremely difficult.[14] Unable to find a job in the highly politicized field of history, he ended up teaching in the less ideologically constrained department of geography at Leningrad State University.

11. For a discussion see Ram (2001); Paradowski (1999); on Gumilev and neo-Eurasianism see a useful set of a conference proceedings *Lev Nikolaevich Gumilev* (2002).
12. For details see the Eurasian university's website, http://www.emu.kz/obshchaya-infor maciya/about-university/.
13. For more discussion on Gumilev's legacy in post-Soviet Russia see a special issue of *Etnograficheskoe obozrenie*, 2006 (3).
14. For Gumilev's biography see Golovnikova and Tarkhova (2001); Lavrov (2000).

Gumilev's major and most famous work, *Ethnogenesis and the Biosphere* (1990), was based on his second dissertation, defended in 1973, for a doctorate in geography (Wagner 1991).[15] The monograph examined the influence of the natural environment on ethnic development. Academic authorities proclaimed the book "too specific" and "of little interest" for a general audience and refused to publish it.[16] Following existing rules, Gumilev deposited the manuscript of *Ethnogenesis* in a state library in 1973, and by 1979 the number of requests for photocopies of the whole manuscript exceeded ten thousand (Shevchenko 2002, 29–30). Despite its obvious popularity, the manuscript was published only in 1989, during the time of perestroika, and quickly turned its author into a major post-Soviet academic celebrity.

Gumilev's theory of ethnogenesis (*etnogenez*) was very similar to that of Bromley, his main academic opponent.[17] For both scholars, ethnic self-awareness was the main principle behind etnos. Closely following Shiroko-gorov, Gumilev emphasized that self-awareness resulted from collective self-juxtaposing of a group of individuals (*osobei*) to all the other groups and collectives (1993, 41). Apart from the group's self-recognition, as Gumilev insisted, there was no single feature that could be consistently used for defining etnos (2002, 93). Not interested in the overt analysis of national political institutions, Gumilev perceived etnos as a "phenomenon of nature" that had little to do with socioeconomic formations. He emphasized that similar social conditions do not produce similar etnoses: the unfolding of social processes and that of ethnogenesis happen in different, "parallel," domains (182, 226). By largely ignoring the impact of political structures and processes, Gumilev associated ethnogenesis mainly with geographical and biological conditions. Etnos was construed as an "independent natural phenomenon," as a "corpuscular system" that shaped and channeled the response of humans to their natural environment (105, 177). Specific forms of adaptation were seen as the most important source of ethnic distinction.

---

15. Since the English translation of *Ethnogenesis* is available only in an abridged form, I use the Russian edition of the book (Gumilev 2002). All translations are mine.

16. In the Soviet Union, very few universities were allowed to have their own publishing houses; the number of published titles was extremely limited. Even fewer university presses could publish popular literature.

17. Among recently published archival documents of Gumilev, there is a list that he compiled in 1987 in order to document the suppression of his views and scholarship from 1975 to 1985. One of the entries is a complaint about Bromley's plagiarism of his work. As Gumilev insisted, at least twenty-nine key arguments of his theory of etnos were borrowed by Bromley without any attribution (Gumilev 2003, 244).

Since the etnos's self-adjustment to its natural context was also accompanied by an active modification of concrete locations, space (*mestorazvitie*) was simultaneously construed as a necessary condition of ethnic evolution (place of development) and as materialized evidence of ethos's being ("the developing of the space") (214).[18]

Drawing on diverse ethnographic and historical material, Gumilev insisted that a new etnos can emerge only as the product of a collision between two (or more) different landscapes, etnoses, or social organisms (2002, 322). A "monotonous" landscape, usually populated by an ethnically homogenous group, tended to resist drastic changes, either by expelling rebels or by incorporating changes with a slow and gradual pace. In contrast to this, landscapes divided by various natural barriers made mutual influence among separate groups relatively difficult; such mosaic landscapes increased ethnic specificity and might eventually lead to the outburst of a new etnos. By shifting the emphasis from exploring societal influences on etnos formation to the scrutiny of anthropogenetic potentials of landscapes, in a series of books Gumilev demonstrated how the terrain of Asia remained an area of major "outbursts of ethnogenesis" throughout several centuries (197, 218).

In Gumilev's case, the analytic split between the ethnic and the political, typical of Soviet ethnology in general, resulted in a peculiar displacement. Ethnic differences were to represent an incommensurability of larger proportions: biopolitical taxonomies (ethnic formations) emerged as a byproduct of physical distinctiveness of geographic areas. The combination of landscape and people was presented as a new form of human unity and human activity—the etnosphere (*etnosfera*) (Gumilev 2002, 39).

In the previous chapter, I showed how Russia's geography was often used by my informants to justify the uniqueness of the Russian national character and Russian way of life. Gumilev's idea of the all-determining significance of the geopolitical juncture provided them with an additional theoretical argument that grounded the source of Russia's cultural and political uniqueness in its transitory location between West and East.[19] Most extensively, the role of this juncture would be theorized by Russian neo-Eurasianists, who would turn a potentially detrimental clash of Russian and Asian civilizations into a productive collision of ascending and descending

18. Gumilev borrows the term *mestorazvitie* (from *mesto*—place, *razvitie*—development) from Petr Savitskii, one of the founders of Eurasianism (2002, 189). For the original discussion see Savitskii (1997, 282) and Miliukov (1993, 66–121).

19. For a useful historical review of Russian views on the Europe-Asia juncture see Bassin (1991).

etnoses.[20] "Geography is our destiny," as Aleksandr Dugin (2004), one of the most vocal current proponents of Gumilev's ideas, framed it.[21]

Gumilev's basic perception of etnos as a product of nature was rooted in a theoretical presumption about the biosphere, understood as a totality of living organisms connected with one another through the circulation of elements and the entropy of energy (Gumilev 2002, 325).[22] The outburst of ethnogenesis, through which a new etnos is usually formed, is a result of a mutagenetic (mutation plus genetic) shift, a deviation from the norm, produced by an excess of energy in the biosphere. Most such genetic mutations, as Gumilev insisted, quickly die out, and only micromutations that manage to resist the pressure of the environment can eventually form an etnos. It is precisely the ability of an organism to persist, its "capacity to withstand purposeful hypertensions," that Gumilev defined as "passionarity" (*passionarnost'*), a drive for change, an urge to break out of the already existing mold (328–29). In 1978, at the height of the Brezhnev stagnation, Gumilev wrote: "Normally, mutation never happens within a whole group in a particular habitat at once. Only a few individual organisms mutate, but sometimes this is enough for a new type of people to emerge. In our case, such a consortium of new people could eventually form itself into an etnos, if the conditions permit. Passionarity of the consortium's members is the mandatory condition for the etnos to emerge" (1993, 288). When there is a sudden emergence of "conquistadors and explorers, or poets and heretics, or such enterprising figures like Caesar or Napoleon," Gumilev insisted, we know that passionarity has become a social factor. "These people are small in number, but their energy enables them to develop or to stimulate an immense activity in any place where history is made" (292).

What happens when the drive for change is worn out? That is to say, what happens when the etnos, objectified in the transformed landscape, reproduced through the transmission of its culture, and guarded with a set of political institutions, has already passed its peak of expansion and is more interested in preserving that which has already been accomplished? As Gumilev indicates, in this situation, the most serious danger for the "descending etnos" usually comes from the neighbors or etnoses that still

20. On the notion of "Eurasia" as a post-Soviet intellectual framework see von Hagen (2004) and Kaganskii (2003). For a discussion of the parallel between Samuel Huntington's "clash of civilization" and Gumilev's collisions of etnoses see Goudakov (2006).

21. On Dugin's political and academic views see Ingram (2001); Umland (2003); and Shlapentokh (2007).

22. Gumilev borrowed the notion of "biosphere" from the work of Vladimir Vernadskii (1998).

retain their initial impulse, still try to adapt themselves to new conditions, and therefore are still capable of expanding the borders of their immediate area of existence (Gumilev 2002, 133).

This expansion of neighboring etnoses does not have to be violent. Sometimes it can take the shape of a chimera, a formation that adapts to a new habitat by mimicking dominant features of native species without seriously modifying its own internal qualities. As Gumilev framed it, when an etnos is devoid or deprived of its own environment, it might turn the ethnic space itself into its own living environment. That is to say, it can use another, "receiving" (*vmeshchaiushchii*), etnos as its primary habitat. Along with animals, plants, and valuable minerals, the native peoples become just another "component of the terrain, which is exploited by the etnos-parasite" (2002, 324). Different from mutually profitable symbiosis or traditional neighboring exchanges, chimera is a form of "ethnoparasitism" (*etnoparazitizm*) aimed at the complete hollowing out of the receiving etnos:

> This is not a simple living side by side, nor is it a form of symbiosis, but... a combination of two different, incompatible systems in one [ethnic] entity. In zoology, an animal's infestation with intestinal worms is called a chimerical construction. The animal can exist without the parasite but the latter will perish without the host. Living in the host's body, the parasite, however, takes an active part in the body's life cycle, increasing the demand for food and altering with its own hormones the organism's biochemistry.... [S]trong, passionary etnoses do not tolerate alien elements in their environment. (2002, 323)

In post-Soviet Russia, Bromley's emphasis on etnos as such, taken together with Gumilev's ideas of passionate ethnic solidarity bound to a particular place of development, suggested a vision of relatedness that exhibited no visible affinity with the discredited framework of Soviet Marxism or the socialist past. Emphasis on the natural, environmental, or extrasocial—a mix of biological concepts, geographical descriptions, and psychological terms—seemed to be the most effective tool to explain ideological flux.

In post-Soviet theories of Russian ethnicity, ideas about ethnic pressure and ethnic passionarity were reactivated by discourses on the Russian tragedy. The nation's recent history was turned into the genocide of the Russian people, and already existing social institutions were alienated further by being invested with threatening chimerical qualities. At the same time, the lack of established or universally shared national traditions was compensated for through the symbolic primacy of individual or collective attachment to space. The Russian terrain, once again, was transformed into a primary site of struggle for the nation's survival. It was Alexander Solzhenitsyn who forcefully (though not single-handedly) drew public attention to these themes.

The Russian Tragedy as the Russian Cross

On May 27, 1994, the Vladivostok airport was besieged by an immense number of journalists, politicians, and gawkers eager to see the landing of an Alaska Airlines plane. The plane carried Alexander Solzhenitsyn, the writer and dissident who had decided to return to Russia after twenty years of exile. The act of return had its own convoluted drama: on the way from Anchorage, Alaska, the plane made an unannounced stop in Magadan, the unofficial capital of the Soviet gulag. It was there that the writer first embraced and kissed Russian soil, inciting rage among the accompanying media crews whom vigilant Russian border control officers trapped on the plane, preventing them from filming the historic event (Ostrovskii 2004).

Back in 1974, following the publication of Solzhenitsyn's *Gulag Archipelago* in the West, the Soviet government had stripped the writer of his Soviet citizenship and deported him. In 1994, taking a special train (paid for by the BBC), Solzhenitsyn spent fifty-six days on a triumphal pilgrimage from Vladivostok to Moscow, familiarizing himself again with the landscape that he had not seen for years (Medvedev 2000, 16). Solzhenitsyn's return to Moscow was televised live for the whole country, and headlines of all the major newspapers announced the long-awaited arrival. The ecstatic reception of the legendary dissident, however, quickly faded away. The highly anticipated speech that Solzhenitsyn delivered in December 1994 to the Russian parliament was met with palpable boredom by the deputies. Solzhenitsyn's weekly TV show on a major Russian network did not succeed in attracting much of an audience either, and it was promptly canceled (Zubtsov 1994, 3). Various attempts to nominate Solzhenitsyn for president of the Russian Federation were preempted by the writer himself, who preferred to concentrate on what seemed to be the more important issues of the day. Neither of his two major books in the 1990s, *The Russian Question at the End of the Twentieth Century* (1995) and *Russia in Collapse* (1998b), managed to provoke substantial public discussion.[23]

Busy with his own historical projects, Solzhenitsyn also preferred to stay away from public discussion of the humanitarian and military disaster

---

23. For a review of the Russian Question, see Tolstaya (2003, 155–67).

in the North Caucasus. Famous for vivid depictions of the horrors of the Stalinist period, in his infrequent comments Solzhenitsyn approached the issue of the Chechen war through the lens of geopolitical interests, mainly pointing to Russia's territorial losses and the "genocide of the Russian people" in Chechnya (Solzhenitsyn 1998a, 17; 2001b).[24]

Increasingly, the mass media presented Solzhenitsyn's return as "grossly belated" or even "mistaken." The writer's decision to reside in a secluded area near Moscow, alongside the traditional homes of the Soviet *nomenklatura,* did not make things easier.[25] For many observers, his dacha, with a tall fence and security cameras, became an apt metaphor for the dissident's aloofness and social awkwardness, for the political irrelevance of the "messiah whom we lost" (Milshtein 2003). The final blow came when the man associated with the "national conscience" for so long and for so many became a persistent target of mocking satire (Voinovich 2002).[26] What had seemed so sacred now became profane.

The situation began to change quickly in the spring of 2001, when Solzhenitsyn published the first volume of *Two Hundred Years Together.* In his new work, the writer promised to "illuminate" years of "the joint life of the Russians and the Jews in the same state" (2001a, 8). The book became a bestseller, and the second volume only increased the temperature of the already heated polemics (Sherbak-Zhukov 2003, 21). Konstantin Borovoi, a flashy entrepreneur and the editor in chief of the glossy magazine *Amerika,* called Solzhenitsyn "an adept of Soviet racism" (2001, 8). Vladmir Bondarenko, a literary critic of Russophile orientation, announced that *Two Hundred Years Together* was just as important for understanding the national tragedy of the Russian people as *Gulag Archipelago* was for understanding the social

24. In 1997, for instance, Solzhenitsyn insisted during one of his rare meetings with people (in a provincial library in Tver') that not granting independence to Chechnya was detrimental to Russia's own interest. For one thing, this political decision made it impossible to insist on resuming Russia's jurisdiction over the Crimean peninsula in the Black Sea, a territory that was conquered by the Russian Empire in the eighteenth century (Solzhenitsyn 1998b, 17). The Crimean region remained a part of the Russian Federation until January 1954, when Nikita Khrushchev decided to change administrative borders and transferred the Crimean region to the administrative jurisdiction of Ukraine. This decision did not change much until the collapse of the Soviet Union, when the Crimea, traditionally populated by Russians and Tatars, became part of a new, independent Ukrainian state. For a discussion see the collection of documents in *Istoricheskii arkhiv* (1992, vol. 1).

25. The dacha in Troitse-Lykovo, which Solzhenitsyn's newly built house replaced, was once the home of the famous Soviet general Mikhail Tukhachevskii, killed by the Stalin regime shortly before the war. The dacha was occupied later by a deputy prime minister of the Soviet government (Dyshev 1993).

26. For reviews of Voinovich's satire see Krasukhin (2003) and Ivanova (2002).

tragedy of ethnic Russians (2001, 7). In various media, letters of support from prisoners of the gulag were balanced by petitions pointing out that Solzhenitsyn's book marked the beginning of yet another round of the anti-Semitic campaign in an increasingly undemocratic Russia.[27]

The book got mixed reviews from historians of Russian Jews. Many of them drew attention to the fact that Solzhenitsyn's study presented neither new documents nor new interpretations (Hosking 2002; Klier 2002). Indeed, it was not the historical dimension of the project that made the book a hot topic. Solzhenitsyn's exploration of the two centuries spent by the Russians and Jews together was an attempt to answer his basic question: "Is such togetherness possible at all?" The former dissident offered his answer at the end of the second volume, anticipating emotional rebukes for the very attempt to draw a line between the two groups.[28] As the writer maintained, the division was already there; the striving of Russian Jews for a complete assimilation—however natural this striving might be—was not really achievable. The reason for this failed "self-dissolution," as the eighty-four-year-old writer put it, had to do "neither with the destiny of one's origin, nor with one's blood, nor with one's genes." For what was crucial in defining one's national belonging in this case was one's ability to decide: "*Whose* pain is leaning closer to your heart: that of the Jewish people or that of the nation in the midst of which you grew up?" (2002, 519; emphasis in the original)[29]

Solzhenitsyn was not the first to appeal to the nation's traumatic experience. As the anthropologist Nancy Ries documented, it was perestroika that brought to life traditional Russian genres of litanies and laments in the late 1980s (Ries 1997). In chapter 1, I showed how similar recollections of past injuries were used by my informants to reactivate or reimagine their bonds with other people and the country. Centered on issues of loss, these communities reintegrated the personal and the collective, providing their members with a feeling of historical continuity that was disrupted by post-Soviet changes. These newly established social bonds were often negatively charged, and their power of emotional attachment was sustained first of all through incessant documenting and reframing of the suffering experienced in the past.

---

27. See, for instance, *Literaturnaia Gazeta,* November 26, 2003, 2; Kadzhaia (2003).

28. Some readers asked in their letters: "What goal, in essence, did Solzhenitsyn have in mind, when he undertook this division?" (Kholmianskaia 2003, 175).

29. See also Solzhenitsyn's response to his critics after the publication of the *Two Hundred Years* (2003, 3). For a general discussion on Solzhenitsyn and the "Jewish question" see Larson (2005).

Solzhenitsyn's vision of national belonging as structured predominantly through the individual and collective recognition of the nation's pain has a lot in common with this everyday patriotism of despair. There is at least one important difference, however. Unlike litanies of perestroika documented by Ries or the cases discussed in chapter 1, in Solzhenitsyn's approach pain does not just produce new forms of emotive connectedness. It also introduces a clear-cut ethnic division. Togetherness and national solidarity, as Solzhenitsyn's book clearly indicates, emerge as two distinctive, if not opposite, categories and practices of national being. Litanies, in other words, acquire specific *ethnic* tonalities.

This ethnic framing, as Solzhenitsyn's example shows, had a particular focus. The discussion of the ethnic differences did not center on the usual figure of a racially or religiously different other—be it the Muslim Chechen in Russia's south or the Chinese migrant in the east. Rather, public debates were animated by the constant quest for the hidden source of heterogeneity within a society that had seemed until recently to be so homogenous. It was an incessant search for signs of the hidden but present difference, a search for manifestations of masked togetherness that permitted the incorporation of tradition and change within the cultural landscape and cultural narrative of the nation.

Solzhenitsyn's history of togetherness did not exhaust the genre of the Russian tragedy, but it did illuminate several crucial aspects of this genre. Its preoccupation with pain pointed to the inescapable failures of attempts to describe once and for all the individual or collective experience of injury. The effort to extricate the nation's history from the history of nations lumped together revealed the retrospective orientation of the overall project. Finally, the fascination with the figure of the Russian Jew highlighted a persistent anxiety about the misleading nature of representation that replaces (Russian) essence with ("chimerical" Russian) appearance.[30] As is shown below, different authors of the Russian tragedy chose to emphasize different themes; yet all of them kept intact the basic desire to read Russia's traumatic past in ethnic terms.

During my fieldwork in Barnaul, my initial introduction to the genre of the Russian tragedy was less academic than I expected. In fall 2002 in Barnaul, I interviewed Konstantin P., an active member of the Altai Slavonic Society (Slavianskoe obshchestvo Altaia). Born in 1978, Konstantin graduated

---

30. Arguably, it was Igor Shafarevich, a Moscow mathematician, whose *Russophobiia*, written in 1978–82 and published originally in *samizdat*, started a recent wave of the tradition to explore the "Russian question" vis-à-vis the backdrop of Jewish history (Shafarevich 2003).

from the most prestigious school in Barnaul (with several subjects taught in English). In 1995, he entered a university, in which both of his parents were teaching social sciences. In 2000, he started in a graduate program in social sciences, working on a dissertation that explored issues of Russian "national self-awareness," as he put it in the conversation.

My interview with Konstantin happened in a local school in downtown Barnaul, in a precinct office that accumulated information about the progress of the 2002 federal census campaign. Along with many other students, Konstantin had been mobilized for conducting actual interviews with people. I asked him about his role in the Slavonic Society, where he had supervised administrative issues since 2000. In Konstantin's words, the society had united the region's intelligentsia since 1994, trying to defend Russian culture and the Russian people in contemporary Russia, as well as "to stimulate the development of our national awareness and national culture." Maybe because of the census activity going on in the background, Konstantin started his explanations with statistical data:

> There are 83 percent of us, Russians, in the country. Actually, I think that Ukrainians and Belorussians who live in Russia are no different from the Russians at all. So if we add them, it would be more than that, 85 percent, if not more! But despite all that, our own situation is very far from being ideal, from the way it should be in principle. Especially, when it comes to culture. Real national culture is emasculated [*vykholashchivaetsia*]. And this is true not just about the Russian people, but about all the native [*korennye*] peoples of Russia. Real national culture is practically absent on TV and radio, and it is not represented in the necessary fashion in literature and newspapers....How often can you hear a Russian song on the radio (never mind the TV)? I mean a *genuinely* Russian one. Not one that is just written in Russian language, but one that is a source of pride of our people....All this is not limited to cultural infringement only; we should say it directly—[ethnic] Russians are inadequately represented in the power structures, too. Be it the state parliament or something else....This can be explained by the fact that, instead of expressing the interests of the majority of the population, the authorities in our country express the interests of transnational capital, of those oligarchs who predominantly have dual citizenship or at least are oriented toward foreign countries.

Konstantin's point had several parallels with the theories of etnos discussed earlier. In the cited passage, the theme of Russian ethnicity emerged vis-à-vis other, unnamed but clearly nonnative, ethnic units. The existing cultural institutions (ethnosocial organisms) were seen as socially and ethnically different from the Russian etnos itself. Konstantin's explanations seemed to be motivated by an understanding that his own Russian experience, be it imaginary or practical, was not a part of the public domain; it was not a part of the commonly shared picture. However, the (inadequate) mechanism of representation was not questioned here. Instead, the feeling of cultural and political nonpresence was used as a starting point for examining how "the Russian culture proper" was replaced by someone else's culture. The social environment was framed as a location of increasingly alienated and alienating cultural coexistence, as a place of forced disengagement from the institutions of power. Subsequently, the very metaphor of common space was undermined by references to transnationality or the dual citizenship of those who were supposed to represent the interests of Russians. Togetherness was turned into duality and duplicity.

There is another important theme articulated by Konstantin—namely, the misleading nature of the easy equation of Russian culture ("genuine Russian songs") with Russian language ("songs in Russian"). In Konstantin's interpretation, the Russian language acquired the hollowed-out quality of the receiving etnos described by Gumilev: without a proper grounding in "the traditions of the Russian people," as Konstantin put it, the Russian language has no particular national value. Struck by this unusual split between the deceptive Russophonic and the genuine Russian, I asked him about these grounding traditions. In response, Konstantin listed three main qualities of the Russian people: universal communion (*sobornost'*), collectivism, and the love for one's neighbor.[31] It is precisely these qualities that are currently being threatened, if not already replaced, by a troika of individualism, cosmopolitanism, and the cult of money, my informant concluded.

This juxtaposition of Soviet spiritual collectivity and post-Soviet money-driven individualism is familiar from the previous chapter. Konstantin's story adds a crucial component that links the collapse of the country with the collapse of the nation. Fully agreeing with the general perception of post-Soviet changes as detrimental to Russian culture, Konstantin told me about the concept of the "Russian cross." Apparently, the concept had been around for quite some time, but it became especially popular in the local media during the discussion of the first results of the 2002 census.[32] As the general story goes, since 1992, Russia's population has been steadily decreasing every year. There are two major demographic reasons for this.

---

31. There is no exact English equivalent for *sobornost'*, which literally means *collectivity* (from *sobrat'sia*—literally—to get assembled). The word also has a strong religious connotation: *sobor* in Russian means "cathedral." Julia Kristeva translates *sobornost'* as "universal communion" (2000, 134), and I follow her approach here. ·

32. For details see *Altaiskaia pravda* (2003); Popova (2003a).

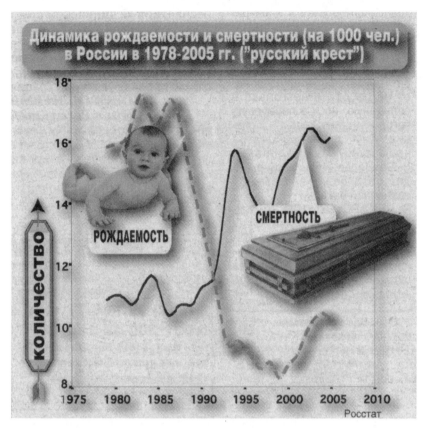

Fig. 2.1. The Russian Cross: babies vs. coffins. Artist: Andrey Dorofeev (www.bestcollage.ru). Source: *Argumenty i Fakty,* no. 22, 2006. Courtesy of the artist.

One is the general increase in the number of deaths in Russia; since 1999 seven hundred to nine hundred thousand people have died annually. The other major factor that contributes to Russia's depopulation is a declining birth rate. The diagram illustrating these two processes has been labeled the "Russian cross" (Popova 2003a; Bateneva 2003) (figure 2.1).

Since 2002, the topic has become standard in Russia's mass media. Regardless of political leaning or professional orientation of the specific outlet, most treatments of the Russian cross have been framed by the rhetoric of mourning over actual and hypothetical losses.[33] For instance, the liberal

33. See different interpretations of the theme in Anisimov (2004); Bakhmetov (2004); Bateneva (2003); *Na strazhe Rodiny* (2002); *Morskaia gazeta* (2002).

daily *Nezavisimaia gazeta,* quoting a deputy minister of health, provided the following grim statistics:

> Every year, the population of Russia is shrinking more and more. Every day we lose almost two villages. Every year a small province is gone. During last thirteen years, 11,000 villages and 290 towns have disappeared from Russia's map; 13,000 more villages that are still on the map in fact have no actual villagers anymore. Taking a pessimistic stance, one can predict that in 50–60 years the number of Russians will reach 70 million.... This phenomenon has already received a grave label: "the Russian cross." (Pokrovskii 2004)[34]

Sovetskaia Rossiia, an oppositional Communist newspaper, used the same trope for its own rhetorical purpose. In the editorial published before June 1, the Day of Children's Protection, the newspaper bemoaned, "June 1 is the only day in our country when the state authorities think about children. But even then never would you hear that the number of kids in our country has dropped from 40 million boys and girls in 1991 to 30 million in 2004. Conducted ceaselessly by the ruling regime and the government, the war against its own people has taken its toll: the lives of 10 million children will never be recovered" (*Sovetskaia Rossiia* 2005).

The provinces that are gone annually and the millions of lost lives of children (who were never born in the first place) are, of course, statistical tricks, aggregate numbers used to visualize general demographic trends and to evoke a necessary emotional reaction from the reader. Taken by itself, this preoccupation with the biological reproduction of the nation is not unique.[35] The Russian cross, not without a certain twist, illustrates a typical tendency of modern political regimes to legitimize themselves through a discourse, in which "every people is doubled by a population," as Giorgio Agamben put it (1999, 84). The conflation of demographic and religious meanings in the concept of the Russian cross adds an important dimension to this traumatic narration. The conflation is instrumental in moving a discussion of technical issues of social policies, health and child care, or the epidemic of alcoholism toward the predictable fascination with the nation's suffering.[36] In the process of this conflation, the fact of Russia's depopulation is often transformed into stories of deliberately conceived and purposefully implemented ethnic extermination (Elizar'eva 2002). For

---

34. By the end of 2005 Russia's population was 142.8 million (*Kommersant,* January 24, 2006).

35. For a similar post-Soviet tendency in Ukraine see Petryna's discussion of the concept of "demographic scissors" (2002, 146).

36. For a useful exception see Khalturina and Korotaev (2006).

example, Gavriil Popov, a former mayor of Moscow and one of the most active prodemocratic politicians of the perestroika period wrote:

> I think there was a Russian Holocaust. It was organized by the Soviet state and the Communist Party, which was in charge of it. Burning humans alive is not the only way to constantly reduce their number. The people could be burned at the construction sites of Communism. Or—in fights with imperialist aggressors. Or—in a process of collectivization....Overburdened with inhumane tasks by the leader, the people could be killed in a doomed experiment of building Communism in an isolated country. The people could be destroyed by the Soviet ideology that mercilessly deadens their minds and dries out their spiritual energy, persistently extirpating the century-old foundations of the people's life. The demographic data and predictions regarding the future of ethnic Russians are nothing but evidence of a holocaust. (Popov 2000b)

In this version of the Russian tragedy the story about the dying nation is predominantly a retrospective project. The primary function of the tragedy is to delineate the path that has brought the nation to its current (miserable) condition. A Barnaul journalist suggests exactly the inverse correlation between the Soviet state and resistance of the Russian etnos, framing it as a question: "Is it a mere coincidence that [the Russian cross emerged] exactly in the period when the previous [Soviet] state order was broken down, and new reforms started?" (Popova 2003b; also Glaz'ev 1998) In turn, Aleksandr Prokhozhev, a philosophy professor from the Altai State Pedagogical University, bluntly identifies the "perpetrators of the genocide" in his book *The Shadow People: On the History of the Jews in Russia* (2002): "The decade of complete Jewish dominance in Russia has resulted in the surplus of deaths over births. Every year the population of Russia shrinks by one million. Two million homeless children wander around the country. There was nothing similar to that even after the Great Patriotic War [in 1941–45]. Now, Russia is in a debtor's prison, totally subordinated to Jewish bankers from the International Monetary Fund" (255).

Regardless of their particular political preferences, each of these versions of the Russian tragedy is rooted in the same rhetorical attempt to juxtapose the natural life of the Russian etnos and the development of its national institutions. Each of them is motivated by the same question: Who is responsible for the Russians' diminishing ability to resist the pressure of alien etnoses and institutions?[37]

---

37. In the spring of 2006, the Russian government, apparently alarmed by the level of nationalist rhetoric associated with the demographic data and by the grave demographic

The Bomb That Killed Russia

Aleksandr Zinoviev, a logician from Moscow State University, instantly became a dissident when in 1978 he published abroad his sociological novel *The Yawning Heights* (1979). The Brezhnev regime (rightly) perceived the book as a form of open criticism of the Soviet state, quickly classified Zinoviev as anti-Communist, fired the fifty-six-year-old professor from his university position, and stripped him of his academic degrees, military awards, and finally citizenship. Cornered, Zinoviev left the USSR and spent more than twenty years in exile in western Europe, teaching and writing about the Soviet Union.[38] In 1990, his citizenship was reestablished, and the philosopher continued to live in Moscow from 1999 until his death in 2006. During that period Zinoviev published a steady stream of texts that were extremely critical of post-Soviet changes. In *A Russian Tragedy (The Death of Utopia)*, a "sociological novel" that came out in 2002, he wrote, for instance:

> When the "bomb of Westernism" exploded in Russia, it hollowed out not only the governmental, economic, ideological and cultural spheres, but also the very human material of the society....Designed as a weapon against Communism, the "bomb of Westernism" turned out to be much more effective. Only recently, this powerful community of [Soviet] people...was the second superpower on the planet, trying to perform a hegemonic role in world history. Now it is destroyed down to its very human foundations. But these human foundations had nothing to do with Communism whatsoever. The bomb was aimed at Communism but it killed Russia. (234)

How did this tragedy become possible? Given the power of the Soviet community, why did it collapse so quickly? What was it in the very national foundation that precipitated its quick dissolution? Why were the evil plans of the outsiders so successful? For Zinoviev the main reason had to do with the "moral, psychological and ideological disintegration" of the population (2002, 213). Inspired by Western ideas and disgusted with the state of the Soviet economy, the Russian people embraced the changes, and by doing so, they in fact were pushed by "irresponsible leaders" to "commit suicide" (30).

---

tendency itself, decided to take control of the situation. A new federal council on demographic policies was instituted, and a large-scale system of pronatalist measures was implemented. The intensity of the nationalist rhetoric was significantly toned down—the "Russian cross" was quickly replaced by the "demographic cross" (Ivanov 2006, 6).

38. For an overall review of Zinoviev's earlier work see Kirkwood (1993).

Zinoviev's description interweaves several of the strategies I have outlined earlier. The "human material" (etnos) and communist history became symbolically independent of each other. The disintegration of the Soviet state, encouraged by the West and from above, was turned rhetorically into the Russian people's suicide. The conflation of two symbolic frames—the suicide of the people and the genocide of the people—resulted in yet another version of the Russian cross. Issues of political accountability were transformed into depictions of the people's martyrdom, while post-Soviet institutions were perceived as being appropriated by someone else. To quote Zinoviev again,

> What we have is a state of criminals and Mafiosi, incapable of any productive work. This state is defenseless before its external enemies. It can't consolidate the popular masses around itself. State leaders can't grasp the notion of Motherland. They have corrupted the people, especially children and youth. There is no trace of legality in the country; criminality of all kinds is flourishing. And people, devoid of any protection from the state, are at the mercy of the gangsters;…the previous system of spiritual and moral values has totally collapsed.…All that was done consciously; it was even justified "theoretically" as a necessary step in the process of "the initial accumulation of capital." (2002, 226–27)

It is important to see how alienation emerges here as a major way of engaging with perceived reality. No area or activity has been spared, and nothing remains safe: the external world, the internal government, both the individual and collectives selves are either corrupted or collapsed. It appears that the work of negation itself is the only maintenance mechanism that can anchor the individual after the collapse. Following familiar lines of conspiratorial thinking discussed in the previous chapter, the quotation endows post-Soviet changes with a deliberate (although hidden) logic and simultaneously marks the source of individual or collective agency as unreachable.

The bomb of Westernism was not the only type of anti-Russian weapon identified by the authors of the Russian tragedy. The Moscow ethnographer Viktor Kozlov offered an emblematic attempt to frame the tragedy within the context of demographic discourse in his book *The Russian Question: The History of a Great People's Tragedy* (1995). A colleague and frequent coauthor of Bromley, Kozlov has had a successful academic career at the research Institute of Ethnography of the Russian Academy of Science. He is widely published in Russian and in English on the theory of etnos and on demographic processes among various ethnic communities in Russia and beyond. For his academic work Kozlov twice received the State Prize, the highest annual award of the Soviet government.

Kozlov's post-Soviet publications were focused mainly on "ethnic sustainability" and "ethnic ecology" (1991; 1994). Some of them had a very pointed political message. When in 1996 Kozlov revised *The Russian Question,* the new edition of the book was dedicated "to all the anti-Russophobes" (1996). The book and Kozlov's own controversial public activity caused several waves of heated, if localized, debates among anthropologists and ethnographers of Russia. Many participants in the "Kozlov affair" drew attention to the undisguised racism and anti-Semitism in his work. Some raised questions about the limits of academic freedom of expression and the proper academic response to it. While agreeing with his critics, I believe that Kozlov's writing—like many other texts discussed in this chapter—should also be approached as an example of a particular genre of academic nationalism that emerged within a broader social context in post-Soviet Russia.[39] The importance of these narratives is not in their (predictable) search for the subject of blame. To recall Wittgenstein, it is not the expression of pain that matters here but the painful place that generates these expressions (1958, 101). In other words, these narratives allow us to localize the injury and to trace the experiences that have been manifested through cries of pain.

Kozlov's analysis of the Russian question was determined to a large extent by his basic understanding of etnos as a relatively closed biological group that reproduces itself through transmitting language, culture, and "ethnic orientations" to the new generations, conceived "predominantly within ethnically homogenous marriages" (1995, 15). In Kozlov's interpretation, the Russian question is a combination of two main problems. The first one points to the decreasing vital abilities of the Russian etnos. The other problem stems from aggravating relations among different etnoses in Russia. Despite identifying his own writing as a form of "ethno-demography," Kozlov's analysis is deeply steeped in historical reconstructions. Hence, the Russian question is a consequence of anti-Russian politics that started with the October Revolution of 1917. According to Kozlov, the absence of the proper Russian "national statehood" was the major reason for the ethnic degradation of the Russians in the Soviet Union. As Kozlov maintains, revolutionary changes in the first two decades of the twentieth century managed to successfully consolidate etnoses that previously had not had their own

---

39. For the history and discussion of the Kozlov affair see Tishkov (1998). See also comments and responses published in the same issue of *Current Anthropology,* 40(4) (1999): 525–28. For a general survey of post-Soviet historiography and anti-Semitism see Rock (2001).

"fully developed" state. As a result, the majority of other etnoses in Russia (as well as in the USSR) were protected by their own forms of statehood: the Tatars in the Tatar republic, the Bashkirs in the Bashkir republic, the Kalmyks in the Kalmyk republic.[40] However, these changes failed to produce the Russian nation-state. Therefore, within the limits of the USSR, ethnic Russians never enjoyed the status of subjects but were used as objects by other nationalities in order to fulfill their own interests (1995, 119). Moreover, ethnic statehoods were often used by particular etnoses as a political ground for demonstrating increasing hostility toward ethnic Russians who could not defend themselves by relying on similar ethnically based political institutions (1995, 5; 1999, 339–40).

It is important to see how Kozlov reproduces in his narrative the logic outlined by Shirokogorov and popularized by Gumilev. The distinction introduced by Kozlov—Russians vs. other etnoses—generates a usual double split. First, it creates an environment of separate ethnic units within one nation, and second, it places the Russian etnos outside available forms of national statehood. Devoid of its own political institutions, the Russian etnos, then, is nothing but a part of the ethnic milieu, to be utilized by other etnoses. In Kozlov's narrative, Shirokogorov's ethnic "self-maintenance" is negatively translated into decreased "vital abilities" of the Russians. Correspondingly, etnos's ability to withstand the pressure of neighboring etnoses within the ethnic milieu is recast as "the worsening of intraethnic relations." This theoretical continuity (albeit not acknowledged directly in Kozlov's work) illuminates how a generic situation was rhetorically appropriated and subsequently turned into a personalized traumatic story.

Apart from lacking an ethnic Russian state, another important factor that contributed to the ethnic degradation of the Russians in the USSR was a long-standing, centralized campaign against Russian culture (Kozlov 1995, 120). As Kozlov maintains, "the ethnic being of a people [*etnicheskoe bytie*] is mainly determined by their language and their unique culture" (120). Consequently, as the argument goes, any harm to these fundamental elements would have inevitable consequences for the etnos's self-awareness. The rest of his argument is based on the structural split between the misleading Russophone speech (*parole*) and the tradition-bound Russian language

---

40. Following the Soviet legacy, the administrative structure of the Russian Federation combines two major principles: there are so-called national administrative formations (republics and provinces with a significant number of non-Russian ethnic groups) and administrative territories that tend to be populated by Russians, where political institutions are usually perceived as ethnically nonspecific or at least ethnically inclusive.

proper (*langue*). As Kozlov maintained, active attempts by the early Soviet government to turn the Russian language into the dominant tool of linguistic communication produced mostly negative results. Appropriated by ethnic minorities, the language was cut off from its vital (Russian) cultural content. The "weakening of the internal unity and lingual-cultural being" of the Russian etnos was aggravated by wide dissemination of the Russophone culture (123). Kozlov defines the predictable subject of this "chimerical" ethno-ventriloquism:

> It should be recognized that most of the Jews, who knew the Russian language pretty well (according to the 1926 census half of the Russian Jews named the Russian language as their "mother tongue"), experienced a certain hostility toward traditional Russian culture and its historical monuments. Hence they played a prominent role in the uprooting of Russian culture, and in substituting for it a "proletarian" ("Soviet") Russophone culture. Mostly, this activity was conducted through the national Committee of Education, and through the press, where the majority of the journalists were Jewish. (143)

As a result, Kozlov insists, by 1991, the Russian Federation was the only republic in the USSR where the struggle for independence and sovereignty of the late 1980s and the early 1990s was motivated by universal democratic liberties and political ambitions of the leadership, rather than by the ethnonationalism of the dominant nation so typical of other republics (228). The Russian etnos could not transform itself into a "collective form of the survival of the fittest" (284). Nor was it able to resist the "toxic influence" and "infiltration of the so-called mass culture of the West" (1996, 209). The "insufficient ethnicity" of the Russian intelligentsia only aggravated the grim conditions of the ethnic Russians (275).

Kozlov's argument suggests that this obsession with the incessant production of obituaries for the nation can be seen as an important cultural device, as an effective apparatus through which people in post-Soviet Russia conceptualized a sudden and unexpected collapse of the order of things, of forms of communication, and of types of collectivity that had been developed and refined for decades.[41] These exercises in writing ethnohistories of the Russian tragedy evidence a slow and painful disinvestment from previously important connections and attachments. The actual location of the object of blame, as I demonstrated, can be radically different—be

---

41. On the link between funeral rituals and the end of political regimes see Borneman (2004a) and Verdery (1999).

it the bomb of Westernism in the writing of the former dissident or the detrimental influence of other etnoses described in the work of the Soviet ethnologist. Yet the result produced by this alienation is the same: a grim picture of a hollowed-out culture and devastated country.

Stirring the Memory of Feelings

How has this history of ethnotrauma relate to other types of symbolic production? How is it integrated with other forms of knowledge and genres of narration? To answer these questions, I rely on published materials and my own conversations with Vasilii Filippov, an active member of the Altai Slavonic Society, and chair of the Philosophy Department at Barnaul State Pedagogical University. A graduate of the Department of Philosophy at Moscow State University, Filippov was assigned to teach in Barnaul during the Khrushchev Thaw and has remained there ever since. From the middle of the 1990s, in cooperation with Vasilii Goncharov, rector of the university from 1973 to 1997, Filippov authored a series of books that examined various aspects of Russian "national self-awareness."[42] Most of these texts were published by the university's press. Except for the most recent book, all of them were peer-reviewed and recommended for publication by professional scholars.[43] Some of the publications were designed as textbooks for university courses in philosophy, history of education, and anthropology; many are used by Filippov in his own courses. The print runs for these publications are between five hundred and fifteen hundred copies, but given the lack of a distribution network, they have not traveled far. I bought two of the most recent publications in local university stores; most of the previously published books have never been reprinted and are available now only in libraries.

During a conversation, I asked Filippov about his intellectual and public activity. He summarized it as an attempt to "open up for [the Russian] people a path to their self-awareness," a path that was "close to nonexistent." As in many other cases described here, this path to self-awareness started with introducing an internal split into the temporal and spatial continuum: the task

42. As Filippov explained in an interview, the cooperation is merely technical—he writes the texts, while the coauthor helps with publication.

43. The usual formula that accompanies most academic books in Russia states that "the book was recommended for publication by such and so." The book that came out in the fall of 2004 states something very different: "This is the authors' edition [*sobstvennaia redaktsiia*] of a book that is based on an independent research of the most brutal and vicious aspects of the expansion of Zionism in Russia in the shape of Trotskyism and Yel'-cynicism" (Filippov and Goncharov 2004, 2).

of defining one's own past was frequently associated with describing someone else's presence. This shift produced an interesting consequence. As Filippov put it in one of his books, "'We' now know much better who 'They' are. Whether 'They' want it or not, 'They' will have failed to extract from us, dominated by 'Their' leadership, more than 'They' have already extracted from us and our Fatherland" (1999, 79). Predictably, "They" in Filippov's version of forced togetherness are predominantly Jewish. To be precise, they are Zionists. Even more often, Filippov uses the hyphenated label "Zion-Fascists" (*siono-fashisty*). His texts, though, always have a paragraph that defines the line between the "Jewish people" and the "Zion-Fascists" (Goncharov and Filippov 1996, 422; Filippov and Goncharov 2004, 31). Yet Filippov's references to the "faces of Zion" make the distinction misleading (Filippov 2000).

Political alienation was not the only result produced by this rhetorical juxtaposition of the "ruling Them" and the "dominated Us." In a similar fashion, Filippov distanced himself from other social institutions. What was distinctive about his approach, though, was his attempt to link the cultural erosion not so much with the demographic decline of the nation but rather with the activity that aimed at altering the very consciousness of Russians. The political alienation is supplemented by linguistic, cultural, and psychological ones. In fact, for Filippov, this "altered state" is precisely the reason that there was no significant reaction on the part of the Russians to the radical worsening of their living conditions. For instance, in his *Russia and the Russian Nation: A Hard Path to Self-Awareness* (1999), descriptions of grim living conditions of the Russian people in the post-Soviet era were followed by the following explanation:

> Ruling today in our Motherland, politicians of foreign descent have subjected Russia and the Russian nation to global looting. But to be able to realize the scope of this act of looting one has to be able to construe the type of relation that looting and violence imply. In order to relate, to suffer, to strive for changes for the best, the individual has to possess the object of this experience in his memory of feelings. If this memory is empty, or if it is stuffed with other motives and strivings, then this individual is incapable of thinking about socially meaningful factors. (63)

Why is one's own "memory of feeling" not reliable anymore? Why does it not retain anymore the object of the traumatic experience? What made this "incapacity of thinking" possible? Filippov explains:

> There are very, very few people thinking seriously about the causes of the current sufferings, which are taking place in a time of peace....Why don't

many people want to look beyond their own nose? They don't look because they don't know. They don't think because their memory of feeling
is stuffed with emotions of a different kind. The Yeltsinoids' regime [*rezhim
yel'tsinoidov*] turned us into zombielike TV viewers. Month after month, year
after year the social values of the *Santa Barbara* "heroes" are more important for us than our own national values and passions. By substituting our
values and passions with totally foreign desires, the regime—just like a circus
magician—manipulates the individual and collective consciousness of Russia's peoples. It is the *method of hermeneutics* that serves as the main tool of
this manipulation (1999, 64; emphasis in the original).

The lack of reaction on the part of the nation, in other words, is construed
as a result of emotional amnesia and rhetorical brainwashing: anesthetized
memory of feelings is reinforced by a manipulated consciousness. The process of self-alienation does not stop here; the destabilization of interpretive
ability is extended further onto the physical qualities of the Russian etnos
itself. Alienation becomes total.

In his *Contemporary Scientific Conceptions of Man*, published in 1997 by
Barnaul State Pedagogical University as a textbook in anthropology, Filippov follows closely Gumilev's work in order to document how the Zionists
exterminate Russians by forcing them to exhaust their passionarity (Filippov and Goncharov 2004, 237). As Filippov suggests, during this pressure,
the genotype of the nation—its "internal code"—remains intact. The destruction is realized through encouraging the formation of a new ethnic
phenotype, a new set of individual features and qualities of the organism.
By turning "mutagenetic" (mutational plus genetic, *mutagennyi*) vices such
as "homosexuality, lesbianism, alcoholism, drugs, prostitution, laziness"
into its way of life, the Russian etnos undergoes an enforced transformation
and completely loses its human face (Filippov 1997, 195–98).

The physical disappearance of the Russian etnos is accelerated by active
interventions of alien forces in two major spheres—work and education.
Referring to Marx, Filippov describes how the work of an average Russian
was transformed into "penal servitude [*katorga*] and plague" from "the process of creative, active, initiative labor." A flight from servitude—a reasonable reaction on the part of average people—could hardly lead to liberation,
though. As Filippov puts it, fleeing from the formative effect of labor brings
the Russian people even "closer to their animal ancestors that evolve into
humans precisely because of labor" (Filippov 1997, 196–97; Goncharov and
Filippov 1996, 309–13).

Correspondingly, education, having been split from labor, became a target
of a global "psychological war" (Filippov 1997, 207). Foreign "foundations

and committees," either through active participation in the post-Soviet re-
vision of textbooks and educational programs or through support for the
desired activity of local educators with grants and stipends, managed to
"completely twist and deform the history of Russia" by neglecting centuries
of the struggle for Russia's independence and unification (203).[44]

Given such an entrenched worldview and a traumatic perception of the
nation's history, is there any hope or a solution? In an interview, Filippov
insisted that current deformations of the Russian language and culture, the
state of "Yel'-cynicism," as he calls it (Filippov and Goncharov 2004), could
mean only one thing: Russians are "doomed." Without their own—ethnic
Russian—government, state, culture, and education, the Russians have no
future and can only temporarily sustain themselves as a "dead-end nation."

In this state of intellectual deadlock and patriotic despair, it is the basic
links of relatedness that manage to deliver a positive symbolic effect.[45] In
2000, at the conference on Effective Education at Universities and Schools,
Filippov maintained that "not only logic educates. Blood educates too.
What the logic of education might be able to solve only in several years,
blood can deliver instantaneously" (2000). In the philosopher's view, it is
the method of "ethnopedagogy" that can bring together the logic of education and the educational effect of blood relations: "Every student was born
as a grandson and will die as a grandparent. School must see and take into
account the fact that every student carries with him the spiritual and moral
link with three or four generations, at least. . . . no revolutions, no reforms,
no constructions or reconstructions can break up this ethno-genetic chain"
(2000). Kinship, family, and generational ties not only connect the individual to his or her habitat. In Filippov's view, they also "determine the basic
biosocial and ethnological vectors of being and behavior." Hence, the purpose of ethnopedagogy is not dissimilar from the goals of the authors and
practitioners of the *Sufficiently General Theory of Governance,* discussed in

44. In January 2000, at a roundtable discussion of patriotic education that was organized
at Barnaul State Pedagogical University by the International Academy of Pedagogical Education, Filippov maintained that "our textbooks have been reflecting the matrix of the market-
driven approach to education, as well as to the principles of postmodernism that are established
throughout the postsocialist terrain. . . . Such an antistate and antinational expansion of a huge
army of sold-out educators amounts to nothing else but a loss of the national security of Russia
and the Russian people. . . . It is time to get out of our trenches, it is time to start an open fight
for the honor and dignity of our Motherland and our education. . . . We have been retreating
in silence for way too long. There is no place for retreat anymore. Beyond us is only nonexis-
tence" (2000).

45. For a similar tendency in other parts of Russia see Rudakov, Kornfel'd, and Baranov
(2000, 9).

Fig. 2.2. The cover of Vasilii Filippov's book
*Russia and the Russian Nation: A Hard Path to
Self-Awareness* (Barnaul: GIPP Altai, 1999).

chapter 1: both want to ensure a stable reproduction of vectors of being
and behavior—either in the process of education or through informational
pressure. Used as an instrument of internal homogenization, ethnopedagogy is meant to foster the intraethnic cooperation of collectivities "with
the same ethno-genetic value orientation," and to ensure a stable reproduction of behavioral patterns, as well as "psycho-physiological reactions" that
are common for the members of the given etnos (2000). One of Filippov's
books provides a striking image of what the actual content of this "ethno-
genetic value orientation" could consist of. The cover of his *Russia and the
Russian Nation: A Hard Path to Self-Awareness* presents the Russian nation
as an intergenerational collective of warriors: dressed as medieval knights,
this militarized community is protecting, and is perhaps inspired by, the
Russian Orthodox church behind them (figure 2.2).

Against this intellectual background, it is easier to understand the value
of historical ethnotraumas. The Russian tragedy shapes post-Soviet experience in the familiar language of the negative and the traumatic. The

Vic N brither gurding around.
Russin m obres, 7 work m more public

114   The Patriotism of Despair

unintelligibility of profound changes, aggravated by a lack of familiarity with new conceptual tools and mechanisms that these changes have
brought about, has resulted in multiple narratives of loss and a rejection
of the recent past. References to the alienating and alienated mass media,
repeated in many interviews during my fieldwork, similarly suggest the lack
of a positive symbolic vocabulary that could make the changes of the last
two decades understandable. Reproducing—albeit in a reverse way—the
logic of Soviet solidarity projected in a utopian future, authors of the Russian tragedy again and again create pictures of "the Russia that we've lost,"
to use the title of a famous perestroika documentary (Govorukhin 1991).
In these ethnotraumas, the commonality of loss in the past (*"we've* lost")
suggests the commonality of victims in the present. Locating post-Soviet
changes within the context of negative experience and traumatic emotions,
the trope of the Russian tragedy cements yet another community of loss.

These stories about lost national culture, degrading language, stolen national wealth, or statehood colonized by the culturally different others cannot be reduced solely to a search for a scapegoat, a search called upon to
mobilize the nation through the activation of "archaic" representations and
everyday stereotypes.[46] Instead, these traumatic narratives should be construed as a painful practice of "unmaking" the Soviet way of life (Humphrey
2002b), as a sociosymbolic operation of disinvestment from previously important contexts and practices that vanished within a very short period.

The main problem with this form of dealing with the past and present
is its dependency on the negative. Despite all the biopolitical divisions and
gaps introduced by histories of ethnotrauma they fail to produce a desired
reference point. Ethnic divides that are imagined in the process of rewriting
the recent and remote past are hardly used as a new beginning, as the constitutive "cut" that could finally outline the range of the subject's symbolic
and identificatory possibilities (Lacan 1978, 206). Rather, the discourse of
the Russian tragedy, structured by repetitious operations of division and
separation, recalls the figure of a stray *deject* described by Julia Kristeva, "A
deviser of territories, languages, works, [he] never stops demarcating his
universe whose fluid confines...constantly question his solidity and impel
him to start afresh" (Kristeva 1982, 8).

For authors of the Russian tragedy, a similar questioning of their borders
and location was often inspired by the attempt to produce a comprehensive
cartography of their alienation—from language, consciousness, culture,

---

46. For an example of such archaic interpretation see Gudkov (2005, 7–80).

power, economy. Devoid of a previously stable social position, these de-
jecting subjects, paradoxically, conducted the unceasing (and unsuccessful) search for the ultimate "anchoring point" that could stop the "endless
movement of signification," and render the nation's experience meaningful
(Lacan 1977, 303). Filippov's writings vividly demonstrate this tendency.
On the one hand, the inability to explain or accept fundamental transformations in the country outside the frame of ethnotrauma leads to the endless production of fragmented portraits of the abject other, who is held
responsible for changes and for their incomprehensibility. On the other
hand, the same situation pushes his writing toward a post-Soviet hermeneutics of suspicion, to a profound mistrust of the emerging social order
and failure to recognize its representations. The discursive flow is sustained
through an incessant compulsion to keep describing the feeling of a gap, the
feeling of noncorrespondence between accessible (Russophone or Western-
ized) frameworks for desires and one's own values and passions (which remain unrepresented). In turn, the shrinking interpretive space is perceived
as a product of "an expansion of the ideology of cynicism and hypocrisy"
(Filippov and Goncharov 2004), as a "large-scale aggression against the
human mind and feelings" created by "the social lie" (Filippov 1997, 207).

Despite their differences, histories of ethnotrauma discussed here demonstrate a persistent return of the same narrative device. Stories about Russian
tragedy are a result of the operation of traumatic split, of painful differentiation. Historical or ethnic experience dissected by this split is often different, varying from the presocialist past to postsocialist changes, from one
ethnicity to another. What seems to be constant, though, is the significance
of trauma—imagined or experienced—in forming post-Soviet narratives
about the nation. Historical ethnotraumas focused on the injuries of the
remote or recent past. The next section explores how a group of Altai ethnovitalists managed to convert recollections of the trauma into a basis for
a new will to live. The concepts of "vital forces" and "vital environment"
allowed them to weave together subjectivity, space, and organic teleology of
the national development.

Forces of Vitalism

With their persistent attempts to introduce a foundational divide in the
historical continuum of the nation, these narratives of the Russian tragedy
polarize audiences. Barnaul was no different in this respect, but the heated
national polemics that accompanied the publication of Solzhenitsyn's *Two
Hundred Years Together* had a more localized tone. In Altai, debates about

national traumas and ethnic differentiation were initiated by a local publication that merged Solzhenitsyn's affective study of togetherness with Kozlov's thinly disguised anti-Semitism. In 2002, shortly before the first volume of *Two Hundred Years Together* became available, Aleksandr Prokhozhev, a philosophy professor at the Altai State Pedagogical University, the oldest educational institution in the region, published *The Shadow People: On The History of Jews in Russia* (2002).[47]

In the 1980s, Prokhozhev was the secretary of the Altai Regional Committee of the Communist Party, responsible for "ideological issues." After the collapse of the party-state system, he started his academic career, actively defending patriotic values in his multiple publications and speeches. Pointing to a perceived lack of historical studies of Russian Jewry (in Russian), the former Communist Party functionary presented his book as an attempt to get rid of a "taboo of sorts" and directly address an overlooked problem—namely, why it is that "among more than 120 nations and ethnicities in the Russian Federation only Jews have no written history of their own; only Jews do not use their own language, and constantly try instead to present their own national Russophonic culture as the culture of the Russians, or as a national culture of [the Russian Federation]?" (2002, 3). The answer to this riddle followed pretty quickly. Listing already familiar arguments, on page 4 of the book Prokhozhev puts it bluntly:

> In our opinion, the most important reason for such a silencing of the history of the Russian Jews is the detrimental role that a part of the Jewry has played and continues to play in Russia. One could always find Jews implicated to some extent in every turmoil, revolution or counterrevolution, or in any other cataclysm that happened to our state. The main executioners of Russia almost always are non-Russian; most of them are Jews. Against this horrifying backdrop of Russia's grief and misery, any productive input of the majority of the Russian Jews, who built and defended our country together with many other nations, looks pale. (4)

The rest of the 278-page text is devoted to the portrayal of this grim backdrop. Prokhozhev's recitation of a detailed list of Russian sufferings concludes with an appeal that these "unprecedented crimes of the Zionist-Jewish fascists against the Russian people and other peoples of Russia

47. Typically for publications of this kind, the publisher is not specified here. The number of printed copies indicated in the book is nine hundred. The book was reviewed for publication by a professor of economy and a professor of philosophy. It is not available in regular bookstores but can easily be bought in the local university bookshops and kiosks.

should be condemned by the International Court [of Justice?] in the Hague" (2002, 258).

While the "Prokhozhev affair" did not produce any new arguments, it helpfully demarcated positions of local intellectuals in regard to ethnic difference. More important, these debates drew attention to local academic projects in which relations between the etnos and the state were envisioned quite differently from narratives of the Russian tragedy. The debates illustrate one of the most advanced local attempts to theorize the role of current changes in the history of the Russian nation.

In the summer of 2002, the Altai Slavonic Society awarded one of its annual prizes to *The Shadow People* in the category "science and education." Staged in the regional public library, the award ceremony was the culminating point in celebrating the Days of Slavic Script and Culture[48] and was meant to acknowledge people and institutions that had demonstrated "faithfulness [*vernost'*] to national traditions" in their recent work (Tokmakov 2002). In a conversation with Filippov, a member of the society's board and a colleague of Prokhozhev, I asked him about the academic value of *The Shadow People*. My question had a very practical underpinning—in Prokhozhev's book Filippov is listed as "the academic editor." Deflecting responsibility, Filippov described the publication as a product of conspiracy. "This is not [Prokhozhev's own work]. He was just framed. Everything came from Moscow....He was just given money" to publish it. Filippov also criticized the use of the word "shadow" in the title, pointing out that Prokhozhev "should not have used it. We, the Russians, have even more shadows." The philosopher, however, never articulated this opinion in his own writing. Instead, in his latest book Filippov strongly defended Prokhozhev against criticism in the local media, referring to it as yet another "clear example of the inflaming of anti-Semitism among the Altai people by some local intellectuals of Jewish descent" (Filippov and Goncharov 2004, 216–17).

Members of the Slavonic Society's award committee were not the only ones who found the publication of Prokhozhev's book important. In the

---

48. Since 1986, Russia has annually celebrated the Day of Slavic Script and Culture (*Den' slavianskoi pis'mennosti i kul'tury*) on May 24. Originally the Day of the Russian Saints Cyril and Methodius, the founders of the Slavonic (Cyrillic) alphabet, the celebration was officially recognized in 1991 by the state and now enjoys unique status as a religious and civic holiday (*tserkovno-gosudarstvennyi prazdnik*), so far the only holiday of its kind in Russia's calendar. Usually the celebration consists of book exhibits, performances of choir music, and conferences on various aspects of Slavic culture. Highly infused with patriotism and the self-congratulatory rhetoric of national exceptionality, the Day of Slavic Script and Culture is often used as an opportunity to revisit the brightest pages of national history.

fall of 2002, Sergei Danilov, a Barnaul lawyer, requested from the regional prosecutor's office a judicial opinion about the book, citing as his legal ground Article 282 of the Russian Criminal Code, which criminalizes attempts to provoke national and religious hatred. The regional prosecutor asked several professors from the School of Sociology at Altai State University to provide their scientific opinion of the book, including a linguistic, psychological, and historical analysis of the text. Partly on the basis of these reports, the prosecutor deemed Danilov's request to be groundless. One of these experts, a department chair, told me that the case was a "politically motivated event" since the book was an academic project and had nothing in common with hate speech or inflammatory accusations. In the official letter from the prosecutor's office publicized in the fall of 2002, the book was cited as an example of "freedom of thought and speech" granted by the Constitution, and was qualified as neither insulting anyone in particular nor threatening to violently undermine the state order (the two types of hate speech with clearly defined legal consequences) (*Svobodnyi kurs* 2002).

The story did not end there. On the basis of Danilov's appeal, the general prosecutor of the Russian Federation initiated a lawsuit against Prokhozhev, citing the same article of the Criminal Code (Negreev 2004).[49] Reacting to this news, several Altai organizations, the Slavonic Society among them, created the Committee for Defense of A. Prokhozhev. The newspaper *Vitiaz'* (The Knight), published by the Slavonic Society, supported Prokhozhev's publication and labeled the criticism a witch hunt organized by "illegal or semi-illegal Zionist organizations" in the region against those writers, academics, and journalists "who describe the objective and honest history of the Jewish etnos in Russia" (Belozertsev 2004).

More significantly, the book was also supported by Sviatoslav Grigor'ev, dean of the Faculty of Sociology at Altai State University at the time, and the main leader of the Slavonic Society. His defense was not a small matter given the faculty's prominent position in the region. In an interview with the university newspaper *Za nauku!* (For Science!) Grigor'ev said:

> It is true that I spoke in favor of this book and, in favor of literature of this sort in general. That is to say, in favor of the literature that does not call people to pick up an axe [*ne prizyvaet k toporu*] but educates them. This real education is not about things that have happened and are happening with the Jewish people; I would not even frame it this way. It is all about the Zionist expansion in the world in general and in our country in particular.

49. The case has been pending for years, and no official decision has been made.

The Zionist danger is no less fearsome than the Communist danger, which created the situation of castration of the Russian national self-awareness and of the Russian culture in our country, which created a situation of the global crises of Russian national statehood, Russian culture. As a sociologist, a citizen, and a Russian person, I am concerned, and this concern is justified historically as well as practically, because the takeover of property and power in the 1990s by the Jewish ethnic minority has resulted today in a very conflictual situation. (2004)

As in many cases discussed earlier, the exercise of biopolitical division in this quote produced a double effect: the ethnic split also introduced a political one. The traumatic Russian experience was extricated from the Communist past first and then was juxtaposed with it. Difference was turned into dichotomy.

For the Altai ethnovitalists—by contrast with many authors of the Russian tragedy—the documenting of the nation's trauma was not an end in itself. Grigor'ev's appeal to the educational merits of "literature of this sort" in the interview was symptomatic. Throughout the 1990s, the Faculty of Sociology at Altai State University was actively developing a comprehensive, albeit often confusing, sociological theory in which issues of ethnic difference became a prominent tool for explaining Russia's current condition. The "situation of castration," as Grigor'ev called it, the recognition of irreversible loss, seemed to mark a starting point for narrating not just the past but also the future of the Russian etnos. The genre of historical and/or political blame was transformed into educational readings, social policies, and methodological ruminations.

How were these stories about horrifying grief and misery translated into an analysis of the etnos's vitality? How did this particular "system of marks"—to use Derrida's definition of racism—outline "space in order to assign forced residence or to close off borders" (1985, 292)? In other words, how did the situation of castration help to organize a community? The rest of this chapter discusses the "sociological theory of vital forces" (*zhiznennye sily*) that was developed under Grigor'ev's leadership at Altai State University.[50] It explains how this version of ethnovitalism manages to render

50. In many cases no exact English translation of the categories created by these sociologists is possible. "Vital forces" is one of them. The Russian word *zhiznennye* (from *zhizn'*, life) could be rendered as "life-giving." The Altai sociologists also use "vitalism" and "vitalist sociology" (*vitalistskaia*) to describe their approach. Following their practice, I will use "vital forces," even though the term implies a connection with the European ideas of vitalism that the Altai sociologists do not have.

dramatic changes meaningful and to articulate a posttraumatic vision of the Russian national identity by using a biopolitical divide as the foundation for a bigger picture of the nation, the country, and the world.

The "sociological school of vital forces," as this intellectual movement is often known, emerged in the 1990s as a network of educational institutions and publications at Altai State University. Despite its provincial location, this is not a marginalized movement on the periphery of the discipline. Rather, it represents a mainstream tendency in official Russian sociology. The influence of ethnovitalists is not limited to the Altai region. The school (both the movement and the faculty) is recognized nationally, and is increasingly cited in national academic journals as an example of a growing field of the "sociology of life."[51] In 2007, Russia's major publisher of college textbooks printed a book by Grigor'ev in the series *National Social Education of Russia in the XXI Century: The Basics of Quality,* presenting the "famous Russian sociologist" as the author of a new "sociological paradigm" (Grigor'ev 2007). Liudmila Gusliakova, chair of the Department of Social Work at the time and a driving force of the faculty, told me that the school's national standing could be easily described by the formula "You may not like us, but you cannot not take us into account."

The intellectual and organizational shaping of the faculty was possible to a large extent because of perestroika. At the end of the 1980s, sociology was a very limited academic field in the Soviet Union. Only three universities (in Moscow, Leningrad, and Kiev) had master's programs in this discipline. There were no doctoral degrees in sociology, and dissertations with sociological topics or methods would usually be written and defended only as a part of the training in scientific Communism or philosophy. The first major breakthrough happened in 1990 when nineteen universities in the former Soviet Union accepted nine hundred students in sociology. Altai State University was among them. A small laboratory of applied sociological studies of youth, started by Grigor'ev in 1989, was officially reformed as the Department of Sociology with an MA track.

The novelty of sociology at the time, combined with the political savvy and good administrative skills of several young professors, quickly turned the department into a large educational industry. The faculty was instituted as the "Educational, Academic, and Practical Complex of Sociology, Psychology, and Social Work" (*uchebno-nauchno-proizvodstevnnyi kompleks*). Along with its seven departments, the complex includes a College of Social

---

51. For some examples see Bolgov (2003); Dalnov and Klimov (2003); Guzalenko (2003); Nemirovskii and Nevirko (2002); Reznik (2000).

Sciences, a Crisis Center for Men, and several smaller centers of psychological counseling for children and families (Rastov et al. 2000, 118–24).[52] The faculty also has a permanent Dissertation Council that is certified to grant the highest academic degrees of candidate of science and doctor of science necessary for an academic career (Grigor'ev was the council's chair and had to sign off on each dissertation.)[53] With all its divisions, more than a thousand students, and dozens of scholars pursuing advanced degrees, the faculty is the largest institution of sociology in Siberia and claims to be the third largest sociological institution in the country (109). The faculty is also the major local educational institution that supplies cadres for regional administrations, institutions of social work, and educational organizations in Altai. It significantly influences the makeup of the regional intellectual elite and the nature of the intellectual climate in the region. In spring 2004, Grigor'ev even had a chance to give his sociological theory a political test, when Mikhail Evdokimov, the governor, appointed him a vice governor of the regional administration in charge of social issues.[54]

This extensive institutional growth of Russian sociology, however, happened while the discipline was repeatedly questioning its academic legacy and standards. Scholars of different generations and theoretical orientations were increasingly suggesting that Russian sociology as a professional and academic field still lacked an intellectual identity.[55] In that respect, the sociology of vital forces, often branded as a "regional scientific school of thought" usefully outlined the scope of tools and approaches that were perceived instrumental for creating a new intellectual community in a post-Soviet province. It is symptomatic that issues of national identity became a major motivating factor in this seemingly academic project.

52. The school includes seven departments: General Sociology; Empirical Sociology and Conflict Studies; Social Work; Social Technologies, Innovations, and Management; Psychology; Psychology of Communications and Psychotechnologies; and Mathematical Methods in Social Sciences.

53. To illustrate the scope of the Altai Dissertation Council's intellectual influence: in July 2004, during its summer session the council held several public meetings in which one doctoral and seven candidate dissertations were publicly defended by three scholars from the Altai region, one from Vladivostok; two from eastern Siberia; and three from different regions of western Siberia (Degtiarev 2004).

54. Ultimately it did not quite work. After less than a year Grigor'ev resigned, following the unexpected death of the governor who appointed him. In March 2006, he moved to Moscow, accepting a double offer from a Moscow university and department of social development and environmental protection of the Russian government (*Altai Daily Review* 2006). This assignment did not last long either, and in a few months Grigor'ev returned to Barnaul.

55. For different interpretations of the disciplinary crisis see Toshenko (2002); Bikbov and Gavrilenko (2002, 2003); Shpakova (2003); Malinkin (2006); Filippov (2006).

In spite of dozens of monographs, collected volumes, textbooks, curriculum standards, and conference proceedings published by the faculty, it is not that easy to grasp the concepts behind them. Published texts often contain little factual material. Most of them are written in a genre of academic reflection upon a theoretical or methodological issue. Articles tend to be structured self-referentially, with a few often recurring foundational passages and definitions used to justify rather than explain the key terms and ideas of vitalist sociology. Academic recycling seems to be the major strategy that ensures the high volume of the faculty's publications; with minor or no changes at all, the same texts are reproduced under different titles.[56]

In 1999, in a text that Grigor'ev coauthored with Iurii Rastov, a senior sociologist of the faculty, the scholars traced their epistemological evolution. Citing their own studies of migration and employment patterns conducted in the 1970s as a source for their later generalizations, the sociologists claimed that "each subject of social life has in his or her possession a different set of potentialities of subjecthood [*nabory potentsii sub"ektnosti*]." As the sociologists observed, the practical realization of these potentialities depends on three major elements: particular "features of the social space," the subject's "ability to comprehend" these features adequately, and a "system of factors called vital forces" (Grigor'ev and Rastov 1999, 8). The individual or group's ability to purposefully utilize their vital forces indicates their level of "subjecthood" (Grigor'ev and Matveeva 2002, 58–81).

In the absence of a Russian equivalent for the English "agency," the subjecthood of ethnovitalism was understood first of all as an essentialist entity, "the self-ness" (*samost'*) that gradually unfolds itself in time and space, as I was reminded in conversations with Altai scholars. Regardless of its exact content, the ethnovitalist subjecthood did help to move sociological studies from lifeless Marxist analyses of relations of production to the "human-centeredness" and "culture-centeredness" (*chelovekotsentrichnost', kulturostentrichnost'*) of individual and group interactions. In other words, the notion of subjecthood was instrumental in overcoming the limits of the traditional "dialectical relations" between base and superstructure, firmly established in Soviet-style social analysis (Grigor'ev 2003a, 79; 2003c, 20). Later, the primary analytic focus of the school was shifted from subjecthood to vital forces that actually help to make the subjecthood real (Grigor'ev and Subetto 2000, 91).

---

56. The faculty has a small publishing division; it also edits and publishes *Sibirskii Sotsiologicheskii Vestnik* (Siberian Sociological Courier). The number of articles published by the faculty's sociologists in the nationally recognized academic journals is extremely low, however.

As Altai vitalists often stress, the analytical task of the category of vital forces is far from discovering or even describing some hidden essence of the human being. Vital forces is a sociological rather than a philosophical category; hence, its main purpose is to help explain how the "individual or collective subject of life-implementation" exists in actual space and time (Grigor'ev and Subetto 2000, 103; Grigor'ev 1999a, 26).

The major impetus for developing the concept of human vital forces came from yet another sociological study done by a group of Altai sociologists in the early 1990s. The study traced the regional consequences of the nuclear test explosions conducted in the neighboring Semipalatinsk region (Kazakhstan) from 1949 to 1962.[57] The detrimental impact of the tests was certainly known to the Soviet officials and the local population, yet until perestroika there was neither discussion of this case nor social services for the people who suffered from these explosions. The sociological project was a part of the general policy of openness started by Gorbachev in the mid-1980s, and it was meant to provide the government with practical recommendations that would enable it to minimize negative social consequences of the Semipalatinsk tragedy (Grigor'ev and Rastov 1999, 11). In a 1994 report titled *The Sociologist in the Region of Ecological Insecurity,* two prominent members of the faculty concluded that along with "obvious manifestations of genetic instability among the offspring" of those who had experienced the influence of the explosions in 1949–62, there also was a "multiple and diverse decrease of the vitality (*zhiznestoikost'*)" of the cohorts in question. The population at large was "negatively affected" (Grigor'ev and Demina 1994, 15).

This traumatic origin of Altai vitalism is important, as is the original combination of issues of environmental disaster, health, and political responsibility, on which the initial project was based. By the end of the 1990s, the traumatic foundation of the concept was generalized; references to a specific politico-environmental disaster were replaced by a version of the Russian tragedy. Traumatic experience acquired the force of an intellectual matrix and became an effective interpretive and narrative device. To quote Grigor'ev:

> The transformation of the general order of social life, mass alcoholism, criminalization of both daily life and the governmental sphere, living standards

---

57. During these years, Semipalatinsk was used as the main site for testing nuclear bombs above and under ground. For more than a decade, the population in Altai was exposed to the flow of radiation from the testing ground.

below the sustenance level—all that provoked illnesses, increased mortality, and decreased life expectancy among all native people of Russia.... This situation not only brings up questions of national and state security in Russia, but also [it points toward] the numerical decrease in the national-cultural community [of the country] of the state-forming etnos [*gosudarstvoobrazuiushchii*]—that is to say, Russians and other native peoples. (Grigor'ev 1999b, 36)

Significantly, in the process of this generalizing shift, the split between the etnos and ethno-social organisms—that is to say, the split between the nation and the state so typical of late Soviet theories of ethnicity—was somewhat overcome. The state emerged as a direct continuation of the etnos, or, perhaps even more important, the state was now construed as a primary condition for the etnos's survival. True, there were plenty of appeals to Russian ethnic statehood in the work of Kozlov or Filippov discussed earlier. Ethnovitalist constructions radically changed the context of these appeals. The state was no longer construed as a contested apparatus of classes or etnoses. Instead, as Tamara Semilet, another prolific scholar of the vital forces school puts it, the state reflected "the ethnopolitical status of the people," being "a form of vital activity of the 'social body' of culture" (Semilet 2003a, 71). To use Shirokogorov's language, the state was turned into part and parcel of the ethnic milieu, into a biopolitical institution that helped to maintain "the vital forces of national communities" (Grigor'ev 1999b, 42).

Within the framework of ethnovitalism, survival of the Russian etnos was no longer constructed only as an issue of significant cultural and historical proportions. It also became a matter of the socioecological security of the state and the nation (Grigor'ev 2003a, 182–83), as well as a burning question of "ecology of individuals and etnoses" (Grigor'ev and Subetto 2003a, 101–7). Correspondingly, the main task of the nonclassical sociology of vital forces, then, was no less than "the creation of theory and practice of the civilization of the managed socionatural [*sotsio-prirodnaia*] evolution" (Grigor'ev 2000b, 131).

Such intertwining of biological metaphors and sociological analysis, as the anthropology of science has demonstrated, often reflects the emerging character of a new discipline. For instance, in her study of American immunology, Emily Martin showed how the vocabulary of the new field of research was created largely through borrowing images and metaphors of the nation-state: "As immunology describes it, bodies are imperiled nations continuously at war to quell alien invaders. These nations have sharply defined borders in space, which are constantly besieged and threatened" (Martin 1990, 421). For Martin, the popularity of this somatic nationalism reveals two major dynamics. A lack of a developed analytic language in the new discipline forced scholars to look for ready-made tropes and interpretive tools elsewhere. At the same time, the familiarity and metaphorical transparency of traditional images of the nation-state turned the language of the "state war" into a terminological prosthesis ready to fill the symbolic vacuum.

What is crucial in such borrowings, as Martin suggests, is the ideological work that this imagery does: violence is inscribed in the very core of daily life and is envisioned as a part of the body's function (Martin 1990, 417). The attractiveness of somatic nationalism is not determined only by the all-permeating nation-state discourse, however. By naturalizing the nonorganic or the social, bodily tropes also turn the organismic logic into a self-sustaining and perpetually unfolding narrative: the organic organization of the etnos is construed as the primary mode of ethnic being and as the primary purpose of its existence.

In their attempts to strengthen the language of sociology with the terminology of the nation-state, Altai ethnovitalists seemed to follow the model described by Martin. Images of health and illness were dominant, yet the application of these images was reversed. It was society and sociology that were expressed now in naturalized terms. As a result, the academic project was increasingly construed as a corrective discipline. Grigor'ev even published a text that outlined the necessity of instituting "social therapy" as a new branch of contemporary sociology (2000, 134). The new field of academic social therapy is still in its infancy; a therapeutic function, however, clearly underlies vitalist sociology as a whole.

The generalization of traumatic experience also modified the construction of the agent of this experience. Original demographic groups ("victims of radioactive exposure") evolved into "national groups" and "national-ethnic communities" (Grigor'ev 1999b, 42). Statistical populations were turned back into ethnic peoples, to reverse and rephrase Agamben (1999, 84). Implicitly following Gumilev, Altai vitalists reproduced and theorized further the link between ethnic passionarity and ethnic place of development: the basic category of vital forces was supplemented by its spatial counterpart—the category of the "vital environment" (*zhiznennoe prostranstvo*). The categorical production eventually resulted in "culturevitalism," a peculiar amalgam of organic metaphors and cultural categories that brought together the biological, the ethnic, and the territorial.

Society-Organism and Its Enemies

Within the nonclassical vitalism of Altai sociologists, the specific origin of vital forces is not exactly clear, as was also the case with the more classical European vitalism of the eighteenth and nineteenth centuries (Wheeler 1939; Cimino and Duchesneau 1997). Gumilev's theory of passionary etnoses is often acknowledged as extremely significant (Grigor'ev 2003b, 29), and many ethnovitalists do explore various aspects of energy exchange between nature and human beings. Different types of energy, it is said, are absorbed from nature through the senses, then transformed and accumulated as psycho-energetic systems in the nervous system and brains (Bobrov 2000, 56; see also Soboleva 2000). Others talk about *Homo vivens*, "a bio-psycho-social being with inherent physical, psychic, and social forces as a source of this being's life" (Rastov 2003, 99). As a particular example, Iurii Rastov, a sociologist of conflict, cites his study of "poor categories" of people who are rarely inclined to protest, despite their objectively bad living conditions. As he concludes, this incoherence reflects the "predominance of physically and psychically defective people" among these categories: "It is impossible to multiply forces when one has none" (100).

In Grigor'ev's own work, the social racism that equates possession with access and, conversely, associates dispossession with degeneration acquired a somewhat different form.[58] It was not the inherent life sources that become problematic for the scholar. Referring to the history of the Slavic etnos as his evidence, he insisted that traditionally the key organizing principle in Slavic history was not blood or kinship but the territorial community (*obshchina*) that sustained the viability of the etnos (Grigor'ev 2001, 121). Following closely Gumilev's argument about the crucial importance of the place of ethnic development, Grigor'ev insisted on securing the unique configuration of vital forces that were shaped by each national-ethnic community in the process of a very particular "interaction with the vital environment, habitat, and the means of livelihood" (2000b, 47).

It is precisely this ability of ethnovitalists to translate the narrative of the Russian tragedy into a narrative about inalienable cultural property, cultural protection, and defense that moved them beyond the preoccupation with past injuries and suffering. The familiar trope of the region in danger acquired pragmatic tones. Histories of ethnotrauma were finally relocated within the context of national security. In her study of *Culture-*

---

58. For more on latent and overt racism in post-Soviet social sciences see Voronkov et al. (2002).

Vitalism, published in 2004 by Altai State University and used as a course book for philosophy students, Tamara Semilet, a philosophy professor, outlined the problem of "national cultural security" and provided a list of "threats to the vital forces." The list, in fact, succinctly summarizes grievances about the current state of Russian culture frequently voiced in the mass media. External dangers to national culture, for instance, include the domination of foreign languages, alien religions, foreign-born ideals and standards, external attempts to dominate the internal political life of the country, radical modifications of patterns of social ties and interactions, imposition of a "cultural inferiority complex," and the "apathy of despair" (2004, 63–64). The mutual pressure of etnoses reappeared here as cultural intrusion, and ethnosphere became a stage for the global competition of etnoses (Koltakov and Moskvichev 2001).

Geopolitical scenarios of Altai ethnovitalists did not escape a touch of historicizing called upon to visualize the steady diminishing of the vital space of Russian culture. For instance, during the conference "Vital Forces of the Slavic People at the Turn of Centuries and Worldviews: The Multifacetedness of the Problem," organized in December 2000 by the faculty of Altai State University, presenters listed multiple facts that could easily be summed up in the following quotation: "On average, from the times of Ivan the Terrible until the middle of the nineteenth century, our country's territory was increasing daily by one square kilometer. In the second half of the nineteenth century, Russia entered a process of slow shrinking. Back then it occupied one-fifth of the world's land surface; now it can barely claim one-seventh of it" (Rastov N. D. 2001, 38).

In more up-to-date versions of a similar narrative, "etnoses of the G-7 [countries]"—often referred to as the "gold billion" (*zolotoi milliard*)—are portrayed as being deeply invested in reducing "the Russian, and predominantly Slavic, population to 40–50 million" (Koltakov and Moskvichev 2001, 136) to be used as a cheap labor force in order to "serve the interests of the world capital-elite," with Russia itself becoming a deindustrialized country with no control over its natural resources (Subetto 2001, 63).[59]

This combination of issues of security, ethnicity, and territory brought back Gumilev's ideas about the importance of the specifically Eurasian place of development. Space and power were firmly linked. As some ethnovitalists like to claim, historically Russia-Eurasia was located *between* the East and the West, occupying simultaneously "the middle and 'the heart.'" The vital

---

59. For a detailed discussion, see the previous chapter.

position determined Russia's role as a "cultural mediator" between different cultural poles, and a "synthesizer" of different cultural logics (Ivanov 2001, 281; Grigor'ev 2000b, 99–100). Such a location means that the collapse of Russia would not be a problem of the Russian or even Slavic etnoses only:

> As the Eurasian civilization, Russia is the center of world stability and instability. If the strategic plan [of the world's master minders, *mondialisty*] to confederate Russia were to succeed…instability would settle here. The West and the East would clash; China would make a geopolitical shift toward Siberia. Germany would "shift" towards the East; the Islamist fundamentalism would also "shift" along the axis of the Volga–River-the North Caucasus-Kazakhstan. A geopolitical disturbance [*smuta*] of grand proportions would then happen. And humankind would hardly succeed in getting out of it, because "portable nuclear bombs," not to mention other weapons of mass destruction, have become a reality these days. (Subetto 1999, 12)

To stop a potential worldwide catastrophe, as Grigor'ev and Subetto have suggested, one needs to understand that the model of personality developed throughout the course of the Russian history is opposite the liberal model (2003a, 105). Within the framework of ethnovitalists, the primacy of collectivity (*sobornost'*), the unity of the individual, society, and the state that was claimed to be typical of the Russians, emerged as a product of a particular Eurasian location, with its specific climate and extensive landscape. Survival and preservation of the Russian "society-organism," they claimed, should begin with introducing an "ecology of the Russian people" and with developing a study of "social virology" as a "special scientific field" that could explore and prevent a "special type of 'sociopsychological war' aimed at destroying the backbone of the ethnos's social memory, its basic value system, and its worldview paradigm" (101–2).

With its bio-psycho-social ethnic body, its organic culture, and its rhetorical "violence in the name of the vital," as the anthropologist James Faubion calls it (2003, 78), the administrative and academic success of vitalist sociology is symptomatic of a process through which communities were imagined and institutionalized in post-Soviet Russia. To some degree, this example revealed an experimental situation: a group of scholars with a background in social sciences and humanities, with extensive experience of international academic travel, and with access (however limited) to world academic literature set about to create a new framework for their sociological data. Starting from scratch, without institutional support or intellectual constraints of the discipline, the school of vital forces in a short time managed to consolidate people and financial resources around the persistent production of quasi-academic narratives, which were structured around the idea of ethnic division.

The traumatic origin of vital forces, the therapeutic goal of ethnovitalist narratives, and the underlying striving to create a protective discursive shield of ethnic cohesion cannot, however, hide the main logical flaw in this theory. The social therapy of this vitalism could sustain itself only through securing a constant production of objects-symptoms for its own application: from the situation of castration of Russian culture to the viral infection of the etnos's backbone, from the global competition of etnoses to the broken genetic code of the national culture.

As this chapter has demonstrated, the ethnovitalist approach is far from being a marginal one in Russia. This analysis of Soviet theories of ethnicity has showed how the analytic separation of the etnos from the state both prefigured current ideas of ethnic solidarity rooted in a particular terrain and helped to frame post–cold war relations as a geopolitics of etnoses. In turn, a discussion of different versions of the Russian tragedy made obvious how metaphors of national pain often led directly to searching for the subject of blame, to defining an institutional, ideological, or ethnic entity that could be held responsible for the trauma of the nation. Yet this delegation of responsibility for the nation's history, this alienation of the past, which only recently was a part of everyone's biography, could also be interpreted as a historically specific affective mapping, as a symbolic tactic used by communities of loss that found themselves in a radically changing environment without any accommodating tools or navigating charts. Blame acts here as an operation of registering the ungraspable without understanding it, as a gesture of recognition of one's own inability to interpret emerging differences and shifting boundaries. By breaking a population into distinctive groups, by separating out some groups, these xenophobic discourses of ethnic difference created the desired effect of intelligibility when dealing with the nation's unpredictable past and rapidly changing present.

3 Exchange of Sacrifices

State, Soldiers, and War

Russia doesn't pay us much—in money or in glory.
But we are Russia's only soldiers.
Hence, we must hold out, until the very death.
Forward! Forward![1]
—"ATY-BATY," a popular song

—What did you fight for [in Chechnya]?
—I know only whom I was fighting against.
—From an interview with a veteran of the Chechen war, Barnaul, 2003

"Article 0" of the Constitution

The shared discourse on imaginary or experienced pain framed within the genre of the Russian tragedy brought the wounded together; it established emotional bonds; it provided authority. In the narratives of traumatic identities described so far, the state was largely missing. Notions of "sociality," "totality" or "wholeness," which were to endow post-Soviet changes with some sense of order, were usually linked with metaphors of land, space, cultural property, or organismic versions of collectivity. When the state did emerge in these stories, it was envisioned either as an institution colonized by outsiders or as an imaginary guardian that was expected to shield individual and collective identities produced elsewhere.

Given Russia's past, this disappearance of the state from post-Soviet narratives seems startling—as if it took only few years to completely erase decades of the involvement of the Soviet state in every aspect of public and private life. Of course, the state did not vanish in Russia. While certainly limited in its activity, the post-Soviet state assumed a peculiar social position. Roughly until 2004 radical changes and dramatic decisions implemented by the state would not be followed by any institutional support or

1. Rossiia nas ne zhaluet ni slavoi, ni rublem/ No my eio poslednie soldaty/ I, znachit, nado vystoiat', pokuda ne umrem/ Aty-baty, aty-baty.

well-coordinated policies. The new Russian state lacked resources, professionals, and more important, any relevant experience in dealing with massive political and economic changes. In addition, the post-Soviet state followed the same striving for immediate transactability described in the first chapter. The discussion of long-term social and political consequences was put aside or at least it was dominated by urgent short-term considerations. In this respect, the metaphor of "the 'kamikaze' team" that Yegor Gaidar, the head of the government that radically transformed Russia's economy in 1992, routinely used in his memoirs and public interviews to describe Russia's first non-Communist, captured well the dominant principle of post-Soviet governance (Gaidar 2003, 89). By definition, the primary task of a kamikaze team is to deliver a lot of shock, not to deal with its consequences.

To put it differently, it was not the state's disappearance that my informants' narratives revealed. Instead, these stories usefully documented the state's disengagement from the processes that it had initiated. In this chapter, I explore a very specific example of this disengagement. I examine how people experienced the state's withdrawal from their lives by using interviews with veterans of Chechen wars and war-related materials that I collected in Barnaul. Being directly involved in shaping the military identity of Russian veterans, the state quickly abandoned veterans after their service was over. The ambiguous legal status of the Chechen war aggravated the veterans' social conditions further. The public indifference or hostility to the outcome of the war left no ground for signs of social respect that ex-soldiers expected.

The Chechen war became, perhaps, the most vivid metaphor for the lawlessness (*bespredel,* literally a lack of any rules) of the 1990s and early part of the next century in Russia.[2] It exposed the least attractive features of the post-Soviet state: its cruelty, its indifference, and its lack of responsibility. War is never an organized event; and the history of every generation of war veterans is always a history of trauma, confusion, and disillusionment. Yet the Chechen war, like the Korean and Vietnam wars in the United States, added to these veterans' traumatic biographies a profound feeling of being betrayed—by the Russian state, by the military leadership, by the general public.[3]

This case is more than the familiar story about yet another generation of soldiers and officers misused by their government. In a concentrated form,

---

2. See Volkov (2002, 82) for a concise discussion of the notion of *bespredel* in Russia's post-Soviet politics.

3. For a detailed discussion of the public perception of the Korean and Vietnam wars see Hynes (1997, 180); Severo and Milford (1989, pts. 7–8).

this group shows what happens to strong state-oriented identities when the state suddenly removes its legal, economic, and symbolic support. With some obvious limits, the relationship between veterans and the state described in this chapter has an obvious parallel with the situation created by the collapse of the Soviet state in 1991. Back then, the lifting of the pressure of the paternalistic state did clear a lot of space for free action. At the same time it undermined the basic conventions that for several decades had regulated a large variety of social relations. Even more important, it made meaningless the identities of those who had been taking the state and its institutions seriously and forced these individuals and groups to redefine and renegotiate their self-perception and their social position in radically changing conditions.

In his study of the last Soviet generation Alexei Yurchak (2006) usefully reminds us that not everybody in the USSR took the Soviet state at its word. It is revealing, though, that even in his discussion of bohemian artists or Komsomol activists from late Soviet Leningrad Yurchak emphasizes the importance of formalized symbolic structures and ossified social conventions through which the Soviet regime inadvertently provided these socially and culturally advanced groups with a legitimate cultural ground for their subversive or opportunistic activities. Such dependency on "authoritative discourse" seems to be even stronger in the cases described here, given that the noninvolvement with the state-organized forms of life, so paramount for Yurchak's informants, was an unaffordable luxury for the majority of my interviewees.

My point, to repeat, is not that the existing Soviet system was good or effective. Its internal flaws were hard to hide. Rather, I want to stress the fact that the late Soviet society did have a set of guidelines and road maps that could deliver predictable social outcomes. The removal of these guidelines did not immediately generate alternative patterns of exchange, interaction, and recognition. And my interviews with veterans demonstrate not only their reaction to the normative vacuum but also their attempts to overcome the absence of workable social conventions by creating a new community of loss.

Given the ambiguity with which the Chechen war was presented in the Russian media, it is perhaps understandable that very few Russian officers used the war as a ground for substantive criticism of the state's military policy. Some approached it as a business opportunity; few resigned quietly. The majority of Russia's higher officers preferred to follow orders silently, ignoring—at least in public—the increasing number of the dead and injured civilians and soldiers. There was no equivalent of Vietnam Veterans against the War in Russia. Nor was there anything comparable to the investigations through which American veterans ("winter soldiers") challenged the U.S. military and civic authorities in 1971 (Stacewicz 1995, 188–252). A possible antiwar stance as a way to create a *post*war identity was replaced by a different symbolic framework: after their return from the war veterans increasingly couched their appeals for public recognition, assistance, and compensation in the language of patriotism. At times, this uneasy attempt to establish an economic equivalent of patriotic values produced unexpected results: veterans' search for recognition of their financial and social entitlements implicitly pushed the state to define the war in Chechnya in terms that exceeded the borders of purely economic issues. The following example illustrates this trend.

In January 2005, a regional court of the Orel province in central Russia overturned the previous decision of a lower court that had obliged the Ministry of Defense to provide a pension and financial compensation to Gennadi Uminskii, a retired ensign. In 1996, he was severely wounded while performing contracted military service for the Ministry of Defense in Chechnya. As the new court decision concluded, "war conditions" made it impossible to determine "the real agent of harm." Therefore, there was "no ground for any claim about the state's responsibility for injuries and disabilities incurred" (Zorin 2005).

As a contract serviceman, Uminskii had participated in a particularly bloody battle when Grozny, Chechnya's capital, was stormed by federal troops at the end of the first Chechen war (December 1994—August 1996). On August 6, 1996, with his platoon positioned outside Grozny, Uminskii (with 202 other servicemen) was ordered to unblock several checkpoints in the city's downtown and to rescue several journalists as well as a general captured by the rebels. As soon as the platoon entered the city, the soldiers were immediately encircled. Most of them were killed on the spot, yet fifty managed to survive, hiding in a ruined building nearby. Despite the rebels' multiple demands that they surrender, the soldiers continued to fight back, turning the building into a defense ground. On August 10, 1996, however, the besieged soldiers were startled by a radio news report: their commanders had announced an official mourning service to commemorate the annihilated platoon. As the soldiers learned later, the regiment's bureaucracy had even issued official "funeral letters" (*pokhoronki*) to inform the soldiers' relatives about their deaths. Although all the besieged soldiers were seriously wounded, not all of them were killed. Some managed to stay in the building for several weeks until a ceasefire between Russia and Chechnya, signed on August 31, 1996, effectively stopped the first Chechen war and put an end to their defense post's blockade (Zhdakaev 2005; Ostroushko 2005).

Having survived the siege, Uminskii spent the next year in hospitals, recovering from concussion and shell shock. He was released in 1998 with the diagnosis of "physical disability of the second degree," which allows for very limited employment under medical supervision (Smetanin 2005). Uminskii's attempts to secure a pension from the Defense Ministry failed. As he learned, his original contract with the ministry had been voided due to his "prolonged absence." Moreover, his military division was disbanded, and in the local office of the Ministry of Defense in Orel, his hometown, he was informed that the person listed under his name was still "missing in action" (Zhdakaev 2005).

Widely publicized by the Russian media, this case was not unique. Throughout the country, veterans and victims of the Chechen wars tried to settle their disputes with the state in courts (Ziuzin 2000). Although still rather small, the number of these cases has been increasing gradually. Uminskii's case, however, was significant not only as an indicator of legal consciousness in Russia. The case was also a clear example of the legal and political uncertainty that has been associated with the Chechen war. *Krasnaia Zvezda* (Red Star), the official newspaper of the Ministry of Defense, bitterly pointed out that it was not just the ministry that should be held responsible. Taken aback by the fact that the ministry was being sued for compensation, the paper insisted that it was "the duty of the whole state to take care of the people who defended its territorial integrity" (Mokhov 2005).

This deflection of responsibility through splitting the ministry from the "whole state" is revealing. Indeed, the Chechen war has been first of all a political, not a military event. Memoirs and interviews of Russian soldiers and generals replay this theme even more strongly. As officers claim, the army was used as a tool in a political game, used irresponsibly and unjustifiably to carry out a humanitarian and military disaster. A commandant of the Russian troops in Chechnya, for instance, complained to a popular magazine in 1996: "The army, the interior troops, the police never do anything because of their own desire or will. They follow orders....It is a shame, it is a pity...that nobody has any idea what our army, our people, our guys are dying for" (Medved 1996, 14:53–54; also Noskòv 2001).

In 2002, in the midst of the second Chechen war (1999–), the situation was not that different. By that time the question "What are our guys dying for?" was toned down, and the army switched from relying on largely untrained conscripts to using contracted volunteers, reservists, and professionally trained military. However, this move changed relatively little; new forms of state-organized violence revealed the same lack of basic organization. In January 2001, a regional Altai newspaper reported on a group of

350 Altai policemen who were to leave for a three-month assignment in Chechnya.[4] The report included an appeal made by the Chamber of Local Entrepreneurs to the broader business community. Describing the poor equipment of the Altai policemen, the chamber asked for contributions: "The Federal [government] provides for the troops while in Chechnya, but it is up to the troops themselves to take care of their personal equipment and gear. [Our policemen] have neither modern helmets, nor bulletproof vests, nor portable radio sets. And without our help—they never will.... We ask you for your help in equipping our guys so that they could at least remotely resemble the technical level of the [Chechen] fighters [*boeviki*]" (*Altaiskaia pravda* 2001).[5] A week later, the newspaper listed some contributions: sheet metal and welding machines from a metal company, five sacks of spaghetti from an individual, a three-month supply of cookies and bottled water from a businessman, first aid sets from a hospital, portable wood-burning ovens from a factory, cash from companies and private citizens—all "for those who go to Chechnya" (Namedni 2001).

This commodification through which the war becomes a part of the public discourse is crucial for sustaining the war itself. Devoid of political context, the war emerged as a story of individual and collective sacrifices, as an everyday practice of perseverance that radically transformed people's lives. Commodities here are the symbols of an imagined community that is shaped by a shared understanding of everyday survival. As if epitomizing the essence of this depoliticized approach to the war, a local newspaper headlined its report about Altai soldiers in the North Caucasus: "Chechnya: The everyday [*byt*], work, life, and death" (Kochevnikov 2000, 16). A veteran of the Chechen war makes a similar point in his recollection:

> Some people like to say—it is not possible to forget this service [in Chechnya].... Of course it is possible. At least, it is possible in my case. For me it all became like a dream now; a very distant night dream. Actually, I do have dreams about Chechnya. Not about fights, though. Just daily life there: mud

4. In 2001 regular troops in Chechnya were replaced officially by professional divisions of the Ministry of the Interior. Chechnya was divided into eighteen temporary zones that have been policed on a rotating basis by professional officers brought from all over the country (*Altaiskaia pravda* 2001).

5. *Boevik* is routinely used in Russian in regard to Chechen rebels. Russian soldiers also use this word to describe themselves. The word has a common root with the word *boi* (combat) and is sometimes translated as "fighter," "hit man," or "assassin." However, unlike a hit man or assassin, *boevik* also implies belonging to an organized group beyond state control or even opposed to the state. There is a certain similarity to the mafia, but the *boevik*'s professional identity, unlike the mafioso's, is solely defined by the production of violence.

Fig. 3.1. From a series on Chechnya by Vladimir Bychkov: "The Dreaming Soldier," 1996. Courtesy of the photographer.

up to my knee; lice. I brought an undershirt from there. My buddies left their signatures on it. But I dropped it into mud, so it turned out that I brought home some Chechen soil. (Somov 2001) (Figure 3.1)

Through distant dreams or soiled shirts, such displacement of the war memory helps to encapsulate traumatic experience. Bitter irony makes it easier to keep a sane distance. It also provides some form of rationalization, as in this military joke told by a veteran:

—What does Article 0 of the Constitution say?
—Is there such an article at all?
—Yes, there is. It says that the officer must suffer! (Agalkov 2003, 210)

Yet this forgetting and distancing—ironic or desperate—does very little to change the lives of veterans and victims after the war. Unwilling to frame the Chechen war in legal terms (as opposed to the politicized rhetoric), the state provided no recognizable juridical language through which survivors could frame their claims and complaints under existing law. Unlike the soldiers who participated in the Soviet invasion in Afghanistan in 1979–89, the Chechen war veterans were not covered by the existing law on veterans. Technically speaking, the war in Chechnya has never been officially classified as a war. From the legal point of view this military campaign is a limited "antiterrorist operation" in the North Caucasus. The status of the operation required no special parliamentary approval but also implied no special support for those who were harmed while carrying it out.

The general impasse in defining the legal status of the war's participants and victims produced two main outcomes. First, the government's persistent unwillingness to address issues of financial and political responsibility for the consequences of the ongoing war was exacerbated by the courts' inclination to rationalize and institutionalize the situation of ambiguity even further. Second, the war's participants and refugees, suffering from physical and psychological injuries, reacted to the lack of any substantive support with bitterness and anger. Often, in their reaction veterans combined a clear recognition of their extreme alienation from the state with a sense of profound dependency on the state's welfare policy.

When the Orel court dismissed—because of the "unlocatability" (*neustanovlennost'*) of proof—"any possibility for compensation of disabilities incurred by the combatants during their participation in military operations in the Chechen republic" (Zorin 2005), frustrated veterans complained: "We are actually being told that we should demand compensation from [the Chechen leaders] Maskhadov and Basaev. It appears that protecting the Motherland is just citizens' own private business [*chastnoe delo grazhdan*]" (Zhdakaev 2005). In turn, human rights activists quickly pointed out that the Orel regional court had finally acknowledged a practice that had been pursued by the Ministry of Defense for years: claims for compensation filed by refugees affected by the war in Chechnya were consistently undermined by the ministry's demand to provide proof of the fact that the harm has indeed been caused by the federal army. As one activist put it, "It might take fifty years or so to make the state recognize its own responsibility. It was just the same with compensation for survivors of the Nazi camps" (Sunlianskaia 2005).

Yet, as Uminskii's case demonstrates, the state's disengagement could not be limited to issues of material compensation. Also, such a withdrawal resulted in a serious crisis of recognition: without the ideological and legal support of the state, the soldier's military experience could easily mutate into an act of banditry. To put it differently, the state's retreat from performing a necessary symbolic work stripped its subjects of categories of perception and rituals of recognition that were used to legitimize the experience through which these subjects were constituted in the first place. What kinds of symbolic practices were available to veterans in this case? How did they communicate their experience to the broader audience—without established narrative scripts and reliable legal frameworks?

Veterans' dependence on public acknowledgment of their military past significantly distinguished their self-presentation from other forms of the patriotism of despair discussed in this book. Monological and self-absorbed trauma stories of Altai neo-Communists or isolationist narratives of ethnovitalists were transformed here into a more outward-directed discourse. Indeed, recognition requires a dialogue, however limited it might be. Hence, practices and metaphors of exchange became crucial in veterans' attempts to evoke signs of social respect. Following Georg Simmel (1978), I call this symbolic strategy "exchange of sacrifices." Closely weaving together loss and gain, judgment and emotion, interaction and interconnection, exchange of sacrifices is a dialogical event through which distinctive values are simultaneously represented and recognized. Sheet metal, sacks of spaghetti, supplies of cookies, or cash enter this exchange, trying if not to balance, then at least to acknowledge, the value of soldiers' lives. Delineating yet another community of loss, the exchange of these sacrifices points to a seemingly shared cultural assumption about the universality of "Article 0" of the Constitution: the officer must suffer.

Reclaimed Traumas

Recent studies of the Chechen war seem to agree that the war has not created a strong version of any collectivity able to mobilize the Russians against the Muslim Chechens. The expected production of enemies certainly has taken place. But it has not become a basic model of national or ethnic identification (Gudkov 2005b; *Byt' chechentsem* 2004).[6] The war in the Caucasus—like the Soviet war in Afghanistan before it (Liakhovskii 2004; Tamarov 1992)—has not precipitated an immediate surge of Russian nationalism, nor has it led to Russian national self-consciousness. In fact, as Anatol Lieven pointed out in his analysis of the first Chechen war, the absence of a clearly defined Russian ethnic identity was a major factor in preventing

---

6. See Russell (2005) for a somewhat different interpretation.

potential conflicts between nations and ethnicities within the Russian Federation, as well as between Russia and its neighbors (1999, 266–70). Public polls, unreliable as they are, similarly suggested that at least until September 2001, high prices, poverty, crime, and unemployment concerned the Russian population more than wars on terror, be they local or global (O'Loughlin, O'Tuathail, and Kolossov 2004, 308; Gerber and Mendelson 2002, 278). To explain this distancing from the war, this section presents the general timeline of the ongoing conflict. My intent here is not to reconstruct the history of the war or to provide a comprehensive list of reasons that caused it. Rather, I summarize some background material, mostly available in Russia during my fieldwork, in order to provide a larger historical context for my informants' comments.[7] The timeline of the war also helps us see how the erratic political decisions in the middle of the 1990s were gradually replaced by the policy of Chechenization of the conflict, in which the federal government actively supported the loyal local cadres while minimizing its own direct participation in the political stabilization of the region.

Available accounts of the Chechen war suggest different perspectives and different starting points. Despite some variations, the tendency to historicize the conflict is dominant. Thus, flyers distributed among Russian soldiers in Chechnya emphasized that from the sixteenth century onward, the Chechen people had always defended their independence, cherishing patriotism as one of their "oldest traditions," just as their "ancestral highlanders" did.[8] Some Russian authors trace the origin of this patriotic tradition as far back as 1559, when the first Russian fortress was set up in Chechnya, signaling the onset of more than four centuries of confrontation between the expanding Russian Empire and the Chechen people (Eremenko and Novikov 1997, 209–32). Others limit the conflict to two centuries, locating its starting point in a series of attempts by the Chechen religious elite to create a unified Chechen state at the end of the eighteenth century (Blinskii 2000, 13). In all cases, the assumed immutability of a recalcitrant Chechen "mentality" (Arutiunov 2003, 9–16) rooted in the "tribal body [*rodovoe telo*] of the Chechen ethnos," as a prominent Russian

---

7. There is a large body of literature that offers detailed accounts of the Chechen war. For a balanced and informative analysis see Evangelista (2002). For a useful review of scholarly and popular literature on the Chechen war in Russian see Khadzharov (2005).

8. The flyer does indicate that there are "various social factors" that shape patriotism and that a "distorted understanding of the patriotic might result in nationalism, chauvinism, self-conceit [*chvanstvo*], arrogance [*kichlivost'*], and national egotism" (Archive of the Altai State Museum of Local History, Arkhiv Altaiskogo Gosudarstvennego. Kraevedcheskogo Muzeia [AAGKM], Op. 17062/10, L.25597).

ethnologist of Chechnya puts it (Chesnov 1999, 91), rhetorically paralleled Russia's aggressive imperial politics.

While these retrospective interpretations are quite common today, many scholars view the current war in Chechnya as the product of a much more recent history. The main point of disagreement in this case has to do with the role that the Soviet past of the Chechen nation has in the post-Soviet context. As with many Soviet nations, the Chechen people went through drastic political and economic transformation before World War II. Within two decades Chechnya was subjected to intensive urbanization, collectivization in agriculture, and industrialization built around oil and gas extraction. Creating an industrialized nation also presupposed a local version of the "cultural revolution." To accomplish universal literacy among non-Russian groups, the Moscow government typically elevated a particular local dialect to the status of the linguistic norm, and then would replace the local script with Cyrillic.[9] These massive transformations in the region peaked in 1936 with the creation of a new national and administrative formation, the Chechen-Ingush Autonomous Republic.[10]

Rapid changes imposed by the early Soviet regime predictably caused some dissatisfaction and protest. The Wehrmacht's advance in the Caucasus during the Second World War lessened the pressure the Soviet regime exerted on the Caucasus and activated already existing anti-Soviet feelings and groups. While a few of these groups apparently did establish some contacts with the Germans who parachuted into the region during 1942–43, the scale of these contacts was extremely limited. No "mass [*pogolovnoe*] collaboration" of the Chechens and Ingushes with the Wehrmacht troops, used by the regime as a rationale for their collective deportation in 1944, was ever documented (Polian 2007, 167–68). Yet on February 23, 1944, the entire population of the Chechen-Ingush Autonomous Republic was rounded up, and within eight days, 478,479 Chechens and 91,250 Ingushes were shipped to Central Asia and Kazakhstan (Beria 2000). In March 1944, the republic itself was abolished, and the evacuated territory was repopulated with people from nearby regions of Russia.[11] Khrushchev's campaign of de-Stalinization later reversed the situation.

9. The original Arabic-based script was replaced with the Roman script in 1925. In 1938 it was turned into Cyrillic. For more on this see Tishkov (2001, 73–76).

10. For a useful discussion of the Soviet nation-building process see Martin (2001) and Suny (1993).

11. Massive relocations of nations started in the USSR before World War II. For instance, to secure its western border, in 1934 the leadership of the Ukrainian Republic orchestrated a campaign aimed at deporting 8,500 families of Poles and Germans from the borderland areas,

In 1957 autonomy was restored, and within two years 432,000 Chechens and Ingushes returned to the Caucasus (Tishkov 2001, 102). As some scholars maintain, it was precisely this trauma of deportation, this experience of genocide that significantly determined the Chechen ethnic *passionarity* and the extremely high level of Chechen national self-consciousness after the collapse of the Soviet Union.[12] Working through the national trauma, however, would have been impossible without a specific configuration of sociopolitical and cultural forces that emerged at the end of the 1980s in the Soviet Union.

The first relatively free elections of the deputies of the Supreme Soviet of the USSR (the Soviet parliament) were conducted in the spring of 1989. They galvanized public opinion and public activity throughout the country. Inspired by glasnost and democratization, people became passionately engaged in local politics, nominating alternative candidates for various offices. In many places this led to sweeping personnel changes within the local leadership of the Communist Party. In the Chechen-Ingush Republic, a revived public interest in politics brought about a dramatic transformation of the political scene. In 1989, for the first time in Soviet history, the highest position in the regional political hierarchy was occupied by a native Chechen. Reversing a long-standing Soviet tradition of appointing ethnic Russians for such prime political posts, Doku Zavgaev became secretary of the regional committee of the Communist Party (and later the head of the regional parliament).

At the same time, considerable change was taking place in the Russian Federation itself. In the course of the political struggle between Mikhail Gorbachev, who epitomized the "federal center" of the Soviet Union, and Boris Yeltsin, who defended the interests of the Russian Federative Republic, Russia's parliament (the Supreme Soviet of Russia) approved the Declaration of State Sovereignty of the Russian Federation on June 12, 1990. The declaration proclaimed its independence from the Soviet Union, leaving no legal ground for Gorbachev's control over Russia itself. This pattern was quickly replicated throughout Russia's regions. Old Soviet institutions were fragmented, and new competing power structures (*vlastnye struktury*) started emerging. The early 1990s became famous as a period of the "parades of sovereignty" (*parad suverenitetov*), when Russia's administrative

accusing them of "anti-Soviet agitation" (Brown 2004, 133). Polian (2003) provides a comprehensive review of Soviet practices of mass deportation.

12. For different versions of this approach see Derlugian (1999, 207); Shnirelman (2006a, 338); Malashenko (2007).

and national provinces insisted on the near complete withdrawal of the central government from local affairs.[13]

As part of this trend, a new nongovernmental organization, the Chechen National Congress, was created in Chechnya. On November 23–25, 1990, at the first session of the congress, three thousand delegates declared that Chechnya was a sovereign state. The momentum created by an organization with no legal status or official mandate forced the Chechen parliament to make a similar move. On November 27, 1990, the regional parliament adopted the Declaration of State Sovereignty that advanced the independence of the Chechen-Ingush Republic and totally omitted any reference to the existence of the USSR ("Deklaratsiia" 1997, 7–10). In 1991, the national congress evolved into the main alternative power structure in Chechnya. Dzhokhar Dudaev, a retired Soviet air force general with real war experience in Afghanistan, was elected as the head of the congress. In June 1991, during the congress's second session, Dudaev announced that the Chechen parliament and the official leadership of the republic had lost the "moral ground" for representing the Chechen people, and he declared the executive committee of the congress the interim power institution that would control the republic until the new presidential and parliamentary elections were held. The Ingush part of the Chechen-Ingush Republic decided to split, and on September 15, 1991, the Ingush Republic within the Russian Federation was formed.

Dudaev's position within Chechnya strengthened during the August 1991 crisis in Moscow, when several high-profile Moscow politicians staged a putsch to oust Gorbachev. The putsch failed within a few days, but Zavgaev's leadership supported the organizers, giving Dudaev's forces a good reason to physically displace them. In early October 1991, Dudaev's supporters occupied the building of the regional parliament, local TV stations, and the KGB arsenals. At the end of October, the executive committee of the congress conducted presidential and parliamentary elections. Successfully elected, on November 1, 1991, President Dudaev confirmed the sovereignty of the Chechen Republic, leaving no doubt that this time "sovereignty" was to mean total independence from both Russia and the USSR.

Busy with undermining Gorbachev's position, Yeltsin's government in Russia had neither the time nor the resources to deal with the situation in Chechnya. Several attempts to influence the situation failed. When on

---

13. For debates at the time of this process see Solnik (1996, 13–25) and Drobizheva (1994, 45–55). Pain (2003) and Filippov (2004) locate this process in a larger political and theoretical context.

November 7, 1991, Yeltsin signed a decree that introduced a state of emergency in Chechnya, he could not implement it. As soon as military planes with federal troops landed there, they were blocked by Dudaev's soldiers. Embarrassed and humiliated by the whole affair, the Russian parliament revoked the emergency decree as "inexpedient" four days after its announcement ("Ob Ukaze Prezidenta RSFSR" 1997, 33). Yeltsin's decree produced a result opposite from that intended; it consolidated anti-Moscow groups vis-à-vis both the disintegrating Russia and its aggressive yet disorganized leadership. Within a short time, Dudaev and his followers created a national guard ("Ukaz Prezidenta" 1997, 34) and restored the right of Chechen citizens to buy and possess firearms, a right that had been "taken away by the totalitarian regime," as Dudaev's decree put it ("O prave grazhdan Chechenskoi respubliki" 1997, 36).

From 1992 to 1994, the Russian government alternated between supporting the anti-Dudaev opposition, led by Zavgaev and other ousted Chechen politicians, and negotiating with Dudaev's leadership. All Russian troops stationed in Chechnya before the declaration of sovereignty were hastily withdrawn in 1992. Most of their weapons, however, were either seized by Dudaev's government or were officially transferred to him by Russian military generals.[14]

Armed and funded by the Russian government and Dudaev's own forces, Chechnya became a highly unstable place by the fall of 1994. Migration of professionals radically increased (Shnirelman 2006a, 349). Feeling increasingly uncomfortable, the non-Chechen population started fleeing en masse: from July 1992 to December 1994 eighty-nine thousand ethnic Russians left the republic (Regent 1998).[15]

Apparently misinformed, the Kremlin increasingly perceived the Chechen opposition to Dudaev as a realistic force. Convinced by the leadership of the Ministry of Defense, on December 11, 1994, Yeltsin signed a decree aimed at restoring "constitutional legality in Chechnya" and "disarming the illegally

14. A special investigative commission of the Russian parliament (Duma) created later, published a collection of documents on the Russian-Chechen conflict. As one of these documents signed by the Ministry of Defense indicates, half of all weapons and equipment were officially transferred to the Chechen Republic. In practical terms this meant that all 260 training airplanes, 5 destroyers, 42 tanks, 14 armed troop carriers were left (or illegally sold by Russian officers, as some sources suggest) to the Dudaev regime (Anishenko et al. 1995, 38–39; also Tishkov 2001, 215).

15. In 1991, there were 240,000 ethnic Russians registered in the Chechen Republic (Bugai 2006, 314). In 1991–93, before the war, 90,000 people left the republic; the majority of the migrants were ethnic Russians (Tishkov 2001, 218; Regent 1998). By 2007, the number of Russian migrants from the republic exceeded 200,000 (Malashenko 2007, 9).

armed formations." On the same day, the Russian troops rolled into Chechnya. The first Chechen War started.[16]

The first major and most brutal operation of the Russian military troops came on New Year's Eve with the storming of the Chechen capital, Grozny. Poorly planned and disastrously implemented, it revealed the deteriorating state of both the Russian army and Russian political influence. In his memoirs, Gennadii Troshev, a general who was in charge of the Forty-Second Corps that participated in the attack (and who was commander of the North Caucasus Military District in 1995–97), recalled that the Ministry of Defense was so confident about the quick success of the campaign that it even did not bother to give it a name. The original advancement of the Russian troops was supposed to scare off the Chechen separatists rather than turn into full-fledged combat (2001, 28, 13). The army lacked weapons, servicemen, and leadership.[17] Radio communication between different divisions was paralyzed; their coordination was virtually nonexistent (Troshev 2001, 29). To quote an eyewitness account of an Altai soldier in Grozny, "It was very hard to continue military operations in the city. We didn't know the city at all. We carried the war on according to maps published in 1981, so we had to get oriented on the spot" (*My zhdali vas* 1999, 30). What was supposed to be a quick and impressive operation was turned into a major campaign with massive losses among civilians and soldiers.

The archive of the Altai State Regional Museum (Barnaul) has a set of letters from soldiers who participated in the first war in Chechnya. In a letter to the mother of a fallen comrade, one of these soldiers described the beginning of the war:

Dear Elena Viktorovna,
    This is Andrei. Yes, I knew [your son] Sergei, since we served half a year in the same battalion. The whole business started in December. First they [the commanders] were taking [to Chechnya] only those who had driving licenses, but later our turn came up, too. Sergei then was an assistant to the superintendent of the army officers' dormitory, so he was summoned to the headquarters and was told where we would be sent. He told me that his hands started trembling after this news. He said he did not want to fight against anyone. He even went to talk to the commander of the battalion. But nobody

16. For different accounts of the war see Furman (1999, 150–76); Shchekochikhin (2003); Tishkov (2001); Trenin and Malashenko (2004, 15–48); *Informatsionannaia voina* (1997).
    17. Before the war, 540 Russian generals, senior officers, lieutenants decided to resign rather than participate in the Chechen campaign of 1994–95 (Mukhin and Yavorskii 2000; Troshev 2001, 19; Oliker 2001, 35).

would listen to him. He even said that he'd run away, but they told him, "Just not from here." So they put all of us in a car and took us over there. But first they took us to the Taman division where they wanted to regroup all the soldiers. To make it short, they decided to turn us, tank men, into infantry.

And the whole battalion was dispersed among several other detachments....So with some other guys I went to the headquarters and told them that we are tank men, and that we do not want to fight as infantry. They told us that they would sort it out and took us aside (all the others were already boarding the plane). The next day they flew us to Vladikavkaz [the capital of the Ingush Republic], where we were told that we would be fighting as tank men. Two days later, they gave us twenty tanks and we moved toward Grozny....Only six tanks came back, and during the storming of the city I did not meet a single person from my battalion. (AAGKM, F. 17060/3)

This general situation of a total mess at the beginning of the war—*nerazberikha,* as General Troshev put it (2001, 13)—has been confirmed many times by other accounts and testimonies.[18] As another soldier explained, many deaths were caused by the fact that conscripts had no training whatsoever: "Instead of automatic guns, we have been mastering sledgehammers and spades [in the army]" (AAGKM, F. 17060/17).

The New Year's Eve storming of the "presidential palace" in Grozny lasted more than three weeks.[19] But even by the end of February 1995, the city was not fully under the control of the Russian army, despite a radical increase in the number of troops from the initial six thousand to thirty thousand (Mukhin and Iavorskii 2000; also Baev 1996, 141–49). "The Haiti-style, small victorious war," as a high-profile Russian official envisioned the military campaign in Chechnya, did not happen.[20]

There were several attempts to start negotiations between Dudaev's and Yeltsin's circles. But the final position, "We do not negotiate with terrorists," articulated in January 1995 by then Prime Minister Chernomyrdin in an interview to a Russian TV channel, eliminated this option (Orlov and Cherkasov 1998, 44). Throughout the spring of 1995, federal troops managed to

18. *Nerazberikha* (from *razbirat'*—to understand, to take apart) literally means something that cannot be "sorted out" or structured.

19. The storming of the presidential palace in Grozny brought back memories of the storming not only of the White House in Moscow in October 1993 but also of the presidential palace in Kabul by the Soviet troops almost exactly fifteen years earlier. For a thorough documented recollection of the Kabul storming see Liakhovskii (2004, 258–314).

20. The citation is from a conversation between Oleg Lobov, the secretary of the Security Council in 1992–96, and Sergei Yushenkov, a deputy of the State Duma (Shchekochikhin 2003, 162).

push the Chechen forces to the mountainous border with Georgia, establishing control over the valley part of Chechnya and most of its mountain terrain (54).

It was a terrorist attack in the nearby Stavropol' region that forced the Russian government to start negotiations with the Chechen side. On June 14, 1995, a group of Chechen terrorists led by Shamil Basayev took about 1,500 hostages in a hospital in the town of Budennovsk. Chernomyrdin's negotiations over the phone with Basayev were televised live. Most of the hostages were eventually released, yet 129 of them were killed in the assault and in failed attempts by Russian troops to free them (Ladnyi 2005; *Washington Post* 1995a, 1995b). The Budennovsk raid inaugurated a series of prolonged consultations between the Russian government and Chechen rebels. In the beginning of 1996 the situation was somewhat balanced: neither the Russian troops nor the Chechen fighters could immediately change the course of events.

The 1996 presidential campaign in Russia significantly changed the attitude of the Yeltsin government toward the Chechen war. The ongoing war aggravated even further the extremely low popularity of Yeltsin. Negotiations seemed to become more urgent, and in May 1996 Yeltsin visited Chechnya, his only trip to the republic. Dudaev's death in April 1996 made this trip significantly easier.[21] However, August 9, 1996, the day of Yeltsin's second inauguration, was marred by another major battle over Grozny, started by Chechen rebels. Huge losses of Russian soldiers, comparable with the 1995 New Year's Eve storm, precipitated a cease-fire, despite active protests by army generals (Orlov and Cherkasov 1998, 84; Mukhin and Iavorskii 2000).

In 2001 in Barnaul, I interviewed Viktor Z., a paratrooper who participated in the August 1996 storm of Grozny. Together with his airborne unit, Viktor was to block a main exit road from the city. Simultaneously, another federal detachment was ordered to push the Chechen fighters toward Viktor's checkpoint, ready to open fire. "It was supposed to be really a large-scale operation," he said. "It would have been the final point in the Chechen campaign. No second Chechen war would have been needed after that." The cease-fire changed it all: within twelve hours Viktor's detachment was withdrawn from Grozny. Soon after that he retired from the army. I asked Viktor about soldiers' attitudes toward the cease-fire. He responded: "It was negative. Everyone understood that if we were to fight, there would be lots

---

21. The general was killed on April 21, 1996, by a self-guided missile, apparently while he was talking on a radio phone with a member of the Russian parliament. For details and different versions see a special issue of *Novaia Gazeta*, April 21, 1997.

Fig. 3.2. A bullet-ridden poster from the 1996 presidential election campaign. The line on the poster reads, "Choose with your heart." Vladimir Bychkov, a Chechen war veteran who took this picture in June 1996 in Serjen-Yurt, Chechnya, provided his own title: "Our beloved president." Courtesy of the photographer.

of losses because almost all the *boeviki* had gathered there, in the city.... But they [the government?] decided to sign the cease-fire. So, there must have been a reason. We were all disappointed. Everyone was in a mood to fight [*uzhe nastroilis' vse*]" (figure 3.2).

Following negotiations between Aleksandr Lebed, the head of the Russian Security Council, and Aslan Maskhadov, former Soviet colonel and the Chechen military commander, the cease-fire agreement was signed on August 31, 1996, in Khasavyurt. Debates about the constitutional status of Chechnya were postponed. As the agreement specified, the issues about the legal status of Chechnya had to "be resolved" by December 31, 2001. The parties also agreed to create a joint commission that would oversee the withdrawal of federal troops and the reconstruction of Chechnya (Eremenko and Novikov 1997, 185).

The agreement had a significant political impact on both sides. By the end of the year, federal troops left Chechnya; in January 1997 Aslan Maskhadov was elected president of the Chechen Republic, and a peace treaty between Russia and Chechnya was signed in May 1997 (Orlov and Cherkasov 1998, 88). Despite its initial positive effect, the Khasavyurt agreement did not resolve the main question about the status of the Chechen Republic in relation to the Russian Federation. Nor did it produce any stabilizing effect within Chechnya itself. The secular political system was quickly replaced with religious-based institutions. In 1998–99, under the leadership of Shamil Basayev, Chechen insurgents attempted to create an Islamic state by unifying Chechnya and the neighboring Dagestan Republic (Maksakov 1999; Trenin and Malashenko 2004, 34). In August 1999, Basayev's group undertook a raid in Dagestan, where it quickly established control over several villages (*Nezavisimaia gazeta* 1999).

In the wake of this development, many in Russia started viewing the Khasavyurt agreement as a political mistake, as an unnecessary compromise, even as treason. Gennadii Troshev, the field general, described it bluntly: "Never before were generals in Russia so limited in their rights and in their authority by the pressure of the civilian leadership, complete dilettantes in military issues. The profaning of the Chechen campaign reached its apogee here" (Troshev 2001, 129). As in the Afghan war, massive losses in the army were perceived to be the result of political games and large-scale errors.

The understanding that a peace treaty by itself would not radically change the situation in Chechnya, combined with clear evidence of the conflict's proliferation by radicalized Islamic groups, precipitated the second Chechen war. The "counterterrorist operation," as the second Chechen war is officially known, was also justified by a second reason. Basayev's raid on Dagestan was never officially condemned by Aslan Maskhadov, the president of Chechnya. Maskhadov's conspicuous silence was interpreted by the Kremlin both as a sign of his tacit endorsement of the hostage taking and as evidence of Maskhadov's own inability to control the so-called field commanders (Barakhova and Bulavinov 1999). On October 1, 1999, Prime Minister Putin met with leaders of the pro-Moscow Chechen opposition and insisted that there would be no negotiations with Maskhadov's government. As before, the Russian leadership decided to follow the tactic of creating a parallel power structure by supporting the Chechen politicians who opposed Dudaev and Maskhadov (Kolesnikov 1999). On the same day, Russian troops entered Chechnya again, continuing the massive mop-up operation (*zachistka*) started after Basayev's early raid on Dagestan. The second Chechen war had begun.

Through a combination of air raids and prolonged sieges, the federal army eventually managed to establish overwhelming control over the region. In February 2001, the Russian minister of defense announced that the "resistance of bands (bandformirovaniia)" was completely broken down (*Nezavisimaia gazeta* 2001, 2). Soon after that, the counterterrorist operation was declared over, and control over the campaign in Chechnya was officially transferred to the Ministry of Interior. From then on, military operations were conducted mostly by *kontraktniki* and rotating police divisions, mobilized from all over the country. Since 2001, there have been no large-scale battles, and the continuing counterterrorist operation has been mostly aimed at eliminating dispersed groups of Chechen *boeviki*.

Important political events between 2002 and 2005 made ideas of Chechnya's independence less and less realistic. Two high-profile hostage takings by the Chechen terrorists—a Moscow theater siege in October 2002 and the Beslan school hostage crisis in September 2004—firmly placed the situation in the North Caucasus within the context of a perceived global war on terror, radically undermining sympathy for Chechnya's claims to independence. The (heavily managed) referendum on the Chechen Constitution conducted on March 23, 2003, in Chechnya affirmed the status of Chechnya *within* the Russian Federation. Presidential elections in Chechnya on October 5, 2003, provided the Moscow-oriented government in Chechnya with statistical legitimacy, however contested it might be. Akhmad Kadyrov, a former mufti and anti-Russia rebel was allegedly supported by 80 percent of the voters. Through the politics of Chechenization, the Russian government started actively transferring the burden of the actual rebuilding and policing of the region onto loyal Chechens. The initial practice of appointing Moscow envoys was replaced by a deliberate reliance on available local cadres, backed by Moscow's money.[22]

Yet this tightly controlled transition was far from smooth. On May 9, 2004, during a parade conducted in Grozny to celebrate the anniversary of Victory Day, President Kadyrov and several of his colleagues were blown up by a hidden bomb. Alu Alkhanov, the newly elected president, continued the politics of close cooperation with Moscow until he was officially replaced in March 2007 by the thirty-year-old Ramzan Kadyrov, a son of Alkhanov's predecessor. The chain of these puppet leaders hardly brought the rule of law to Chechnya, yet it helped to turn the problem of the Chechen war into the Chechens' own problem.

---

22. For a review of the practice of Chechenization see Human Rights Center Memorial (2006).

Forgotten Wars

In Russia, the war in Chechnya has remained on the margin of the public's attention. No influential public mobilization—be it prowar or antiwar—has been triggered in the course of the Chechen war. Episodic attempts of politicians and public intellectuals to raise larger issues about the state's military policy or the public's indifference to it have done little to bring people together.[23] With few exceptions, there have been no major public protests or political campaigns against the war. Neither the grim fate of thousands of refugees from Chechnya nor tragic reports about victims of suicide bombings and hostage-taking outside the region have mobilized the public. The military draft has provoked no mass revolt on the part of potential conscripts. The deaths of soldiers seem to concern no one outside the circle of relatives and close friends. No federal organization that could defend the rights and interests of the Chechen war veterans and their relatives has emerged either. Instead, relations between the state and the war consequences were usually mediated by private, individual efforts while the war itself has been symbolically relegated to the remote geographic province. It appears that the war has become an integral and imperceptible part of the post-Soviet informational landscape. Inevitable and yet hardly noticeable at the same time, the Chechen war has been transformed into yet another grim fixture of post-Communist society, along with corruption, organized crime, poverty, and general lawlessness.

NTV, an independent Russian TV channel, which provoked the anger of the Yeltsin government for its antiwar reporting from Chechnya during 1994–96, succinctly summarized the general attitude on December 11, 2004, in a televised event designed to commemorate the tenth anniversary of the outset of the war. As the ceremony's presenter framed it in the opening line, "The war has not vanished into history yet, but the authorities and society have already forgotten about it" (NTV 2004).

This public amnesia is striking, given the post-Soviet context of the war. Unlike secretive military involvements of the Soviet army in East Asia, Africa, or Latin America in the last half of the twentieth century, the Chechen war is not a minor-scale operation that could be kept confidential (*Rossiia i SSSR* 2001). Nor is there anything similar to the all-pervading censorship

---

23. Until her murder in 2006, Anna Politkovskaya (2001), a Russian journalist, was a persistent yet rather isolated critic of the war in Chechnya. Memorial, an independent human rights network, is yet another prominent institution that steadily assembles evidence of atrocities in the North Caucasus (Baisaev and Grushkin 2006, 2003; see also Memorial's official website at http://www.memo.ru).

and propagandistic machine that so successfully turned the Soviet invasion in Afghanistan in 1979–89 into a hidden and unannounced war (Borovik 1990; Gai and Snegirev 1991). Persistent attempts by the Yeltsin and Putin governments to restrain the coverage of the Chechen war in electronic and print media certainly took place. But it is misleading to directly link these efforts to control information flow with the public's indifference, as some scholars have suggested (Gerber and Mendelson 2002), not only because such a view overestimates the dependency of public opinion on post-Soviet *agitprop* but also because it seems to ignore the extensive experience of dealing with censorship that the Russian audience acquired during the Soviet period. Important as they were, several Moscow-based TV and radio stations, which were shut down or radically restaffed after their antiwar reports, could hardly compete with the impact of personal war accounts shared by refuges or ex-combatants. By the spring of 2006, there were at least one million soldiers and officers who had taken part in the "combat activity in the North Caucasus region," as the war in Chechnya is officially known (Moshkin and Savchenko 2006). While rarely represented in the mainstream media, oral and written stories of their war experience did circulate among civilians, undermining the government's desire to fully control the war coverage. Moreover, despite its attempts, the regime of "managed democracy," often associated with Putin's government, could not suppress independent newspapers, information agencies, human rights organizations, or electronic Listservs that were willing and able to deliver available information.

In other words, it was not primarily the lack or distortion of information about the war that produced the public amnesia. Sources of this indifference lie elsewhere. What was crucial in public perception of the Chechen war was its deep political ambiguity and the overwhelming distrust that this ambiguity caused. Throughout the 1990s, the Russian government rapidly changed its policies toward Chechnya and radically shifted its support and alliances, producing a deep-rooted feeling of suspicion about the underlying goals of the war. The initial war for independence was quickly transformed into a large-scale *razborka* (sorting out), into a war "between gangs in Moscow and those in Grozny" (Rigi 2007, 38). The clear tendency of Putin's government to emphasize the link between Chechen rebels and radical Islamist organizations was instrumental in presenting the second Chechen war as a part of the global war on terrorism.[24] Yet even these political efforts

---

24. For a useful review of this symbolic reframing of the war see Wood (2007, 113–45).

have done little to undermine a popular belief that the terrorist attacks and hostage taking carried out by Chechen rebels outside Chechnya would have been impossible without the direct or indirect involvement of Russia's own corrupt military and state bureaucracy. In 2002, an Altai newspaper voiced a well-shared feeling of ambiguity about the war in Chechnya: "It has already been eight years since our country entered a state of civil war in the North Caucasus, but there is still no clear definition of what is happening. As a result, all that is going on out there touches the foul line" (Dmitrienko 2002). In 2006, twelve years after the war started, a Moscow-based newspaper summed up the current attitude in a similar way: "The authorities themselves cannot quite determine whether Russian soldiers are dying [in Chechnya] to restore the constitutional order or to fight international terrorism" (Moshkin and Savchenko 2006).

Contradictory accounts of war casualties that circulate in the Russian mass media have increased this uncertainty further. The exact number of people killed, wounded, and displaced during the war is still hard to estimate. In November 2004, Taus Djabrailov, the head of the (pro-Moscow) Chechen State Council, for instance, reported that more than 200,000 inhabitants of the republic had been killed since 1994 (*Moscow News* 2004). The exact number of casualties among the Russian military remains unclear. In February 2003, citing the North Caucasus Military District as its source, a Russian information agency reported that 4,739 servicemen had died in military operations in Chechnya during 2002 alone (along with 13,108 wounded and 29 missing in action). The Moscow leadership of the Ministry of Defense denied the numbers and insisted instead that 4,572 Russian soldiers had been killed in Chechnya during *three* years—from the fall of 1999 to the end of 2002 (*Chechnya Weekly* 2003). Sergei Ivanov, the defense minister at the time, made the picture even more confusing by stating that in 2002 the number of servicemen killed in the North Caucasus was 480.[25] In 2007, the Defense Ministry revealed yet another number, reporting that since 1999 it had lost 3,613 soldiers (Mukhin 2007, 8).

Human rights activists and NGOs rely on different statistics. Valentina Mel'nikova, chair of the nongovernmental Union of the Committees of Soldiers' Mothers, indicated in her interviews that from 1999 to 2004 the second Chechen war took the lives of about 13,000 soldiers (Novosti 2004). Correspondingly, since December 1994, the overall number of servicemen who were killed in combat, who died later from their wounds, or who committed

---

25. According to Ivanov's report, during January–October 2004, 148 troops were killed in the North Caucasus (with 499 in 2001 and 291 in 2003) (*Moscow News* 2004).

suicide after returning from Chechnya is approaching 25,000 (Mel'nikova 2004; Moshkin and Savchenko 2006). Regardless of the overall number, suffice it to say that by the end of 2006 in the Altai region alone the number of servicemen who died in Chechnya had reached 238, radically exceeding the number of the Afghan war's casualties (*Altaiskaia pravda,* 2006a).

Permanent public disputes over numbers of the dead do not just demonstrate different ways of counting bodies. They inevitably reconfirm a public distrust of any official information regarding the war. Often this distrust is amplified by the highly unreliable means of communication between Chechnya and the rest of Russia. Even the official destination of soldiers deployed in Chechnya reveals a radical yet accepted discrepancy between reality and its symbolic framing: all correspondence sent to soldiers must be addressed to "Moscow-400" (AAGKM, Op. 17399/26, L. 31930). In Barnaul, in the archive of the Altai Museum of Local Wars, I discovered a set of letters sent by soldiers from Chechnya to their parents in Altai during the first war. Some soldiers were absolutely convinced that gaps in correspondence were not an accident but the result of official policy. As Petr Nikonov put it: "Mother, the letters that we sent from the front line have been burned. Do not get upset if there is no news from me" (AAGKM, Op. 17399/26, P.31930).

Breaks in written correspondence were aggravated by a traditional bureaucratic attitude of military officials. A commander writes to a soldier's parents from Altai:

Good afternoon!
   This is the commander of the detachment where your son, Aleksei Vladimirovich Noskov, served. I am in a hospital myself, in Saratov [a city in Central Russia]. In my bag, there is a whole bunch of letters that did not find their addressees. Now, when I write this letter to you, I hold in my hand letters dated Jan. 19 and Jan. 31 [that you sent] from the [Altai] town of Biisk. I do not know whether you know it already. Your son was killed on Jan. 4 in Grozny. I did not see his body myself. It was reported to me by the commander of the platoon. Your son died in a military car that was hit by a grenade. It happened early in the morning on Jan. 4., when they tried to protect a medical compound located at the intersection of Pervomaiskaia St. and Chekhov St. This is all I wanted to tell you.
   Respectfully yours,
   Captain Yashin. Feb. 12, 1995 (AAGKM, Chechen war veterans' folder)

Communication with the military rarely became more reliable when parents tried it in person or via the phone. One Altai mother, concerned with the lack of news about her son drafted into the Chechen war, tried to obtain reliable information from military officials for several weeks. Her phone calls to army headquarters were met with the same answer—son was "alive and well" (*zhiv-zdorov*). "My son had already been dead [for several weeks]," the mother recalled later. "But they kept telling me that he was alive and well....Now, I think my whole life was wasted. What was the point? What did I raise my children for? To lose them in Afghanistan or Chechnya?" (*My zhdali vas* 1999, 71).

This shift to viewing soldiers' deaths in terms of personal loss, of family rather than state responsibility, is telling. As the next chapter points out, the domestication of loss, while often being effective on a personal level, at the same time reveals the limited scope of institutional and symbolic means for mediating traumatic experience. The profound feeling of distrust narrows this scope even more: efforts of the nongovernmental media to raise public awareness about the war were met with the same combination of profound suspicion and confusion. Reports of human rights activists on atrocities and devastation produced by federal troops in Chechnya were frequently dismissed as biased by those who stressed in their competing narratives of victimhood the lack of any significant attention to the plight of thousands of Russian refuges who had to leave Chechnya in 1992–94, to morbid public executions of Russian soldiers, or to the slave trade industry organized in Chechnya by the rebels.[26] The participation of foreign donors in funding a limited number of antiwar organizations was used as a clear indicator of their anti-Russian prejudices.[27]

Discarding official and alternative sources of information as mere propaganda, people more and more often resorted to personal narratives, rumors, contradictory testimonies, and popular culture (cinema, song, memoirs) in order to make sense of the war. Suspicion often took the form of stories about oil interests that some Moscow politicians had in the Caucasus, about Russian officers who sold arms and soldiers to Chechen rebels, about massive misappropriation of funding allocated by the federal government for military and civic programs in Chechnya, and so forth. Bordering on the edge of military folklore, these stories were as numerous as they were unsurprising. Focused on conspiracy and exchange, they drew attention to clashing systems of ethical and political coordinates that were activated by post-Soviet changes.

---

26. Bugai (2006); Pokrovskii (2006), and Tishkov (2001) provide different versions of this approach.

27. For examples see Noskov (2001, 96) and Alksnis (2004); on links between foreign foundations and antiwar activists see Gerber and Mendelson (2002, 302).

Our Own Apocalypse

Throughout the 1990s, Russia's cultural industry demonstrated the same distancing attitude to the war in Chechnya. Concerned with this situation, the July 2000 issue of *Iskusstvo kino* (*The Art of Cinema*), an influential Russian journal of film theory and criticism, asked film and TV directors working on the topic of the Chechen war to explain the lack of "an adequate" representation of the regional wars of the 1980s–90s (Afghanistan, Chechnya, Tadjikistan, Georgia, Moldova) in Russian cinema. Comparing the omnipresence of Vietnam in the American film, the journal pointed to the fact that in Russia there were "literally four or five films" that dealt with recent wars ("Na toi voine" 2000, 5).

Responses fluctuated between two poles. On the one hand, the lack of attention to recent wars was interpreted as a clear sign of denial. As Sergei Govorukhin, a Russian film director, framed it, "We should not just talk, we should scream about things happening in Chechnya. Instead we put on the appearance that nothing serious is happening.…It is regrettable that society doesn't want to know the truth about this dirty campaign" (Govorukhin 2000, 7). On the other hand, the same situation was associated with difficulties of the process of symbolization itself. As Sulambek Mamilov, a film director born in the Chechen-Ingush Republic, observed, "The point in question is neither a lack of civic temperament on the part of film directors, nor their infantilism…rather it is a state of shock that they are experiencing. The horror reported on TV, the blood, the suffering, the refugees are so shocking that it takes time to restore your capability of comprehending this tragedy, and to take a stance regarding it" (Mamilov 2000, 11).

The stance was taken eventually. However, the two most notable and commercially successful films of 2002–5 outlined a direction that was very different from the one expected by the directors interviewed by *Iskusstvo kino*. *War* (*Voina*, directed by Alexei Balabanov, 2002), a film about Russian soldiers and British journalists taken hostage by the Chechen fighters, presented the war in the Caucasus as a deadly clash of cultures and religions. Framed as a Russian soldier's story about the Chechen war, the film traces the soldier's survival in the midst of total betrayal. It is the tale of an abandoned average Russian Ivan who defends his life with all available legal and illegal means. Often labeled chauvinistic, bluntly anti-Chechen, and anti-Western, *War* was one of the most popular films of the year (Zvereva 2002; "Proshchai, oruzhie" 2002).

Feodor Bondarchuk's *Company 9* (*Deviataia rota*, 2005) was another major attempt to revisit Russia's painful military history. Based on a real story, the film was an epic tearjerker about a group of Soviet soldiers who defended a crucial position in the mountains in the very end of the Afghan war. Simply forgotten by their commanders during the massive withdrawal from Afghanistan, these soldiers died in a fight, unnecessary and unappreciated. The biggest Russian blockbuster since 1991, *Company 9* reinforced the general tendency to portray war as a matter of personal endurance and sacrifice (Kishkovsky 2005). "We have won our own war," emphasized the general message in the epilogue of the film, "We were simply forgotten. Yet we have won it."

Fascinated by the film's artistic quality—"the sublime and cruel" at the same time—the media almost unanimously supported a new trend to depict the "war as it is," leaving disturbing political questions aside (Dolin 2005). Vladimir Putin used the opportunity to make an important symbolic gesture and invited the film crew, key ministers, and several veterans of the war in Afghanistan to the President's residence to watch *Company 9* together. The political importance of the high-level cultural event was clarified in Putin's remarks: "It is about time to stop all this political noise around the events that took place in Afghanistan. Clearly, these events should be…studied by politicians, historians, experts, militaries, and so on. But it is just as clear that those who have fought in Afghanistan have nothing to be ashamed of….You honestly performed your duty, and you are entitled…to expect an adequate reaction…from society and the state" (Politov 2005). Still, the anxiety about the universal captivating effect produced by the film made itself known, even if inadvertently. One of the journalists, comparing *Company 9* with its American counterparts, noticed, "This film has been already called our own *Apocalypse Now*. It seems, however, that it will be our *Apocalypse Yesterday, Now, and Forever*" (Shumiatskaia 2005).

The metaphors of our own war and our own apocalypse are helpful in understanding both the symbolic absence of Chechen (and Afghan) war memory and the attempt to gloss over political issues with images of individual or collective survival. Taken as a separate, isolated phenomenon, the failure to symbolize the war experience implies that other forms of post-Soviet life have already been integrated, appropriately classified, and represented. In this isolationist approach, the status of war memory is usually reduced to gaps in an otherwise smooth narrative. Yet the metaphor of our own apocalypse—just like multiple obituaries for the Russian nation produced by the authors of the Russian tragedy—strongly suggests that there is no smooth post-Soviet narrative to speak of. It was precisely this fragmentation of established forms of signification and exchange that forced people to focus on waging their own local wars. The forgotten Chechen war in this context can be seen as a symptom that helps us understand better contemporary Russian culture, state, and society.

"I Have No Idea How to Make Myself Useful"

Many of my meetings with Chechen war veterans in Barnaul took place during the autumn of 2001. The United States had just started a military campaign in Afghanistan, and there was much discussion in the local press about a supposed plan of the American government to hire veterans of the Chechen and Afghan wars to participate in the U.S. operation in Afghanistan. The source of this idea was not quite clear; nonetheless several veterans were interviewed by local media about possible contracted service for the U.S. army. My conversation with Vitalii B., a twenty-four-year-old participant in the first Chechen war, took place just a few hours after a local TV channel had taped his comments. Excited by the sudden attention, Vitalii summed up the prevalent attitude to the possible involvement in a new war:

> I'd go to Afghanistan. And there is a very simple reason for this. I have been here, at home, for three years now, and I have no idea how to make myself useful. Yes, we have this [Chechen] veteran movement, and it is all very interesting, but! But the state does not want to help us, it cannot help us. And I am not talking about myself; I am talking about everybody.... There is nothing. There are no elementary things. A guy comes back from the war.... The state gives him some privileges if he decides to study at a university. But no university would ever accept him. Everything he had learned at school, he totally forgot during the war! Everything!... I'd go to Afghanistan. And it is not because I want it. War is foreign to me. But today this is a way to secure my own future.

There are several important themes in this comment. First, Afghanistan does have a special meaning for Russian soldiers. As part of the regular army, 620,000 troops participated in the Soviet war in Afghanistan in 1979–89; more than 15,000 were killed during this time (*Rossiia i SSSR* 2001, 539). Initially neglected, participants in the Afghan war became glorified in the early 1990s, when memorials and monuments were created throughout the country by ex-servicemen and parents of fallen soldiers (figures 3.3 and 3.4).

In that respect, the attraction of the new Afghan possibility, at least to some extent, stemmed from the social recognition that Afghan veterans enjoyed in the first half of the 1990s. The comparison with the Soviet invasion

Fig. 3.3. Memorials to Afghan war veterans: stone of remembrance with the sign "Bagram" in Minsk (Belarus), 2004. Courtesy of Elena Trubina.

in Afghanistan would be used by veterans of the Chechen war as a basic narrative device for structuring their own military experience and postwar claims. There was another, no less crucial, reference in Vitalii's comment that also would become typical. The appeal of a (new) war was rationalized by constructing the following juxtaposition: the extended period of one's own social and professional dislocation was paralleled by a perceived indifference of the state to the fate of its servicemen.

Demobilization emerged as an individual dis-localization vis-à-vis the disengaged state. Nikolai F., a Chechen war veteran, developed this idea further in an interview: "We realize what kind of policy it is. As if a puppy is thrown into a river, and if the puppy manages to get to the surface, it means that it is worthy of living; if not, so be it....We do not like to see the state performing this sort of policy toward us." It appeared that the state-conferred identity balanced on the verge of implosion when the state retreated from its subjectifying function. Hence the trope of abandonment was frequently linked with images of personal deterioration. The question of being worthy of living after the war was turned into a recurrent theme.

Fig. 3.4. "Black Tulip," a monument to Afghan war veterans in Yekaterinburg (Russia), 2007. Photo by author.

In their studies of autobiographical documents and fiction written by Vietnam War veterans, scholars have pointed out that fragmentation of language and personal narrative was one of the main discursive tools that veterans used to describe themselves. Ex-soldiers and literary critics often referred to this conscious aesthetic of disintegration as "fragging," using a term that during the Vietnam War described soldiers' assassination of their officers with fragmentation grenades. In soldiers' prose and poetry, stylistic and narrative disintegration was a way of exploding the official presentations of war. A controlling device of sorts, the discursive fragging worked both as a form of self-defense (self-distancing) and an act of reclaiming language (Bibby 1993, 30; Gotera 1993, 40; Hidalgo 1993, 9).

My informants' stories of collapse and disintegration seemed to follow this general tendency to fragment in order to symbolically control the traumatic experience.[28] In a somewhat similar way, the narrative of self-disintegration was also replayed in war poetry and songs that were widely circulated among the Chechen war veterans. One example of this poetic fragging highlights the theme of postwar collapse.

"Statistics," a song written and performed by A. Musin, opens a special collection of tapes *From One War to Another* (*Ot voiny do voiny* 2002) (figure 3.5). The epigraph on the tape cover spells out the main message: "Songs sung from the heart" (*pesni, spetye serdtsem*). Though the lyrics are mainly focused on the outcome of the Soviet invasion in Afghanistan, they have a clear reference to the current situation: "today" is described as "the time of returning to war, with no one paying for it."

Relying on a single formula, the author (and the protagonist) throughout the song cites statistics for different types of war veterans' behavior. In its aggregated form, this sociopoetic listing represents the collective corpus of war veterans: "Every first [man] who has been there [in the war], will never forget it"; "Every third has no energy to prove anything to anyone"; "Every fourth has not cooled off and is ready to fight"; "Every sixth has retreated from everything, sticking to the Bible or Koran"; "Every ninth screams at night, waking up from a nightmare." And finally:

> Every twentieth sees in his life nothing but vodka and tears;
> And his life is like a vicious circle that makes mourning roses closer.
> Every thirtieth is on a needle, not believing that he is a drug addict;
> And the only thing that could bring him back is yet another portion of stuff.

---

28. For examples of actual fragging during the Second World War and the war in Afghanistan see Merridale (2006, 192) and Alexievich (1992, 41), respectively.

Fig. 3.5. "From One War to Another." The cover of a tape recording of soldiers' songs. DD Music, 2002.

Every two hundredth has no arm or leg; and prosthesis hardly makes sense;
And no benefits could possibly help, no privileges would ever work.
Sometimes, one in a hundred makes his way to prison;
Even this is too many, but this is the only case that we are always reminded about.

This grim archive of available identities is periodically interrupted by a chorus that explains the nature of this deplorable state. There is no mysticism, the song elaborates: "It is just statistics that put a deadly noose around us / Every single one of us is in this trap, only our numbers differ / And those who have not been killed by the syndrome / Are being killed by some other means."

The statistical trap is presented here as a diversely differentiated list. However, what is striking about this gloomy poetics is that the differentiation emerges in "Statistics" as a typology, a set of generalized features. Individual biographies are turned into aggregated qualities; the overwhelming anonymity ("only our numbers differ") pairs with profound pessimism ("a deadly noose"). This anonymity, this self-erasure, is an account of one's own ruin, an outline of one's own "desubjectification" (Agamben 1999, 142). What this poetics of disintegration repeatedly reveals is an implicit recognition of the fact that no symbolic envelope, no positive meaningful receptacle has been able to produce the desired structuring effect (Lacan 1997, 260), as if war horrors have seamlessly morphed into the horrors of everyday life.

It is useful to approach these narratives of self-disintegration through the Althusserian idea about the subjectifying force of ideological state apparatuses. In the essay on ideology and ideological state apparatuses, Althusser linked ideological framings and subjectivity: through rituals of ideological recognition "abstract individuals" are turned into concrete, distinguishable, and irreplaceable subjects (1971, 173). In his oft-cited example, Althusser described how this recognition happens: individuals are walking down the street when a policeman hails, "Hey, you there!" In most cases, an individual turns around, suspecting or knowing that it was he who was supposed to be hailed (174).

In this reading, ideology is not necessarily equal to brainwashing or to a purposeful distortion of reality. Instead, its task is to situate the subject in the midst of this reality by making it "possible to act purposefully" within incomprehensible social situations (Geertz 1973, 220). The goal of ideology is to single the individual or collective subject out of an abstract human mass, to "animate" the subject into existence, as Judith Butler puts it (1997, 25). The anecdote reveals another important moment: hailing (or interpellation) works because it is expected. It is effective because there is a willingness—on the part of the emerging subject—to be addressed.

It is precisely this idea of the hailing expected from ideology that is important in discussing the state's symbolic role in defining veterans' identity. Veterans' stories of fragmentation describe a situation in which ideological state apparatuses have failed to deliver the anticipated call. The stories also outline the general dilemma of having a strong state-related identity in a weak state. The collapse of the context and institutions, which used to support such an identity, rarely activates a search for new identifications. Rather this withdrawal of the basic (and familiar) support reinforces a desire to maintain prior identities as firmly as possible. Imposed by the state and internalized by veterans, military self-perception is transformed into a generative cliché, into a social template that is expected to perform a necessary classifying function in times of peace. In the absence of ideological hailing in the postwar life, ex-servicemen are lost when they face the necessity of reentering a nonmilitarized society. Recurring attempts to reenact the traumatic experience in rituals and militarized employment, the attraction of "banal militarism" as a way of avoiding difficulties of returning to civil life (Cock 2005, 801), are rooted precisely in this lack of nonmilitarized forms of interpellation by the state. It comes from the feeling, to use the veteran's phrase, that "there is nothing" else to hang onto.

In many cases, the malfunctioning of the ideological state apparatuses was revealed through veterans' routine anthropomorphizing of the state: metaphors of the deaf state, the state that doesn't notice or doesn't hear were common in veterans' discussions. Yet what these metaphors displaced was not the demand for being heard but a desire to be hailed, addressed, and differentiated by the state.

During one of my interviews, after a veteran's long tirade about society's "universal indifference" to their postwar lives, I tried to see if veterans themselves would be willing to reverse the dynamic by hailing the state and the public. I asked my interlocutor if he had ever tried to talk to local journalists or intelligentsia to draw public attention to his cause. The answer was negative. As this veteran insisted, people did not really need to know about the ordeal the soldiers had to go through in Chechnya. Instead, I was told, to understand what the veterans' experience was about "everyone should watch *Saving Private Ryan*," a Steven Spielberg film (1998), in which a team of American soldiers is sent to rescue a paratrooper lost during the battle for Omaha Beach in Normandy in June 1944. Nikolai F., a participant in the first Chechen war, translated the meaning of this film about suffering and rewarding salvation in terms of the post-Soviet reality: "If the state managed to turn us, civil people, young guys, into *boeviki,* well, not quite that, let's say, into warriors [*voinov*], into people who know how to fight, then the state should think hard about the way it can turn us back into civilians." These expectations for the authoritative hailing were destined to remain futile. Once again, the state withdrew, unwilling and often incapable of addressing the complicated issue of soldiers' demobilization. The weak state became a state that betrayed.[29]

29. In his study of Zimbabwean soldiers demobilized in the early 1980s after the war for independence, Musemwa (1995) traces a similar tendency: having returned from the war veterans became quickly marginalized and ignored. One soldier summed up a dominant perception of the postwar situation that could be easily heard from the veterans of the Chechen war: "The politicians who made us what we are had ditched us" (51).

Benefits of War

In my conversations with veterans, I was always surprised by their persistent reluctance to discuss the goals of the war in Chechnya (or the U.S. military operation in Afghanistan). My question about the goals of the war was usually dismissed as irrelevant; at best, veterans would simply justify the status quo by saying that there must have been "some reason." Critical opinions were few, and in their attempts to frame relations with the state in terms of business exchange, veterans continued the same old strategy of depoliticizing the war. In displacing these *whys* the veterans of the Chechen war were not original, though. Samuel Hynes (1997) in his historical study of soldiers' narratives has traced the same tendency: soldiers of different wars and different generations have usually preferred to leave these *whys* in the shadow of their descriptions of combat experience. Regardless of the type and timing, war memories seem to be following the same plotline: with some predictable variations, the descriptions of mud, lice, cold, or heat radically overshadow the infrequent questioning of political rationales that determined these wars in the first place.[30]

However, as Hynes insists, "the soldier assumes—*must* assume—that if he did ask that question, if he were allowed to ask it, there would be a rational answer, that what he is doing and suffering makes sense to someone farther up in the chain of command" (1997, 12). What happens when no reasonable explanation can justify one's experience of horror?

When I asked Kirill P., a Chechen war veteran, to describe his perception of people's attitude to veterans, he told me about one incident. The Altai regional government issued free transportation passes for the veterans. Using such a pass, Kirill once boarded a tram, where he was confronted by a female ticket officer.[31] With a big magnifying lens, she closely examined Kirill's pass, deemed it fake, and demanded that Kirill leave the tram. The veteran refused, despite the officer's threat to call the police. As if dismissing the importance of the story, Kirill finished his description with a phrase: "Those who know us, they realize very well that we have already paid our Motherland in full." This instantaneous translation of a failed monetary transaction into a metaphor of exchange and sacrifice was the most characteristic feature of veterans' commentaries. Many sincerely believed that the

30. Catherine Merridale traces these descriptions of daily life during the Second World War in her interviews with Russian veterans (2006); see also Alexievich (1992) and Gorban' (2003) for similar recollections of the participants of the Afghan and Chechen wars, respectively.

31. Apart from the driver, usually each bus or tram has an on-board conductor whose task is to sell passes and check the validity of documents that entitle passengers to free rides.

state had not delivered its part of the deal. As one veteran put it, "the state has not settled the account [with us]" (*gosudarstvo ne rasschitalos'*).

Ironically, by building their postwar narratives around descriptions of literal or metaphorical payments, veterans endowed the notions of money and debt with a strong moral connotation. The theme of compensation, benefits, privileges, and money emerged alongside the theme of patriotic duty. Sometimes both themes complemented each other, and economic benefits were presented as a logical sign of respect and recognition. Sometimes the two themes contradicted and undermined each other, construed as two totally incommensurable ways of acknowledging veterans' war past.[32] What seemed to be constant in both cases was the assumed understanding that the state was ultimately responsible not only for veterans' postwar economic dislocation but also for the crisis of their state-oriented identity. Both themes were deeply rooted in the recent Soviet past. Both also suggested important modifications that allow us to trace changes in relations among individuals, groups, and the state in post-Soviet Russia.

By the end of the 1980s, the Soviet state had created an elaborate (but not necessarily very effective) system of support for the veterans of the Second World War. Organized hierarchically (the type and number of benefits were associated with types of veterans' state awards and/or injuries), the system included special food and department stores for ex-servicemen, as well as personal privileges such as free housing, free or heavily discounted food packages, cars, medicine, health care, transportation, and other in-kind benefits. When in the middle of the 1980s veterans of the Afghan war—*afgantsy,* as they are usually called—started forming their first unions, they aimed at reproducing the benefit system created for the previous war's generation.[33] There was an important difference, however. Afgantsy organizations were created under the institutional auspice of local branches of Komsomol (the Communist Union of Youth), which provided a level of political, financial, and legal support that previous generations had not employed.[34]

At the end of the Soviet Union, Komsomol was the largest youth organization in the country, composed of virtually everyone between the ages of fourteen and twenty-eight. The union was formally and financially independent, yet politically it was tightly connected with the party and the state.

32. Dynin (1990, 59–130) provides a set of diverse examples suggesting that the trope of duty/debt became a central part of the public rhetoric in the late 1980s, after the Soviet withdrawal from Afghanistan.

33. The term *afgantsy* (singular, *afganets*) is normally used to refer to "people from Afghanistan."

34. For an extensive list of examples of the initial stage of the *afgantsy* movement in the USSR see Dynin (1990).

The Komsomol's initial attempts to channel the afgantsy through existing political structures clearly reflected the organization's political aim. The first Union of Veterans of Afghanistan (Soiuz veteranov Afganistana) created in Barnaul in 1985 was actively involved in civic and military-patriotic (*voenno-patrioticheskoe*) education programs, which usually included regional concerts, competitions of military and patriotic songs, boot camps for high school students, and even routine neighborhood watch raids in unsafe areas of the city. At the same time, the union provided its members with medical, social, and sometimes financial help, relying first of all on funds from the Komsomol and state budgets. With the dissolution of the Soviet Union, the immense network of Komsomol institutions and property quickly vanished. There was no immediate institutional backbone to support newly emerging social groups and organizations, nor was there a stable source of financial help.

Unlike the Komsomol, the afgantsy organizations managed to outlast the collapse of the Soviet Union and even to preserve their favorable political reputation. The successful translation of this reputation into financial capital was the key to survival. In the early 1990s, the Russian state, unable to allocate any funding for social programs for Afghan war veterans or to deliver those programs in kind, decided to grant (or was lobbied into granting) significant tax privileges to organizations that united the most vulnerable category, injured and disabled ex-soldiers. In two special decrees in 1991 and 1993, President Yeltsin granted to three major umbrella organizations of Afghan war veterans complete immunity from excise duty on imported goods and foodstuffs and provided them with a set of tax incentives for conducting financial operations and for carrying out various types of entrepreneurial activity ("O Rossiiskom fonde" 1991; "O deiatel'nosti" 1992; "O merakh" 1993).[35] The country was experiencing a sharp shortage of food and consumer products. Hence it was expected that the funds accumulated by the Union of Invalids from these operations would be spent on building housing and providing necessary medical and financial support for veterans.

The actual result was quite different. Investigations conducted into one fund for afgantsy revealed that only a small fraction of its revenues—between 9 and 24 percent by different accounts—was actually spent on the intended purposes (Nikulina 1997; Nedomerova 1995). Tax benefits were

---

35. The list of organizations included the Union of Veterans of Afghanistan (Soiuz veteranov Afganistana); All-Russian Union of Veterans of Afghanistan (Rossiiskii soiuz veteranov Afganistana), and Russian Foundation of Invalids of War in Afghanistan (Rossiiskii Fond invalidov voiny v Afganistane). See Kotenev (1994) and Danilova (2002) for more details.

used mostly to flood the country with cheap vodka and tobacco, while revenues were appropriated by the leadership (Berger 1995). Lacking the initial capital and necessary skills, foundations devoted to handicapped veterans were either colonized by criminals or quickly became criminalized themselves (Volkov 2002, 11–12). Frants Klintsevich, a member of the Russian parliament and a high-profile functionary of the All-Russian Union of Veterans of Afghanistan pointed out in 1997 that because of their cooperation with criminal groups, afgantsy foundations were able to pocket roughly one billion dollars (Shaburkin 1997).

My Barnaul informant, Igor K., a leader of the Union of Veterans of the Chechen War, stressed the same point in a conversation, when he referred to the afgantsy as a path that Chechen war veterans preferred to avoid: "Predominantly, it was not the veterans who took advantage of the privileges that were granted by the state to their organizations. The opportunity was seized by smarter and more competent civilians. Veterans were pushed overboard. And finally all that resulted in the explosions at the Kotliakovo cemetery."

The implied basic opposition, veterans versus civilians, is worth noting, yet even more important is the reference to the cemetery explosions. The explosions consisted of two notorious contract murders that took place in Moscow in 1994 and 1996 on the same day, November 10. Both explosions were associated with the name of Mikhail Likhodei, the leader of the Union of Invalids of the Afghan War, a primary corporate beneficiary of a tax exemption from import operations. On November 10, 1994, Likhodei was killed on the way to his apartment by a bomb planted in the elevator's speakerphone. Two years later, when 157 people gathered near Likhodei's grave at the Kotliakovo Cemetery in Moscow for a commemoration ceremony, another explosive went off, injuring seventy and killing thirteen people (including Likhodei's widow and son) (Savel'ev 1996a).

The timing of the events was not random. November 10 has long been officially marked in the Russian calendar as a professional holiday in honor of the Soviet/Russian police (Den' Sovetskoi/Rossiiskoi Militsii). The holiday acquired special prominence during the late Soviet period and was meant to celebrate close ties among the police, the political leadership, and the Soviet people. Murders staged on this day, in other words, were seen as a clear challenge to the authorities (*Izvestia* 1996). For average citizens, the holiday had a strong association with a lengthy concert that featured national stars of classical and popular genres. The concert was attended by the highest state officials and televised live for the whole country. Public awareness about the 1996 explosion increased even more when on November 10

Prime Minister Viktor Chernomyrdin canceled all the entertainment programs, the concert included, as a sign of mourning. Given that in late Soviet history the concert had been canceled only once, on November 10, 1981, because of Leonid Brezhnev's death, this measure attracted a lot of attention to the murder (Savel'ev 1996b).

In the mass media, the explosions became highly symbolic. Newspapers quickly dubbed the events the veterans' "own Afghan war," which was aimed at "sorting out" afgantsy financial problems and group loyalties.[36] The explosions also marked a turning point in the post-Soviet collective biography of the afgantsy. Tax benefits were drastically reduced (and later eliminated), and veterans themselves became tightly linked in the public imagination with corruption and banditry (Savvateeva 1995; Punanov 1998). The veterans' public image became especially grim when the media reported that both events were apparently contracted for by fellow veterans, competing for access to economic privileges (Oleinik 1996; Sanin 1998).[37] By the end of the 1990s, the figure of the afganets was turned into a cliché standing for an uncontrolled, violent, mafia-connected man, tortured by his military past, "a killing-machine, with big fists, a weak head and no conscience," as an Afghan war veteran put it (Alexievich 1992, 94; also Dubin 1996). Replicating the trajectory of the post-Vietnam "freaked-out loser" from the "Vetsploitation" films of the 1960–170s in the United States, the criminal afganets became a standard feature of Russian mass culture by the second Chechen war (Kern 1988, 43; Dwyer 2002).

Despite the fact that corporate financial benefits for veterans and invalids were eventually abolished, vivid signs of this period persist in Barnaul even now. It was during this time that the Altai Union of Veterans of the Afghan War emerged as an important economic actor in the region, able to privatize several local plants and factories. The Home of Veterans, the union's headquarters, is located in a restored red-brick mansion in the very center of Barnaul, directly across from the regional administration headquarters, powerfully symbolizing the economic and political success of the union in the 1990s.

The post-Soviet evolution of the "Afghan movement," or "the internationalist movement" as it is sometimes called, is interestingly reflected in emblems and signs that the Altai Union of Veterans of Afghanistan displays

36. In 2002, the "cemetery explosions" would be memorialized in a popular television series, *Brigada* (directed by Aleksei Sidorov), a saga about the transformation of late-Soviet bandits into post-Soviet entrepreneurs.

37. In the end, however, the court dismissed the case, and the defendant afgantsy were released (*Vremia Novostei* 2004).

Fig. 3.6. The emblem of the International Movement of Afghan War Veterans. Barnaul, 2003. Photo by author.

on the Home of Veterans, which hosts the organization. The major emblem, created in 1991, is a wrought-iron shield with the sign "Home of the Internationalist Movement." There is a Soviet star with hammer and sickle in the middle and a traditional wreath of tulips meant to evoke the association with the airplanes (called "Black Tulip") that transported coffins with soldiers back to the USSR during the Afghan war[38] (figure 3.6).

The post-Soviet sign, however, displayed above the home's main entrance, contains a different message and a different combination of symbols (figure 3.7). The Soviet star was significantly minimized. Instead, the sign displays the organization's logo, a bullet with the word "AFGAN" in Latin script, and a black tulip next to it. The logo is located under a white line that reads against the green backdrop: "God, Russia, and our Brotherhood are with us!" The most telling elements, however, are the bottom lines, which identify

---

38. The origin of this symbolism is not totally clear. Veterans do not seem to be aware of the fact that in Iran, tulips have traditionally symbolized martyrdom. The version that is dominant among afgantsy associates the black tulip with the name of a funeral bureau in Tashkent, Uzbekistan, that was charged with providing coffins for the army during the war. The name, then, was eventually associated with the four points where bodies of the deceased soldiers were collected for transferring to the USSR. Later, the name became linked with the transport planes themselves (Gai and Snegirev 1991, 278–79). The bureaucratic euphemism for the zinc coffin containing a dead soldier is "cargo 200" (*gruz 200*). Under this name coffins were shipped throughout the Soviet Union; the same term is used for coffins from Chechnya.

Fig. 3.7. Internationalist, Ltd.: "God, Russia, and Our Brotherhood Are with Us." Barnaul, 2003. Photo by author.

corporations associated with the Union of Veterans, the company Internationalist, Ltd., and a construction company with exactly the same name. In a peculiar form, the combination of the two emblems outlines a straightforward vector of development from the military-patriotic Home of the International Movement to the commercially-driven Internationalist, Ltd.

This material legacy of the early 1990s strikingly contrasts with the condition of the Chechen war veterans in Barnaul. When I interviewed them in 2001–2, their organizations occupied half of the first floor in a dilapidated building not far away from Barnaul's center. All activity was concentrated in two small rooms, while two-thirds of the space seemed to have been in a period of prolonged renovation, with nearly collapsed walls and huge piles of junk on the floor. Lacking in finances, the Chechen war veterans could neither finish the renovation nor move to a better location.

Given the rapidly changing political, economic, and ethical background, how could Chechen war veterans—collectively and individually—sustain their military economy in everyday life? I have been suggesting that the exchange of sacrifices between ex-servicemen and the state was largely shaped by practices of recognition that the state had implemented in the recent past. There were still some signs of practices associated with the benefit system designed to support veterans of various Soviet military campaigns. However, a wide-scale implementation of this system was hardly possible even in the late 1990s. Taking the afgantsy model as their main reference point, Chechen war veterans accommodated it to changing conditions.

There was much discussion about mutual support and mutual responsibility between the two generations of war veterans. Despite multiple and very significant differences, a considerable family resemblance between the two generations was obvious: Chechen war veterans often refer to themselves as "younger brothers of afgantsy," and their public identity—*chechentsy,* as they call themselves (that is, Chechens, from Chechnya)—is based on the same toponymic approach.[39] Much of this similarity is determined by institutional proximity: the first groups of Chechen war veterans emerged in Barnaul as informal chapters of local unions of Afghan war veterans. Strengthened financially by privileges granted in the early 1990s, local foundations of afgantsy provided a new generation of veterans with immediate financial and legal support, performing a consolidating function that used to be monopolized by the Komsomol organization. By the mid-1990s, a growing understanding of their own specific interests, taken together with the elimination of economic privileges and the negative public attitude toward afgantsy, resulted in a new organization that united participants of the Chechen war in the region.

The Chechen war veterans' distancing from the previous generation of veterans was also provoked by a traditionally divisive practice of governmentality. Unlike Afghan veterans, whose postwar legal status had been determined by the law On Veterans (1994), which basically equated them with veterans of the Second World War, participants in the Chechen war had no legal framework that could outline or even clarify their postwar rights and entitlements.[40] As previously indicated, the Russian government was careful not to frame the war in Chechnya as a war; officially, it was referred to as a counterterrorist operation, or, at most, as combat or fighting activities

39. Veterans usually refer to ethnic Chechens (*chechentsy*) as *dukhi* (spirits or spooks) or *chekhi,* which appears to be a phonetic amalgamation of *chechentsy* and *dukhi* (*chekhi* literally means Czechs).
40. During the Soviet period, the status of the Afghan veterans was also determined by corresponding legal acts.

(*boevye deistviia*) in the North Caucasus. Correspondingly, there were no war veterans but only participants in combat activities who were not covered by the existing law and were not eligible for the statewide subsidies or assistance that could be relevant in their case.

The unequal legal conditions of the two generations of veterans and the lack of civic identity attributed to Chechen war veterans produced tensions in sibling-like relations. One veteran described the source of this tension with the "Afghan brothers" well: "We are an independent organization, yet we are always together with [Afghan war veterans] on each and every question. The end result, though, is strange: we exist, but as if we don't matter.... We don't want to be in the role of extras anymore." Attempting to play their own independent role, Chechen war veterans in Barnaul founded a regional nongovernmental organization of invalids and former participants of military conflicts, Bratstvo (Fraternity). The organization was created in February 1997 after an annual festival of soldiers' songs established to commemorate the withdrawal of the Soviet Army from Afghanistan.

Despite its name, the main person behind this organization was a woman, Marina Shaul'skaia, who had no military experience but a good deal of expertise in social work. From the early 1990s Shaul'skaia was in charge of the department "social benefits" of the Altai Union of Afghan Veterans. Throughout the 1990s, she also wrote scripts and directed all major public events of the Committee of Soldiers' Mothers, as well as Altai's afgantsy. She managed to bring chechentsy together and to establish a vital connection with local power structures.

When I interviewed her in 2002, Shaul'skaia had already severed her ties with the Afghan and the Chechen war veteran movements. I asked her if there was any visible difference between these two generations. Referring to the idea of a post-Soviet ideological vacuum, she said, "The Afghan war veterans had some limits, they still had something sacred. The younger [veterans of the Chechen war] have nothing of this. They are totally different. There was no ideology, and you could see what happened because of this. The [first] Chechen war was outside of ideology. Everybody was on his own, surviving. What was desired was not victory by any means, but prosperity at any price; a desire to get above everyone else."

Shaul'skaia's comment notwithstanding, this emphasis on prosperity and individualism among chechentsy certainly had some resemblance to the social trajectory of Afghan war veterans. In the Chechen war veterans' case, there was a major financial reason that pushed this individualism even further. With the beginning of the war in Chechnya, financial subsidies to war veterans, abolished in the spring of 1995, returned. This time, however, subsidies came in a very different form: corporate tax breaks and exemptions were replaced with individualized payments. At the end of 1994, the Ministry of Defense doubled the base salary for contract officers and tripled the per diem allowances to servicemen deployed in Chechnya.[41] As a result, a soldier's "combat payments" (*boevye vyplaty*), as they are usually called, could easily come up to $1,000 a month, roughly six times more than an average salary in the country at the time. Normally deployed for up to six months, servicemen often returned from Chechnya with a substantial amount of cash, at least in theory (Zakharov 2000; Mikhailova 1995; *Na strazhe Rodiny* 1997; Agentsvo voennykh novostei 1999). But payments were often delayed. To preclude robbery and murders associated with combat money, the Ministry of Defense started transferring funds to its local divisions that drafted soldiers in the first place rather than paying cash in Chechnya. However, money transfers frequently took several months or even years in some cases. In this situation, demobilized soldiers would get caught up in military red tape, which increased their sense of general dislocation (Ziuzin 2000). The Uminskii case, discussed at the beginning of this chapter, reflects a structurally similar condition. The situation was not that different in Barnaul, where the Union of Veterans of Chechnya (UVC), an umbrella organization that enlisted more than two thousand individuals and several smaller organizations (Bratstvo included), spent a large part of its time helping veterans to secure their combat payments. The legal and accounting work associated with combat payment arrears was organized in the UVC by several women who were girlfriends or wives of veterans (as I was told). Veterans themselves, often not having received the education necessary for such paperwork, usually resorted to direct negotiations with local administrations. The individual nature of these monetary exchanges with the state helps explain why there was little collective action among veterans.

Combat payments significantly modified veterans' assumptions about an exchange of sacrifices: the payments set a clear financial benchmark, a certain level of economic expectations below which veterans did not want to sink. Against the sign of personal financial success epitomized by combat payments, low-income jobs available in the region were not even considered as the starting point of a potential career. Veterans dismissed them out of hand even as a temporary occupation. As Vitalii explained, "Yes, job banks have vacancies; they say there are seven thousand positions available today.

41. The ministry also recalibrated the weight of service time from the point of view of retirement: one month of combat service in Chechnya was equal to three months of regular service (Ivanuk 1995); the same system was used during the war in Afghanistan (Dynin 1990, 135).

But, excuse me, a guy who went through all that [war experience], he just would never even think about this job, this "occupation" for 600 rubles [$20] a month. He would never think about it. Because he knows his own price."

The quick conversion of salary into personal worth is instructive. Sacrifice, to recall Simmel, "is not only the condition of specific values, but the condition of value as such . . . it is not only the price to be paid for particular established values, but the price through which alone values can be established" (1978, 84–85). Hence, one's war experience, one's potential sacrifice of his life, was used as the ultimate measurement for other social relations. Interactions, in short, were construed as exchanges. But as in any exchange, this particular desire to gain something else in return for what has been given up brought with it a double-sided conflict. As Vitalii's comment demonstrates, the search for an appropriate equivalent to mediate between one's sacrifice and its external recognition requires an ability to negotiate between different moral accounts. In other words, different "regimes of value," without which exchange would not be possible, are based on potentially conflicting expectations of this exchange; they also produce dissimilar interests associated with similar values (Appadurai 1986, 57; Graeber 2001, 30–33). For Vitalii and many other veterans, competing regimes of value did not represent different points of view about social exchange; rather, these differences were construed as attempts to justify *failed* exchanges—that is, to justify exchanges that devalued the high price originally paid by veterans.

The comment also demonstrates how military identity is resuscitated in the postwar situation: entitlement to a better salary is justified not by better professional skills but by one's experience of war. Significantly, in his attempt to convert the military past into a postwar value, Vitalii failed to find any stable or even positive representation. Heavily rooted in the operation of negation ("would *never even* think"), his rhetorical strategy indexes rather than describes the starting and final points of the argument. Neither the formative war experience ("who went through *all that*"), nor one's own worthiness ("price") provided a graspable explanation.

There were other reasons that made veterans' military identity resurface, too. Postwar failures to find a way of making use of themselves, described by Vitalii, had much to do with veterans' backgrounds. Drafted mostly from rural areas of Altai, these men could hardly find employment after their return.[42] Some ex-servicemen tried to find their way back to Chechnya or other hot spots and signed professional contracts with the

---

42. In this respect, the background of the Chechen war veterans resembles that of soldiers who fought in the Afghan war: the majority of conscripts were children of peasant and working-class families from rural areas (Gromov 1994, 286).

Fig. 3.8. A banner on a building: "Army of Russia—Army of Professionals. Contracted Military Service—It's a Job for Real Men!" Barnaul, 2004. Photo by author.

Ministry of Defense or the Ministry of the Interior. By one local estimate, up to 30 percent of all contracts in the region were signed by veterans of the Chechen (and other post-Soviet) wars.[43] Other men, perhaps following an aggressive advertising campaign organized by the regional office of the Ministry of Defense, signed short-term agreements to go to Chechnya in order to "earn enough money to buy fur coats for their wives, or new TV sets....Or just to save enough money so that they would not have to build their life from the zero-level," as a contract military officer observed (Gurtenko 2002) (figures 3.8 and 3.9).

But military contracts did not come automatically: in 2003 out of two thousand men who submitted their applications, only twelve hundred were able to land an actual job.[44] Yet, as one military recruiter described it, contractors from the Altai region demonstrated a persistently negative tendency. Usually coming from low-income families, these military servicemen were often stupefied when confronted with their relatively high salaries: "When these guys get hold of normal money, they have no idea what to

43. For instance, in 2002, 907 men from the Altai region signed military contracts (*Svobodnii kurs*, April 5, 2001).

44. *Altai Daily Review*, August 16, 2004.

Fig. 3.9. An advertisement for army service: "I choose contract service [in the army]." Barnaul, 2006. Photo by author.

spend it on. So, they "invest" it in alcohol....We don't keep people like that" (Kuleshov and Sagitov 2003).

The majority of veterans, however, did not return to the war and preferred to find a job at home. Still, all veterans with whom I spoke described their immediate postwar time as one long drinking binge, "A 100 percent *zapoi*," as one veteran called it.[45] While not exactly new among Russian men (Pesmen 2000, 170–88), this type of zapoi has its own distinctive economy. Combat payments made these binges financially possible. In turn, a lack of permanent jobs and relatively independent lifestyle (very few veterans are married or have long-term partners) provided social conditions necessary for this type of behavior. To quote Oleg, a veteran of the first Chechen war,

> In 1996, after that [Khasavyurt] peace agreement, we all came back to this normal, civilian life....Nobody even tried to find a job during the first couple

45. The word *zapoi* (drinking binge) comes from the verb *zapit'*, which means both "to start drinking" and "to wash down."

of months because mainly it was zapoi....With veterans, I drank for two–three months. Joy came only in a bottle. The common goal was to get drunk. A common interest was to get drunk, talk about the war; about the way things were then, to recall something from that time, to get totally pissed off at the whole world, and to start a fight with someone while drunk....We had no time for psychological rehabilitation.

Frequently, zapoi would mark an extended period of liminality, with no clear way out. The state of the local economy did not make the situation any better. Apart from Barnaul, the region was predominantly agricultural, with limited demand for a seasonal labor force, low salaries, lack of career perspectives, and unattractive working conditions. This "zero opportunity variant" (*nulevoi variant*), as a veteran aptly termed it, often forced ex-servicemen to move to Barnaul, the biggest industrial center in the region. However, very few veterans had useful connections, marketable skills, or even clear plans for starting new, urban lives. Their job choices were determined by their previous military training. They tried militarized state institutions—police, security service, fire brigades, or tax police—first, usually with no success.

Veterans' lack of success in obtaining professional employment in the governmental sector gave rise to a particular conspiracy theory. Applying for a state job in security-related areas often involved a comprehensive medical checkup. While physical tests are usually passed without any significant problem, mandatory interviews with a psychotherapist often cut veterans off. As Oleg K., an active member of the Union of Chechen War Veterans framed it, "I think, they just had a special policy to get rid of participants [of the Chechen war] during this medical checkup. Simply, they want to get rid of us." Oleg recollected that during the interview with a psychotherapist he was asked to guess a popular proverb from the description suggested by the doctor. The proverb seemed to be hard to recall, and getting anxious about the possibility of failing the crucial test, Oleg asked the doctor if she herself knew the proverb. The reaction was somewhat off-putting: "Don't be rude, young man." A verbal exchange between the psychotherapist and the veteran that followed right after that effectively resulted in the verdict that ended any aspiration for the state-related career: "Not fit for the job" (*ne goden*).

It is because of experiences like this that veterans were reluctant to seek any psychological rehabilitation. Social workers and psychologists from the Men's Crisis Center, which was created in Barnaul precisely in order to help veterans of the Chechen war, unanimously told me that the center did not manage to attract the veterans' attention. Mentioning the "Chechen syndrome," a term widely used in the media to describe the postwar (and posttraumatic) condition of veterans (*Svobodnyi kurs* 2001), could provoke a flurry of negative emotions and angry accusations similar to the one I got during an interview with Nikolai F.: "We veterans need no psychologist at all.... You people have this understanding that if we fought a war it means we are imbeciles [*duraki*]! But in reality, a person who went through a war is prepared for life better than anyone else."

Failed psychological tests were not the only catalyst. Veterans' attempts to find jobs in the private sector provided plenty of similar examples. The military ID (*voennyi bilet*) of each veteran of the Chechen war bears a clear stamp—"participated in combat activity" (*uchastnik voennykh deistvii*)—and usually indicates the number of "combat days" spent in Chechnya.[46] Issued by the state, the ID must be submitted with a job application to a potential employer. Veterans were convinced that this stamp was often read by potential employers as a diagnosis, as another disqualifying stamp: "Not fit for the job."[47]

The area where veterans did succeed in landing jobs was in private industry that required militarized skills. For example, after several months in his own village, with no job and no prospects, Viktor Z., a paratrooper, decided to move to Barnaul. He had neither close relatives nor friends in the city. For some time he managed to share a room with a man whom he had not known at all before, but who was a relative of a friend. His first big job was a security guard/doorman in a bar. In the interview, Viktor emphasized what appeared to be a very unusual fact. His first employer had needed neither recommendations nor background-check phone calls to hire him. Apparently surprised by the act of recognition that required no additional steps, the veteran continued: "On their own, they themselves just personally accepted me [*sami ot sebia lichno menia priniali*]. And I started working; and people liked it. People would come and say, 'Glad to see you.' Even customers did that!" The security job in the bar led to another position. A local businessman offered Viktor the job of a bodyguard/chauffeur. For two years Viktor drove this man and other businessmen around the town, accompanying them on business trips to other cities when needed. After meeting with several veterans who had organized a local Union of Veterans of the Chechen War, Viktor decided to quit the job in order to work full time in

46. The exact number of days is important not only because of the amount of combat payment but also for calculating the retirement package later (*Svobodnyi kurs* 2002).
47. See Vines (1998, 196) for a similar discussion in the Mozambique context.

Bratstvo. As he put it, "We had a discussion among ourselves, and decided that we just didn't like the way it was going on."

Viktor's decision to quit reflected a general feeling among veterans. Practically every conversation that I had with ex-soldiers would eventually evolve into a discussion about friendship ties and military bonds formed by the combat experience. Some of them framed it in terms of nostalgia. "It is not a nostalgia for blood or death that hangs freely around there," as Aleksei T., a veteran of the first Chechen war emphasized. "It is a nostalgia for relations, for situations when people would die for each other; where the collective was one perfect wholeness."

The appeal to an idealized community tested by blood and death is a standard response to one's own dislocation. Studies of American soldiers who participated in the Iraq war similarly indicated that it was "solidarity with one's comrades," the bond of trust developed in the field that motivated the soldiers most. The following quote from an interview with an American soldier in Iraq could be easily paralleled by similar examples from interviews with Chechen war veterans: "Everybody just did what we had to do. It was just looking out for one another. We weren't fighting for anybody else but ourselves. We weren't fighting for some higher-up who is somebody; we were just fighting for each other" (as quoted in Wong et al. 2003, 12). It was exactly this bonding component that was missing from the postwar lives of Chechen war veterans.[48]

The trope of combat brotherhood had an additional meaning in the history of Russia, too. Memorialization of the Second World War, which accelerated in the Soviet Union in the 1960s, capitalized on the symbolic possibilities that the notion of war-tested solidarity provided. Back then, in the wake of Khrushchev's Thaw, the melodramatic tone of war films and the intimate intonation of the so-called war lieutenants' prose helped to extricate the victory in World War II from the messy problem of the Stalinist legacy.[49] In post-Soviet Russia, the intimate discourse of military friendship helped again to move one's attention away from political aspects of the war, from the unimaginable and unjustifiable number of casualties and refugees, from (often) incompetent military leadership. As Viktor's comment

48. See Prilepin (2006) for a semifictionalized description of this combat brotherhood in Chechnya.

49. The term "lieutenants' prose" is used to describe novels about the Great Patriotic War written by low-ranking officers with war experience. These attempts to look at the war from "below" drastically contrasted with the official glorifying canon of the perception of the war. For a discussion of the symbolic importance of this war in producing late Soviet and post-Soviet identity see Gudkov (2004, 20–58).

indicated, this idealized solidarity was precipitated by displeasure with "the way it was going on." What were those negative factors that accelerated the veterans' desire for consolidations?

Minding Their Own Business

Veterans often interpret their unsuccessful attempts to find jobs or otherwise integrate themselves into the community of civilians (*grazhdanskikh*) as a consequence of a prejudice against them on the part of those who did not have the same (war) past.[50] The imposed or imagined experience of nonintegration, in other words, was reframed as veterans' enforced marginalization. Admitting the zero-level opportunity available to them, in their discussions my informants referred to *bezyskhodnost'* (despair)—a feeling of being interminably captured, literally, a situation without exit—as a main source of their own criminality. Deeply aware of their negative public image, very few veterans tried to defend crimes committed by their brothers in arms. But almost every member of the UVC I talked to was strongly compelled to explain the origin of this situation, as in this quote from my interview with a veteran: "We are told all the time: 'Sorry we do not have any job vacancies.' In fact, they just do not want to hire us. But for how long could a man wander about, with no job, with no money?...He won't beg. He'd rather pick up a stem [*stvol*, a gun]."

References to their own special sensitivity and psychological imbalance were used by veterans if not to justify, then at least to downplay outbursts of violent behavior. On a different occasion, I witnessed how the organization attempted to intervene on behalf of its members. My conversation with Oleg K., a leader of the UVC whom I quoted earlier, was interrupted by a phone call. The mother of a girl raped by a drunken Chechen war veteran several days earlier was trying to figure out the circumstances of the case, determined to sue the offender. Asking for forgiveness, referring to the special ("uncontrolled") psychological state of the veteran, and offering to cover necessary medical treatment, Oleg did his best to convince the mother to settle the case without going to court, which would produce yet another criminal charge against chechentsy. The negotiation was long but apparently successful.

In this context, veterans' solidarity rooted in the shared experience was perceived not only as a source of individual and group identity but also as

---

50. For a similar attitude among South African ex-combatants see Cock (2005, 796–97).

an effective preventive tool. Nikolai F., a leader of the UVC, passionately described the essence of this precautionary solidarity in an interview. As he put it, the main goal of the union "is to bring everyone together and to prevent once and forever our guys from any further fighting. Because they still wage their wars here [*prodolzhali voevat' zdes'*]. Some are in criminal gangs, some by themselves. If we let it go in this direction…many lives would have a very pitiful end. Even today many of our guys are behind prison bars, convicted of anything from armed robbery to murders. This is our tragedy."

The criminal trail associated with the chechentsy movement was also seen by veterans as the main thing hindering their economic activity. Veterans' attempts to clarify their own position in this regard were hardly helpful, though. For instance, complaining about a lack of working relations with businesses in the city, Oleg insisted that "important, big entrepreneurs in town think that we are a criminal structure, mafia…but we are people like anyone else. We just try to earn money!"

A combination of this military solidarity with a perceived (or experienced) rejection by the outside world resulted in a peculiar striving for self-enclosure among veterans. Used as a navigating tool in veterans' postwar life, military identity and military experience were projected onto business relations in the form of an idealized military fraternity. The solution to a permanent conflict between potential employers and ex-servicemen was found in the idea of a homogenized environment: a community of war veterans minding their own business. This business, however, had an odd character. Unlike the Afghan veterans, the UVC and similar organizations around the country could not build their organizational structures around institutional tax privileges anymore. Nor could they incorporate themselves as business companies: veterans' unions are registered as "societal" (*obshchestvennaia*), that is, nongovernmental, noncommercial civil organizations. Constrained by these factors, the UVC made persistent attempts to create an infrastructure around the distribution of welfare subsidies allocated in the local or federal budgets. In fact, the UVC performed the role of middleman between two state institutions. Using its own statistics, the UVC compiled lists of participants of the Chechen wars who needed some assistance and then submitted this information to the regional administration that controlled the budget. The administration transferred the money to local welfare offices, which actually handed out the cash according to the lists provided by the UVC. This circulation of documents and money secured for the UVC an important symbolic position, yet it hardly made the organization less dependent: the amount of subsidies and the timeliness of actual payments depended on the constant honing of relations with the local administration. Veterans' dependency on good relations with the administration was all the more important because all the subsidies and benefits came from the regional budget only.

As has been mentioned, the Chechen war veterans were not protected by the existing law on veterans. One important consequence of this situation was the fact that the federal government was not obliged (and has not been willing so far) to provide any special funding for demobilized soldiers. Instead, it recommended that regional governments take care of this issue. Given the generally poor economic condition of the region, I asked my informants where the funding for a limited set of benefits (mostly free transportation and reduced utility costs) was coming from. Viktor Z., responsible for financial issues of the union, explained the sinister economy of redistribution. As he put it, no additional money came from Moscow. However, every year the regional budget would receive from Moscow special funds to cover social payments to the Second World War veteran: "Say, in the beginning of the year there are twenty thousand world war veterans, and there is a corresponding amount of money. Yet, by the end of the year, the number of veterans will diminish.... Hence, we could redistribute among Chechen war vets the money that has not been paid out to those world war veterans" who died during the year.

This source, however, was unreliable and hardly renewable. Moreover, the overall circulation of money and documents, associated with redistribution of funding, did not bring any real funding to the organization itself. What the UVC tried to do in this context, then, was to create various "associate" business projects from which to fund its own budget. This entrepreneurial activity was not always successful. When I interviewed Shaul'skaia, she recalled how during the first years of Bratstvo's existence, the organization became a target of numerous shady offers. Having no business experience, she tried to steer Bratstvo away from commercialism and the corruption associated with it. "Still," as she put it, "Without knowing it, we've got ourselves into hard situations many times, and I had to do a lot to get [these guys] out of prison or to settle issues with the tax police. It was just a horror, a nightmare." In 1998, one year after Bratstvo's creation, seventeen veterans in Altai had been charged with criminal offenses, and another dozen were under investigation (Shaul'skaia 1999, 96). Oleg K., an active member of Bratstvo, recalled the same experience in a more restrained way: "We just tried to be entrepreneurial, without any understanding of how business is run; we got ourselves into a wrong spot and were burned a bit." When I asked him to clarify what this "wrong spot" was about, he reacted: "Business. We just built lots of debt. But it is all fine now."

Perhaps because of these earlier burnouts, the UVC eventually switched to less capital-intensive projects. As a result, its main economic activity was focused on small retail businesses. At the time of my interviews, the UVC owned several stalls located in the city's markets, "bazaar points" (*bazarnye tochki*), as Oleg described them. The stalls were perceived mostly as a modified form of real estate: income came as rental payments from actual sellers. This form of economic involvement allowed the UVC to stay away from issues of financial investment or the supplies of goods. It also produced a different form of occupation: veterans did not sell—they collected the rent.[51] The UVC's other project demonstrated a continuing connection with the afgantsy movement. In an interview with Oleg, who was in charge of the UVC's economic activity, I was told that "older brothers," afgantsy, "gave" (*dali*) the UVC a small fish smokehouse. I tried to clarify whether "giving" meant "leasing." No, Oleg insisted; it was not a lease: "They gave us a possibility to get up from our knees, a chance to accumulate some money."

Within this business and symbolic context, the veterans' idea about enterprises for "veterans only" seemed to be a plausible solution for an extended crisis.[52] I quote an excerpt from my conversation with two veterans, Vladimir V. and Grigorii B. Both actively work in the UVC and participated in the first Chechen war. Explaining the socioeconomic reasoning behind organizing enterprises for veterans, they said:

> VLADIMIR V.: We are trying to raise [*podniat'*] the economic activity [of the UVC], and it would be desirable if the power structures [authorities] would help us in doing this, because it is much easier for veterans to work with other veterans. Look, an average chief manager of a factory would never hire a veteran because he is afraid of him. But I would hire him right away. And there is a simple reason for this. If a veteran is my employee, I could pull very different levers to punish him when he confuses which shore to swim to, so to speak....I would have a moral right to reprimand him. Unlike this chief manager, who most likely is a civilian, with no army experience whatsoever, with no moral right to reprimand....
>
> GRIGORII B.: It is simple. Nobody knows us better than we ourselves. We need only half a word to understand each other. And usually, we don't let each other down, that's our upbringing [*vospitanie*]. And when we do

51. See Volkov (2002, 87) for a similar tendency among post-Soviet bandits to avoid any direct productive activity.
52. Jacklyn Cock in her study of South African ex-combatants indicates a similar trend: 87 percent of interviewed ex-soldiers strongly believe that the government must establish a job creation program that would be aimed specifically at them (2005, 796).

let people down, it is not our fault. If we organize our own working environment, it could help us to avoid situations when a boss would kick a veteran around.... We are trying to pick guys in such a way that in the end there would be a single wholeness. It is not a secret that our brother takes things too close to his heart. If someone on a street gives him a wrong look, he would "define" this person without saying a word.[53] And in principle, he has a moral right to this, even though it is wrong from a legal point of view.

These remarks reveal the clear impossibility of military economics to produce a necessary social effect. Creating a special working environment for young men cannot be justified by the logic of market competition. Instead, the possibility of social self-enclosure, the production of a special niche was constructed through a discourse on morality. It was not the short-term effectiveness of veterans' professional skills that mattered; what counted instead was the long-term preventive social effect that the enclosed environment could deliver.

This image of an enclosed working community brings back utopian fantasies of self-sustained and self-policing phalansteries. Yet what is striking about this particular attempt to create a business environment through military bonds is the underlying belief in the incommensurability of military and civilian experiences. The scope of exchange of sacrifices between the two worlds becomes extremely limited here, producing two parallel domains of value circulation. Like the Altai neocoms, veterans envisioned their own version of the regime of noncoverage that could recognize once and for all the inconvertibility of the values around which their community was built.

As the relationship between the veterans' "moral right" and the civilians' "legal point of view" spelled out by Grigorii B. demonstrates, this dissimilarity of values was also a hierarchy. Perhaps even more important was the discursive gesture by which this contradiction deepened. The supremacy of illegal-yet-moral right was defended, once again, by references to one's military experience—more precisely by references to one's performance of his civic duty.[54] What is crucial for understanding veterans' postwar identity

53. The veteran used the verb *opredeliat'*, which usually means "to define." Here the verb is used in its less common meaning—"to determine the limits," "to size up," but also "to confine."
54. Caroline Humphrey discusses a structurally similar practice of social differentiation among Soviet criminals, where the thieves' law, a set of strict rules of conduct, would bind the community of criminals together (*vory v zakone*) and simultaneously distinguish them morally from the official legal system, as well as from criminals who did not follow such rules (2002b, 103–6).

is the fact that their appeals to moral right had no content apart from patriotic experience. It was precisely the *origin* of this right that the formality of
the law failed to recognize or purposefully ignored.

"What If There Is a War Tomorrow?"

The veterans' rhetoric of a postcombat economy, with their emphasis
on completing the exchanges started between officers and the state, created
a discursive position outside the potentially charged political framings of
the Chechen war. Similar to the language of legality, analyzed by Jean and
John Comaroff, the language of exchange indicated a point of entry into the
field of interaction with the state by suggesting a (somewhat) nonconfron-
tational way of articulating one's social claims and entitlements (Comaroff
and Comaroff 2003a, 457). The limits of this war-as-a-business approach,
however, became very clear when the state refused to recognize its debts to
soldiers—that is, when soldiers' claims to being paid back were simply dismissed as irrelevant or inappropriate. Moreover, effective as it might be in
settling financial disputes, the language of the postcombat economy failed
to evoke signs of social respect, crucial in the post-Soviet situation where
the personal and the economic tend to be tightly intertwined.

The social impasse produced by metaphors of war as a business pushed
veterans to activate a different symbolic strategy in which militarized economics was complemented or overshadowed by patriotic values. In the following quote from my interview with Viktor Z., the financial persistently
echoed and emphasized the patriotic. Our conversation was about the goal
of the Chechen war. Without my prompting, Viktor immediately started
talking about combat payments: "Some people think it is all because of
money. But the amount of money that we get there cannot justify the fighting.... True, it is hard to survive without money. But you know there is a
line that I often recall: "Not for bucks or rubles did our guys fall here, but
in order to be able again to call you, Russia, the Great Rus [*Rus' velikaia*]'.[55]
Average conscripts [*srochniki*] like us, we all had in our subconscious that
we were doing it really for Russia. But I have no idea what the big shots
thought about this."

---

55. "Ne za baksy i rubli zdes' nashi parni polegli / A chtoby tebia, Rossiia, Rus'iu velikoi
zvali." Traditionally, *Rus'* is used either to refer to the first state of eastern Slavs in the ninth century (the Kievan Rus') or to denote the unified Russian state (the Great Rus') that was gradually
taking shape in the fifteenth and sixteenth centuries. In either case, *Rus'* tends to emphasize key
historical fights with outsiders in the process of creating a strong national state.

It is important to see how the initial split, bucks versus death for the Great Rus', was amplified by yet another form of differentiation: average soldiers versus big shots. Eventually these two juxtapositions would be reassembled and reconnected in a different configuration: "Big shots with bucks" would oppose the community of rank-and-file soldiers who "have paid to the Motherland" with blood and life, as another Chechen war veteran put it.[56] Exhibiting the same tendency toward self-enclosure discussed in previous chapters, this splitting once again justified social exclusions/inclusions, this time on moral grounds.

Sometimes, this striving for a close (and closed) community of shared values and experience would take veterans in unexpected directions. In several discussions, I was told that it was prison—or rather, the *zona*, a prison camp—that Chechen war veterans saw as the ultimate moral antidote to the lack of public respect and recognition, a place where veterans could be treated "normally." It was exactly in this social milieu, as Vladimir V. put it, that "veterans are appreciated accordingly." "It is a paradox, but somehow in the zones it is valued a lot that someone has defended his Motherland. Not in school, but in the zone! There is a clear attitude and understanding. These people [Chechen war veterans] fought a war, these are respectable people: they defended the Motherland! I have no idea where this patriotism is coming from. But [in the zones] they managed to preserve the patriotism that the civilians almost completely lost. We should set this as our benchmark."

In this implicit vindication of criminality through patriotism, the seemingly sudden juxtaposition of schools and prisons is jarring only at first. The two institutions, being perhaps the most vivid metonymies of the state, logically point to a third one that remained unmentioned: the army. The implied triangulation usefully outlines the closed circuit of a symbolic economy within which these institutions—along with prisoners of war—are involved and within which patriotism is actively promulgated. Respect for defenders of the motherland is associated with enclosed institutions of state power.

Significantly, attachment to one's country is construed here in terms of one's ability to endure traumatic hardship and the ordeals that this country offers. The hardship of the war experience not only becomes fundamentally formative and life-defining but also untranslatable. In their interviews, songs, diaries, and memoirs, veterans again and again point to the profound

---

56. For a discussion of military honor in the Russian army and its opposition to the "money-grabbing civilians" see von Hagen (1990, 333).

absence of any symbolic equivalent that could render their experience meaningful for outsiders. For instance, recently published notes from a war journal kept by the soldier Aleksandr Zhembrovskii in Chechnya are preceded by the following epigraph: "We found the most loyal friends here. People who have not been here, who never took a risk, would never understand us. Only mother, father, brother, and friend who went through Chechnya or Afghanistan, would understand us" (2003, 235). The experience and memory of war are used as a symbolic shield and a last refuge from the outsiders. As an Afghan war veteran put it in a response to an interviewer, "Just leave [the war] alone. It's ours!" (as quoted in Alexievich 1992, 14).[57]

This perception of an individual or group experience as incomprehensible to others—this adamant insistence on a hermeneutical enclosure of sorts—could be interpreted as yet another version of idealized collectivity. Reminiscent of the song "Statistics," the sociosymbolic cartography of zones (civil versus military, military versus education, education versus camps) helped to structure, classify, and homogenize the post-Soviet experience and environment. It isolated units (mother, brother, friend, big shot). It created connections among them. It rationalized social interactions (bucks, blood) or rediscovered forgotten continuities. Simultaneously emphasizing differences and similarities, this type of zoning pointed to a multiplicity of logics within a fragmented and therefore graspable universe. It also shifted the discursive production from forms of exchange to notions of identity and recognition.

In the remark quoted earlier, the spontaneous juxtaposition of the patriotically inclined zones versus unpatriotic schools was not merely a rhetorical or structural opposition. The reference to the pedagogical system also had a very practical underpinning, just like the veteran's allusion to prisons. Continuing a long-established tradition to appeal to the educational importance of the combat experience, local schools often ask Chechen war veterans to take part in various patriotic events. Traditionally, this participation amounts to veterans' public talks and informal conversations with students. What distinguished the UVC in that respect was a ramified system of so called military-patriotic clubs (*voenno-patrioticheskie kluby*) that veterans started creating in Barnaul after the first Chechen war. As of 2005 there were nine such clubs, each bringing together fifteen to thirty students. Usually, these clubs are based at local schools, relying on schools' gymnasiums as their primary space. The initial motivation for creating these clubs, as I was told by Kirill P., the leader of the "patriotic division" of the UVC,

57. On the impossibility of the secondhand comprehension of war see Hynes (1997, 1–2); for an opposite view see Tatum (2004, chap. 6).

had to do with veterans' conscious attempt to "pull kids from basements, to distract them from alcohol, drugs, and crime." Hence, not all members of a respective club come from the school that hosts a particular club. At times, the presence of "outside" kids with complicated biographies in someone else's school causes tensions between the school's teachers and the veterans. The tension is usually settled through a proven mechanism—reference to the veterans' army training and war experience. "I shame them into submission," Kirill explained.

What kind of alternative do these clubs provide then? How do Chechen war veterans envision the normal or even ideal educational/patriotic environment? By and large, the ordering and normalizing effect of this education is associated with the incorporation of a militarized structure of conduct. Clubs' activity normally includes assembling and disassembling Kalashnikov automatic rifles, shooting, hand-to-hand combat, body building, and games (basketball, volleyball, soccer). There is a strong symbolic component in this activity too. All cadets (*kursanty*), as they are called, are expected to memorize and recite on request the actual Rules of Army Conduct (*ustavy sluzhby*). All cadets know their respective place in the hierarchy, determined by a respective rank. Periodically, the UVC organizes boot camps in the nearby Altai mountains. In a long interview, Kirill described the most recent trip to the mountains:

> In the mountains, we rely on a two-volume *Encyclopedia of Survival.* I know, it might sound cruel, but everyone has to have this sort of lesson in life. Once, at 4:00 a.m. we woke up all the kids (between twelve and twenty years old) to do an endurance test. They did not manage to get up in forty-five sec, so we put them back, and did it again. Then I made them jog. It was raining, but I decided not to make any exceptions.... Three or four kilometers. They were all wet and I was telling them that if there was no steam coming from their bodies, it meant that they weren't running hard enough, and that they'd get sick. So, everyone ran. Girls cried, but ran, still. You have to be firm to make them interested, you have to be tough.... If they are interested, the percentage of drug users and drunks [among youngsters] would drop right away.

Fantasizing, the twenty-four-year old Kirill also told me about his two biggest dreams. Getting enough real Kalashnikovs was one of them. The veteran was going on, describing how these guns could be arranged nicely on a special ladderlike stand, how an armed cadet would be put on guard next to it; how cadets would get busy with cleaning and assembling rifles, each with a specially assigned number. Acting as an important sign of group belonging, the Kalashnikov was invested with some educational capacity as well. "When they handle these rifles, they become more responsible: it *is* a gun after all! This way, they take themselves more seriously, too." Kirill's second biggest dream was about getting enough uniforms for each cadet: army boots, sailor's vests, and camouflage suits.

For anyone familiar with Soviet history, there is very little new in these pedagogical fantasies of war-oriented patriotism. Similarly organized militarized communes and colonies, associated with the name of Anton Makarenko, a famous Soviet educator, were widespread in Soviet Russia in the 1920s and early 1930s. Back then a militarized daily routine and a strong emphasis on the uniform were used as a way of providing homeless, abandoned, and often criminal children with a definite performative backbone. The activity-driven self that emerged in these conditions, the flexible organism of Soviet modernity, was extremely effective in responding to the constantly changing sociopolitical environment. One's primary investment in the performative and the procedural (drills and routines) to a large extent allowed for staying away from the constant necessity of defining one's own location in ideological terms. In this context, the uniform, this socially accessible cultural layer, usefully gestured toward a recognizable subject position within the historically available field of relations (Oushakine 2004).[58]

Apart from some historical adjustment, the system of cadet training designed by Kirill P. was not that different from the "colonies" of the early Soviet period (cf. von Hagen 1990, chap. 7). Struck by this similarity, I asked if he knew anything about the pedagogical experiments of Makarenko. His answer was negative: "We just teach what we know, from our own experience." Rooted only in secondary school education and the army, this teaching amounts to the reproduction of the most clichéd forms of army life: regularized behavior in nonregular situations.

There was yet another resemblance between the two different historical situations that produced a similar form of social organization. Interested in understanding the specifics of the "patriotic" part in the "military-patriotic" name of clubs, I tried to get some explanations. The initial answer was quite formal: "The task is to love our Motherland [*Rodiny liubit'*]." I pressed further, asking him to elaborate. "The Motherland, as I understand it, is about one's own home, mother, relatives. What if something happens? Who is going to defend us? If you are a real man, you could just pick up an automatic rifle [*avtomat*], and would go to protect." The explanation quickly

---

58. See Theweleit (1989) for an analysis of a similar obsession with the body and the uniform among soldiers who participated in the suppression of the Communist insurrection of 1919–20 in Germany.

changed into a discussion about the legacy of the Chechen and Afghan wars. "We are not trying to impress upon cadets any specific view about Afghanistan or Chechnya. We just teach them how not to be afraid of the situation that we are in.... It is not easy. But who has an easy life today? And what if there is a war tomorrow?"

This structural dominance of the logic of siege is emblematic of the chechentsy movement in general. The impact of the war experience on veterans is obvious. What is unexpected, however, is the shift in emphasis in the process of reclaiming this experience *after* the war. As mentioned earlier, the war past was rarely turned into a starting point for an antiwar or war-preventing activity in the present, as was common in official Soviet pro-peace propaganda. Instead, it was the idea of being ready for a possible war, the perception of the region in danger that brought people together and organized them in their postwar life. It was in the process of this shift, as the quote indicates, that the task of loving the motherland was straightforwardly and unproblematically equated with the training of how not to be afraid of the current situation.

Phalansteries, boot camps, zones—these images of enclosed spaces, in which experiences are (forcefully) homogenized and values are shared—emerged as idealized forms of safe havens in my informants' comments. These regimented social and symbolic settings were envisioned as places where exchanges were completed and sacrifices did not remain unnoticed. As if mirroring the disengaged state, veterans discovered solutions of their problems in various forms of departure from the public sphere. In a reversed form, these militarized metaphors and practices of enclosed but understanding brotherhood provided striking illustrations of veterans' own notion of "exit-less-ness" (*bezyskhodnost'*): an experienced lack of entry into the world of the civilians was transformed into fantasies of a community of loss that walled itself off from the outsiders.

Ritualizing the Recognition of Loss

This book has described how similar communities were built around values of loss, which cannot be transposed into other symbolic regimes or moral accounts, and has suggested that such attempts point to a persistent lack of positive symbolic frameworks that could shape narratives about post-Soviet life. The local nature of these communities and the metonymic character of their self-presentations highlight an important aspect of postsocialist development: a collapse of the general social context (symbolic order) within which actions and identities used to make sense.

It is important to stress the formal aspect of this collapse: the downfall of socialist ideology in the 1990s cannot be limited to the disintegration of a particular value system. It also rendered meaningless the existing rituals of recognition. One's social status, social achievements, and social biography suddenly became ostensibly devoid of familiar prescriptive clues.

Perhaps most strikingly, the disintegration of established practices of signification and recognition manifested itself in the failure to come up with adequate categories for new types of experience. The post-Soviet uncertainty made the production of new typologies and classifications—that is, those symbolic hierarchies that could provide some structuring effect in the changing condition—especially hard. The ambiguous status of the Chechen war, coupled with the state's persistent attempts to keep the war within a closely regulated symbolic context, added to the post-Soviet uncertainty yet another layer. As a result, in the absence of normative frameworks or routinized practices for making the Chechen war personally and socially meaningful, both people and institutions tended to resort to the strikingly mechanical application of Soviet-style symbols.

At times, the symbolic impact of such reliance on Soviet signs could be chilling. For instance, a young Altai serviceman, severely wounded during the first Chechen war, described how in 1996, upon his return from Chechnya, the city's government issued an identification document to prove his entitlement to such benefits as free local transportation and reduced rent. The unclear legal status of the Chechen war, its participants, and victims, however, resulted in a category impasse: the ID listed the soldier as an "invalid of the Great Patriotic War [*Velikaia Otechestvennaia voina*], with a second-degree disability." Yet, as pointed out in chapter 1, the term "Great Patriotic War" is used in Russia to refer to the period of the Second World War from the moment of Germany's invasion in the USSR on June 22, 1941, until Victory Day on May 9, 1945. While being literally out of sync with reality, the use of this term by the local bureaucracy to describe the Chechen war veteran's status was by no means meaningless. From the economic point of view, this identity, granted by the state, equated the soldier with other generations of veterans entitled to welfare benefits. Inevitably, this accent on the formal and the procedural created a tension. As the veteran observed, "Some people give me a crazy look when I show this ID. Once in a while, [someone] will sneer: "So, how exactly did you manage to take part in [the Great Patriotic War]?" (*My zhdali vas* 1999, 31)[59]

59. The theme of misrecognition and misreading of the veterans' status and awards was originally shaped during the Afghan war. Soldiers' interviews, memoirs, poetry, and songs

The story brings to light the uneasy nature of recognition. Being the subject's fundamental need, recognition by others has a crucial "supplementary dimension"—reciprocity, as Jacques Lacan liked to point out (1991, 247). Reciprocity is not the same as mutuality here; rather, it is a commitment to the same set of imaginary positions from which one's particular location and one's particular experience can be seen, described, and thus acknowledged (1997, 51). Within this context, public indifference to the fate of Chechen war veterans (and to the signs of their presence) reveals a lack of a common vocabulary of public symbolism. To a large extent, this lack stems from veterans' own double symbolic strategy—namely, from their attempt to address simultaneously the state and the "outside community" by activating two contradictory discourses of postcombat economy and patriotic values. One example illustrates the point. Complaining about social indifference, the veteran told me,

> Today, a certain group of people is at war, defending the state. Meanwhile, here people burn down their lives in pubs, take drugs, and steal.... So the person who shed his blood, defending the Motherland (and all those who live here) comes home. What does he see? Not just a lack of respect. There is no understanding whatsoever. These people, who basically lived for two years in pubs and clubs, they could not possibly realize what this person has done; what he has done for them personally, too! And it is not a question of [soldiers'] benefits [*l'goty*]; we need to think how to start paying respect to people like him.

Sometimes veterans' complaints about the lack of respect for veterans bring the two blamed parties together, as in this remark by Igor K.: "There are no morals.... Practically, people have no morals, no education whatsoever. And where is it all coming from? From the state!... Because it is the state that organizes people."

Against this background of the incomplete exchange of sacrifices between the veterans and the state, as well as between the veterans and the audience, ex-combatants created a new sociosymbolic context by reclaiming

---

frequently contain bitter observations about people's blaming the veterans for being impostors, liars, or opportunists. Often in these texts, the clarity of the war experience is contrasted with the baffling nature of civilian life, as in an excerpt from the song "Ordena ne prodaiutsia" ("Awards Are Not for Sale") by the Afghan war veteran Yuri Slatov: "I was told by an old woman at a train station / "Shame on you, son! Don't start your life with a lie! / Put this medal away / Give it back to the one you have bought it from / You are so young, yet already lost all your conscience!" /.../ What could tell I her in response? / I have no strength to make excuses / Hiding medal with my arm / Protecting it from insult / I recall the Afghan sky.../ My transparent sky..." (as quoted in Smirnov 1990, 100).

and reappropriating the legacy of Russia's previous wars in their public rituals. The production and reproduction of ritualized actions—be they the songs or the militarized drills described earlier—had their own transformative effect. A gap between existing categories and daily practices often resulted in veterans' attempts to reestablish their control through "symbolic reformulations" and concerted rituals (Vygotsky and Luria 1994, 109–11; Comaroff 1985, 120).

As mentioned earlier, discursive fragging was one of the ways through which veterans tried to resume their control over language and narrative. Songs also provided them with a literary framework in which narrative continuity became possible. Ritualized performances of songs were often used as a way of joining and confirming *in public* previously isolated or even nonexistent forms of relations. As a result, the link between the Great Patriotic War and the Chechen war that seemed so strikingly out of place in the mid-1990s became the rhetorical norm ten years later. Images of suffering soldiers of the Second World War were unproblematically conflated with descriptions of veterans' experiences in the Chechen war. Such activation of the war trauma, foundational for Russia's national self-perception after the collapse of the USSR, generated instant sympathy. By appealing to the legacy of the Second World War, the current generation of veterans invoked memories of loss, experienced in 1941–45 almost by every family in Russia. Crucially, it was not the type or the purpose of a particular war that became acknowledged in this newly created ritual of recognition. Nor was it a victorious end that was celebrated. Rather, patriotic values were evoked as a particular state of emotions, as a repetition of a familiar configuration of painful events. For an example of this public remembering, let us return to an event discussed earlier—the commemoration of the tenth anniversary of the beginning on the Chechen war that was organized by NTV, a major Russian television network.

The event was broadcast on December 11, 2004, exactly ten years from the day when Boris Yeltsin signed a decree calling for the restoration of "constitutional legality" in the Chechen Republic. Staged in a big concert hall filled with veterans and their families, the event drew attention to the forgotten war, to the sad plight of hostages, soldiers, and their relatives. Personalized stories of officers and civilians and various award ceremonies were interspersed with performances of professional and amateur singers. Newly written songs about the war in Chechnya were supplemented by the active recycling of Soviet songs about the Great Patriotic War.

In the very end of the event, building up the emotional and symbolic coda, the two anchors of the ceremony tried to connect all historical dots in a linear narrative. As one of them put it, "The Great Patriotic War lasted four years; the war in Afghanistan—nine; the Chechen war just opened up its tenth-year page, and nobody knows how long this morbid book of war will last." The ceremony, then, made an unpredictable move. Addressing the audience, the presenter continued: "There are no victories in civil wars, yet all of you—those who are here today, and those who are not with us anymore—all of you, have won your own victory. Selflessly and loyally, you served your Fatherland, at a time when the Fatherland is not going through its best period." The second host of the event followed the theme and praised the soldiers in the room, emphasizing the fact that they had done everything they could to ensure that "our country would regain its previous dignity and grandeur" (*dostoinstvo i velichie*). The presenter concluded by personalizing the historical link between different generations: "Veterans of the Great Patriotic War are looking at you. Because only to you they could entrust the country that they have saved from Fascism, along with the banner of the Victory, which they carried throughout the Great Patriotic War from Ukraine to Germany. The banner that was raised on the top of the Imperial Chancellery in Berlin on May 2, 1945." The banner was carried in, accompanied by a guard of honor. Then followed a short video clip, spelling out historical parallels that might have been left unnoticed otherwise. Black-and-white images of Soviet cities and Berlin, destroyed during the Second World War, were seamlessly blended with images of the devastated Chechnya. The footage of the Russian flag raised in Chechnya was carefully preceded *and* echoed by archival shots of a Soviet flag, waving above the Reichstag in Berlin. The effect of the video narrative was amplified by the soundtrack, the song "Despite it all, we've won" ("I vse-taki my pobedili") from a late Soviet film about a veteran of the Great Patriotic War:

> Things weren't easy at the start; I won't lie about it.
> Tugboats sat silent on that shore
> On the shore where we were, too.
> We were abandoning our hometowns
> Leaving our souls to stay there forever.
> Despite it all, Despite it all
> Despite it all we have won.
> The scarlet snow was blackened by lost hats
> And lips became numb on the shore.
> On the shore, where we stayed
> Where we stayed back then.
> There was a Stalingrad behind every back
> There was no retreat from frozen trenches.

Despite it all, Despite it all
Despite it all we have won.
The salt of sweat discolored soldiers' shirts
That salt of return is like honey for us.
On the shore, on the shore
Where we stayed back then.
Regardless of how many of us are still alive
The voice of our dead buddies is here.
Despite it all, Despite it all
Despite it all we have won.[60]

Originally written in the early 1980s, this song about the Great Patriotic War provided back then a striking contrast to the state-supported canons of war representations. "Despite it all" lacked both the paralyzing melancholy so typical of Soviet war songs and the ostentatious self-glorification that dominated in the official epic version of the war during the Brezhnev period. Released during perestroika, the song suggested a different way of remembering the war: it downplayed its overall scale and focused instead on telling details. The overall fragmentation of the song's narrative emphasized the "order of urgency," not the logical consequences of the war experience.[61] Providing neither striking metaphors nor memorable images, it portrayed the war as an incoherent ensemble of everyday fragments of the war life, a disjointed collection of metonyms of loss, and a "confused story of confusion" (Hynes 1997, 153). Unlike some songs written during the war, it had no patriotic fervor. Nor did it exploit the usual theme of family ties, which was supposed to inspire the soldiers. Suggesting no clear and complete narrative, the song presented the victory as a broken-up story of individual perseverance, regardless of the surrounding circumstances. Anchored in multiple yet disjointed elements (tugboats, hats, lips, shirts), the war experience was, at the same time, disconnected from larger political and social aspects of the war.

In its post-Soviet incarnation, in the course of the commemorating event, the song was suddenly imbued with a different significance. Not only did it reduce—again—the war experience to the personalized ability not to give up, but it also endowed the post-Soviet disaster in Chechnya with some of the historical dignity of the victory in the Second World War ("one's own Stalingrad"). As a performative act, the song not only reminded the

---

60. "I vse-taki my pobedili," lyrics by Grigorii Pozhenian; music by Piotr Todorovskii.
61. On the order of urgency versus order of logic in survivors' narratives see Levi (1993, 9–10); for a discussion in a larger historical context see Tatum (2004, 2–3).

participants about shared values, experience, and relationships but enacted this commonality in a totally new context.

The fragmented perception of the Great Patriotic War offered in the song provided a frame of comparison but also a method of writing a new military history. In the post-Soviet situation, the avoidance of any overarching symbolic frameworks turned out to be quite appealing. The original deliberate escape from glorifying ideological clichés of the late Soviet period resulted in a peculiar form of military ahistoricism twenty years later. Songs about the Chechen war in a similar way would downplay overall context in order to highlight meaningful details. However, this metonymic remembering would be accompanied by a historically specific will to connect that linked similar fragments of dissimilar wars. Stringing different wars in a seamless line, songs would recontextualize military experiences in both the past and the present. More important, such songs would target a much larger audience. Building the Chechen war experience into the inherited narrative of war, this poetic activity somewhat broke down the existing public indifference toward the war and its veterans. Following is one example of this approach, although the trend could be easily extended.

The song "Everything Is Cool" ("Vse puteom," by Roman Bulgachev) is a part of the fourth volume of the CD series *Black Tulip*. The CD is dedicated to "those who have fought and who still fight, carrying out the Motherland's orders." Using the accompaniment mostly as background, Andrei Vasil'ev, a singer with a husky baritone, narrates (rather than sings) the story in which the same situation is repeated in three different geographical places at three different periods of time:

> Leaden snowstorms were finally over
> And the time of war was ended, too.
> Trains were running home from the West
> Spring in May excited every mind.
> Often, in a local neighborhood
> Brightened by the evening moon,
> Veterans commemorated those
> Who failed to return.
> Sitting at the table outside
> Slightly muted by a lack of noise
> "It's over," everybody thought
> And everything will be cool
> In our postwar country.
> Time is spinning quickly all its wheels

Time is setting pain and wounds apart.
The unusual word "Afghan"
Settles in our lives.
Carrying bitter scars in their souls
Foreign cities left behind,
Veterans commemorated those
Who failed to return.
Sitting at the table outside
Slightly muted by a lack of noise
"It's over," everybody thought
And everything will be cool.
In our postwar country.
Guys have not been born to look
At the world from their knees.
Dressed in a dusty T-shirt
Wearing soldier's boots,
The son of the soldier
Who took Kabul
The grandson of the soldier
Who took Berlin
How did you celebrate the New Century
In the burned-out Chechen land?
Sitting at the table outside
Slightly muted by a lack of noise
"It's over," everybody thought
And everything will be cool
In our postwar country. Everything seemed so cool.

In his discussion of the main difference between writing poetry and writing history, Reinhart Koselleck, a German historian, pointed to the long-standing tradition of juxtaposing the synchronicity of events in poetry and diachronic sequencing of events in history. Unlike a historian, who is concerned with the time-bound relationships and constellations of things, the poet "is able to cluster incidents as closely as he wishes" (Gotthold Ephraim Lessing as quoted in Koselleck 2004, 205). This logic of poetic clustering was certainly fully employed in the song, demonstrating how the postwar was never realized, how "a lack of noise" was always interrupted. The joining of different historical periods and locations, the constructing of an alternative chronotope—Grozny-Kabul-Berlin, West-East-Caucasus—produced a generational continuity. To be more precise, this joining of generations transformed the horizontal unity of brothers in arms into a vertical unity of ancestors. The symbolic rezoning of events and generations turned military brotherhood into a paradigmatic unit, a pillar that supports a newly written history. The double symbolic effect of this clustering not only allows for the domesticating of wars, for making them into a part of everyday life ("at the table, outside"). More important, it locates them on the same plane; continuity as repetition downplays crucial differences and emphasizes formal resemblances, the shared biographical contour ("Son of the soldier who took Kabul/Grandson of the soldier who took Berlin").

The genre of the war song became a major cultural device through which Chechen war veterans could reach a large audience by appealing to the commonality of loss in Russian society.[62] Performative and narrative at the same time, songs not only emerged as instruments used by yet another generation of veterans to inform their audience about a forgotten or marginalized war (Mosse 1990, 20) but also, and more important, as an invitation to join the act of narration. The social and sociological importance of this genre is hard to overestimate. Songs are indeed actions. They are performances in which people take part. From this point of view, songs, like any ritual, can be seen as a pattern of actions in which "shared concepts of relations…are affirmed, explored, and celebrated" (Small 2001, 346–47). Suffice it to mention that Bratstvo, the first organization of the Chechen war veterans in Barnaul, emerged precisely as the result of a festival of soldiers' songs (Shaul'skaia 1999, 95–96).

Emotionally charged, these songs about the brotherhood of men who have been able to sustain the continuity of their military profession do reach people who have not been necessarily affected by the Chechen war. In December 2002 in Barnaul I attended a concert of a vocal group, Slaviane (Slavs). The group is a frequent participant in events organized by the Altai Committee of Soldiers' Mothers and veterans of local wars; it also had a tour in Chechnya, giving concerts for policemen and military deployed there. Slaviane's show had a title: "Songs of Russian Squadrons" ("Pesni russkogo voinstva"). The six soloists, young men in their early twenties, all dressed in black, were accompanied by a full-fledged orchestra of "folk Russian

---

62. This generation of veterans was not the first one that tried to follow this path. Starting in the 1960s, Soviet soldiers participated in such military operations as the Arab-Israeli war (1967), the Soviet-led intervention in Czechoslovakia (1968), and the clash between the USSR and China over Damanskii Island (1969) and used the medium of the popular song to narrate the experiences, which were not otherwise represented by the press. During perestroika, the genre went through a revival: the politics of openness provided veterans of the Afghan war with unusually wide access to a large audience. For an extensive treatment of war songs in Russian culture see Lipatov (2006).

instruments," as the playbill explained it. Among a diverse assortment of war songs from different periods of Russia's history, the song "Officers" by Oleg Gazmanov was dedicated to participants of recent wars. During its performance, there was a clear emotional rapport between the singers and the audience. People started rising from their seats when Slaviane began the chorus line: "Officers, officers your hearts are a target / For Russia and freedom without end / Officers, Russians, let freedom shine / And make our hearts beat in unison." It was hard not to follow this collective emotional impulse; it was almost impossible to ignore it. By the middle of the song, there were four hundred or so people standing in the hall and silently looking—in unison—at the stage.

It is precisely this binding social power of publicly performed rituals that veterans appealed to in their attempts to get their message to different groups. Providing quotable symbolic formulas, songs frame discursive intonation and channel emotions. They reshape—however temporarily and locally—practices of perception and often result in signs of respect for the military. Limited in their effect by time and space, songs nonetheless offset established social hierarchies by pointing to possibilities that have not been realized or by negating those that have already been implemented.

We should not overestimate the impact of these (and other) rituals in reshaping the public attitude toward Chechen war veterans in particular and toward the war in Chechnya in general: the usual lifetime of these songs is quite short, and commemorative rituals are not yet routine. Yet through these microforms of symbolic recognition veterans have managed to achieve a public status that the state has denied them for a decade (figure 3.10).

These emerging public rituals were the very first successful attempts to break the silence and amnesia associated with the Chechen war. The breakthrough came with a price: new symbolic frameworks tend to be excessively sentimental; they are twisted in their chronology; they are dubious in their comparisons; and they are overstretched in their implications. Moving from one war to another, they flatten and militarize history. The choice of their symbols is restricted: from "our own apocalypses" to "one's own Stalingrad," from Berlin to Chechnya. Despite these drawbacks, this version of the patriotism of despair seems to be winning over a large audience, or at least it has been able to mobilize an expected emotional response from the audience that that seemed to have forgotten about the war in Chechnya.

THIS chapter has traced discursive moves, metaphorical tropes, and symbolic practices through which Chechen war veterans attempted to redefine

Fig. 3.10. "The voice of our fallen buddies is here." A grave monument to a Chechen war soldier. Barnaul, 2006. Photo by author.

their relations with state and society in Russia after returning from the war. It suggests that a combination of the symbolic legacy of the Soviet period and post-Soviet uncertainty resulted in a situation where the exchange of sacrifices emerged as an effective mediating tool between veterans' war experiences and their claims for recognition from the increasingly disengaged state. As the chapter pointed out, discourses on postcombat economics and patriotic values became dependent on the constant reproduction and reconstruction of militarized identities, on keeping the war alive. This cultivation of identity rooted in the war experience often led to practices of self-enclosure or hostile distancing from those who were unable to share memories of war. Simultaneously, this primacy of military identity resulted in attempts to rewrite the nation's history either as a chain of accidental military successes or as a succession of personal and societal traumas. This dominance of a traumatic narrative to describe the postwar life might be seen as a sign of the general state of the post-Soviet symbolic order: solidarity emerges in the process of sharing losses, and communities are built around practices of incorporating past suffering in the present.

4 Mothers, Objects, and Relations

Organized by Death

I am always telling everyone and everywhere: as long as the memory of our sons is alive, they are alive too. As soon as this memory is forgotten, they are dead in a real sense of this word. Today, there are people around who still remember them....And my life was devoted exactly to this....The war veterans call me "Mother Sveta," and I am proud of this. I think my life was not spent for nothing.
—SVETLANA PAVLUKOVA, Founder of the Altai Committee of the Soldiers' Mothers, Barnaul, 2002.

Memory is, achingly, the only relation we can have with the dead.
—SUSAN SONTAG, *Regarding the Pain of Others*

Communicating in sorrow is still communicating.
—ÉMILE DURKHEIM, *The Elementary Forms of the Religious Life*

"Today Our Family Got Bigger"

June 1 is a peculiar date in the Russian calendar. Throughout the Soviet period it was officially marked as International Children Protection Day (Mezhdunarodnyi den' zashchity detei). Not having a ritual or a symbol of its own, the day usually amounted to a stream of publications and video materials aimed at raising awareness about the problems of children around the world. The postsocialist history of this day has acquired more localized meanings. In Barnaul, June 1 also became a day to commemorate soldiers killed in military conflicts since the Second World War. This shift from protecting children to commemorating deaths of "children's protectors," as a local newspaper framed it, happened on June 1, 1991 (Dmitrienko 2004). On that day two regional organizations—the Union of the Afghan War Veterans and the Council of Mothers whose sons died in Afghanistan in 1979–89—opened a public memorial, which still remains the largest complex of its kind in the former Soviet Union.[1] Unlike similar memorial sites, the Altai complex is not limited to the traditional combination of

1. Initially, the official name of the mothers' organization was the Council of Mothers of Warriors-Internationalists Who Died in the Republic of Afghanistan (Sovet materei pogibshikh

Fig. 4.1. Metal plaque with names of Altai soldiers who died in the Afghan war. Barnaul, 2006. Photo by author.

a monument and the eternal flame. In Barnaul, the memorial also includes the Regional Museum and Archive of Military History, as well as the headquarters of the veterans' union and the mothers' committee. The central wall in the building's courtyard is covered with a large metal plaque that lists the names of 144 Altai soldiers who died during the Soviet military invasion in Afghanistan. Below the plaque there is a stone of remembrance brought by war veterans from Afghanistan to symbolize their link with the country in which they fought.[2] Located in the very center of the city, the memorial was originally dedicated to "perished warriors-internationalists" (figure 4.1).

---

voinov-internatsionalistov v Respublike Afganistan); it was changed later to the Committee of Soldiers' Mothers.

2. See Mosse (1990, 83) for an exploration of the historical link between the stone of remembrance and the altar.

The "international" component of the dedication reflected the political terminology of the time: in the 1980s the presence of Soviet troops in Afghanistan was officially billed as a form of Soviet "international help" to Afghanistan's people and government.[3] The symbolism of the memorial was gradually evolving throughout the 1990s, yet from the very beginning, the place was devoid of ostensibly Soviet imagery. Instead, religious representations were much more prominent: a wrought-iron silhouette of the Orthodox dome above the courtyard provided the public space with a Christian undertone (figure 4.2). The martyrdom connotation of the setting was additionally emphasized by the pavement, which had the color of spilled blood.

Five years later, on June 1, 1996, yet another public ceremony commemorated deaths of children's protectors. The memorial complex was about to change its name: the list of warriors-internationalists who had died in Afghanistan was supplemented by the names of soldiers from Altai who were killed in Chechnya, Tajikistan, Moldova, or Abkhazia in what became known as "local wars" of the 1990s. Many people gathered in the city's main square in front of a big screen on which an image of Russian churches was crossed by the line "Hello, Mother!" (*Zdravstvyi, mama!*). War songs from loudspeakers were soon interrupted by the noise of an arriving armed personnel carrier. The city's officials, veterans, and mothers would use it later as an improvised stage (figure 4.3).

Speeches about fallen soldiers were interspersed with veterans' songs and poems about their military brotherhood and lost comrades. Yet there were clear differences between the ways in which local officials and representatives of the mothers' council framed these tragic losses in their speeches. Nikolai Shuoba, a veteran of the Afghan war appointed by President Yeltsin as his permanent envoy in the region, urged people to refrain from quick and simple conclusions about the reasons for the new deaths. As the veteran put it, "Let's stay away today from political evaluations. We are here to express our humane attitude to what these soldiers did.... There might be different political opinions [about the conflicts] but we have done here everything we could... to commemorate the people [who died]."

Following Shuoba, Svetlana Pavlukova, the head and founder of the Altai Committee of Soldiers' Mothers, whose own son had died in Afghanistan, refrained from making a political statement in a less direct way. "Today

3. Unclassified documents of the Politburo indicate that from the very beginning of the invasion, the Soviet government was particularly conscious about using the language of "help" and "assistance" to frame the war. See the Politburo's decision "On the propagandist framing of our action in respect to Afghanistan" (Odnokolenko 1992, 4).

Fig. 4.2. Memorial to Fallen Soldiers of Local Wars. Barnaul, 2004. Photo by author.

our big family got bigger. In addition to the four thousands boys who fought in Afghanistan and the 144 families who lost their sons there, we now have soldiers who fought or died in Chechnya; 76 people who were killed and about 2,000 of those who came back."[4] She then unveiled several memorial plaques with the names of fallen soldiers. A thoroughly scripted

---

4. I quote Shuoba and Pavlukova from the amateur video chronicle of the event that I obtained during my fieldwork.

Fig. 4.3. "Today our big family got bigger." Meeting of commemoration in Barnaul. June 1, 1996. A still from a video.

and choreographed event quickly changed into an unruly scene of despair, wailing, and tears. Parents and veterans rushed to the wall plaques; several aggrieved parents stroked metal letters that made up their sons' names. A few women tried to attach candles and flowers to the names. Everybody wept, but even through this sobbing one could still hear the piercing cry of a mother who demanded that her husband get closer to their son's name and kiss "the son," as she put it. The wailing gradually calmed down with the appearance of a local orthodox priest who performed a religious service. By the time the priest's meditative prayers were replaced by fireworks and a concert by a nationally famous rock band, the public event seemed to be back to its script.

Military losses such as these, while certainly not a new phenomenon in Russia, acquired a somewhat unusual dimension after the collapse of the Soviet Union. Caused by state-sponsored violence, the deaths of soldiers in hidden and forgotten wars, as well as in the army in general, were ostensibly devoid of the justifying ideological context that was so prominent, for example, in public representations of the losses of the Second World War

(Tumarkin 1994; Schleifman 2001). The absence of an authoritative interpretation of the consequences of state military politics produced an uncommon cultural and political situation. The task of cultural "enframing" and "emplotment," which could render soldiers' deaths socially and personally meaningful, was actively taken up by the mothers themselves.[5] Their striving for public recognition of their losses and their own identities often resulted in a complicated ethical situation: attempts at assigning a wider social meaning to their traumas became fundamentally entangled with a public rationalization of the state's military politics (Danilova 2004).

Previous chapters outlined the different forms of the patriotism of despair that emerged around imagined or experienced loss. They traced how the fragmentation of Soviet networks and the radical transformation of state institutions in the 1990s forced people to search for graspable meanings that could be attached to confusing and dislocating changes. A few of my informants attempted to reformat Soviet history by splitting off its unpleasant or problematic parts ("History already loves you"). Some preferred to frame Russia's development as an example of ethnic demise ("Russian tragedy") or as a painful process of rediscovering the true sources of the Russian nation's vitality. The same search for explanation pushed other groups to produce conspiracy narratives able to link incoherent facts and incompatible processes into sufficiently general theories of governance. Yet others established new rituals of recognition and sociosymbolic exchange in order to create relations of reciprocity and feelings of connectedness, which they had lacked. In all these cases, a traumatic experience became generative. Wounds originated stories, identities, and communities. The feeling of personal or collective loss was transformed into the main integrative principle around which the "social edifice" was built, as Slavoj Žižek put it. Lack became positivized (Žižek 2001, 149, 143; Huyssen 2003, 49–71).

A particular "work of the negative" (Green 1999) described in this chapter highlights yet another form of the patriotism of despair. Pavlukova's appeal to the symbolism of family ties, quoted earlier, was not unusual. Indeed, among Afghan and Chechen veterans Pavlukova herself is often referred to as "Mama." During my fieldwork I also observed how the activists associated with the Altai Committee of Soldiers Mothers (CSM) in their conversations and public presentations routinely addressed soldiers and conscripts as "little sons" (*synki*). It was also common for the committee's staff to use the informal and domestic terms *mamochki* or *mamashi*

---

5. On the structuring role of "enframing" and "emplotment" in narrative production, see Heidegger (1969, 19–23) and White (1973, 5–11), respectively.

(mummies, moms), rather than actual names, when talking to the women who came for consultation. The following discussion examines the Altai mothers' tendency to "domesticate" the field of social relations and explores how these women dealt with political traumas in a situation when public opinion about the causes that led to these traumas was ambiguous if not polarizing. Rather than describing this "familiarization" of social relations as a gendered reflection of the increasing political apathy in Russia's provinces (Yanov 2003; Levada 2003), the chapter considers the Altai mothers' practices of enactive mourning as a historical example of the "politics of pity" (Boltanski 1999, 3). That is to say, they provide an example of a use of affect through which a community of loss could be organized, sustained, and publicly represented. This affective economy to a large extent became possible because of a particular form of material production. By marking their losses with a series of artifacts, the Altai mothers produced a network of "transitional objects" that firmly linked memories of the past with mourning practices in the present and imaginary pictures of the future. Metonymies of death, these newly created objects could never fully represent the mothers' trauma, yet they were instrumental in demarcating its presence in public and private spaces.

In 2001–2, I interviewed a group of activists associated with the Altai Committee of Soldiers' Mothers; I observed their interaction with conscripts and their parents. I read their documents. In addition to the transcripts of my conversations with these women, in this chapter I also use a set of letters that I discovered in the archive of the Museum of Local Wars. The set includes about two hundred letters, which soldiers' mothers sent to Svetlana Pavlukova from 1990 to 2000. In 2000, Pavlukova deposited them in the archive; crammed into two plastic bags, they sat there for about two years, frequented by mice. Besides written and oral documents, I rely on several amateur videos that I collected during my fieldwork. Videos range from 1991 to 2000 and document various memorial and funeral rituals organized by the Altai mothers.

By using these diverse materials, I trace how grief and pain shaped personal narratives, created social networks, and modified public landscapes in post-Soviet Altai. I analyze practices and rituals through which these women redefined public space and objectified their experience by inscribing signs of their sons' deaths into civic and quasi-religious settings. My study of sensory inscriptions of loss documents a situation in which the traditional "trajectory of historical redress, therapeusis, and completion" (Feldman 2004, 166) failed to deliver its curative effect. For most of the 1990s, tropes of martyrdom, human rights frameworks, practices of political activism, and healing scenarios of trauma studies were largely neglected or perceived as inapplicable for framing deaths caused by the Russian state's military politics. In this context, the discourse on family ties and family-related identities appeared an effective way of claiming publicly recognizable positions for women whose traumatic experience had been neglected, dismissed, or forgotten.

Organized by Death

As with many other nongovernmental organizations, the national CSM emerged during perestroika.[6] From its very beginning, the CSM, an umbrella association that now includes about three hundred local branches across the country, was concerned with the secrecy that accompanied losses of soldiers drafted for the war in Afghanistan. The Soviet government did not disclose information about casualties, and some soldiers' graves from the 1980s still bear the trace of this secrecy even today. Using the typical euphemism, grave monuments proclaim that soldiers "died while fulfilling international duty (pogib pri ispolnenii internatsional'nogo dolga)" (figure 4.4). In response to social indifference and to the state's politics of nonrecognition, the committees built their practices of solidarity around issues of death. As the slogan of the Moscow-based legal organization Mother's Right (Pravo materi) phrases it, "Information about dead sons unites their parents."

The link between information and death is crucial here. Unknown causes of soldiers' deaths were only part of the problem. Sometimes a lack of basic information was aggravated by the mothers' protracted fights with the military authorities over the identification of dead bodies. Beginning with the Afghan war, a new funeral ritual emerged: distrusting the officials, parents started insisting on opening zinc coffins upon their arrival. In some cases, the "cargo 200"—as zinc coffins became known in bureaucratic language—contained the wrong bodies. In others, coffins had no bodies at all, just rocks or earth. Rare as they were, these grim cases were well remembered by parents. Yet such incidents did not always reflect a deliberate attempt of army officials to mislead the parents. War veterans explained to me that sometimes a massive explosion followed by a fire could leave very few, if any, remains. In such situations, rocks put in the coffin were a clumsy attempt to

6. Literature on Committees of Soldiers' Mothers is quickly growing. For the English-language studies see Caiazza (2002, 123–46); Sperling (2003); and Hemment (2004).

Fig. 4.4. The grave of a soldier who "died while performing international duty." Barnaul, 2006. Photo by author.

avoid the uneasy task of explaining the details of the body's destruction by creating the appearance of its presence in the coffin (figure 4.5).

Occasionally the committee was able to help mothers with finding or identifying the bodies of their sons. More often, the CSM provided an outlet for articulating mothers' concern and disgust: in their public appeals and open letters, the CSM's branches demanded that state authorities punish those army officers who had ordered that soldiers' relatives be sent coffins "with the wrong bodies or stones," as one mother reported (Tarasova 1991, SPPF).[7]

The overall political context also had an impact on the prominence of death in the mothers' activity: by and large the mothers expressed a strong

7. Unless noted otherwise, all letters that I quote here come from the Altai State Museum of Local History (Altaiskii Gosudarstvennyi Kraevedcheskii Muzei, AGKM), the Svetlana Pavlukova Papers Fond (Barnaul, Russia). Letters were not cataloged; some of them were not signed or dated. Therefore, when citing these documents, I indicate whenever possible the author's name, the year the letter was sent, and the abbreviation of the archive that holds these letters (SPPF).

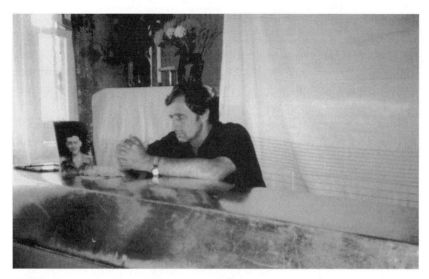

Fig. 4.5. Father at a zinc coffin holding the body of his son who died in Chechnya. 1995. AGKM, OF. 168121/3, F.-6466. Courtesy of the Altai Museum of Military History, Barnaul.

resistance toward the changing framing of the Soviet invasion in Afghanistan. The Soviet interpretation of the war as an example of "international duty" had been completely discarded by the end of the 1980s. Instead, the invasion was seen as a "grave error" of the irresponsible government. Very few wanted to admit that their sons had become victims of "a political mistake" (Alexievich 1992, 78). Many parents of fallen soldiers perceived this change of meaning as a personal insult. As a result, a new cult of the dead, an active construction of new commemorative rituals, sites, and symbols became the main way through which the mothers could reinscribe their losses in the changing social and symbolic environment. One of these mothers succinctly summarized the connection between the memorialization and the perceived disgracing of their lost sons. She wrote to Pavlukova in 1991, "I think the most important legacy that we could leave behind is the Memory of our children. It is the memory of the glaring misdeed [*zlodeianie*] that they were subjected to. Maybe sometime in the future people will sort everything out about this war. Right now, everything is covered with dirt, dirt, dirt [*griaz'*]" (Inna L., 1991, SPPF). Even in 2000, one of the soldiers' mothers bitterly complained to a Moscow newspaper, "Our sons performed their duty [in Afghanistan] with dignity," but the state "besmirched" (*oporochilo*) them, when it proclaimed this war a mistake (Tuchkova 2000, 13). One important consequence of this failed battle against the new interpretation of the Afghan war was the mothers' attempt to depoliticize it altogether. In the process of the incessant multiplication of memorial sites, the mothers displaced the traditional Russian search for the culprit by commemorating practices: the question "Who is to blame?" was overshadowed by the question "How do we remember?"

The CSM's memorializing activity should be kept in perspective, though. As I found out during my fieldwork, there seemed to be a clear distinction between the types of activities performed by the CSM's offices located in large industrial centers and those carried out by the CSM's chapters working in the provinces. The preoccupation with monuments, eternal flames, and elaborate mourning rituals was largely typical for remote regions. For the CSM's most active offices located in Moscow and St. Petersburg, the memorializing activity was not their main priority at all. Instead, in the early 1990s, these offices were very effective in finding information about missing soldiers. The mothers helped to rescue soldiers held captive by the Afghan military. The committee constantly defended hazed conscripts who deserted from their divisions. When the Chechen war began in 1994, the CSM's leadership took an active antiwar position, demanding that the government withdraw Russian troops from Chechnya and threatening to completely disrupt the annual conscription campaign. As in the previous war, the CSM again helped to find lost soldiers, this time in the North Caucasus. A few mothers came to Grozny and even conducted direct negotiations with the Chechen rebels (Pyasetskaya and Brander, 1998). They also organized demonstrations and marches against state military politics in Chechnya. Several local offices associated with the mothers' movement were able to translate issues of state-organized violence into terms of political and financial responsibility. For example, in 2004 lawyers of the Moscow-based foundation A Mother's Right took part in 130 trials around the country, seeking financial compensation for families who had lost their sons in the army ("Otchet o deiatel'nosti" 2004).

It is precisely this combination of a critical political stance with the experienced use of legal instruments that has become emblematic for the CSM movement in Russia and abroad (Hemment 2004). For this humanitarian activity the national CSM was nominated for the Nobel Peace Prize. The CSM's vocal position got these women into trouble, too. The group's increasing independence (and its support from abroad) was grudgingly accepted by military and state officials. Yet in their public comments, officials persistently emphasized the excessive emotionality and, by implication, the irrationality of the mothers' claims and demands. As some military officers insisted, military issues should be approached *s umom i serdtsem*, not just with the heart but also with the mind (Biletskii 1996, 3). Army officers also liked to point out that the CSM's interests were fully in sync with the army's own concerns: both mothers and generals wanted to take care of the soldiers (*khlopochut za soldat*); both wanted to abolish mandatory conscription and switch to a professional army; both wanted to get rid of hazing and humiliation in the army. The difference—as the official newspaper of the Ministry of Defense, *Krasnaia Zvezda*, put it in 1995—was that the army commanders just did not have enough resources to "meet all these needs" (Popov 1995, 4).

The CSM's strong antiwar position in the mid-1990s produced a set of counterarguments that became a mandatory component of the state's reaction to the mothers' movement. Military officers' articles and interviews repeatedly voiced their suspicion about the CSM's "real" intentions. In their own way, officials followed the widespread tendency of the time to see any post-Soviet public activity as manipulated and/or corrupt. For example, only two months after the humanitarian disaster in the December 1994 storming of Grozny, two lieutenant colonels wrote in *Krasnaia zvezda*:

> Somebody uses mothers' tears to gain political capital....Their grief [*beda*] has been made into an idée fixe [*vozveli v ideiu*], which is used as a banner of the crusade against "the criminal generals." When these "crusaders" urge soldiers' mothers to come to Grozny...they do not fathom [*ne vnikaiut*] how a soldier's mother from Vladivostok could find money to get to Chechnya. How could she get there? Would she be able to get there safe and healthy at all?...they just sent these mothers forward. So that later these crusaders could go to the West...and lecture about human rights. (Popov and Stasovskii 1995, 4)

The names of the "crusaders" were not revealed in this article, yet their pro-Western leaning (or even Western origin) was clearly demarcated. By the end of the 1990s, this effort to present the CSM as an icon of foreign influence only strengthened. Officials questioned the sources of funding that provided the CSM with relative independence from the state, unusual in the cash-strapped Russia of the 1990s. In 2004–2005, when the Putin government started a strict policy of monitoring the financial activity of nongovernmental organizations, the level of attention to possible links between foreign money and soldiers' mothers became especially high. The development reached its highest point in 2004, when Viktor Alksnis, a Communist deputy of the Russian parliament, officially requested the prosecutor general and Ministry of Justice to investigate the CSM's activity. As

Alksnis (2004) explained it, "My request has to do with the fact that for more than ten years we have had a very active organization that is funded by the West.... Given that this organization conducts an active antiarmy campaign, I have all reasons to believe that this organization carries out political orders of those who fund it.... These women have no relation to soldiers' mothers whatsoever; these women are professional politicians, who work for money; who have hundreds of offices around Russia; and who are very effective in spreading their propaganda around."

Alksnis's representation of the mothers' movement exaggerated the dominant attitude of state institutions toward the CSM only to some extent. These exaggerations, however, did preserve the general discursive logic that shaped this attitude. As the quoted excerpt demonstrates, the mothers' attempts to frame their work as a direct reflection of their maternal responsibilities were dismissed as a rhetorical ploy. Then their collective identity was narrowed down, politicized, and read through a patriotic lens: the committee's antiarmy critique was interpreted as anti-Russian and therefore pro-Western" (and, at times, pro-Chechen). Political activity was understood here almost exclusively as a set of relations between the state and a collective or individual subject. The very idea that politics could also be extended to personal and group attempts to negotiate their own interest outside the state's immediate control was totally dismissed. Politics without the state was seen as an antistate politics.

Mothers' Politics of Survival

Originally, my own views about the CSM were entirely formed by the Russian mass media and Western academic writings. When I started my fieldwork in Barnaul in 2001, I expected to see the much described protest and antiwar activity spearheaded by the local committee. I anticipated meeting the mobilized group of women who were willing and able to question the state's military disaster in Chechnya. This never happened.

The first local chapter of the federal CSM was organized in Barnaul in 1989, when Svetlana Pavlukova, a waitress from a local hospital, started bringing together mothers who had lost their sons in Afghanistan. In the late 1980s, Pavlukova's two sons were drafted into the army to participate in the Soviet invasion. In 1988 one son was killed in combat and was awarded posthumously the medal of Hero of the Soviet Union, the highest military distinction available in the Soviet Union. The death of the son was neither hidden nor ignored, and perhaps because of this fact, issues of commemoration became more important for Pavlukova than issues of justice.

In 1991, yet another chapter of the committee was founded in Barnaul, in this case by mothers whose conscripted sons had died because of hazing and abuse in army (*neustavnye otnosheniia*). Eventually this chapter became a part of the unified Altai committee, but it remained socially and geographically distinctive. Needless to say, the picture of the cash-abundant NGO painted by Alksnis and some mass media outlets was far from reality too. Both committee branches in Barnaul had very modest working environments. Pavlukova's office was hosted (and paid for) by the Afghan war veterans' organization. The other chapter occupied two small rooms in a rundown concrete structure. When I interviewed women who worked there, their major concern was the threat of their local utility company to cut off electricity for unpaid bills. None of the offices had a computer (or people who were comfortable with working on it). All the correspondence with parents and army officials was done by hand; the use of the old typewriter was reserved for especially important occasions. The notions of the Internet and grants were virtually unknown to these women.

Unlike their more politically driven colleagues in other CSM branches around the country (see Popkova 2004), the Altai CSM never translated soldiers' deaths into a language of political responsibility and legal compensation. The Altai committee had not initiated a single court case throughout its history. Having neither a professional lawyer, psychologist, nor social worker among its staff members, the CSM mostly sustained its activity by relying on volunteer mothers. Both chapters were concerned primarily with commemorating dead soldiers, assisting their families, and providing consultations to potential conscripts. Issues of memory and mourning became the dominant organizing principle for the mothers' activities. The memorial that was opened to the public in 1991 was followed in 1992 by the book *Sons of Altai* (known as the "Memory Book"), which contained the photos and biographies of all Altai soldiers killed in Afghanistan. In 1994, the committee organized a reburial of soldiers and consolidated all the remains in a specially allocated section of a local cemetery. In the second half of the 1990s, with the Chechen war in progress, the situation was repeated. In 1996, the CSM unveiled memorial plaques with names of Altai soldiers who had died in military conflict in the Caucasus and Central Asia. In 1999, Altai mothers published a new book of obituaries for the Altai troops killed in Chechnya. Between 2001 and 2006 the committee and the local museum of war history were busy compiling a new edition of the obituary books—for all the soldiers who died while in the army. The strong tendency toward preserving the memory of deceased sons could be traced on the individual level, too: in their letters, the majority of mothers wrote about their successful or failed attempts to properly "perpetuate their sons," as they put it.[8]

In the midst of this memorializing activity, the Chechen war was not quite forgotten in Barnaul. But as Olga K., one of the leaders, told me, in the mid-1990s the Altai CSM deliberately decided to "help soldiers" instead of actively "sabotaging" the government's war policy. The Altai mothers did provide help, collecting money, food, and clothes donations for the army. They even raised enough resources to buy a circular saw and several truck-loads of lumber to make soldiers' life in Chechnya a bit easier. The mothers also offered consultations to war veterans after their return from Chechnya. They just stopped questioning the very reasons that made their work neces-sary. Survival was viewed "in relation to death itself, not in relation to dying for something" (Koselleck 2002, 312).

Alksnis's vitriolic and highly politicized campaign against the committee helps to explain why the Altai mothers preferred to avoid taking a clearly marked political position. There was an additional reason for their reluc-tance. Ironically, as suggested by Alksnis's comments, it had to do with money. By law, parents of soldiers who died while in service are entitled to financial benefits from the state. For instance, mothers over fifty years old and fathers over fifty-five can receive additional early retirement benefits.[9] Retired parents or otherwise dependent relatives (siblings, grandparents) also can apply for a pension to compensate for the loss of the provider. Depending on the local legislature, families of dead soldiers can be granted discounted medical prescriptions and a 50 percent cost reduction for tele-phone and state-provided utilities (gas, water, and electricity). The benefits were stipulated by law, yet very few parents knew about them. The commit-tee discovered this situation rather inadvertently. In 1990, Pavlukova started compiling the book of obituaries for soldiers who died in Afghanistan; she contacted soldiers' parents, asking them to provide stories and photographs. Along with collecting this information, she also inquired whether parents were getting any financial compensation for the sons they lost. It turned out that only a few families did. As a result, the Altai CSM started instructing parents about their rights.

The situation has been changing very slowly, though. Almost a decade later, the branch of the Altai committee that deals with non-war-related

---

8. In their interviews and letters, the mothers routinely described their memorializing activi-ty by the Russian word *uvekovechit'* (from *vek,* century), which literally means to memorialize forever, to perpetuate.

9. Usually the retirement age for women is fifty-five, for men, sixty.

deaths in the army decided to publish a similar book of obituaries for soldiers. As Pavlukova had done earlier, the committee included in its letters, along with a request for soldiers' photos and biographies, a questionnaire about parents' pensions and compensations. I quote one of the common responses: "Dear women from the committee of soldiers' mothers. You asked me if I receive any benefits or pension for my son who died in the army. But you are the first people who told me that I could have any benefits. My son has been dead for more than fourteen years already, and nobody ever told me that I could apply for any support" (Serdiuk 2000, SPPF).

Things were not easier when parents did learn about their rights and entitlements. Impoverished local budgets, combined with the severe liquidity crisis of the 1990s, radically limited local administrations' abilities to pay even regular salaries and pensions, let alone to cover unpredictable expenses caused by casualties in the army. This dire financial condition became one of the main topics of the mothers' exchanges in the 1990s, linking the loss of sons, the disengaging state, and the loss of their own economic security together. A mother wrote to Pavlukova on Christmas Eve 1998, "Svetlana, we have not been paid our pensions for five months in a row. Why? I do not know. They say on TV that money has arrived. But where did it arrive to? Who knows. What are we to do? What about you? Do you get your pension every month or not? And who is responsible for all this? Can you find out?...Do you get any food packages? With a discount? If you live like us, when everything must be paid in full, it must be really hard. They killed off our children, and now they want to starve us to death. It was fine when pensions were paid every month; now it is just hell" (Biletnikova 1998, SPPF).

This overall poverty was crucial for the mothers' painful recognition of their own dependency on the state. But perhaps even more frustrating was their experience of the state's nontransparency, when the authorities purposely would not disclose parents' legal entitlements or when they would withhold parents' pensions without explanation. A mother whose son died in Chechnya explains, "It took such a long time to find out what I was supposed to get that I even became ashamed of myself. Everybody was telling me that I was supposed to get nothing. It was painful, and it hurt the memory of my son; we are not used to complaining, or demanding something for ourselves" (M. Kolesnik 2000, SPPF).

The key role of the regional and district administrations in providing (or withholding) subsidies to the mothers was not entirely new in Altai. Given the region's poor economic condition, the power of local authorities was traditionally rooted in their ability to distribute welfare funding that came from Moscow. What post-Soviet economic changes added to this was

a high degree of arbitrariness with which local administrations would conduct their politics of redistribution. Pressed by various groups and strapped
by limited budgets, local politicians were extremely selective and divisive
in their treatment of mothers. Thus, all the mothers I interviewed in Barnaul were keenly aware of the social "category" to which they belonged.
A mother whose sons died in Afghanistan and Chechnya was provided by
local administrations with an additional 100 rubles per month ($3 in 2001)
and a fixed monthly food package, which was sometimes supplemented by
such seasonal supplies as cabbage, poultry, flour, or oil.[10] Mothers whose
sons died because of accident or hazing received nothing. In an interview,
Tatiana M., an active member of the committee raised the question for
which many mothers still do not have an answer: "What difference does it
make where the soldier died? We all sent our sons to the army in the same
way. Kids are all the same. Mothers are the same, too. Why does it matter
that one soldier died on the battlefield and the other in the barracks?"

The significance of these subsidies should not be misread. The mothers
had no illusions that a hundred-ruble payment or an extra can of vegetable
oil could make much of a difference in their lives. What they did make clear
in their interviews was the fact that these material objects were indeed read
as an authoritative gesture of their social recognition. The mothers' affective
reading of signs of respect significantly changed their own self-perception.
The public attention they received (or the lack of it) was construed as a
symbol of commemoration of the lost soldiers, as if the mothers became
living representations of their dead sons. To a large extent, the mothers'
unwillingness to question the Russian state's military and social politics was
determined by their awareness of the fact that state authorities were often
the only institution that endowed them with a socially meaningful public
identity. Nadezhda S., whose son was killed in the army by his fellow soldiers, described it to me in the following way: "When on March 8 [Inter-
national Women's Day], the authorities give a flower to a mother, it means
a lot for the soul with many wounds [*izranennaia dusha*], you know....Not
the gift itself but the attention. The fact that they still remember her son.
And herself, too. Some mothers get this regularly. They are surrounded by

---

10. Documents from the regional archive of the Communist Party (AGKA) specify how a
monthly food package looked in the early 1990s in Barnaul. From the late 1980s to the early
1990s, an average food package for war veterans (or their parents) included one kilo of smoked
sausage, one chicken (of the "first category of quality"), two jars of canned meat, one jar of
canned fish, 200 grams of tea, 600 grams of hard candies, and one kilo of butter (AGKA, F. 1,
Op. 158, D. 110, L. 104).

attention from the regional administration. As far as we go ... we are on our own pretty much."[11]

These appeals to justice validated by death illustrate the mothers' remarkable insistence on equality understood as sameness. Granted, these appeals were not entirely universal, and I will discuss later the mothers' own attempt to differentiate among various degrees of grief. Distinctive features of the mothers' losses were not quite discarded here, but they were radically pushed aside. Unlike the Chechen war veterans who persistently stressed the untranslatability of the war experience that forever had set them apart from the world of civilians, the Altai mothers approached the problem of recognition in a very different way. In their letters, speeches, and private interviews these women stressed again and again the idea of death as an equalizer: a similar loss might indeed happen to anyone. After all, "mothers are the same, kids are the same." Hence they construed their grief as necessarily universal. In turn, the experience of loss provided them with a recognizable public identity. The social self-isolation practiced by Chechen war veterans was replaced in the mothers' cases by a strong desire to synchronize their affective experience with the affective state of their audience. The perceived commonality of loss, once again, was envisioned as a main foundation of community.

"Let the Mother of the Dead Hero Speak!"

Explaining the history of the Altai committee, Svetlana Pavlukova described to me how the committee had decided to bring together in 1989 all the Altai mothers whose sons were killed in Afghanistan, "We needed this gathering of mothers, because it had been ten years since the war started. And all these years, people were as if totally forgotten. You know, everyone was by herself, and suddenly they all got together and they were told about their rights and that there were other people, similar to themselves; that there were people with a similar grief." This theme of unnoticed grief and ignored pain dominated the oral and written narratives of my informants. Similar to the complaints of the Chechen war veterans, the mothers' descriptions of their social invisibility also pointed toward the withdrawing state, dysfunctional institutions, and a general feeling of social collapse typical of the first post-Soviet decade. Soldiers' deaths did not create this

11. In her study of groups affected by Chernobyl, Adriana Petryna describes how financial compensations provided by the Ukrainian state were used by Chernobyl sufferers to create a recognized identity after the collapse of state socialism (2002, 107–14).

experience of disintegration, but they did exacerbate it. Some letters that mothers wrote to the committee throughout the 1990s provided horrifying firsthand evidence of the vanishing state. A mother from an Altai village recollected her ordeals:

> My son was drafted on July 7, 1991....First he spent several months in the Sverdlovsk region [in the Urals] in a boot camp. In October 1991, he was transferred to Germany, but troops started withdrawing, and from August 1992 he was stationed in Tallinn, Estonia. By spring 1993, his tank detachment was moved from Estonia almost completely, except for my son's unit. In the very end of May, he sent us a letter, saying that he'd be back home by June. On July 16, we got a telegram, saying that he was dead. At this time, there was no communication between Russia and Estonia, because Russia had cut off all supplies of electricity, oil, and gas to this country. So, it was next to impossible to get the coffin with our son's body from Estonia. Only the Chief military prosecutor could do it in the end. But even then it happened only because our son was transported as a civilian person, not as a military officer....We did not ask questions about his death when we got the coffin; we just had no energy to do any investigation. As it turned out, we missed our chance. My son's commander retired, and the one who replaced him told me that he was not responsible for other people's business....Please, help me find out how my son died; I did not just pick him from a tree....Sincerely yours. Nadezhda L. (n.d., SPPF)

It is precisely this personalized experience of the collapse of the Soviet Union that the institutional analysis of the USSR's disintegration often tends to overlook or ignore. Cases like this make it easier to understand why the disappearance of the "empire of evil" would be seen as a tragedy by those who lived on the eastern side of the Iron Curtain. The ideological, anti-Communist component, which dominates interpretations of the end of the USSR, tends to overshadow the fact that the breakdown of state socialism in a peculiar fashion combined the tearing down of the Berlin Wall with the simultaneous erecting of smaller walls and barriers in places that used to be obstacle-free. For groups described in this book, the dramatic confirmation of the internal vacuity of Soviet ideology could hardly justify their personal ordeals associated with releasing a son's body from a country that had just become independent or with securing mortuary benefits stipulated by law. The institutional collapse of the country, in other words, was also experienced as a fundamental rupture in people's *daily* lives.

However, it was precisely these personal losses and traumas that produced a set of discursive genres and symbolic practices able to frame—however incompletely and partially—a major sociopolitical event of the twentieth century. In the mothers' case, the unexplained deaths and unacknowledged losses provided them with a historically specific social position from which they could address others. Grim as it was, for many of these women their identity as mothers of dead soldiers was often the last argument in their attempt to claim social significance. This identity became all the more important in light of their devalued professional status and impoverished economic condition. In 2000, a single mother whose son had died in Chechnya lamented in her letter to Pavlukova that the local administration had completely forgotten about her and her dead son. The mother then described her interaction with the village officials. She had asked local authorities for assistance with replacing the faulty piping in her private house. With a very small salary (which she had not been paid for more than a year), she could not bear any expenses. The administration had provided the pipes for free but had refused to pay for the installation. As a local official pointed out, given her small salary the mother could not afford such a replacement even if her son were alive. The mother described her response as follows: "If my son were to come back alive I would have lived happily even in a dugout. I have no firewood, no coal, and cannot do anything about it....I am not a drunk or something, I am a decent person, and they have no money for me anyway. I have never received even the child benefits that they have owed me since my son was little. My son is already grown up, and even dead" (M. Shafranova 2000, SPPF).

Another mother similarly anchored her identity and feeling of personal worth in the loss of her son. In a letter to Pavlukova from the early 1990s, she described a local commemoration of the withdrawal of Soviet troops from Afghanistan. Several drunk Afghan war veterans, who also attended the event, began a brawl by the monument. Trying to restrain them, the mother pointed out that she and her husband had come to the square to commemorate the fallen soldiers, not to witness a fight. The comment provoked an angry reply from one of the veterans: "You are lucky, you've got a husband; some are less fortunate." "Yes," the mother responded, "I have the best luck of all because my son enjoys the greatest benefit possible: he lies under the gravestone. And you are still alive. You forgot about this kind of benefit" (S. Alekseeva n.d. SPPF).

It is impossible to verify or disprove the stories that the mothers told in their letters and interviews. However, it is not the evidential quality that is important about these narratives of loss. What they do document quite convincingly is a particular way of shaping and confirming these women's identity, their way of self-positioning in a society that has ceased to have clear norms of respect, unambiguous meanings of sacrifices, or positive forms of representation. In this case, death, loss, and absence became an experiential and symbolic foundation around which new social interactions were created. Death and loss anchored the identities of the survivors. They were evoked to offset challenges, too. The assumed self-description—a dead soldier's mother—was originally intended to signify these women's social position. However, eventually this metonymy evolved into a metaphor, into a powerful cultural code that successfully merged the political and the domestic without hiding the traumatic void at the core of this merging.

Apart from its identity effect, the theme of ignored death and unnoticed grief also worked as a major organizing device that helped to bring the mothers together. The ability to express their pain or, perhaps more precisely, to express their pain in public produced a powerful binding experience that, in turn, resulted in creating a community of "sisters in pain and grief," as one Altai mother characterized it to me. In her studies of mourning women in Greece, Nadia Seremetakis traced a similar tendency to form social groups through the sharing of emotions. For Seremetakis, such an "affective enclave" functions as "a value-charged site" that allows women to symbolically reframe the existing social order. Truth claims are constructed here as a direct continuation of "the emotional force of pain" (1993, 146, 148). The power of this force was certainly realized and understood by the Altai mothers.

Pavlukova told me a story from the early 1990s when, unable to find a truck to bring printed copies of the book *Sons of Altai* from St. Petersburg, she decided to attend a public meeting with a foreign "lord," as she called him. The lord brought to Barnaul several wheelchairs for handicapped veterans as a sign of gratitude to the soldiers who had rescued his relative from a swamp. Pavlukova knew no details about the lord or the event, but she decided to attend it anyway. As she recalled,

> I was sitting in this meeting with my friend and had no idea whom to ask for the truck I needed. But I have a book in which there were photos of my sons [who were in Afghanistan]...So I raised the book above my head. As soon as a soldier-hero finished talking, I raised the book. I was all in tears myself but managed to say: "Let the Mother of the Dead Hero Speak" [*Daite materi geroia, kotorogo net v zhivykh, slovo!*] So I explained that others have such books, and that I also want one, that our guys are no worse....It was a shock for me back then. I cried then. Afterwards, I asked the friend [who came with me]: "Did I speak clearly?" She said—"No. Nothing was clear at all, except for one thing—you needed something."

It is interesting to see how Pavlukova (retrospectively) describes the process of constructing a dialogical environment. Her insistence on public speech, her demand for communication—"Give the word to the mother," as a literal translation from Russian would have it—happened in a situation where her potential addressee was unknown. It was the emotionally charged word; it was a direct evocation of the dead that was supposed to create a context for dialogical exchange in the process of a mother's public articulation of her pain.

This case also makes evident the fact that the mother's insistence on having the word worked as a point of entry rather as a means of explanation. The mother's activation of the affective meaning of speech preempted an attempt to explain.[12] Or as Julia Kristeva put it, "uncertain and indeterminate articulation" dominated here the attempt to provide comprehensible representations (1984, 24). Yet the representational aspect was not completely lost in this vocalization of pain. The meeting point between the mother and her audience did emerge through the "medium of signs," as Voloshinov called it ([1929] 1998, 12). The failure of Pavlukova's speech to convey content was compensated for by a different form of symbolization. An acoustics of pain was to echo photographs of the sons from the book.

For Seremetakis (1993), it is the interplay between domination and resistance or, correspondingly, between pain and truth that is of key importance for understanding the way in which "affective enclaves" frame their demands (see also Robben 1995). While agreeing with the anthropologist's structural logic, I want to draw attention to a different side of this communication between those who suffer and those who do not. What I find important in the mothers' activity is the picture of the "social order" that appears from their emotionally invested subject position. Pavlukova's comments seem to indicate a reversal of the traditional Durkheimian understanding of mourning as an outcome of the moral pressure that society exercises in critical times over its members in order to strengthen social solidarity. In *The Elementary Forms of the Religious Life* Durkheim writes, "A family which allows one of its members to die without being wept for shows by that very fact that it lacks moral unity and cohesion: it abdicates, it renounces its existence. An individual, in his turn, if he is strongly attached to the society of which he is a member, feels that he is morally held to participating in its sorrows and joys; not to be interested in them would be equivalent to breaking the bonds uniting them to the group; it would be

12. On affective meaning see Kristeva (1995, 104).

renouncing all desires for it and contradicting himself" ([1912] 1967, 446; also Bloch and Parry 1980).

However, the mothers' active creation of social bonds, which never existed before, *preceded* collective assemblings for rituals of mourning. The *commonality* of "a common misfortune" and the *collectivity* of "collective sentiments," crucial for the Durkheimian view of society, had to be established first before they could be renewed in the process of collective effervescence (Durkheim [1912] 1967, 445; Shilling and Mellor 1998). To put it differently, in the process of articulating their grief, the mothers did not merely address or support the existing social order. Rather, they negotiated and constructed a new social context from the available fragments (Kaneff 2002). It was precisely the structural possibility of an emotionally charged site of enunciation, the mothers' insistence on "having a word" in public in the name of the dead son, that made this negotiation effective.

Metonymies of Death

Sharing loss and suffering resulted in a series of practices through which personal pain was converted into collectivized memory, which was in turn materialized as an arranged amalgam of objects, places, and rituals, as "material sites of affective experience" (Flatley 2001, 91). Katerina M., an active participant in the Altai CSM, told me how she spent several months in an exhausting struggle with the local administration, trying to get some help in building a grave headstone for her son who "drowned" while in the army, as official documents put it.[13] Contacted by the committee, she visited a conference of parents: "It was such a conference! Every mother expressed her own pain: how her son died, all these details. I sat through it, we all cried there a lot. You know, to listen to this pain, what kind of death people had, how they were buried....We sobbed and wailed, of course, and after that I started coming here once in a while. And one day I was told, "We need a Room of Memory [*komnata pamiati*]." I promised to do it, because my [other] son is an artist. And this is how it all started."

This recollection usefully outlines the common trajectory that expressions of pain assumed in mothers' remarks. Social isolation was broken down by making one's suffering visible, tangible, and heard. Yet isolation was hardly overcome. Multiplied in personal narratives, loss was nonetheless

---

13. As the Altai mothers are convinced, references to direct or indirect "suicides" (such as "drowning" or the "mishandling" of guns) are used by officials as cover-ups to hide the real reasons for soldiers' deaths (such as fights, rapes, and murders).

rarely presented as a public issue. Predominantly, it was framed as a traumatic experience with which outsiders could identify themselves. Loss, to repeat, was not translated here into narratives that could prevent its repetition. Yet it was contained, first of all, spatially: as a room of memory, a row of graves, or a home of veterans. The creating of a "micromoral setting" (Kleinman 1995, 123)—a site of mourning or a community of loss—and the physical rearranging of the space of the community's existence suddenly became more prominent than the identities of those who died and the causes of their deaths.

As suggested above, the tendency to localize losses caused by state-organized violence to a large degree was shaped by the absence of shared legitimizing political scripts and public rituals of recognition. However, this absence does not explain why the depoliticization was realized as the active production of deep emotional connections between an individual and material objects. The theory and practice of object relations developed by Melanie Klein (1975; see also Segal, 1974; Kristeva 2001) and her followers provides an important frame that helps to highlight some aspects of this process. It is useful to mention here a few of the concepts elaborated by the British psychotherapist Donald Winnicott (1971).[14]

In his work on patterns of identification Winnicott drew attention to a particular mediating role that objects can play in linking the individual's internal and external worlds. At certain moments of life a toy, a blanket, a tune, a word, or a mannerism can become a crucial tool in the individual's defense against anxiety (1971, 4). These transitional phenomena, as Winnicott called them, assume a borderline position, acting simultaneously as a screen for projecting one's illusions and emotions (fears and fantasies) and as a part of the autonomously existing material world. In the process of such "object-relating" the individual invests an object with some significant memories and associations, and by creating this bond of attachment, Winnicott points out, "the subject is depleted to the extent that something of the subject is found in the object, though enriched by feeling" (1971, 90). Being a part of shared reality, such "transitional objects" offer a meeting ground between the individual imagination and the outside world.

It is not this everyday fetishism, however, that interests Winnicott. The importance of the transitional object is its ability to provide a secure link with the outside, to map out safe trajectories of possible relations beyond

---

14. For a discussion of object relations and the self see Csikszentmihalyi and Rochberg-Halton (1982); Born (1997, 1998); Schattschneider (2000); Mohkansing-den Boer and Zock (2004); on object relations and trauma see Davoine and Gaudilliere (2004).

the realm of the imaginary. Transitional objects, in other words, work as a form of reality testing before the rules and contours of this reality become fully graspable. These objects outline "the intermediate area" that allows the development of a relationship between "what is objectively perceived and what is subjectively conceived of" (1971, 11).

As Winnicott emphasizes throughout his work, the transition from the imaginary object-relating to the realist object-usage presupposes confidence in the environment, the ability of the subject to decode various contexts in which objects of identification are immersed. Successful navigation of this space of transition, Winnicott concludes, "depends on experience that leads to trust" (1971, 103).[15] In the absence of such confidence, in a situation where such a transition is blocked, the individual might rely on an excessive "exploitation" of the object of attachment and become "cluttered up with persecutory elements of which he has no means of ridding himself" (1971, 103). The transitional object, then, could be institutionalized as a place of permanent escape.

Winnicott's model has a lot in common with the Freudian distinction between mourning and melancholia (Freud [1917] 1963). As with object-usage, mourning, understood as a gradual process of detachment from a lost object, presupposes a growing differentiation between the individual's attachment to the object and the object itself. In turn, in melancholia, the individual's refusal to admit loss is sustained through a repetitive reproduction of imaginary relations with and material substitutions for the missing object (Kristeva 1989; Butler 2004, 19–49). What is significant in Winnicott's version of the object-relations theory is the shift from transformations of the individual's self-perception to modifications of the object with which the individual associates himself or herself. This refocusing not only highlights the process of differentiation among available objects that the individual must go through in the process of building his or her attachment but also points to social conditions ("trust") that can stimulate or hinder the individual's move from one type of object relations to the other (see Winnicott 2000, 341–68).

While not exhausting the list of all possible reasons, Winnicott's model helps to conceptualize the mode of symbolization of loss employed by many mothers. In the absence of trust and shared discursive tools, these women created their identities by recontextualizing the losses: mortuary replacements for lost sons were saturated with feeling and built into the

15. On the role of transitional space in building trust see Robben (2000, 73).

structure of their everyday order of things. Metonymic object-relating, in other words, acted as an important connecting link that could ground emotions in particular material things but could not signify the meaning of these objects.[16]

The mothers' preoccupation with graves and grave memorials for their lost sons was one of the most striking forms of object relations that I observed during my fieldwork. Russian graves traditionally tend to be decorative, architecturally complex, and strikingly individualized. Smooth lawns of graves with identical stone plaques, so typical, for instance, of American military graveyards, are completely unknown in Russia. Nor has there been anything similar to the park cemetery movement that radically transformed funeral practices in the United States and Europe in the middle of the nineteenth century by turning cemeteries into aesthetically organized landscapes (Mosse 1990, 41–42). Instead, grave sites in Soviet and post-Soviet Russia have been constructed as semiprivate settings, carved out of public space. Normally, graves are clearly separated from one another by low fences or metal chains. The grave plots, however, are usually allocated by the local administrations and are not owned by the relatives of the deceased, though the relatives do transform them into highly personal spaces. Graves vary in their aesthetics, but there seems to be a set of generally shared conventions: a vertical wooden, stone, or concrete monument normally has a portrait and the name of the deceased. In some cases, the top of the headstone has a star or a cross. Post-Soviet graves tend to have more elaborated inscriptions, too. In the Barnaul cemetery that I visited, some headstones had quotations from popular songs and poetry; other monuments bore short commemorative lines. Frequently graves were accompanied by small tables and benches that turned the site into a place of communion between the deceased and the survivors; it was not uncommon for visitors to leave food and even a half-full shot of vodka next to the grave monument.

The sociocultural legacy of Russian funeral customs certainly influenced the mothers' strong disposition toward this kind of memorialization through objects. Their active production of sites and objects of mourning also stemmed from the fact that the materiality of symbolic objects allowed these women not only to mark the last traces of sons who had passed away but also to evidence the loss that was ignored. The mothers' active and deliberate proliferation of memorial practices and sites seems to fully support the conclusion formulated by Stanley Cavell: "Studies of social suffering

---

16. For more on metonymic logic and object relations see Lacan (1977, 164).

must contain a study of society's silence toward it" (1997, 95). By performing various death rituals, the mothers evoke an expression of public support and succeed in constructing a "good death," that is a death that has
witnesses and does not fall into oblivion (Serematakis 1991, 101; Danforth
1982, 125).

Evoking public support was not easy to accomplish, though. By law, fu-
nerals of soldiers who died while in service should be covered by the state
budget (distributed through local offices of the Ministry of Defense), but
the actual post-Soviet practice added its own correction to the rule. Payments were often delayed, disputed, or rejected. A mother whose son died
in Chechnya in 1997 wrote to Pavlukova, "Getting money for the grave
monument takes my last energy. Officials from the regional office of the
Ministry of Defense are totally heartless; they lie all the time. I'm ready to
spit right in their eyes. Last time they demanded that I submit the original
death certificate [instead of a copy], as if I am trying to reserve in advance
a grave monument for my eighteen-year-old-son [who is dead]. They say,
maybe by the end of the year they'd have money for this. And for the funeral
they had no money either. This damn war will never end" (N. Pakhomova
1997, SPPF).

Sometimes there was a compromise: instead of money, local administrations would provide parents with prefabricated monuments. In such cases,
many mothers continued to demand equal treatment and insisted on uni-
formity of gravestones, whenever it was possible. I was told in interviews, for
instance, that marble headstones were especially sought after and therefore
in a short supply. As a result, the mothers formed one of the saddest queues
of their lives: a "queue for marble gravestones" [*ochered' na mramornye pa-
miatniki*], as one of them described it to me.

The gravestones erected by the mothers symbolized their losses in several
important ways. Imbued with emotions, grave monuments were construed
not so much as reminders but almost as substitutions for the lost sons. The
mothers' affective attachment to these physical objects turned them into the
central piece that sustained their imaginary connection with the deceased.
Svetlana Alexievich in her book of interviews with Afghan war veterans and
their parents has a striking explanation of this tendency by the mother of a
soldier who died in Afghanistan: "When I come to the grave I always bow
to him, and I bow to him again when I leave. I am only home if people are
coming. I feel fine here with my son. Ice and snow do not bother me. I write
letters here. I go home when it's dark....I greet every little flower, every tiny
stem growing from his grave: 'Are you from there? Are you from him? Are
you from my son?'" (1992, 179–80).

In their letters, Altai mothers told of similar experiences. The mother of a soldier fallen in Afghanistan wrote, "My heart is bleeding, when I think that there will finally be a time when I won't come to my son's grave. Coming to this grave again and again is the only thing I'd live for [*tol'ko by radi etogo zhil by i zhil*]. Though I do have grandchildren and other children" (G. Alekseeva G.1992, SPPF). Yet another mother makes the symbolic equation between the lost son and the newly found object of attachment even more directly: "We raise our sons with our own hands, and now with our own hands we have to take care of the gravestones to our boys" (L. Fursova 1992, SPPF).

And they do take care: the erecting of monuments rarely marks the completion of the mourning process; rather, it starts a long and profound relationship between the mother and the grave site. Initial mortuary arrangements and structures are often supplemented by new elements. Plaques are modified. Portraits are changed. Fences are replaced. Tables and benches are added. The materiality of the process of memorialization provides mourning with its own dynamic, which firmly roots within the same symbolic field physical objects, mothers' memories of their sons, and mothers' own identities. The mourning process, in other words, does not fade away. It is not supposed to fade away. Transitional objects map out no transition, and materialized traces of loss are instrumental in keeping this mourning intact. In some cases, mortuary practices associated with the graves of deceased sons find their logical resolution: parents often insist on being buried next to their sons, and quite a few original graves of soldiers have been extended to meet these requests (figure 4.6).

In its own way, the post-Soviet context also influences this incessant production and reproduction of material signs of death. Graves are vandalized. Memorial plaques and fences made out of metal get stolen. Grave trees get cut down, as in this case described by a mother whose son died in Afghanistan:

On January 2, together with my husband, we went to the son's grave. When we came there, we realized that all six blue spruces that I had planted five years ago had been cut down. I cried so much that I had to stay in bed for a whole week....I had spent so much time taking care of these trees. I rented a car at least six times to bring the trees there. I kept saving all these buckets and jars so that I could bring water for the trees. I even collected water on the road, from a puddle after the rain. And now they are all gone. Cut to the very root. I do not know what to do. To plant more? To plant different trees? Such a pain. Nothing is sacred anymore. (Z. Lipovaia n.d., SPPF)

Fig. 4.6. The grave of a soldier who died "performing his international duty" in Afghanistan (1985), and the grave of his mother (2005). Barnaul, 2006. Photo by author.

In an interview, Svetlana Pavlukova told me about another outrageous case. In the mid-1990s, somebody stole metal plaques with the names of fallen soldiers and a metal emblem of the Veterans' Union attached to the walls of the memorial complex in downtown Barnaul (the scrap metal could be sold). The Altai CSM and veterans had to raise money to replace the signs. To avoid potential repetitions of the theft, they replaced bronze with cast iron.

What these examples show is how the very materiality of symbolic objects strengthens people's affective attachments to them: managing the social biography of these traces of loss becomes just as important as taking care of the loss itself. The transitional character of these traces—their borderline location between the world of internal emotions and the world of external objects—makes it possible to use, sometimes inadvertently, the privatized and domesticated ritual as a way of creating a new community.

In an interview, Pavlukova explained how she decided to start a massive rearrangement of the cemetery where soldiers who died in Afghanistan were buried. As she recalled it, originally soldiers were buried on the edges of the cemetery because the authorities were trying to hide evidence of the unpopular war. The mothers brought all these soldiers together. "In the center," as Pavlukova emphasized. She then added, "Some parents did not want to do it in the beginning but then, several years later, they realized how nice it is when all the boys are commemorated at once, and also reburied their sons. We always have a memorial service [*panikhida*] on February 15 [the day when the Soviet troops finally left Afghanistan]....There is a small chapel at the cemetery now, so we all come, put up candles, stand a bit, nobody gets cold; then we walk through the cemetery and then go back home and lay a memorial table there [*pominal'nyi stol*]."

As if streamlining history, all the graves were rearranged in a neat row, regardless of the actual dates of death. A massive stone of remembrance served as a gateway to the alley, evoking a shared sense of being torn apart by the necessity to recall the dead and the inability to find proper words to do so. The short poem carved on the stone read:

> Recall everybody who died over there
> And this memory shall be endless
> Let silence sound instead of words
> As an eternal moment of grief.[17]

This mortuary rearranging of space concerns more than the dead, of course. As the anthropologist Katherine Verdery suggests, (re)burial creates and reorders community by reaffirming mourners' identities but also by narrowing and bounding the borders of this community (1999, 108; also Winter 1995, 147). Funeral practices demarcate a community of loss and closely connect the reconfiguration of landscape and the reorganization of society (figure 4.7).

In this respect, the mothers' active reorganization of space associated with dead bodies can be seen as a form of taking control over the situation

---

17. "Pomianem vsekh pogibshikh tam / Pust' pamiat' budet beskonechnoi / I tishina vzamen slovam / Zvuchit minutoi skorbi vechnoi." By Valerii Burkov, http://avtomat2000.com/tv.html.

Fig. 4.7. Demarcating a community of loss: public funeral of a soldier who died in Chechnya. Barnaul, June 1995. AGKM, OF.16804/2, F.-6447. Courtesy of the Altai Museum of Military History, Barnaul.

in which their role was previously reduced to that of a passive bystander.[18] Establishing the sociospatial connectedness of the dead is mirrored here by the sociospatial production of the community of loss.[19] As Pavlukova vividly explained it, the relocation of the remains produced a public landscape (cemetery) that offers a ground, a literal place ("a chapel") for the survivors. The place also determines the trajectory of their behavior: as Pavlukova puts it, "we all come," "put up candles," "stand a bit."[20] In this newly created topography of death, the assumed identity—mother of a soldier who is dead—intertwines the world of family, the world of politics, and the world beyond one's reach. It is also instructive to see how this reorganization of landscape/society—from the sociosymbolic margin to the sociosymbolic center—was reflected on the level of naming. In interviews, soldiers' mothers and those who associated with the veteran movement in

18. On control and memorial sites see Bradbury (2001, 221–24) and Koselleck (2002, 294).
19. On implicit and explicit parallelism between creating a "society of the dead" and recreating one's own society see Hertz (1960, 71) and Seale (1998, 65–67).
20. More on the reconfiguration of public space as a reflection of the post-Soviet changes see Flatley (2001); Grant (2001) Papernyi (2004); Revzin (2006); Ryklin (2002).

Barnaul routinely referred to this row of graves as the Alley of Glory (*alleia slavy*), completely disregarding its official title, the "Memorial Alley."

In his study of postutopian societies, the anthropologist John Borneman suggested the metaphor "Death of the Father" to conceptualize the end of "totalizing and patricentric" regimes. Pointing to a strong preoccupation with the deaths of authority figures, Borneman traced a change in the pattern of identity construction: previous identifications with the "father of the nation" were replaced in postutopian societies by rituals of his symbolic decapitation, which could potentially open a path for new configurations of political authority (2004b).

The practices described here similarly rely on mortuary rituals for marking the end of the totalizing authority in Russia. However, the striving toward a large-scale symbolic deposition is less prominent here. As I have tried to show, it was the public recognition of the mothers' loss rather than their implicit or explicit participation in rituals of symbolic annihilation of political leaders that became crucial for new configurations of authority, emerging in these affective mortuary practices. The end of the political regime manifested itself here as a patchwork of mourning rituals through which Altai mothers objectified traces of personal loss in public. Perhaps unwittingly, they marked the end of the regime as a physically rearranged space called upon to materialize an "eternal moment of grief." The gradual evolution of the Barnaul cemetery was a good indicator of this process. Pavlukova's attempt to claim the central social location for the memory of the dead (within the limits of the city's main cemetery) in the early 1990s became the norm a decade later. The cemetery's two most central areas are occupied by the graves of soldiers who died in local wars. Graves of officers killed in Chechnya are located near the main entrance, right next to the chapel that anchors the whole cemetery. The expensive and imposing headstones radically contrast with the peripheral and marginalized status of the Chechen war in people's daily lives (figure 4.8). Prominently displayed at the cemetery, they serve as monumental evidence of the forgotten war.

Domesticating Loss

The absence of public consensus about military history in late Soviet and early post-Soviet Russia, the polarizing effect that discussions of the Chechen and Afghan wars tended to produce, and the mothers' own dependency on local administration made it almost impossible for the committee to count on the support of people outside their immediate circle. As has been suggested, the Altai mothers' inability and unwillingness to articulate

Fig. 4.8. Graves of military officers who died in the Chechen war. The sign on the stone reads: "Forgive [us] for not being able to safeguard you with our prayers, nor resurrect you with tears from our eyes." Barnaul, 2006. Photo by author.

a discourse of civic rights and political responsibility or a therapeutic discourse of social help and rehabilitation led them to an active elaboration of the discourse on commemoration. Caused by state-organized violence, losses became incorporated in the mothers' daily lives by activating what André Green, a French psychoanalyst, called an "objectalizing function" (1999, 85).

I have demonstrated how through meaningful investments loss was inscribed on such material objects as headstones and memorial plaques that could sustain mothers' sense of self and secure continuing bonds with the dead (Klass, Silverman, and Nickman 1996). This enactive remembering was not explicitly aimed at reexamining the meaning of the past. Rather, it was aimed at incorporating the traumatic past into daily practices of the present. The following excerpt from a mother's letter outlines well how metonymies of death were domesticated and discursively stabilized in the private context. The letter was written in the early 1990s by a mother whose son died in Afghanistan.

> Svetlana, how are you [?] How is your health [?] Svetlana we live little by little, I cry a bit and live again. We must live on for the memory of our sons. Svetlana, my dear, [your son] Kostia is forever alive in our family and he lives together with our own son. In the evening, I put them asleep, all my sons, and in the morning I wake them up and live through the whole day, remembering them....Svetlana, we just got an apartment from the local division of the Defense Ministry; [we have to pay only] 50 percent of the rent. We move in around November 7 [the anniversary of the Bolshevik Revolution of the 1917]. You are very welcome to come and stay with us. Svetlana, can I ask you to send me a photo of Kostia. I have one, but it is so tiny. I am compiling an *Album of Memory to Those Boys Who Gave Their Lives for Freedom of Afghanistan.* And I need Kostia also on my nightstand. All of them I put on the nightstand, in frames with flowers around. Apt. is on the ninth floor in a twelve-story building in downtown Omsk, two rooms, 32 square meters of living space. Larisa is a second-year college student; she spent two months in the Krasnodar region as an intern, collecting vegetables and fruit. She returned on the 29th. Write me, tell me how your life is going. How your grandsons are. Did [Kostia's widow] Liubushka write to you at all [?] If you write her, pass my big maternal greeting and tell her that we remember Kostia and herself and cannot wait to see [her] in our place. Svetlana, my dear, take care of yourself, do not cry too much. An extra day of life is the best memory for our sons. It is an extra flower planted on the graves of our sons. It is hard. There is nothing to say about it. But we must live on. Grit our teeth from pain and live, live, live. Live for the memory of our sons. All the best, my dear. I hug you firmly and wait for your reply. Liuba, Omsk. (Furtseva n.d., SPPF)[21]

This text was by no means an exception among about two hundred letters that I discovered in the Altai Museum of Local Wars. Written throughout the 1990s by mothers whose sons were killed in local wars, these letters intertwined the theme of loss and pain with descriptions of daily chores, illnesses, new refrigerators, TV sets, or harvests of potatoes. Trauma constantly resurfaced there, being broken into multiple objects of attachment.[22] Loss was expressed as a circulation of emotions through the vehicle of material things. Instead of being isolated and mourned—or, as many trauma studies suggest, instead of remaining a blank spot, a void that cannot be symbolized

---

21. Whenever possible, I have tried to preserve the original style and syntax in my translations of the mothers' letters.

22. For more details on death and objectification see Harrison (2003, 55–71).

(Caruth 1996; Homans 2000; Winter 1995)—traumatic loss became here the main structuring principle of the text, the main narrative device that stitched together a fragmented story of loss (Eng and Kazanjian 2003, 5).

This normalization of loss, through its localization and fragmentation, should not hide a corresponding process through which metonymies of death were inscribed in the everyday life here—namely, a series of exchanges (apartment, photos, visits, flowers) that was persistently originated by the loss. Neither forgotten, nor overcome, loss was transposed here to a different plane. Exchanges were not about compensation—that is to say, they were not about finding an acceptable equivalent to represent the depth of the loss or justify it. Rather, they functioned here as "a *mode of symbolizing* that is both economic and significant" (Goux 1990, 4; emphasis in the original). Exchanges worked here as a serial act of recognition that drew public attention to the loss but failed to convey the degree of its importance. Strikingly, the mothers' understanding of exchanges had little in common with the exchanges of sacrifices practiced by the Chechen war veterans, discussed in the previous chapter. The overarching metaphor of debt and the logic of the implicit contract between soldiers and the state, so crucial for sustaining the veterans' claims to compensation and recognition, were almost entirely absent in the mothers' stories. Instead, their exchanges appeared to be built into a multiplicity of short-term transactions encapsulated by the flow of daily life. For instance, another mother whose son died in Afghanistan wrote in 1999:

> Dear Svetlana Grigor'evna…On February 15 we went to Kliuchi [the administrative center of the district] to commemorate our children. We were given money there; we visited a church and put up candles, went to the cemetery and to the monument and after all that we went to a diner.…There was a concert, they sang songs about Afghanistan. The sovkhoz's administration gave us two kilos of millet, one kilo of buckwheat, one box of tea. Widows lay flowers on the graves and I did too. As far as medication goes, nothing will work because we are about to start our vegetable garden. I should just go to Kliuchi and get this medication to lower my blood pressure but I was told that I could buy my medication with a discount only once a year. And then they do not have it anyway. So much for medication. As long as we can walk we walk, when we cannot walk we start taking care of ourselves. I live with my [other] son, he is single, no wife. And he is about to plough fields, so I have to prepare his lunch bags to take to the steppe. That's it. Good-bye. (Zhabina 1999, SPPF)

The conflation of the symbolic and the material/economic in these exchanges (money-candles-dinner-songs-buckwheat-flowers-medication) had an additional underlying cause. The mothers' appeal for recognition, for acknowledgment of their trauma took place when cognition and knowledge of what happened were often impossible. In many cases, the mothers had no information about the circumstances of their sons' deaths; sometimes they never saw the bodies. A mother whose son died in the first Chechen war wrote to Pavlukova, "We still cannot believe that Iurii exists no more— since we have not seen or touched him [since his death]. I still think I will get a letter from him" (L. Moroz 1998, SPPF). In this case, the domestication of trauma, its depoliticization, and its relocation within the familiar context of everyday life seemed to be the only narrative strategy that made sense. Loss and remains became inseparable; or, as another mother put it: "All that is left of my son is my pain, my pride and [his] award" (Furtseva n.d., SPPF).

"How Do We Remember?"

This strategy of retaining and reproducing objects that mattered was actively used by relatives of fallen soldiers for constructing postmortem biographies of their sons. Obituaries of the soldiers from Altai who died in Afghanistan and Chechnya were written by parents, friends, or schoolteachers and were collected by the CSM. Some families even created their own family albums to commemorate lost sons (figure 4.9).

The first collection was published in 1992 as the book *Sons of Altai*; the second, titled *We were waiting for you, sons…*, came out in 1999. The CSM's women usually referred to these publications as books of memory (*knigi pamiati*). Similar books (with similar titles) have been published by many regional CSM chapters throughout the country. In a decentralized and autonomous manner, these local lists of fallen soldiers continued the official late-Soviet tradition of compiling and updating local and national records of those who died during the Second World War. In Barnaul, *Sons of Altai* was the first regional publication of this type. Usually, books of memory are limited to very basic information; they rarely go beyond the traditional catalog of names and dates of soldiers' births and deaths. *Sons of Altai* was quite different in this respect; soldiers' photos and date were accompanied by their short biographies-obituaries. The book united the dead without reducing them to an anonymous group (see Hallam and Hockey 2001, 89). As Pavlukova told me, it was this book that gave her the idea to consolidate the actual graves of soldiers. To some extent, the first book of memory became the textual equivalent of a portable memorial site. It was frequently used as a powerful visual argument in discussions; veterans often took it to public

Fig. 4.9. To commemorate their lost sons, some families create their own albums of memory. A page from an album compiled by a sister of a soldier who died in Chechnya. Barnaul, 1997. Photo by author.

meetings and rituals. The book was proudly displayed in the main office of the mothers' committee and was often mentioned both in the mothers' letters and in veterans' interviews.

The production of *Sons of Altai* was not a small event. Initiated in 1991 by the committee and the Afghan Veterans' Union, the publication was supervised by two women, a local journalist and a curator from the Altai Museum of the Local Wars. Together with Pavlukova, they asked soldiers' parents to send in obituaries for their sons. As the curator explained to me, the original obituaries were edited during the preparation of the publication. In some cases the initial texts were supplemented with additional materials collected during interviews with people who knew the fallen soldiers. Pavlukova did not participate in the textual part of the project but was actively involved in solving all kinds of technical issues. In a conversation, she recalled different stages of the book's production. Struggling with funding, she decided to ask for help from local deputies and went to a session of the regional parliament. As she put it to me ten years after the event, "I did not even know back then what the word "session" meant....But I came to see all these men; only men were sitting there....So I told [the deputies] right away: "Here you are, guys, all of you are sons of your mothers. How do you treat your mothers? Kindly?! Do the same, when soldiers' mothers come to you for some help. Even if you cannot help, can you say it in such a way as not to offend them?...Use some nice words, even if you have no money to help."

This appeal to family roles seemed to work—many regional factories and organizations contributed money to the project. Yet the mechanical production of the book turned into a long saga. Originally, the book was to be printed by a publishing house in St. Petersburg. In 1991, when visiting the publisher, Pavlukova was told that she herself needed to find the ten tons of paper necessary for the book. The Soviet Union was nearing its end, and the centralized system of quotas and distribution was being replaced by more individual and market-driven approaches. Pavlukova managed to secure a quota for a certain amount of paper that had to be reclaimed in Omsk, a city in Siberia. However, in Omsk, Pavlukova was told that the allocated paper could not be available immediately and could not be available for money, which was increasingly losing its value because of inflation. After a couple of trips to Omsk, Pavlukova was finally offered a deal: she could have the paper in exchange for either a hoisting crane or several tons of starch. As she recalled in an interview, this was how she learned the meaning of another word—"barter." The exchange did not go in this direction, though: confused, puzzled, and agitated by the whole affair, Pavlukova fainted during the negotiation of the contract, which prompted the owner of the paper to supply it on less convoluted terms, that is, in exchange for money.

Stylistically, *Sons of Altai* was a combination of two long-standing traditions of commemoration rooted in the Soviet past. The official canon included booklets, postcards, and albums in which images of soldiers who had died in World War II were accompanied by short impersonal descriptions of their heroic feats. The second, much more informal canon is associated with the popular tradition of the "soldier album," a handmade collection of stories, pictures, and poems traditionally prepared by soldiers before returning home (Bannikov 2002, 205–16; Karasik 2001). Most obituaries published in the book of memory had a plotline similar to this one:

> Before Sergei was drafted into the army, he built a well: "This is for you, mother, remember me every time you draw water from it." Aleksandra Ivanovna [the mother] also keeps the watch that Sergei bought when he got his first salary, after summer work during his vacations in grade seven. He did not like to waste time, he always kept himself busy—watering or putting grass in the silo. He did not shy away from the work around the house, either. After the eighth grade, he entered a local college and was certified as a professional tractor driver. The New Year of 1980 Sergei was in Afghanistan. But his parents found this out only in March. Before that, they were getting letters with strange return addresses. In his last letter, which came in June, Sergei mentioned that his military unit had moved toward the border with Pakistan. Right after that, they got a letter from his commander: "We cannot disclose all the details, but I can say one thing: your son demonstrated a model of courage and bravery when performing a military task.... Because of various reasons [*po riadu obstoiatel'stv*], no personal things survived him, I will try to send a photo, though." This was the style of "death notices" back then.
>
> Junior sergeant Mazurin was a gun-layer. Places of his service: Kabul, Kandahar, Gaznee. Died from excessive bleeding on the battlefield.
>
> Buried in his motherland, in the village of Veseloiarsk, Rubzovskii district. Awarded the Order of the Red Star (posthumously). (Khramtsova 1992, n.p.)

Personalized but short on individual details, these posthumous representations contained almost no political message or an attempt to justify the deaths by depicting heroic acts, an approach somewhat unusual for the Soviet tradition of war memorialization. During my work in the archive of the Museum of Local Wars, I realized that this absence of implicit or explicit political messages did not come about naturally. The archive also had a collection of draft obituaries that were originally written by parents or, in some cases, by teachers from the high schools where soldiers studied before they were drafted. Often these unedited texts were quite dissimilar from the obituaries finally included in the book. Yet surprisingly, it was the original obituaries that were full of ideological clichés of the time.[23] I give only one example to illustrate the point; the list, however, could be easily extended.

---

23. Catherine Merridale discovered the same tendency during her interviews with the World War II veterans in Russia. Frequently veterans' recollections were saturated with images borrowed from books or films (2006, 48).

A two-page handwritten obituary for Aleksei Larshutin described his life in the following way:

> Larshutin Aleksei Germanovich was born on February 8, 1968. Like any village boy he loved horses and other animals. He was very industrious. Every summer he helped with hay mowing. He started school in 1975, and graduated from the high school in 1985. After that, he began his degree in a forestry college in Biisk [a city in Altai]. Aleksei started driving tractors and other cars when he was only twelve years old, because his father was a car mechanic....In the spring of 1986 he was drafted into the Soviet army. He volunteered to go to Afghanistan. On April 26, 1987, the Afghan people celebrated Revolution Day, but the Afghan opposition began shooting at a peaceful rally. Leaders of the Gulbachar province asked [the Soviets] to help protect the common people. On this festive day Aleksei was severely wounded by a deadly shell fragment when he was defending people in the street. But the peaceful people were not harmed. For his combat Aleksei was awarded posthumously the Order of the Red Star. When he died, he was nineteen years, two months, and eighteen days old. (Anonymous n.d., SPPF)

The obituary for Larshutin published in *Sons of Altai* did not necessarily misrepresent his life, but this version of his life and death emphasized somewhat different things. Below is a slightly abridged version of the published obituary:

> In one of her letters Maria Larshutina would write: "It is so good that our sons have been withdrawn from Afghanistan; now thousands of mothers could sleep well." Maria lost her son, and she knows what sleepless nights feel like, and what it means—to wait in vain the return of your son from the army....
> Aleksei played guitar and accordion really well; his fellow soldiers wrote that his songs were very uplifting and they kept them in a good mood....He was kind, jovial, and outgoing. As a private, he was a mortarman, and took part in four major operations and ambushes. His death was not easy. The fight went on for an hour and a half. He was wounded by a phosphoric shell. Such shells turn people into torches. Soldiers put the flame out and flew Aleksei to a hospital by helicopter. Doctors could not save him, however. His body was severely burned. Aleksei's commander wrote later to his parents that their son, despite the pain, kept smiling. "He was always smiling," his mother said. "He loved animals, preferring horses and dogs. During his summers, he trained baby horses. He liked hiking. He could drive a tractor. He participated in a competition for the best plowman and was awarded a prize. What a son we have lost." Aleksei graduated from a secondary school, and studied for two years in the Biisk forestry college.

> Buried in his motherland, in the village of Cheposh.
> Awarded the Order of the Red Star (posthumously). (Khramtsova 1992)

Allusions to martyrdom and stoic suffering (living torch, smiles despite pain, etc.) replaced here the original attempts to justify death through sociopolitical reasoning (protecting the common people of Afghanistan). Throughout the book references to Afghanistan in general and political connotations of the invasion in particular were radically minimized. This erasure strikingly contrasted with the multiple documents that evidenced a very different historical perception of the invasion. Many mothers shared the feeling that their sons had gone to Afghanistan with a liberating mission. In turn, veterans themselves often stressed in their recollections and memoirs the motivating force of the "Afghan people's revolution," which was so prevalent in the late 1970s in the USSR (see Alexievich 1992, 29–31, 73; Smirnov 1990, 114).

The successful domestication of loss was reached here through the downplaying of the foreign character of the war. The war once again was turned into a story of individual perseverance. To some extent, it was this politics of representation in the early 1990s that later provided a necessary symbolic ground for framing Soviet and Russian involvement in military conflicts abroad as "local" wars while turning wars themselves into a matter of daily life.[24]

What I find significant in this clear attempt to obliterate the political detail and clichés of the time from soldiers' obituaries is not the ideological motivation of the editor (I could not tell when editorial corrections were made). In fact, edited obituaries only made more salient the mothers' overall tendency to ground the memory of the soldiers fallen "over there" in the familiar details of the everyday. As the published obituaries also demonstrated, stories about the sons' short lives were seamlessly interwoven with stories about their mothers. For many mothers, the obituaries for their sons encouraged them to streamline their own biographies. Turning the narrative of loss into a biographical genre, in their letters some mothers would string together different periods in their past by highlighting a historically specific, yet seemingly inescapable, experience of deprivation or suffering. A mother wrote, responding to Pavlukova's invitation,

> Sorry I could not come to the [commemorative] event that you've organized. We had lots of snowstorms around here. I wanted to call you but all the

24. See chapter 3 for details.

equipment from the local telephone station was stolen exactly around that time. There are no limits to what people can steal now. People are so heartless these days. It would have been fine. But it's just such a pity. I was only one year old when my father was drafted into the Finnish war [of 1939–40]. Then there was the Great Patriotic War, he never came back from. Still missing in action. Nobody knew what happened. Ours were retreating, and he was wounded. We grew up with a mother only; then there was a stepfather. Mother was sick all the time, and stayed home.…Only life started getting better a bit, the death of my son [in the army] totally ruined my health. My husband is totally ill, too. Without a vegetable garden we would not survive.…But we'll manage somehow. As long as there is no war. (Gavruseva 1992, SPPF)

In the absence of a mythologizing frame or an ideological support, the narrative of loss emerges as a story about an ordinary, private life that was periodically split or interrupted by a traumatic event. Often this everyday mélange of traumatic things and events was used as a model of civic activity. For many mothers the community of emotional support, built around mortuary rituals, became the only social link that led them out of their isolation. Katerina M., a woman who designed and decorated a room of memory for a local committee, recollected in her interview:

When we put all these photos [of dead soldiers] up, we invited all the parents to come. A priest came too. He gave us this icon, the Blessed Virgin, Assumption of the Blessed Mary. He blessed the room. And after that, parents started coming. Well, not everyone, but a lot. You know, imagine [a mother,] she stays at home and there is nobody to remember her son with. Her soul gets sick, she is lacking something, so she comes here. She comes, with her little bundle, you know, cookies, candies, sometimes, a bottle, not without it. So, we sit down, each gets fifty grams, we do not drink here, really. As Olga puts it, "Only symbolically, fifty grams to each!" So, we drink. Commemorate her child; hers and the rest of them. Then, we light the candles, stand for a while, and this is it. And this mother, after all that, she wipes her tears and smiles. And she goes home in a better mood, a lighter one.…

Now this committee is my life. I race to get here all the time…sometimes— two, three times a week. It depends what happens at home, in the garden…now [in winter] the garden is over, so I race here all the time. I miss all these women and boys…I come after work, stop by, and tell [my boy] something about home and it gets better. I put up a candle, get closer [to the picture of my son] and stroke him. Initially they had put his picture on the very top, it is better there, but I moved it later to a different place, lower. So that now I can reach him, my son.

Facing death without established traditions or rituals often means that "the authority offered in the face of death is the authority not of tradition but of the self" (Walter 1994, 188). There is no coherent style of mourning or convention of remembrance to follow. Hence, when I visited the room of memory, I saw a large board covered with army fatigue fabric that served as an improvised post-Soviet iconostasis: icons of Blessed Mary and St. Nicholas occupied its top corners, and the center of the board was covered by a large red star. Plastic red carnations, a silent reminder of a Soviet revolutionary tradition, were left side by side with Russian Orthodox candles. A large slogan above these artifacts read: "Eternal Glory to the Sons—The Pain of Loss Will Not Be Washed Away by Tears."

This seemingly haphazard ensemble of incompatible signs and symbols was more than an example of bricolage, though. Despite their overall randomness, all the fragments made perfect sense. Each of them pointed to a predictable symbolic code. However, the Altai mothers' practices and narratives also clearly revealed that no positive symbolic framework other than the overarching narrative of pain of loss could have turned these fragments into a coherent mosaic.

Moreover, the metonymic logic of these remnants produced an additional fragmenting effect. As Jacques Derrida put it in a somewhat similar context, this logic "divides the referential trait, suspends the referent and leaves it to be desired, while still maintaining the reference" (2001, 61). To put it somewhat differently, what became critical in this "affective economy of the detail" (Miller 2003, 122) was an ability to retain the links with multiple signifiers of the deceased—transitional objects of sorts—while knowing full well that neither the signified nor the referent was available anymore. In a situation when crucial details could not be disclosed and no personal things survived, attempts to understand what was lost were replaced by a striving to realize what remained (Eng and Kazanjian. 2003, 2).

Oscillating between different scales of generalization and analysis, metonymy necessarily suggests a constant movement between part and whole, large and small, close and distant (Ferme 2001, 121). More crucially, the metonymic signification relies on one's ability to condense the whole in a remnant. Or, to reverse the proposition, it presupposes one's willingness to unpack the fragment in order to trace missing links. It is precisely this "semiotic volunteerism" (de Certeau, Giard, and Mayol 1998, 32), this fragmented yet contiguous object-relating that helped the Altai mothers find meaning in their loss in an environment devoid of shared symbolic conventions. Traces without referents, objects that mattered but did not necessarily provide a consistent logic or a picture, these fragments nonetheless demarcated a field of social relations, provided a context, and sometimes suggested a guideline for action (Humphrey 2002a, 83). The production of objects replacing loss might also explain why mourning was not followed by an expected disengagement from the loss. It is by constantly oscillating between material references and the absent referents that soldiers' mothers remain connected with "the boys" and sustain the circulation of their emotions in public (Klass, Silverman, and Nickman 1996, xviii).

The Hall of Memory (Zal Pamiati), a part of the permanent exhibit of the regional Museum of the Local Wars, was perhaps the most vivid realization of the Altai mothers' tendency to perceive or even to construct public space through an intense patchwork of symbolism and domesticity. Opened in the early 1990s, the two-room hall displayed some standard Soviet devices of memorialization. There was a traditional case of capsules filled with earth from the graves of the soldiers buried in the Altai region. There was a wall of soldiers' pictures. There was a poster with an anonymous poem titled "To the Motherland" that read: "Commemorate us, Russia, in a December frost / Just before you all gather at the holiday table / Commemorate those, who were faithful to the military oath / Who vanished in eternity but protected you forever."

At the same time, the rooms contained things that were not very common for a traditional museum exhibit. One corner presented a real tent in which soldiers slept during their service in Afghanistan. A glass case on an opposite wall contained a death notice sent to parents, with pictures of a soldier's funeral and a mourning mother. The windows in the rooms were structured as crosses with wrought-iron silhouettes of black tulips that symbolized the airplanes that transported coffins with bodies from Afghanistan (figure 4.10). Religious symbolism was also reflected in the lighting fixtures on the ceiling, arranged in the shape of a large cross (figure 4.11). On the wall of pictures, each photo of a soldier was accompanied by a small candleholder that could be used like votive candles in Russian Orthodox churches (figure 4.12). The curator of the exhibit warned me, though, that this prominence of religious symbolism (in a state museum) should not be read literally: multiple crosses were meant to symbolize "hope in a broad sense of this word." In turn, one of the mothers tried to assure me that earth in the capsules was indeed brought from real graves: "We go [to the Hall of Memory] every holiday, and could light a candle for each soldier. You know, music starts—Ave Maria or something like that—and after that it all begins." The lack of a civic narrative and an analytic distance was replaced by a sentiment-provoking choreography of visual and audio media usually performed within the circle of close relatives and friends. State violence was

Fig. 4.10. One hundred forty-four capsules with earth from soldiers' graves and black tulips in the cross-shaped window frames. Barnaul, 2006. Photo by author.

turned into a private trauma, and a museum was transformed into a site of mourning, into a peculiar amalgam of a quasi graveyard and a secular church.

Performing the Politics of Pity

The specifics through which Altai mothers objectified their "imagined community" are significant, for they indicate how these women modified existing traditions for deploying suffering in politics. Many scholars studying post-totalizing and postsocialist reconfigurations of public space view such changes as a part of a larger process of "reordering morality." The new spatial order is often turned into the moral foundation of a new life by "pursuing accountability and justice around dead bodies" (Verdery 1999, 111; also Gal 1991; Borneman 2004a; Paperno 2001; Etkind 2004). To some extent, the mothers' mortuary practices underscored a similar tendency.

Fig. 4.11. A lighting cross in the Hall of Memory. Barnaul, 2006. Photo by author.

Their attempts to establish a new form of collectivity for the dead—in the museum or in the cemetery—presented a striking contrast with the official Soviet practices of war commemoration in which *common* graves and tombs of *unknown* soldiers were implicitly juxtaposed to elaborate individual grave sites of the Soviet political and cultural elite such as Lenin's Tomb or the Novo-Devichii necropolis in Moscow.[25] Along with this, there was another, very different tendency, suggesting that the transition from practices of mourning to building a new moral order, outlined by Verdery, is far from universal. A politics of justice—that is, a politics aimed at "settling accounts" (Borneman 1997)—could be effectively blocked by the "politics of pity" (Boltanski 1999), rooted in a powerful desire to preserve "wounded attachments" (Brown 1995, chap. 3). This section examines a theoretical framework that helps to understand this modification.

Hannah Arendt in her analysis of political genealogy of "the social question" points out that since the French Revolution an emphasis on people's suffering has been a major driving force in politics. Usually, it produces two

25. On funeral practices in the Soviet period see Binns (1979, 1980).

Fig. 4.12. Candleholders and photos of soldiers killed in Afghanistan. Barnaul, 2001. Photo by author.

types of outcome: compassion, an ability "to be stricken with the suffering of someone else as though it was contagious" and pity, a generalized sentiment that fills up the space between those who suffer, on the one hand, and the "community of interest with the oppressed and exploited," on the other (1963, 85, 88). Rooted in the immediacy of response, compassion, Arendt observes, is curiously muted and awkward with words, unlike "the eloquent pity" that is able to reach out to a broader audience in its glorification of the suffering of others (85, 88).

For the purpose of this analysis, two points are important in Arendt's interpretation of politicized suffering: the first has to do with the sentimental and arranged quality of pity; the second emphasizes the mediating character of pity able to connect—without conflating—those who suffer with those who observe them. To put it in Arendt's words: "[W]ithout the presence of misfortune, pity could not exist, and it therefore has just as much vested interest in the existence of the unhappy as thirst for power has a vested interest in the existence of the weak" (1963, 89). Following Arendt's distinction between compassion and pity, Luc Boltanski in his work drew attention to the crucial role of distance in sustaining a politics of pity: the spectacle of remote suffering undermines the urgency of the commitment by separating knowledge from action (1999, 33).

For Arendt and Boltanski it is crucial that the politics of pity has a hierarchical nature; the object of pity (the sufferer) and the subject of pity (the observer) are socially and experientially split. The Altai mothers' experience, however, radically reverses this order of things. Unlike Arendt's *hommes faibles,* whose misery justified the political radicalism of the French Revolution (1963, 88–90; Spelman 1999, 82–89), or images of distant suffering that charity campaigns use to convince those who are *not* desperate (Boltanski 1999; also Kleinman and Kleinman 1997), the soldiers' mothers were far from being the passive objects of someone else's politics inspired by their pain. Instead, their representations of pain, their experience of suffering, and their emotionally driven attempts to negotiate new social positions are merged here. Firmly rooted in their loss, soldiers' mothers *themselves* perform an emotive micropolitics of pity in order to produce a recognizable identity in a situation where more conventional forms of identification, political representation, and the rules of social exchange either cease to function or only start to emerge. By taking control over the public display of their loss and suffering, the mothers nonetheless kept intact major features of the politics of pity: the border between the unfortunate and fortunate was increasingly solidified, mothers' presentations of their suffering were progressively ritualized, and histories of loss were more and more removed from any action that could prevent those losses from happening again.

The mothers' investments in the constant production of a value-charged subject position and their involvement in the public circulation of emotion, which this position usually entails, had its consequences. As Wendy Brown put it in a similar context, "Politicized identity…enunciates itself, makes claims for itself, only by entrenching, restating, dramatizing, and inscribing its pain in politics; it can hold out no future—for itself or others—that triumphs over this pain" (1995, 74). This inscribing of pain in politics can also produce a different—unifying—experience. Commonly associated with the politics of pity, a distinction between those who suffer and those who do not (Arendt 1963, 88–89) persists in the Altai mothers' activity, too. It has, however, an authorship and a function that are different from the politics of pity described by Arendt. Preoccupied with the emotional network that articulations of trauma stories produce, the Altai mothers did not succeed in turning language into "their non-violent weapon to capture the public consciousness" of those outside their immediate circle, as did, for example, the Argentinean Mothers of the Plaza de Mayo, who actively unmasked the junta's practice of abduction and the murders of the disappeared (Bouvard 1994, 131). The Altai mothers' activity seemed to follow a trajectory that was also used by the Committee of Mothers of Heroes and Martyrs of Matagalpa in Nicaragua in 1979–84. Unable to successfully challenge the existing system of power or to form an active oppositional movement, they did accomplish a lot of changes by transforming *their* environment and *their* own network of meaningful relations (Bayard de Volo 2001, 209).

For Altai mothers, the presumed commonality and universality of suffering functioned as a unifying framework, and as the main tool of exclusion. The outside world was viewed as "imaginary extensions of the subject" (Born and Hesmondhalgh 2000, 35), as "an externalization of the interior" (Boltanski 1999, 82). Establishing connections with a broader community was defined by the effort to find one's own traumatic experience reflected in other people's lives.[26] Exceeding the usual intention to become an object of someone else's emotional reaction, the mothers' politics of pity tried to erase the difference between feeling sorry for someone and feeling someone else's sorrow. Empathy, *sochiuvstvie* (literally, cofeeling) was turned here into *sostradanie,* cosuffering. A purposeful coordination of affect, in other words, required a corresponding coordination of experience (Eagleton 2003, 156). One comment from a mother's letter helpfully clarifies this somewhat abstract point. Complaining to Pavlukova about another leader of a regional CSM, a mother summed up her qualifying principle: "Her behavior disappoints me a lot. She has no room for grief [*net goria v nei*]. She is just obsessed with glory and heroism, while the maternal pain is hardly noticeable in her" (Irina L., SPPF).

During my fieldwork, I observed how Tatiana M., an active member of a local branch of an Altai CSM that deals with abuses in the army, instructed mothers who came for advice. During one of my visits, I witnessed Tatiana's long conversation with a mother who came from a nearby village. The mother's son had been drafted to a remote military base, and for several weeks there had been no news and no telephone calls from him. Alarmed by

26. For a theoretical discussion see Young (1997, 257–58).

the situation, she sold a cow, bought train tickets, and went to the base. As she discovered, the son had been hospitalized for some time; his feet were infected and had started "rotting," as she put it. She commandeered her son and brought him home. Realizing that such an act could easily qualify as a criminal offense, she came to the committee. In the conversation with the mother, Tatiana first suggested that she get a divorce. According to law, a family with a single mother and only one son can be granted an exemption from the service by the Ministry of Defense. This solution was not really plausible (the mother had another son). Having explored other, even less realistic possibilities, Tatiana finally resorted to what seemed the most effective tool: she told the mother how to talk to the military officials, since one has to find a "common language even with the enemy." As Tatiana framed it, "You have to cry. Cry as only a mother can do it." Several weeks later, in an interview, she revealed the origin of this approach (without any connection with this particular case): "When I came here, I did not know what to do.... There was this permanent grief all the time, so.... But Olga K. [the head of the CSM's branch] told me: "Sit at the table. A mother comes, she cries, so you cry with her, too.... This is how I started it in 1994."[27]

It is exactly this conscious "recourse to a shared, and relatively fixed set, of public gestures" as opposed to unmediated empathy—the political production of "a chain of communication of feeling," as Arjun Appadurai put it (1990, 110, 107; also Skidmore 2003, 9)—that seems to enable the Altai mothers to conduct their emotive politics of pity. One consequence that this distancing politics of pity tends to produce was quite surprising. The Altai CSM is indeed a committee that brings together only mothers. Fathers' participation is infrequent and irregular; moreover, all the mothers I interviewed were either widows or remarried to someone other than the dead son's father.[28] Even more striking was the fact that soldiers' widows or sisters were not involved in the committee's activity either. The mothers' unfriendly comments about their daughters-in-law regularly popped up in their conversations and letters, making the younger women's participation in the committee even less likely. Pavlukova's frequent correspondent, a mother whose son died in Afghanistan, reflects this attitude in her letter: "The young ones [widows] could not care less about our problems; they are young and healthy. They find new husbands, and live without legalizing

27. For a very different treatment of grief and pity in the Indian context see Clark-Decès (2005, 40–49).

28. Feitlowitz traces a somewhat similar tendency in her studies of terror in Argentina (1998, 96).

the marriage so that they will still be entitled to death benefits.... This is why we have called our organization the council of *parents*.... It is parents' destiny to carry out the political struggle" (Irina L., SPPF; emphasis in the original).

In part this resentment was economically driven: soldiers' widows were entitled to bigger social benefits than soldiers' mothers. There were signs indicating that the symbolic hierarchy of traumatic experience was just as important as the material one. Altai mothers might not have been familiar with Solzhenitsyn's appeal to rely on the differentiating function of pain in structuring communities (discussed in chapter 2), but they were certainly familiar with the consolidating effect that such a differentiation could deliver.

As we have seen, the regional administration was instrumental in dividing mothers into different social categories according to the circumstances of their sons' deaths. Yet the mothers themselves were painfully discriminating in following the social typology of loss that underlay their collective rituals. Thus, for a long time commemorative gatherings in the city brought together only mothers whose sons died in Afghanistan. Mothers of soldiers killed in Chechnya began to be invited to such public events well after the second Chechen war started. Significantly, the mothers whose sons died because of abuse and negligence in the army were completely excluded from these commemorative rituals. One of these mothers, Olga K., whose son was apparently killed by his fellow soldiers, described to me how she tried to attract the attention of the local authorities in these circumstances:

In 1991 we... became a civic organization. And the first thing I did was to introduce myself to the local administration; I had worked before in a research institute and never socialized in such high circles [*vysshie krugi*].... Usually I would come and say that I am a mother whose son died in the army in a time of peace. They would open their eyes wide and say, "Is it true that there are cases like that?" I'd say, "Of course, there are! What are you talking about?" Later I put together an album, you know, an album in which all our deceased are. In which our pain is, mainly. An album of pain. Pictures, photos, things like that. So, I would come to the officials to introduce myself and I would show them portraits from the album, so that they could have a look, and I could see their reaction. If they looked at the portraits with some attention, then I would talk to them. If they only leafed through the album, I would take it back and leave right away. People often would ask me in such cases, "Lady, why did you come, then?" So, thanks to this album, I found people who are interested. And not just interested but also helpful. They understand our pain, they help us.

This story usefully outlines the internal mechanism of the politics of pity. The dialogical exchange between mother and official is triangulated: the emotional response is expected to be triggered by the "organized" evidence of loss—an album of pain. Empowering and voyeuristic at the same time, the spectacle of suffering and the witnessing of others' reaction to it become inseparable here.[29] Containing the loss, the album demarcates and mediates the distance between the mother and the official. This medium of signs radically changes the modality of this exchange, too. The articulation of pain is overshadowed by the mother's "emotional *reading*" of her interlocutor (Ahmed 2004, 26; emphasis added). Generating a structure for attention and remembering (Kleinman 1995, 124; Saunders and Aghaie 2005, 16), this conflation of affect and media makes rhetorically and socially inappropriate any questions about the political conditions that produced these losses in the first place. What is shared here is not a piece of information or a view, which can be contested, but rather an intimate space for emotional commitment to the dead (Boltanski 1999, 42; Tsintjilonis 2004, 376). Vocalization of pain and exchange of opinions about tragic losses become discursively, socially, and spatially separate.

And yet this reliance on synchronization of affect and media—not unlike the similar attempts of Altai neocommunists or Chechen war veterans discussed earlier—often faced its limits when the mothers tried to get their message beyond the boundaries of their emotional enclave. The mothers frequently construed this lack of public attention as people's reluctance to return the grief projected onto them caused by their inability to imagine themselves in the same situation. Svetlana Pavlukova complained in an interview that mothers of potential conscripts usually did not even bother to attend special meetings about military drafting that the committee organized periodically: "These people, they think, 'It is your son, not mine, who has to go to Chechnya. My son is too little to do this.' But in the end, it is our common pain. Today your son is little, but the war....It lasts, it goes forever. And as a result, even your grandsons might be drafted....I do not even know what to do, but today our sons go there, tomorrow our grandsons. And somehow, somewhere...there is no peace yet."

When I asked her to describe why there was a need to go to this war in the first place and what was to be defended there, she was confused. Struggling with words, she finally framed her answer as a series of short phrases: "You know...How should I put it? How should I say it?...Before, there was

---

29. See Hesford (2004) on the simultaneity of empowerment and voyeurism in testimonies.

something we all supported. And now, well, there is somehow no ideal to live for. But you know, in general, I am a patriot of my Motherland, and Russia for me, well, always remains my Motherland." The retreat into an abstract patriotism as the last and self-explanatory reason revealed the context in which this sudden politicization happened: a lack of ideals to *live* for and the inability to justify *deaths* were framed in terms of national belonging or, to be more precise, in terms of the nation space that must prevail.

The Blood That Forgets Nothing

At the end of the 1990s, trying to break away from a seeming state of isolation and simultaneously to keep good relations with the local authorities, the mothers framed soldiers' deaths within a more overtly political context. The second book of memory, *We were waiting for you, sons…* (*My zhdali vas* 1999) was instrumental in changing the CSM's tone. The book came out in the fall of 1999, shortly after Putin's government started the second Chechen war. The book used a very different way to narrate the war and its losses. Unlike the first book of memory, it had an extended collection of critical accounts of the Chechen wars written by journalists from local Altai newspapers. At the same time, the "memorial" part, the actual list of fallen soldiers, was radically modified. Personalized obituaries were gone; instead, the section titled "Requiem" included color photographs of fallen soldiers accompanied by a few dry lines that briefly described their places of birth, death, types of military forces in which they served, and—when applicable—the awards they received, usually posthumously. Though devoid of any strong emotional messages, the book did contain one editorial piece that let the anger be heard. A two-page afterword with the subtitle "Who Is to Blame?" spelled out what seemed to be the dominant attitude of the time. As if drawing a line under the social and political disaster caused by the war in Chechnya, the text insisted that "President [Yeltsin's] main fault [was] not in his decision to move troops [into Chechnya]. No. His main crime [was] in destroying the state, along with this state's ability to protect its own people" (*My zhdali vas* 1999, 269).

The public presentation of the book made this gradual transformation of the politics of pity into a politics of blame even more obvious. The event was staged in a local theater in downtown Barnaul and was attended by the mothers, veterans of local wars, politicians, and journalists. The ceremony was opened by a short video, in which endless images of churches and pictures of Russian landscapes put a peaceful, spiritual cast on the last hundred years of Russia's history. The video was accompanied by a narrative that had a very different message. The peaceful visual backdrop was in a radical contrast to a story that presented the century as a lasting chain of external attacks and internal treachery: from the Russian-Japanese war of 1905 to the plan of psychological war against Russia allegedly created by Allen Dulles in the 1950s; from Germany's invasion in 1941 to Russia's current battles with Islam in the Caucasus. The century of history emerged as a century of heroic struggle and resistance to alien forces, a resistance that is "deeply rooted" in Russian tradition, as one of the presenters put it. The main slogan of the ceremony reminded the audience of the purpose of this lesson in history: "To Remember in Order to Live" (*Pomnit', chtoby zhit'*).

Taken out of its immediate political context, the war in Chechnya was located within a larger historical narrative that radically marginalized the war's own specific aspects and causes. The political framing of losses, in other words, became possible as a result of a metaphorical operation, already familiar from songs about the Chechen wars discussed in the previous chapter. However, unlike veterans, the mothers were not interested in a genealogy of military glory ("a son of the soldier who took Kabul, a grandson of a soldier who took Berlin"). Instead, sons killed in local wars were presented as a link in the chain of ancestors who died defending their Motherland from a long-standing "campaign of Russia's dismembering [*raschlenenie*]" initiated by various hostile forces. The poem read at the opening of the book presentation—a simultaneous message to a "distant ancestor" and to a close descendant ("son")—summed up this interplay of outside pressure and internal resistance well:

> The battlefield is ablaze
> My ancestor, now I recall our tie
> It is my blood
> That you shed on the Kulikovo battlefield…
> Our blood is intact
> Even though it has been shed many times
> It forgets nothing
> Remember, son, you share the blood of your ancestors. (Artem'ev n.d.)

This poem about the shared substance through which communities are established and maintained in a succinct form brings together the main tropes that sustained the patriotic narratives discussed in this book. Soil, blood, war, and history link sons and ancestors in a perpetually unfolding narrative of national loss. The Kulikovo battlefield mentioned in the poem had a special meaning in this bloody amalgamation of the national and the spatial. Located in central Russia (the Tula region), the battlefield was the place where on September 8, 1380, Russian soldiers, led by the Moscow prince Dmitrii Ivanovich, for the first time in history defeated the troops of the Golden Horde.[30] The battle is traditionally seen as a crucial moment in the process of the liberation of Rus' from Tatar domination and as a powerful step toward the emergence of a consolidated Russian state. The political importance of the battle was reemphasized in 1996, when the Russian government issued a special decision that outlined a series of events aimed at commemorating the six hundredth anniversary of the event.[31]

During the book presentation, the importance of biospatial connections was emphasized in a more politically overt way, as well. When a group of contemporary dancers in black dresses performed their disjointed movements on stage, the screen behind them depicted footage of the Russian deputies voting in December 1991 in favor of dissolving the Soviet Union.

The voice-over simultaneously gave the dictionary meaning of the word "cosmopolite" as a person who does not recognize the specificity of the relationship with the motherland, thus bringing back sinister associations with the Stalinist anti-Semitic campaign against "kinless cosmopolites" (*bezrodnye kosmopolity*). Aleksandr Surikov, governor of the region at the time, attended the presentation, too; he sponsored the publication of the book of memory and even authorized the introduction to it. In his short speech he linked the theme of cut-off roots with the idea of alienated state institutions. As the governor put it, the soldiers' deaths were the "price for the betrayals" that began with the splitting of the Soviet Union. "It is a bitter price. But this is the price we have to pay for the life of our state. We've got no other state."[32] Justified by a lack of choice, the life of the state became associated with deaths in families, while the rhetoric of grief helped to

30. In his canonical *History of Russia from the Ancient Times*, written in the nineteenth century, Sergei Solov'ev indicates that about four hundred thousand soldiers participated in the battle. The number has been disputed, but regardless of the actual figure, the battle is often presented in Russian historiography as an ultimate "fight between Europe and Asia" (1963, 2:286–87).

31. As a part of this memorialization campaign, the Russian government decided to open "a military-historical and natural park-museum" on the site of the battle (*Kulikovo pole* n.d.). The tendency to reinstate victories of the past in the post-Soviet period was reconfirmed in the fall 2004, when the Duma, the Russian parliament, adopted a new law on national holidays. The traditional celebration of the Bolshevik Revolution (November 7) was abandoned. Instead, the Duma pronounced November 4 as the Day of Popular Unity (Den' narodnogo edinstva) to commemorate November 4, 1612, when armed peasants and merchants liberated Moscow from the Polish interventionists and stimulated the consolidation of power in Russia (the Romanov dynasty was elected in 1613).

32. I quote the governor from a videotape of the event that I obtained during the fieldwork.

transform the state violence in Chechnya into a self-victimizing discourse on the history of betrayals.

This search for a political justification of the military deaths marked a significant break with the symbolic strategies of the early 1990s. Back then, as the curator of the Altai Museum of Local Wars told me, she wanted to finish the exhibit about the Afghan war with the question "What for?" This question "simply went away," as the curator put it, but the strong necessity for an answer remained. By the late 1990s, this quest for explanation acquired the shape of a discursive self-victimization. By reinterpreting and reenacting previous conflicts and wars, the historicization of suffering helped to bridge the gap between past violence and violence in the present (Schröder and Schmidt 2001, 9; Hoepken 1999; Senjkovic 1993). By exteriorizing perpetrators, the mothers established a new common space inside: a "sociomoral" environment (Comaroff and Comaroff 2000, 13) shared by ancestors and descendants. Designed originally to commemorate fallen soldiers, the presentation was turned into another story about the nation's injuries.[33]

It is hard to tell whether this retreat to the patriotism of despair, with its predictable references to blood and soil, was a conscious political choice or an example of the Altai mothers' "strategic use of essentialism," as Gayatri Spivak defined it some time ago (Spivak 1993, 35). In my interviews with the CSM's women, they rejected any association with existing political groups and movements.[34] Regardless of these women's own intentions, the book presentation clearly showed the limits of their metonymic signification: the emotional inscriptions of pain in politics could be easily appropriated by more politically and rhetorically skillful groups, able to transform the politics of pity into a politics of blame.

By drawing attention to the symbolic strategies of dealing with deaths caused by state-organized violence, this chapter demonstrated how women in a Russian province formed a network of support in a situation of drastic social changes and dysfunctional institutions. Stories about suffering articulated by the Altai mothers created a community of loss that acted as the main author and simultaneously the main target of their politics of pity.

---

33. On the exclusion of perpetrators in the process of building a community see Borneman (1997, 22–23) and Girard (1986).

34. In 2004, the Moscow office of the CSM tried to transform the loosely organized committee into a political party, the United Party of Soldiers' Mothers. The party was short-lived—by 2005, it had merged with the Republican Party, which ceased to exist several months later.

By creating a space for the traumatic experience in their narratives, biographies, and environment, this group of women learned to live in a state of grief.

We have seen how the domestication and personalization of loss, as well as the localization of wars and violence, were used first of all as a means of organizing otherwise amorphous groups. At times, the Altai mothers' search for public recognition of their losses and their own identities resulted in a complicated ethical situation: attempts at finding a wider social importance in the deaths of their sons became fundamentally entangled with a public rationalization of the state's military politics. Yet predominantly, the post-Soviet ambiguity, with its lack of unifying civic discourses and shared standards, was overcome by the mothers in two major ways: issues of political responsibility and individual recovery were overshadowed by a powerful discourse on relatedness ("the mothers of dead soldiers") and memorialization ("How do we remember them?"). Unable (and unwilling) to rely on political metaphors, the Altai mothers narrated their losses within the genres of biographical stories and emotionally charged events. By displaying their suffering in public, the mothers created affective local enclaves. At the same time, their rituals of metonymic memorialization both reproduced material evidence of their traumas and assigned symbolic meaning to their sons' deaths. Providing a poignant framework for the postsocialist experience, losses caused by state military politics were turned into a primary form of subjectification. Perceived in quasi-familial terms of individual and group loyalty, public space and the nation's history eventually became the source of an emotional striving for revenge and retribution rather than for accountability and justice.

Conclusion

"People Cut in Half"

"We ended up in between. Not old, not young....We did not become patriotic. We did not become cosmopolitan, either. We were filled with hatred for *Sovok*. But for some reason, every New Year's Eve we still sing *Unbreakable Union*" (Minaev 2007, 7; emphasis in the original). *Sovok* is a pejorative term for the Soviet Union; the song about the "Unbreakable Union of Freeborn Republics"—is the old Soviet anthem. The quotation is from the introductory essay that Sergei Minaev, a successful writer and businessman from Moscow, wrote for an edited collection of texts by his peers—Russian authors born between 1970 and 1976. Presented as a countercultural phenomenon, the anthology is devoted mainly to the remembrance of the USSR (Litprom.ru 2007)

There is a paradox connected with the Soviet legacy in contemporary Russia. Attempts to revisit, retain, and reconstruct traces of this vanishing period are increasing as the USSR is becoming more and more the property of professional historians. Multiple polls have traced a steady tendency: more than half of Russians (*rossiiane*) regret the disappearance of the Soviet Union. A third believe that the collapse was inevitable. But there is still no general agreement about the causes of this collapse, almost two decades after the event. About a quarter of those who were polled in 2007 pointed to "the irresponsible behavior" of Boris Yeltsin (Russia), Leonid Kravchuk (Ukraine), and Stanislav Shushkevich (Belarus), who on December 8, 1991, agreed to end the USSR. About 20 percent cited "the people's disappointment" with the Soviet government led by Mikhail Gorbachev. Yet others referred to the "hostile conspiracy of foreign forces" (16 percent) or to the "total exhaustion" of the Communist ideology (15 percent). Strikingly, despite the strong attachment to the Soviet past, only 16 percent said they would welcome the resurrection of the USSR in its previous form.[1]

Nostalgic feelings, predictably, are decreasing among younger generations, yet they are still very prominent among those who have been shaped in the 1990s, both during and by the collapse of the USSR.[2] The generations that ended up in between are already determining the country's cultural development and will increasingly influence its political agenda as well. Their investment in the past should not be misread, though. Most of these children of reform have no illusions about state socialism, and they have learned their lessons about purges, repressions, and the gulag. But they have also experienced their own share of the Soviet experiment, associated mostly with the Politburo's elderly members rather than with Stalin's iron fist. Their socialism was more domestic than political, and their Soviet legacy is one of the very few sources through which they can explain, if not understand, the historical forces that so dramatically split their lives into Soviet and post-Soviet segments.

Given Russia's current development, this basic cultural inclination to come to terms with the recent past (or even to find appropriate terms for it) will perhaps only become stronger. The "rowdy 1990s" (*likhie devianostye*), as this period is labeled retrospectively in Russia now, passed too quickly to have established a stable ground or produced a cultural demand for any serious self-reflection.[3] The relative "stability" of the first decade of the new century provided both a time-out and a historical distance, necessary for taking a probing retrospective look at the recent past.

It is remarkable that in these increasingly frequent attempts to capture the meaning of the post-Soviet liminality, the children of reform appealed to the primacy of traumatic experience. In the late 1980s, the magazine *Ogonek* made glasnost real by opening important debates about Stalinism. In 2007, the magazine reexamined the changes started by perestroika by publishing

1. For details see the report "What Do Russians Regret about the Collapse of the USSR?" based on a sociological poll conducted in December 2007 by the Levada Center, a major Russian polling firm, http://www.polit.ru/research/2007/12/24/ussr.html.

2. Among Russians between twenty-five and thirty-nine years old, 40 percent regretted the collapse of the USSR. The proportion is higher among older people ("What Do Russians Regret?").

3. *Likhoi* has a double meaning in Russian—the root, *likho,* means "evil," but it can also be used to describe something unrestrained, bold, and dashing.

a review of Minaev's edited collection. Epitomizing a larger trend, the essay was titled "I Have a Trauma." Andrei Arkhangelskii, a literary critic, wrote,

> We are used to talking through our problems one on one, but never—as a country....Therefore, every generation carries its own trauma with it, unspoken. When compared with the war or repressions, the wrecking [*razval*] of the USSR is nothing special, of course. Just do not try to tell this to my generation....Yes, we managed to catch the late Brezhnev; and possibly, we were the most loyal Soviet kids ever. The childhood we had was not very affluent but it was peaceful; and we loved that country for it—in our own way, no doubt, but sincerely, nonetheless. In 1991 those who taught us to cherish the motherland as the apple of one's eye informed us that the country had ended—for objective reasons. "Objective" is a good word, but can anyone be objective during the funeral of one's own mother? (2007)

In his interview with the *New York Times,* Minaev himself appealed to similar metaphors in his description of the generation of those who were destined forever to remain ex-Soviet: "We are people cut in half. We were born "v Sovke" [in the Soviet Union]. Then in the 1990s they drastically changed everything. They said, 'OK, now we're watching another channel. We're not watching this one anymore." They said forget about all the heroes, forget about the entire cultural heritage, forget about everything. We've changed the picture. Now survive.' It's like throwing house pets into the forest" (as quoted in Kishkovsky 2007).

This book has attempted to show how this language of trauma articulated by "people cut in half" gradually emerged in Russia as the main symbolic framework for describing radical changes of the 1990s and their consequences in the following decade. The end of the country provoked multiple discourses and rituals, in which personally felt dramatic events wove identity, loss, and the nation into a plausible narrative—with a collapsed state, radical economic reforms, dramatic transformations of social values, and changing cultural patterns in the background. For many of my informants "trauma" was more than a striking image for sudden and inexplicable ruptures in their lives. In many cases there was nothing metaphoric about violence, deaths, or suffering. Yet what unites experience-based trauma and imaginary trauma is a profound desire to get beyond objective reasoning in order to transform the transitional experience into something very tangible: headstones, leaflets, theoretical frameworks, or war songs.

In some cases, elaborate rituals of mourning and memorialization created a lasting link with the past. In others, the recognition of loss led to the incessant production of obituaries able to retain in words (or to provide an account of) what had been lost. In yet other cases, the search for a meaningful connection resulted in establishing emotional attachments with dramatic events that had not been witnessed and emotional memories that had never been shared. The production and circulation of such narratives and rituals frequently led to a particular form of collectivity—communities of loss. There is, of course, not that much new about this type of belonging in Russia. Consider again Viktor Shklovsky, a Russian formalist, who compared St. Petersburg after the Bolshevik Revolution to a group of men after an explosion: their insides have been torn out, but they sit and keep on talking (2004, 133–34). Separated from Shklovsky by several wars, seventy years of state socialism, and almost two decades of market reforms, during my fieldwork in Barnaul I had a chance to witness people talking after yet another "explosion." These retrospective conversations provided a historical bookend, a culturally specific narrative of closure—for the regime and the country but also for the experiment that gave birth to the Soviet way of life.

Structured by the recollection of personal or historical traumas, the communities of loss discussed in this book habitually framed their relations in naturalizing terms, be it soldiers' brotherhood, mothers' committees, ethnic milieus, or various organic metaphors for the Russian national body. New forms of social kinship emerged through a vocabulary of shared pain: the memory of blood and the memory of suffering seemed to merge in these forms of connectedness. It was this patriotism of despair" that brought the country, the nation, and the traumatic experience together. A wounded attachment, the patriotism of despair deflected rather than healed pain. It was a promise of a community bound by the solidarity of grief. A community of loss, no doubt, but a community, nonetheless.

References

Acar, Keziban. 2004. "An Examination of Russian Imperialism: Russian Military and Intellectual Descriptions of the Caucasians during the Russo-Turkish War of 1877–1878." *Nationalities Papers* 32 (1): 7–21.

Agalkov, Aleksandr. 2003. "Khozhdenie za tri goroda." In Gordin and Grigor'ev 2003, 209–19.

Agamben, Giorgio. 1999. *Remnants of Auschwitz: The Witness and the Archive.* Trans. Daniel Heller-Roazen. New York: Zone Books.

———. 1998. *Homo Sacer: Sovereign Power and Bare Life.* Trans. Daniel Heller-Roazen. Stanford: Stanford University Press.

Agenstvo voennykh novostei. 1999. "Uchastnikam boev v Chechne gosudarstvo budet vyplachivat' okolo 1000 dollarov SShA v mesiats." October 1999.

Ahmed, Sarah. 2004. "Collective Feelings Or, The Impression Left by Others." *Theory, Culture and Society* 21 (2): 25–42.

Akaev, Askar. 2002. *Kirgyzskaia gosudarstvennost' i narodnyi epos 'Manas.'* Bishkek: Uchkun.

Alexievich, Svetlana. 1992. *Zinky Boys: Soviet Voices from the Afghanistan War.* Trans. Julia and Robin Whitby. New York: Norton.

Alksnis, Viktor. 2004. "Deputat Gosdumy RF Viktor Aksnis obviniaet Soiuz komitetov soldatskikh materei v vypolnenii politicheskogo zakaza so storony Zapada." Interview, October 20. Radio *Ekho Moskvy.* http://echo.msk.ru/news/211841.html.

Altai Daily Review. 2006. "Byvshyi vitse-gubernator i dekan sotsiologicheskogo fakul'teta AltGU budet rabotat' v Moskve." March 16. http://www.bankfax.ru/page.php?pg=34365.

———. 2004. "'Kak vtorgalis' na Altai': Vospominaniia ochevidtsa o zagadochnom charternom reise 3–4 aprelia. 2004." April 12.

———. 2003. "Defitsit konsolidirovannogo biudzheta Altaiskogo kraia v 2004 g. uvelichitsia v dva raza." November 28. http://www.bankfax.ru/page.php?pg=22254.

Altaiskaia pravda. 2006a. Pomiani nas, Rossiia, v dekabr'skuiu stuzhy! December, 27.

———. 2006b. "Namedni." September 2.

———. 2003. "Russkii krest." January 22.

Altaiskaia pravda. 2001. "Otriad osobogo naznacheniia." January 24.

Althusser, Louis. 1971. *Lenin and Philosophy and Other Essays.* Trans. Ben Brewster. New York: Monthly Review Press.

Analiz. 2004. *Analiz protsessov privatizatsii gosudartsvennoi sobstvennosti v Rossiiskoi Federatsii za period 1993–2003 godov.* Moscow: Olita.

Anderson, Benedict. 1991. *Imagined Communities: Reflections on the Origin and Spread of Nationalism.* London: Verso.

Anderson, David. G. 2000. "Surogate Money and the 'Wild Market' in Central Siberia." In Seabright 2000, 318–44.

Andreev, Andrei. 2002. "Manipuliatsiia soznaniem: Rossiia ne mozhet pogibnut'." *Pokolenie,* no. 12: 5.

Anishenko, G., A. Vasilevskaia, O. Kugusheva, and O. Mramornov, eds. 1995. *Komissiia Govorukhina.* Moscow: Laventa.

Anisimov, E. 2004. "Rossiia ostanetsia bez russkikh?" *Komsomol'skaia pravda,* May 4.

Appadurai, Arjun. 1990. "Topographies of the Self: Praise and Emotion in Hindu India." In *Language and the Politics of Emotion,* ed. C. Lutz and L. Abu-Lughod, 91–112. Cambridge: Cambridge University Press.

———. 1986. "Introduction: Commodities and the Politics of Value." In *The Social Life of Things: Commodities in Cultural Perspective,* ed. A. Appadurai, 3–63. Cambridge: Cambridge University Press.

ARD. 2005. "Interview of Vladimir Putin with German television channels ARD and ZDF, May 5, 2005." http://www.kremlin.ru/text/appears/2005/05/87570.shtml.

Arendt, Hannah. 1963. *On Revolution.* New York: Viking.

Arkhangelskaia, Natalia, Maxim Rubchenko, and Ekaterina Shokhina. 2005. "Monetizatsiia l'got: Falshstart." *Ekspert* 3: 12–17.

Arkhangelskii, Andrei. 2007. "U menia est' travma." *Ogonek,* December 3, 53.

Artem'ev V. n.d. "Pamiat'." http://www.akm1917.org/music/text/pamyat_rus_sssr.htm.

Arutunov, Sergei. 2003. "Vpered nazad, k estestvennomu pravu." In *Rossiia i Chechnia: Poiski vykhoda,* ed. Yakov Gordin, 9–16. St. Petersburg: Zvezda.

Arvedlund, Erin E. 2005. "Celebrating the U.S.S.R. in Song. Uncle Joe and All." *New York Times,* May 7.

Asad, Talal. 2003. *Formations of the Secular: Christianity, Islam, Modernity.* Stanford: Stanford University Press.

Baev, Pavel K. 1996. *The Russian Army in the Time of Trouble.* London: Sage Publications.

Baisaev, U., and D. Grushkin, eds. 2006. *Zdes' zhivut liudi. Chechnia: khronika nasiliia.* Pts. 2–3. Moscow: Zven'ia.

———. 2003. *Zdes' zhivut liudi. Chechnia: khronika nasiliia.* Pt. 1. Moscow: Zven'ia.

Bakhtin, Mikhail. 1981. *The Dialogic Imagination: Four Essays.* Trans. Caryl Emerson and Michael Holquist. Austin: University of Texas Press.

Bakhtin, Mikhail, and Pavel Medvedev. 1991. *The Formal Method in Literary Scholarship: A Critical Introduction to Sociological Poetics.* Trans. Albert Wehrle. Baltimore: John Hopkins University Press.

Baktmetov A. 2004. "'Russkii krest'—na vsiu zhizn'." *Profil',* November 15, 34–35.

Balibar, Étienne. 1994. "Subjection and Subjectivation." In *Supposing the Subject,* ed. Joan Copjec. London: Verso.

Bannikov, Konstantin. 2002. *Antropologiia ektsremal'nykh grupp: Dominantnye otnosheniia sredi voenno-sluzhashchikh srochnoi sluzhby Rossiiskoi armii.* Moscow.

Barakhova, Alla, and Ilia Bulavinov. 1999. "Chechenskie vlasti voiny odobrili." *Kommersant-Daily*, October 2.

Bar-on, Dan. 1999. *The Indescribable and the Undiscussable, Reconstructing Human Discourse After Trauma.* Budapest: Central European University Press.

Barthes, Roland. 1981. *Camera Lucida. Reflections on Photography.* Trans. Richard Howard. New York: Hill and Wang.

Basilov V. N. 1992. "Etnografiia: Est' li u nee budushchee?" *Etnograficheskoe obozrenie,* 4: 3–17.

Bass, Alan. 2000. *Difference and Disavowal: The Trauma of Eros.* Stanford: Stanford University Press.

Bassin, Mark. 1991. "Russia between Europe and Asia: The Ideological Construction of Georaphical Space." *Slavic Review* 50 (1): 1–17.

Bateneva, Tatiana. 2003. "Russkii krest" nuzhno popravit'. *Izvestia,* May 17.

Bayard de Volo, Lorraine. 2001. *Mothers of Heros and Martyrs: Gender Identity Politics in Nicaragua, 1979–1999.* Baltimore: Johns Hopkins University Press.

Belozertsev, Iurii. 2004. "Kazaki v zashchitu uchenogo." *Vitiaz,* no. 2: 3.

Beria, Lavrentii. 2000. "Letter to I. Stalin from March 1, 1944. Dokumenty iz arkhiva Iosifa Stalina." *Nezavisimaia gazeta,* February 29.

Berger, Mikhail. 1995. "1 347 172 715 572 rublei. Etu summu ne poluchila kazna iz-za l'got odnim tol'ko sportivnym organizatsiiam." *Izvestiia,* February 21.

Bibby, Michael. 1993. "Fragging the Chains of Command: GI Resistance Poetry and Mutilation." *Journal of American Culture* 16 (3): 29–39.

Bikbov, A., and S. Gavrilenko. 2003. "Rossiiskaia sotsiologiia: Avtonomiia pod voprosom. Part 2." *Logos* 2: 51–87.

———. 2002. "Rossiiskaia sotsiologiia: Avtonomiia pod voprosom. Part 1." *Logos* 5: 186–210.

Biletskii, Andrei. 1996. "Soldatskie materi. Umom ili serdtsem?" *Na boevom postu,* July 17, 2.

Binns, Christopher. 1979. "Changing Face of Power: Revolution and Accommodation in the Development of the Soviet Ceremonial System. Part 1." *Man* (N.S.) 14 (4): 585–606.

———. 1980. "Changing Face of Power: Revolution and Accommodation in the Development of the Soviet Ceremonial System. Part 2." *Man* (N.S.) 15 (1): 170–87.

Blinskii, A., ed. 2000. *Rossiia i Chechnia: 200–letniaia voina.* St. Petersburg: Satis.

Bloch, Maurice, and Jonathan Parry. 1980. "Introduction: Death and the Regeneration of Life." In *Death and the Regeneration of Life,* ed. M. Bloch and J. Parry, 1–44. Cambridge: Cambridge University Press.

Bobrov, Mikhail. 2000. "Zhiznennye sily cheloveka (problema vzaimodeistviia sostavliaiushchikh)." In Grigor'ev and Demina 2000, 56–62.

Bocharov, V. V., and V. A. Tishkov, eds. 2001. *Anthropologiia nasiliia.* St. Petersburg: Nauka.

Bogdanov, K. A., and A. A. Panchenko, eds. 2001. *Mifologiia i povsednevnost': Gendernyi podkhod v anthropologicheskikh distsiplinakh.* St. Petersburg: Aleteiia.

Bolgov, Vladimir. 2003. "Sotsiologicheskii analiz novykh form sotsiokul'turnoi zhizni." *Sotsiologicheskie issledovaniia* 2: 28–39.

Boltanski, Luc. 1999. *Distant Suffering: Morality, Media, and Politics.* Cambridge: Cambridge University Press.

Bondarenko, Vladimir. 2001. "Solzhenitsyn protiv Marka Deicha." *Zavtra,* November 21, 7.

Born, Georgina. 1998. "Anthropology, Kleinian Psychoanalysis, and the Subject of Culture." *American Anthropologist* 100 (2): 373–86.

———. 1997. "Modernist Discourse, Psychic Forms, and Agency: Aesthetic Subjectivities at IRCAM." *Cultural Anthropology* 12 (4): 480–501.

Born, Georgina, and David Hesmondhalgh. 2000. "Introduction: On Difference, Representation, and Appropriation in Music." In *Western Music and Its Other: Difference, Representation, and Appropriation in Music,* ed. G. Born and D. Hesmondhalgh, 1–58. Berkeley: University of California Press.

Borneman, John. 2004a. "Theorizing Regime Ends." In *Death of the Father: An Anthropology of the End in Political Authority,* ed. John Borneman, 1–32. New York: Berghahn Books.

———, ed. 2004b. *Death of the Father: An Anthropology of the End in Political Authority.* New York: Berghahn Books.

———. 1997. *Settling Accounts: Violence, Justice and Accountability in Postsocialist Europe.* Princeton: Princeton University Press.

———. 1992. *Belonging in the Two Berlins: Kin, State, Nation.* Cambridge: Cambridge University Press.

Böröcz, Jozsef. 2000. "The Fox and the Raven: The European Union and Hungary Renegotiate the Margins of 'Europe.'" *Comparative Studies of History and Society* 42 (4): 348–80.

Borovik, Artyom. 1990. *The Hidden War: A Russian Journalist's Account of the Soviet War in Afghanistan.* New York: Grove Press.

Borovikov, Dmitry. 2002. "Chto takoe pobeda." *Pokolenie,* no. 8.

Borovoi, Konstantin. 2001. "On genial'no ugadal potrebnosti vlasti." *Komsomol'skaia pravda,* July 18.

Bourgois, Philippe. 2001. "The Power of Violence in War and Peace: Post-Cold War Lessons from El Salvador." *Ethnography* 2 (1): 5–34.

Bouvard, Marguerite Guzman. 1994. *Revolutionizing Motherhood: The Mothers of the Plaza de Mayo.* Wilmington, DE: SR Books.

Boycko, Maxim, Andrei Shleifer, and Robert Vishny. 1996. *Privatizing Russia.* Cambridge, MA: MIT Press.

Boyd, Richard. 1979. "Metaphor and Theory Change: What Is Metaphor For?" *Metaphor and Thought,* ed. Andrew Ortony. Cambidge: Cambridge University Press.

Boym, Svetlana. 2001. *The Future of Nostalgia.* New York: Basic books.

Bradbury, Mary. 2001. "Forget Me Not: Memorialization in Cemeteries and Crematoria." In *Grief, Mourning and Death Ritual,* ed. J. Hockey, J. Katz, and N. Small. Philadelphia, PA: Open University Press.

———. 1999. *Representations of Death: A Social Psychological Perspective.* London: Routledge.

Bromley, Yulian. 1989. *Theoretical Ethnography.* Moscow: Nauka.

———. 1976. *Soviet Ethnography: Main Trends.* Moscow: USSR Academy of Sciences.

Bromley, Yulian, and Viktor Kozlov. 1975. "National Processes in the USSR." In Bromley 1989, 142–69.

Brown, Kate. 2004. *A Biography of No Place: From Ethnic Borderland to Soviet Heartland.* Cambridge, MA: Harvard University Press.

Brown, Michael. 2004. "Heritage as Property." In *Property in Question: Value Transformation in the Global Economy,* ed. K. Verdery and C. Humphrey, 49–68. Oxford: Berg.

Brown, Wendy. 1995. *States of Injury: Power and Freedom in Late Modernity.* Princeton: Princeton University Press.

Bruszt, Laszlo, and David Stark. 2003. "Who Counts? Supranational Norms and Societal Needs." *East European Politics and Societies* 17 (1): 74–82.

Buchowski, Michal. 2003. "Coming to Terms with Capitalism: An Example of a Rural Community in Poland." *Dialectical Anthropology* 27: 47–68.

Bugai, N. F. 2006. *Chechenskaia respublika: Konfrontatsiia, stabil'nost', mir.* Moscow.

Buldakov, Vitalii. 2002. "Bezobidnaia" psikhologiia. *Pokolenie,* no. 13.

Burawoy, Michael. 2002. "Transition without Transformation: Russia's Involuntary Road to Capitalism." *East European Politics and Societies* 15 (2): 269–90.

Burawoy, Michael, and Krotov Pavel. 1993. "The Economic Basis of Russia's Political Crisis." *New Left Review* 198: 49–70.

Burganov, Agdas. 2002. "Izvechnye russkie voprosy v zerkale sovremennosti." *Sotsiologicheskie issledovaniia* 4: 97–102.

Butler, Judith. 2004. *Precarious Life: The Power of Mourning and Violence.* London: Verso.

———. 1997. *Excitable Speech: A Politics of Performativity.* New York: Routledge.

Byt' chechentsem: Mir i voina glazami shkol'nikov. 2004. Moscow: Memorial—Novoe izdatel'stvo.

Caiazza, Amy. 2002. *Mothers and Soldiers: Gender, Citizenship, and Civil Society in Contemporary Russia.* New York: Routledge.

Campbell, Matthew, Jacqueline M. Labbe, and Sally Shuttleworth, eds. 2000. *Memory and Memorials 1789–1914. Literary and Cultural Pespective.* London: Routledge.

Carsten, Janet, ed. 2000. *Cultures of Relatedness: New Approaches to the Study of Kinship.* Cambridge: Cambridge University Press.

Caruth, Cathy. 1996. *Unclaimed Experience: Trauma, Narrative, and History.* Baltimore: Johns Hopkins University Press.

———, ed. 1995. *Trauma: Explorations in Memory.* Baltimore: Johns Hopkins University Press.

Cavell, Stanley. 1997. "Comments on Veena Das's Essay 'Language and Body: Transactions and Construction of Pain.'" In Kleinman, Das, and Lock 1997, 93–98.

CBS. 2005. "Interview of V. V. Putin by CBS anchor Mike Wallace." May 9. http://www.kremlin.ru/text/appears/2005/05/87802.shtml.

Cheah, Pheng. 2003. *Spectral Nationality: Passages of Freedom from Kant to Postcolonial Literatures of Liberation.* New York: Columbia University Press.

Chechnya Weekly. 2003. "Casualty Figures." February 20. http://www.jamestown.org/publications_details.

Chernykh, Evgenii. 2005. "Oleg Gazmanov: Mne zapreshchali pet' v Kremle pro Sovetskii Soiuz." *Komsomol'skaia pravda,* April 7.

Chernyshev, Iurii. 2005. "Evolutsiia politicheskogo rezhima v Rossii i 'fenomen Mikhaila Evdokimova.'" Altaiskaia shkola politicheskikh issledovanii. http://hist.dcn-asu.ru/ashpi/aspi/research/2005/phnmn.html.

Chernyshev Iurii, ed. 2004. *Dnevnik Altaiskoi shkoly politicheskikh issledovanii.* Vols. 19–20. Barnaul: Izdatel'stvo Altaiskogo universiteta.

Chesnov, Ian. 1999. "Byt' chechentsem: Lichnost' i etnicheskaia identifikatsiia naroda." In Furman 1999, 63–102.

Cimino, Guido, and Francois Dushesneau, eds. 1997. *Vitalisms from Haller to the Cell Theory.* Firenze: Leo S. Olschki Editore.

Clark, David, ed. 1993. *The Sociology of Death: Theory, Culture, Practice.* Cambridge, MA: Blackwell Publishers.

Clark, Simon. 2000. "The Household in a Non-Monetary Market Economy." In Seabright 2000, 176–206.

Clark-Decès, Isabelle. 2005. *No One Cries for the Dead: Tamil Dirges, Rowdy Songs, and Graveyard Petitions.* Berkeley: University of California Press.

Clifford, James, and George Marcus, eds. 1986. *Writing Culture: The Poetics and Politics of Ethnography.* Berkeley: University of California Press.

Cock, Jacklyn. 2005. "'Guards and Guns': Towards Privatized Militarism in Post-Apartheid South Africa." *Journal of Southern African Studies* 31 (4): 791–803.

Comaroff, Jean. 1985. *Body of Power and Spirit of Resistance: The Culture and History of a South African People.* Chicago: Chicago University Press.

Comaroff, Jean, and John L. Comaroff. 2003a. "Reflections on Liberalism, Postculturalism, and ID-ology: Citizenship and Difference in South Africa." *Social Identities* 9 (4): 445–73.

———. 2003b. "Transparent Fictions; or, The Conspiracies of a Liberal Imagination: An Afterword." In West and Sanders 2003, 287–300.

———. 2000. "Millennial Capitalism: First Thought on a Second Coming." In *Millennial Capitalism and the Culture of Neoliberalism,* ed. Jean Comaroff and John L. Comaroff, 1–57. Durham, NC: Duke University Press.

———. 1992. *Ethnography and the Historical Imagination.* Boulder: Westview Press.

Commander, Simon, and Paul Seabright. 2000. "Conclusion: What Is to Be Done?" In Seabright 2000, 362–74.

Cosgrove, Simon. 2004. *Russian Nationalism and the Politics of Soviet Literature: the Case of Nash Sovremennik, 1981–91.* New York: Palgrave Macmillan.

Courtois, Stéphane, Nicolas Werth, Jean-Louis Panné, Andrzej Paczkowski, Karel Bartosek, and Jean-Louis Margolin. 1999. *The Black Book of Communism: Crimes, Terror, Repression.* Trans. Jonathan Murphy. Cambridge, MA: Harvard University Press.

Csikszentmihalyi, Mihaly, and Eugene Rochberg-Halton. 1982. *The Meaning of Things: Domestic Symbols and the Self.* Cambridge, MA: Cambridge University Press.

Dalnov, Gennadii, and Vladimir Klimov. 2003. "Ob osnovnom poniatii 'sotsiologiia zhizni.'" *Sotsiologicheskie issledovaniia* 4: 12–19.

Danforth, Loring M. 1982. *The Death Rituals of Rural Greece.* Princeton: Princeton University Press.

Danilova, Natalia. 2004. "Pravo materi soldata: instinkt zaboty ili grazhdanskii dolg?" In *Semeinye uzy: modeli dlia sborki.* Vol. 2. Ed. Serguei Oushakine, 188–211. Moscow: NLO.

———. 2002. "Kollektivnye deistviia uchastnikov voiny v Afganistane v kontekste sotsial'noi politiki." Dissertatsiia na soiskanie uchenoi stepeni kandidata sotsiologicheskikh nauk. Saratov: Saratovskii gosudarstvennyi tekhnicheskii universitet.

Das, Veena, Arthur Kleimann, Mamphela Ramphele, and Pamela Reynolds, eds. 2000. *Violence and Subjectivity.* Berkeley: University of California Press.

Davoine, Francoise, and Jean-Max Gaudilliere. 2004. *History Beyond Trauma*. Trans. Susan Fairfield. New York: Other Press.

Dean, Jodi. 2000. "Theorizing Conpiracy Theory." *Theory and Event* 4: 3.

de Certeau, Michel. 1984. *The Practice of Everyday Life*. Trans. Steven Rendall. Berkeley: University of California Press.

de Certeau, Michel, Luce Giard, and Pierre Mayol. 1998. *The Practices of Everyday Life*. Vol. 2, *Living and Cooking*. Trans. Timothy Tomasik. Minneapolis: Minnesota University Press.

Degtiarev, Sergei. 2004. "Sem' kandidatskikh i odna doktorskaia." *Altaiskaia pravda*, July 13.

"Deklaratsiia o gosudarstvennom suverenitete Checheno-Ingushskoi Respubliki." 1997. In Eremenko and Novikov 1997, 7–10.

Derlugian, Georgii. 1999. "Chechenskaia revolutsiia and chechenskaia istoriia." In Furman 1999, 197–222.

Derrida, Jacques. 2001. *The Work of Mourning*. Ed. Pascale-Anne Brault and Michael Naas. Chicago: University of Chicago Press.

——. 1985. "Racism's Last Word." *Critical Inquiry* 12 (1): 290–99.

Dinello, Natalia. 2002. "Clans for Markets, Clans for Plan: Social Networks in Hungary and Russia." *East European Politics and Societies* 15 (3): 589–624.

"Discussing Imperial Legacy: Archaisms and Neologisms." 2005. *Ab Imperio* 4.

Dmitrienko, Tamara. 2004. "1 iunia v Barnaule zashchishchali detei i materei." *Svobodnyi kurs*, June 3.

——. 2002. "Iz plena." *Svobodnyi kurs*, May 23.

Dolin, Anton. 2005. "Voina—Mat' rodna." *Gazeta*, September 28.

Dostatochno. 2003. *Dostatochno obshchaia teoriia upravleniia*. Novosibirsk: NIKA.

Dragadze, Tamara. 1980. "The Place of 'Ethnos' Theory in Soviet Anthropology." In *Soviet and Western Anthropology*, ed. Ernest Gellner. New York: Columbia University Press.

Drobizheva, Leokadia. 1994. "Process of Disintegration in the Russian Federation and the Problems of Russians." In *The New Russian Diaspora*, ed. V. Schlapentokh, M. Sendich, and E. Payin, 45–55. New York: M. E. Sharpe.

——. 1996. "Ispytaniia na sostoiatelnost': K sotsiologicheskoi poetike russkogo romana-boevika." *Novoe literaturnoe obozrenie* 22: 252–74.

Dubin, Boris. 1994. "Kul'turnaia dinamika i massovaia kul'tura segodnia." In *Kuda ideot Rossiia? Al'ternativy obshchestvennogo razvitiia*, ed. T. Zaslavskaia and L. Arutiunian, 223–30. Moscow: Interpraks.

Dugin, Aleksandr. 2004. *"Proekt 'Evraziia.'"* Moscow: EKSMO.

Durkheim, Émile. [1912] 1967. *The Elementary Forms of the Religious Life*. Trans. Joseph Ward Swain. New York: Free Press.

Dunn, Elizabeth C. 2004. *Privatizing Poland: Baby Food, Big Business, and the Remaking of Labour*. Ithaca: Cornell University Press.

Dwyer, Jeremy. 2002. "Telling the 'Real' Story: Interpretation of Contemporary Events in Viktor Dotsenko's Superboeviki." *Soviet and Post-Soviet Review* 29 (3): 221–23.

Dynin, I. M. 1990. *Posle Afganistana: "Afgantsy" v pis'makh, dokumentakh, svidetel'stvakh ochevidtsev*. Moscow: Profizdat.

Dyshev, Sergei. 1993. "Russkii dom Solzhenitsyna." *Krasnaia zvezda*, March 7.

Eagleton, Terry. 2003. *Sweet Violence: The Idea of the Tragic.* Oxford: Blackwell Publishing.

Edinenie. n.d. *The official website.* http://www.kpe.ru/about/.

Ekart, Aleksei. 2003. "Nyneshnie shkol'niki vynosiat prigovor rezhimu 'demokratii.' Moi adres—Sovetskii Soiuz." *Pokolenie,* no. 16.

———. 2002. "Zharennyi petukh—ptitsa mudrosti." *Pokolenie,* no. 13.

———. n.d. "U russkikh net pravykh idei! 'Nash bronepoezd' dlia 'detei reform.'" *Forum.* http://www.forum.msk.ru/files/040122164727.html.

Elizar'eva Tamara. 2002. "Russkii krest." *Vechernii Barnaul,* November 22.

Eng, David, and David Kazanjian. 2003. "Introduction: Mourning Remains." In *Loss,* ed. David Eng and David Kazanjian, 1–28. Berkeley: University of California Press.

Eremenko, I. N., and Iu. D. Novikov, eds. 1997. *Rossiia i Chechnia (1990–1997). Dokumenty svidetel'stvuiut.* Moscow: RAU—Universitet.

Eremicheva, Galina, and Jussi Simpura. 1999. "Nedoverie kak sotsial'naia problema sovremennoi Rossii." *Zhurnal sotsiologii i sotsial'noi antropologii* 2 (4): 145–59.

Erkhov, Anton. 2007. "LV." *Russkii Zhurnal,* http://www.russ.ru/culture/novye_opi saniya/lv.

Etkind, Alexander. 2004. "Hard and Soft in Cultural Memory: Political Mourning in Russia and Germany." *Grey Room* 16: 36–59.

Evangelista, Matthew. 2002. *The Chechen Wars: Will Russia Go the Way of the Soviet Union?* Washington, DC: Brookings Institution Press.

Ewing, Katherine Pratt. 2000. "The Violence of Non-recognition: Becoming a 'Conscious' Muslim Woman in Turkey." In *Cultures Under Siege: Collective Violence after Trauma,* ed. Antonius C. G. M. Robben and Marcello M. Suárez-Orozco, 248–71. Cambridge: Cambridge University Press.

Faubion, James D. 2003. "Religion, Violence and the Vitalistic Economy." *Anthropological Quarterly* 76 (1): 71–85.

Fedoseev, Sergei. 2005. "'Koroli' i 'kapusta.'" In *Lubianka: Obespechenie ekonomicheskoi bezopasnosti gosudarstva,* ed. V. A. Stavitskii, 146–57. Moscow: Kuchkovo pole.

Feitlowitz, Marguerite. 1998. *A Lexicon of Terror: Argentina and the Legacies of Torture.* New York: Oxford University Press.

Feldman, Allen. 2004. "Memory Theaters, Virtual Witnessing, and the Trauma Aesthetic." *Biography* 27 (1): 163–202.

Ferme, Mariane C. 2001. *The Underneath of Things: Violence, History, and the Everyday in Sierra Leone.* Berkeley: University of California Press.

Filippov, Aleksandr. 2006. "Teoreticheskaia sotsiologiia v Rossii." In *Mysliashchaia Rossiia: Kartografiia sovremennykh intellektual'nykh napravlenii,* ed. Vitalii Kurennoi, 185–200. Moscow: Nasledie Evrazii.

Filippov, V. P. 2006. "S. Shirokogorov: U istokov biosotsial'noi interpretatsii etnosa." *Etnograficheskoe obozrenie,* 3: 86–93.

———. 2004. "Asimmetrichnaia konstruktsiia etnicheskogo federalizma." *Etnograficheskoe obozrenie* 6: 74–86.

Filippov, Vasilii. 2000. "Vospitanie natsional'nogo patriotizma uchashchikhsia sredstvami etnopedagogiki." *Pedagogicheskii universitetskii vestnik* 2. http://bspu.ab.ru/Journal/vestnik/ARHIW/N2_2000/list/list144.html.

———. 1999. *Rossiia i russkaia natsia: Trudnyi put' k samopoznaniu.* Barnaul: GIPP Altai.

———. 1997. *Chelovek v kontseptsii sovremennogo nauchnogo poznaniia.* Barnaul: Barnaul'skii pedinstitut.

Filippov, Vasilii, and Vasilii Goncharov. 2004. *Ekspansiia ideologii tsinizma i litsemeriia. Rossiia. XX vek (dokumenty i fakty)*. Barnaul: GIPP Altai.

Fitzpatrick, Sheila. 2005. *Tear Off the Masks! Identity and Imposture in Twentieth-Century Russia*. Princeton: Princeton University Press.

Flatley, Jonathan. 2001. "Moscow and Melancholia." *Social Text* 19 (1): 75–102.

Foucault, Michel. 2005. *The Hermeneutics of the Subject: Lectures at the College de France, 1981–1982*. Trans. Graham Burchell. New York: Picador.

——. 2003. *"Society Must Be Defended." Lectures At the College de France 1975–1976*. Trans. David Macey. New York: Picador.

——. 1997. "On the Genealogy of Ethics: An Overview of Work in Progress." In Foucault, *Ethics: Subjectivity and Truth*, ed. Paul Rabinow, 253–80. New York: New Press.

Franklin, Simon, and Emma Widdis, eds. 2004. *National Identity in Russian Culture: an Introduction*. Cambridge: Cambridge University Press.

Freud, Sigmund. [1917] 1963. "Mourning and Melancholia." In *General Psychological Theory. Papers on Metapsychology*. New York: A Touchstone Book.

Friedlander, Saul, ed. 1992. *Probing the Limits of Representation: Nazism and the "Final Solution."* Cambridge: Harvard University Press.

Furman, Dmitry, ed. 1999. *Chechnia i Rossiia: Obshchestva i gosudarstva*. Moscow: Polinform-Talburi.

Gadlo, A. V. 1995. "Etnicheskaiia istoriia russkogo naroda kak problema otechestvennoi istoriografii vtoroi poloviny XX veka." *Vestnik Sankt-Peterburgskogo universiteta* 2: 3–5.

Gai, David, and Vladimir Snegirev. 1991. *Vtorzhenie: Neizvestnye stranitsy neob"iavlennoi voiny*. Moscow: IKPA.

Gaidar, Yegor. 2003. *State and Evolution: Russia's Search for a Free Market*. Trans. Jane Ann Miller. Seattle: University of Washington Press.

——. 1999. *Days of Defeat and Victory*. Trans. Jane Ann Miller. Seattle: University of Washington Press.

——. 1995. "Russian Reform." In *Russian Reform/International Money*. By Yegor Gaidar and Karl Otto Pöhl. Cambridge, MA: MIT, 1–54.

Gal, Susan. 1991. "Bartok's Funeral: Representation of Europe in Hungarian Political Rhetoric." *American Ethnologist* 18 (3): 440–58.

Geertz, Clifford. 1973. *The Interpretation of Cultures: Selected Essays*. New York: Basic Books, Inc.

Gerber, Theodore P., and Sarah E. Mendelson. 2002. "Russian Public Opinion on Human Rights and the War in Chechnya." *Post-Soviet Affairs* 18 (4): 271–305.

Girard, Rene. 1986. *The Scapegoat*. Trans. Yvonne Freccero. Baltimore: Johns Hopkins University Press.

Gladarev, Boris. 2000. "Formirovanie i funktsionirovanie milieu (na primire arkheologicheskogo kruzhka LDP-DTIU, 1970–2000)." St. Petersburg Center for Independent Sociological Research. http://www.indepsocres.spb.ru/boriss.htm.

Glaz'ev, Sergei. 1998. *Genotsid*. Moscow: Terra.

Goldman, Marshall I. 2003. *The Piratization of Russia: Russian Reform Goes Awry*. New York: Routledge.

Golovnikova O., and N. Tarkhova. 2001. "'Iosif Vissarionovich! Spasite sovetskogo istorika…' (o neizvestnom pis'me Anny Akhmatovoi Stalinu)." *Otechestvennaia istoriia* 3: 149–57.

Goncharenko, A. I. 2004. "Gubernator nadezhdy." In *Dnevnik Altaiskoi shkoly politicheskikh issledovanii, ed.* Iurii Chernyshev, Vol. 19–20. Barnaul: Izdatel'stvo Altaiskogo universiteta, 41–48.

Goncharov, V. N., and V. N. Filipov. 1996. *Rossiia, Lenin i sovremennyi mir.* Barnaul: Barnaul gosudarstvennyi peduniversitet.

Gorban', Valerii. 2003. "Dnevnik ofitsera OMONa." In Gordin and Grigor'ev 2003, 148–208.

Gordin, Ya, and V. Grigor'ev, eds. 2003. *My byli na etikh voinakh: Svidetel'stva uchastnikov sobytii 1989–2000 godov.* St. Petersburg: Zvezda.

Gotera, Vince. 1993. "The Fragging of Language: D. F. Brown's Vietnam War Poetry." *Journal of American Culture* 16 (3): 39–45.

Goudakov, Vladimir. 2006. "Gumilev and Hungtington: Approaches and Terminology." *Diogenes* 210: 82–90.

Goux, Jean-Joseph. 1999. "Cash, Check, or Charge?" In *The New Economic Criticism: Studies at the Intersection of Literature and Economics,* ed. Martha Woodmansee and Mark Osteen, 114–28. New York: Routledge.

———. 1994. *The Coiners of Language.* Trans. Jennifer Curtis Cage. Norman: University of Oklahoma Press.

———. 1990. *Symbolic Economies after Marx and Freud.* Trans. by Jennifer Curtis Cage. Ithaca: Cornell University Press.

Govorukhin, Sergei. 2000. "Obshchestvo ne khochet znat' pravdu." *Iskusstvo kino* 7: 7–10.

Govorukhin, Stanislav. 1991. *Rossiia, kotoruiu my poteriali.* Moscow: Assotsiatsiia Rotatsiia.

Graeber, David. 2001. *Toward an Anthropological Theory of Value: The False Coin of Our Dream.* New York: Palgrave.

Grant, Bruce. 2001. "New Moscow Monuments, or States of Innocence." *American Ethnologist* 28 (2): 332–62.

Green, André. 1999. *The Work of the Negative.* Trans. Andrew Weller. London: Free Associations.

Grigor'ev, Sviatoslav. 2007. *Osnovy vitalistskoi sotsiologii XXI veka.* Moscow: Gardariki.

———. 2004. "Nabolevshaia problema: Opasnost' sionizma v Rossii (K voprosu o sudebnom presledovanii A. A. Prokhozheva)." *Za nauku,* February 19.

———. 2003a. Kul'turologiia razvitiia rossiiskogo universiteta (Izbrannye trudy k 30-letiiu nauchnoi i pedagogicheskoi deiatel'nosti). Barnaul, Moscow: N.P.

———. 2003b. "Vitalizm: Evolutsiia filosofsko-sotsiologicheskikh vozzrenii." In Semilet 2003b, 23–31.

———. 2003c. "Predislovie. Kulturotsentrichnost' analiza evolutsii zhiznennykh sil obshestva i cheloveka: kontekst osmysleniia vzaimosviazi fundamental'nukh osnov razvitiia sotsiologicheskoi teorii i poliparadigmal'nosti eio sovremennykh mirovozzrencheskikh osnov." In Semilet 2003b, 5–23.

———. 2001. Vitalistskaia sotsiologiia: Paradigma nastoiashchego i budushchego (izbrannye stat'i po neklassicheskoi sotsiologii). Barnaul: APNTS SO RAO.

———. 2000b. *Iskry sokrovennogo.* Barnaul: OAO Altaiskii poligraficheskii kombinat.

———. 1999a. "Postroenie sovremennogo fundamenta sotstiologicheskoi teorii zhiznennykh sil cheloveka." In Grigor'ev and Demina 1999, 1: 24–34.

———. 1999b. "Teoretiko-metodologicheskie osnovy i aktualnost' analiza zhiznennykh sil natsional'nykh obshchnostei v Rossii 1990-kh gg." In Grigor'ev and Demina 1999, 1: 35–44.

Grigor'ev, Sviatoslav, and Ludmila Demina. 1994. *Sotsiolog v raione ekologicheskogo neblagopoluchiia: Kontseptsiia, programma, oput podgotovki.* Barnaul: Altaiskii gosudarstvennyi universitet.

Grigor'ev, Sviatoslav, and Ludmila Demina, eds. 2000. *Sovremennoe ponimanie zhiznennykh sil cheloveka: Ot metafory k kontseptsii (stanovlenie vitalistskoi sotsiologicheskoi paradigmy).* Moscow: Magistr-Press.

———. 1999. *Sovremennoe obshchestvo i lichnost' v sotsiologii zhiznennykh sil cheloveka.* Vol. 1. Barnaul: APNTs SO RAO.

Grigor'ev, Sviatoslav, and Ludmila Gusliakova, eds. 2003. *Neklassicheskaia sotsiologiia v sovremennoi Rossii: Nakoplenie metodologicheskogo potentsiala i tekhologicheskikh vozmozhnostei.* Moscow-Barnaul: ARNTs SO RAO.

Grigor'ev, Sviatoslav, and Natal'a Matveeva. 2002. Sotsiologiia obrazovaniia kak otraslevaia teoriia v sovremennom sotsiologicheskom vitalizme. Barnaul: ARNTs SO RAO.

Grigor'ev, Sviatoslav, and Iurii Rastov. 1999. "Sovremennaia istoriia formirovaniia sotsiologicheskoi kontseptsii zhiznennykh sil cheloveka." In Grigor'ev and Demina 1999, 1: 7–24.

Grigor'ev, Sviatoslav, and Tamara Semilet, eds. 1999a. *Dukhovnoe i sotsial'noe razvitie Rossii 1990-kh.: Problema sokhraneniia zhiznennykh sil russkogo naroda.* Barnaul: School of Sociology, Altai State University.

———. 1999b. Formirovanie patrioticheskogo soznaniia russkogo naroda. Materialy regional'noi nauchno-prakticheskoi konferentsii 1999 g. Barnaul: Slavianskoe obshchestvo.

Grigor'ev, Sviatoslav, and Aleksandr Subetto. 2003a. "Kul'turostentrichnost' ekologii lichnosti i etnosa v sisteme obrazovaniia kak problema sotsial'noi virusologii: Kontekst analiza v vitalistskoi sotsiologii." *Sibirskii Sotsiologicheskii Vestnik* 1: 101–7.

———. 2003b. "Osnovy neklassicheskoi sotsiologii: Sovremennyi kontekst analiza." In Grigor'ev and Gusliakova 2003, 7–24.

———. 2000. *Osnovy neklassicheskoi sotsiologii (Novye tendentsii razvitiia kul'tury sotsiologicheskogo myshleniia na rubezhe XX–XXI vekov)* Barnaul: ARNTs SO RAN.

Gromov, Boris. 1994. *Ogranichennyi kontingent.* Moscow: Progress.

Grozovskii. Boris. 2003. "Regiony smogut zarabotat'." *Vedomosti,* November 24.

Gudkov, Lev. 2005a. "Ideologema 'vraga': 'Vragi' kak massovyi sindrom i mekhanizm sotsiokul'turnoi integratsii." In *Obraz vraga,* ed. L. Gudkov, 7–80. Moskva: Novoe izdatelstvo.

———. ed. 2005b. *Obraz vraga.* Moskva: Novoe izdatelstvo.

———. 2004. *Negativnaia identichnost'. Stat'i 1997–2002.* Moscow: NLO.

Gumilev, Lev. 2003. "Spravka. Mekhanizm zazhima publikatsii L. N. Gumileva, doktora istoricheskikh nauk s 1961 g., za period s 1975 po 1985." In *Vospominaniia L. N. Gumileva. Vospominaniia. Publikatsii. Issledovaniia,* ed. V. Voronovich and A. Kozyrev, 237–44. St. Petersburg: Rostok.

———. 2002. *Etnogenez i biosfera zemli.* Moscow: AST.

———. 1993. *Etnosfera: Istoriia liudei i istoriia prirody.* Moscow: Ekonpros.

Gumilev, Lev. 1990. *Ethnogenesis and the Biosphere.* Moscow: Progress Publisher.

———. 1989. *Drevniaia Rus' i velikaia step'.* Moscow: Mysl'.

Guriev, Sergei, and Barry W. Ickes. 2000. "Barter in Russia." In Seabright 2000, 147–75.

Gurtenko, Nikolai. 2002. "Kontraktniki—obratnaia storona medali." *Altaiskaia pravda,* September 1.

Guzalenko, Leonid. 2003. "Nuzhna li sotsiologii zhizni zhivaia lichnost'?" *Sotsiologicheskie issledovaniia* 10: 3–13.

Guzeva, Alya, and A. Rona-Tas. 2001. "Uncertainty, Risk, and American Credit Cards Market Compared." *American Sociological Review* 66 (5): 632–46.

Hallam, Elisabeth, and Jenny Hockey. 2001. *Death, Memory and Material Culture.* Oxford: Berg.

Harding, Susan, and Kathleen Stewart. 2003. "Anxieties of Influence: Conspiracy Theories and Therapeutic Culture in Millennial America." In West and Sanders 2003, 258–86.

Harrison, Robert Pogue. 2003. *The Dominion of the Dead.* London: University of Chicago Press.

Harrison, Simon. 2000. "From Prestige Goods to Legacies: Property and the Objectification of Culture in Melanesia." *Comparative Study of Society and History* 42 (3): 662–79.

———. 1999. "Identity as a Scarce Resource." *Social Anthropology* 7 (3): 239–51.

Hedlund, Stefan. 2005. *Russian Path Dependence.* London: Routledge.

Heidegger, Martin. 1969. *The Question Concerning Technology and Other Essays.* Trans. William Lovitt. New York: Harper Torchbooks.

Heller, Dana. 2007. "t.A.T.u. You! Russia, the Global Politics of Eurovision, and Lesbian Pop." *Popular Music* 26 (2): 195–210.

Hemment, Julie. 2004. "The Riddle of the Third Sector: Civil Society, International Aid, and NGOs in Russia." *Anthropological Quarterly* 77 (2): 215–41.

Hertz, Robert. 1960. *Death and the Right Hand: A Contribution to the Study of the Collective Representation of Death.* Glencoe, Ill.: Free Press.

Hesford, Wendy. 2004. "Documenting Violations: Rhetorical Witnessing and the Spectacle of Distant Suffering." *Biography* 27 (1): 104–44.

Hidalgo, Stephen. 1993. "Agendas for Vietnam War Poetry: Reading the War as Art, History, Therapy and Politics." *Journal of American Culture* 16 (3): 5–13.

Hill, Fiona, and Clifford G. Gaddy. 2003. *The Siberian Curse: How Communist Planners Left Russia Out in the Cold.* Washington, DC: Brookings Institution.

Hirsch, Francine. 2005. *Empire of Nations: Ethnographic Knowledge and the Making of the Soviet Union.* Ithaca: Cornell University Press.

Hockstader, Lee. 1995b. "Mystery of Missing Rebel Imperils Chechen Talks; Russia Seeks Commando Who Led Raid on Town." *Washington Post.* June 27. A12.

Hoepken, Wolfgang. 1999. "War, Memory, and Education in Fragmented Society: The Case of Yugoslavia." *East European Politics and Societies* 13 (1): 190–227.

Homans, Peter, ed. 2000. *The Ambiguity of Mourning and Memory at Century's End.* Charlottesville: University Press of Virginia.

Hosking, Geoffrey. 2002. "Love-Hate Relationship." *Times Literary Supplement,* March 1, 3–4.

Hubbs, Joanna. 1988. *Mother Russia: the Feminine Myth in Russian Culture.* Bloomington: Indiana University Press.

Human Rights Center Memorial. 2006. "The Chechen Republic: Consequences of "Chechenization" of the Conflict." March 3. http://www.memo.ru/eng/memhrc/texts/6chechen.shtml.

Humphrey, Caroline. 2002a. "Rituals of Death as a Context for Understanding Personal Property in Socialist Mongolia." *Journal of Royal Anthropological Institute* 8: 65–87.

———. 2002b. *The Unmaking of Soviet Life: Everyday Economies after Socialism.* Ithaca: Cornell University Press.

———. 2000. "An Anthropological View of Barter in Russia." In Seabright 2000, 71–92.

———. 1998. *Marx Went Away—But Karl Stayed Behind.* Ann Arbor: University of Michigan Press.

Huyssen, Andreas. 2003. *Present Past: Urban Palimpsest and the Politics of Memory.* Stanford: Stanford University Press.

Hynes, Samuel. 1997. *The Soldiers' Tale: Bearing Witness to Modern War.* New York: Allen Lane.

Informatsionnaia voina v Chechne: Fakty. Dokumenty. Svidetel'stva. Noiabr' 1994—sentiabr' 1996. 1997. Moscow: Memorial.

Ingram, Alan. 2001. "Alexander Dugin: Geopolitics and Neo-fascism in Post-Soviet Russia." *Political Geography* 20: 1029–51.

Institute for the Economy in Transition. n.d. http://www.iet.ru/page.php?id=42.

Iskhakov, S. M., ed. 2005. Tragediia velikoi derzhavy: natsional'nyi vopros i raspad Sovetskogo Soiuza. Moscow: Sotsial'no-politicheskaia mysl.

Ivanov, A. V. 2001. "Sovremennoe zvuchanie evraziistva: Rol' i znachenie russkoi kul'tury v polikul'turnom prostranstve kontinenta." In Semilet 2001, 278–88.

Ivanov, M. S. 1976. "Comments." In Bromley 1989, 236–38.

Ivanov, Vitalii. 2006. "Poslanie prezidenta Rossii: Strana ne vymret…" *Izvestiia,* May 11.

Ivanova, Natal'a. 2002a. *No$tal'iaschee.* Moscow: Raduga.

———. 2002b. "Sezon skandalov: Voinovitch protiv Solzhenitsyna." *Znamia* 11: 186–98.

Ivanuk, Ivan. 1995. "General-polkovnik Vasilii Vorob'ev: Uchastniki boev budut zashchishcheny v polnoi mere." *Krasnaia zvezda,* January 18.

Izvestia. 1996. "Bandity perenosiat razborki na kladbishcha." November 11.

Jameson, Frederic. 1988. "Cognitive Mapping." In *Marxism and Interpretation of Culture,* ed. Cary Nelson and Lawrence Grossberg. Chicago: University of Illinois Press, 347–57.

Job, Sebastian. 2001. "Globalising Russia? The Neoliberal/Nationalist Two-Step and the Russification of the West." *Third World Quarterly* 22 (6): 931–49.

Kadzhaia, Valerii. 2003. "'Evreiskii sindrom' sovetskoi propagandy. I do kakoi stepeni veren emu okazalsia Aleksandr Solzhenitsyn." *NG. Ex libris,* Aug. 21, 3.

Kaganskii, Vladimir. 2003. "Rossiiskaia tsivilizatsiia: Krivda i pravda Evraziistva." *Obshchestvennye nauki i sovremennost',* pt. 1, 4: 63–80; pt. 2, 5: 70–83.

Kaneff, Deema. 2002. "Why People Don't Die 'Naturally' Any More: Changing Relations Between 'The Individual' and 'The State' in Post-Socialist Bulgaria." *Journal of Royal Anthropological Institute* 8: 89–105.

Kara-Murza, Sergei. 2002a. *Anti-sovetskii proekt.* Moscow: Algoritm.

———. 2002b. "Ograblenie po Chubaisy." *Pokolenie,* no. 13.

———. 2000. *Manipuliatsiia soznaniem.* Kiev: Oritani.

Kara-Murza, Sergei. n.d. Sergei Kara-Murza. Personal website. http://www.kara-murza.ru/index.htm.

Karasik, Mikhail, ed. 2001. *Dembel'skii al'bom: Russkii Art Brut. Mezhdu ku'turoi i knigoi khudozhnika.* St. Petersburg: M.K. and Kharmsizdat.

Kern, Louis J. 1988. "MIAs, Myth, and Macho Magic: Post-Apocalyptic Cinematic Vision of Vietnam." In *Search and Clear: Critical Responses to Selected Literature and Films of the Vietnam War,* ed. William Searle, 37–54. Bowling Green, OH: Bowling Green State University Popular Press.

Khadzharov, Musa. 2005. "Mech i pero: Knigi o Chechne (2002–2004)." *Neprikosnovennyi zapas* 38. http://www.nz-online.ru/index.

Khairulin, Marat. 2006. "Zhizn' i smert' Shestoi Roty." *Gazeta,* March 1.

Khalturina, Dar'ia, and Andrei Korotaev. 2006. *Russkii krest: Faktory, mekhanizmy i puti preodoleniia demograficheskogo krizisa v Rossii.* Moscow, URSS.

Kharkhordin, Oleg. 1999. *The Collective and the Individual in Russia: A Study of Practices.* Berkeley: University of California Press.

Kholmianskaia, F. I. 2003. "Neskol'ko zamechanii o knige Solzhenitsyna 'Dvesti let vmeste.'" *Voprosy istorii* 5: 174–75.

Khramtsova, T., ed. 1992. *Syny Altaia. Kniga Pamiati.* St. Petersburg: Leninzdat.

Kiewiet, Roderick, and Mikhail Myagkov. 2002. "Are the Communists Dying Out in Russia?" *Communist and Post-Communist Studies* 35: 39–50.

Kirkwood, Michael. 1993. *Alexander Zinoviev: An Introduction to His Work.* Basingstoke: Macmillan.

Kishkovsky, Sophia. 2007. "The Tortured Voice of Russia's Lost Generation." *New York Times,* December 22.

———. 2005. "From a Bitter War Defeat Comes Russia's Latest Blockbuster Action Movie." *New York Times,* October 29.

Klamer, Arjo, and Thomas Leonard. 1994. "So What's an Economic Metaphor?" In Mirowski 1994b, 20–54.

Klass, D., P. R. Silverman, and S. L. Nickman, eds. 1996. *Continuing Bonds, New Understanding of Grief.* Washington, DC: Taylor and Francis.

Klein, Melanie. 1975. *Envy and Gradiude, and Other Works, 1946–1963. The Writings of Melanie Klein.* Vol. III. New York: Fress Press.

Kleinman, Arthur. 1995. *Writing at the Margin: Discourse between Anthropology and Medicine.* Berkeley: California University Press.

———. 1992. "Pain and Resistance: The Delegitimation and Relegitimation of the Local Worlds." In *Pain as Human Experience: An Anthropological Perspective,* ed. Mary-Jo DelVecchio Good et al, 169–97. Berkeley: University of California Press.

Kleinman, Arthur, and Joan Kleinman. 1997. "The Appeal of Experience; The Dismay of Images: Cultural Appropriation of Suffering in Our Time." In Kleinman, Das, and Lock 1997, 1–25.

Kleinman, Arthur, Veena Das, and Margaret Lock, eds. 1997. *Social Suffering.* Berkeley: University of California Press.

Klier, John. 2002. "No Prize for History." *History Today,* November, 60–61.

Kniazevskaia, Tatiana, ed. 1999. *Russkaia intelligentsiia: Istoriia i sud'ba.* Moscow: Nauka.

Kniazkov, Sergei. 2005a. "Praporshchik Uminskii: Geroi ili avantiurist?" *Krasnaia zvezda,* January 25.

———. 2005b. "A praporshckiku neimiotsia." *Krasnaia zvezda,* June 11.

Knight, Peter, ed. 2002. *Conspiracy Nation: The Politics of Paranoia in Postwar America.* New York: New York University Press.

Kochevnikov, Sergei. 2000. "Chechnia: Byt, rabota, zhizn, smert'." *Svobodnyi kurs,* May 4.

Kokh, Alfred. 1998. *The Selling of the Soviet Empire: Politics and Economics of Russia's Privatization. Revelations of the Principal Insider.* New York: Liberty Publishing House.

Kolarska-Bobiriska, Lena. 2003. "The EU Accession and Strengthening of Institutions in East Central Europe: The Case of Poland." *East European Politics and Societies* 17 (1): 259–70.

Kolesnikov, Andrei. 1999. "Chechenskii sindrom-2." *Izvestiia,* October 2.

Koltakov, Konstantin, and Igor Moskvichev. 2001. "Etnicheskaia paradigma i konkurentsiia etnosov kak storona global'nogo mirovogo krizisa." In Semilet 2001, 134–40.

Komy prinadlezhit Rossiia. 2003. Moscow: Vagrius-Kommersant.

Kontsetpual'naia vlast': mif ili realnost'? 2002. Novosibirsk.

Koselleck, Reinhart. 2004. *Future Past: On the Semantics of Historical Time.* Trans. Keith Tribe. New York: Columbia University Press.

——. 2002. *The Practice of Conceptual History: Timing History, Spacing Concepts.* Trans. Todd Samuel Presner et al. Stanford: Stanford University Press.

Kotenev, Aleksandr. 1994. *Neokonchennaia voina.* Moscow: Souz veteranov Afganistana.

Kotkin, Stephen. 2001. *Armageddon Averted: The Soviet Collapse 1970–2000.* Oxford: Oxford University Press.

Kovalev, Sergei. 2004. *NLP effektivnogo rukovodstva, ili kak upravliat' kem ugodno i gde ugodno.* Rostov/Don: Feniks.

Kozhinov, Vadim. 2002. *O russkom national'nom soznanii.* Moscow: Algoritm.

Kozlov, S. Ia., ed. 2003. *Akademik Iu. V. Bromley i otechestvennaia etnologia. 1960–1990-e gody.* Moscow: Nauka.

Kozlov, Viktor. 2001. "Ob akademike Iuliane Vladimoroviche Bromlee—uchenom i cheloveke." *Etnograficheskoe obozrenie* 4: 3–9.

——. 1999. *Etnos. Natsiia, Natsionalizm. Sushchnost' i problematika.* Moscow: Staryi sad.

——. 1996. *Istoriia tragedii russkogo naroda. Russkii vopros.* Moscow.

——. 1995. *Russkii vopros: Istoriia tragedii velikogo naroda.* Moscow.

——. 1994. *Etnicheskaia ekologiia: Stanovlenie distsipliny i istoriia problemy.* Moscow: RAN.

——. 1991. "Zhizneobespechenie etnosa: Soderzhanie poniatiia i ego ekologicheckie aspekty." In *Etnicheskaia ekologiia: Teoriia i praktika,* ed. V. Kozlov, 14–44. Moscow: Nauka.

——. 1969. *Dinamika chislennosti narodov.* Moscow.

Krasukhin, Gennadii. 2003. "'Portret na fone mifa' i ego kritiki." *Voprosy literatury* 2: 77–92.

Kristeva, Julia. 2001. *Melanie Klein.* Trans. Ross Guberman. New York: Columbia University Press.

——. 2000. *Crisis of the European Subject.* Trans. Susan Fairfield. New York: Other Press.

——. 1995. *New Maladies of the Soul.* Trans. Ross Guberman. New York: Columbia University Press.

Kristeva, Julia. 1989. *Black Sun: Depression and Melancholia.* Trans. Leon Roudiez. New York: Columbia University Press.

———. 1984. *Revolution in Poetic Language*. Trans. Margaret Waller. New York: Columbia University Press.

———. 1982. *Powers of Horror. An Essay on Abjection*. Trans. Leon Roudiez. New York: Columbia University Press.

Krongauz, Maksim. 2008. *Russkii iazyk na grani nervnogo sryva*. Moscow: Iazyki slavianskikh kul'tur.

Kudrov, V. 2002. "Za vysokuiu konkurentnosposobnost'." *Mirovaia ekonomika i mezhdunarodnye otnosheniia* 2: 114–18.

Kuleshov, Vadim. 2003. "Voina Sergeia Zamiatkina." *Altaiskaia pravda,* March 21.

———. 2002. "Sotsiologi ob'ediniautsia." *Altaiskaia pravda,* February 20.

Kuleshov, Vadim, and Zakir Sagitov. 2003. "Dobrovol'tsy." *Altaiskaia pravda.* September 23.

Kulikovo pole. n.d. Kulikovo pole. The State Military-Historical and Natural Park-Museum. http://www.kulpole.ru/ENG/N_pan_E.htm.

Kuznetsov, A. M. 2006. "S. M. Shirokogorov i drugie. Vvedenie k diskussii." *Etnograficheskoe obozrenie,* 3: 54–56.

Lacan, Jacques. 1997. *The Psychoses. 1955–1956. The Seminars of Jacques Lacan. Book III.* Ed. Jacques-Alan Miller. Translated with notes by Russell Grigg. London: Norton.

———. 1991. The Seminars of Jacques Lacan. Book I. Freud's Papers on Technique 1953–1954. Trans. John Forrester. New York: Norton.

———. 1978. *The Four Fundamental Concepts of Psychoanalysis.* Trans. Alan Sheridan. New York: Norton.

———. 1977. *Écrits: A Selection.* Trans. Alan Sheridan. New York: Norton.

Ladnyi, Vladimir. 2005. "Strashnaiia doroga k khramu." *Rossiskaia gazeta,* June 14.

Laktionova, Natalia. 2002. "Doroga v tsivilizatsiiu ili liberal'nyi tupik?" *Dialog-OD* 10: 15–25.

Larson, Nathan D. 2005. *Aleksandr Solzhenitsyn and the Modern Russo-Jewish Question.* Stuttgart: Ibidem-Verlag.

Lavrov, Sergei. 2000. *Lev Gumilev: Sud'ba i idei.* Moscow: Svarog.

Ledeneva, Alena. 2006. *How Russia Really Works: The Informal Practices That Shaped Post-Soviet Politics and Business.* Ithaca: Cornell University Press.

———. 1998. *Russia's Economy of Favours: Blat, Networking and Informal Exchange.* Cambridge: Cambridge University Press.

Lemon, Alaina. 1998. "'Your Eyes Are Green Like Dollars': Counterfeit Cash, National Substance, and Currency Apartheid in 1990s Russia." *Cultural Anthropology* 13 (1): 22–55.

Lev Nikolaevich Gumilev. Teoriia etnogeneza i istoricheskie sud'by Evrazii. Materialy konferentsii. 2002. Vols. 1–2. St. Petersburg: Evropeiskii Dom.

Levada, Yuri. 2003. "Obshchestvo i reformy. Stabil'nost' v nestabilnosti." *Obshchestvennye nauki i sovremennost'* 10: 5–11.

Levi, Primo. 1993. *Survival in Auschwitz.* New York: Collier, Macmillan.

Liakhovskii, Aleksandr. 2004. *Tragediia i doblest' Afgana.* Moscow: Nord.

Lieven, Anatol. 1999. "Voina v Chechne i upadok rossiiskogo mogushchestva." In Furman 1999, 250–89.

Likhachev, Viacheslav. 2002. *Natsizm v Rossii.* Moscow: Panorama.

Limomov, Eduard. 2003. *Drugaia Rossiia: Ochertaniia budushchego.* Moscow: Ultrakul'tura.

Lipatov, Vladislav. 2006. *Soldat i pesnia: 300 let vmeste.* Ekaterinburg: Izdatel'stvo gumanitarnogo universiteta.

Litprom.ru. 2007. Moscow: Astrel.

Lopukha, Aleksandr. 2000. *Zhiznennye sily patriotizma.* Moscow: Rusaki.

Lovell, Stephen. 2006. *Destination in Doubt: Russia Since 1989.* London: Zed Books.

Lynch, Allen. 2005. *How Russia Is Not Ruled: Reflections on Russian Political Development.* Cambridge: Cambridge University Press.

Maksakov, Il'ia. 1999. "Govorit' o normalizatsii situatsii v Dagestane poka chto neumestno." *Nezavisimaia gazeta,* August 11.

Malashenko, Aleksei. 2007. "Khotiat li russkie v Chechniu." *Nezavisimaia gazeta,* July 23.

Malinkin, Aleksandr. 2006. "Poliparadigmal'nyi podkhod i situatsiia v rossiiskoi sotsiologii." *Sotsiologicheskie issledovaniia* 1: 114–23.

Maltseva, A. V. 2004. "Tsennosti obrazovaniia kak faktory natsional'nogo razvitiia." In *Russkoe sotsiokul'turnoe prostranstvo: Dukhovnye konstanty i sotsial'nye tekhnologii: Materialy regional'noi nauchnoi konferentsii, posviashchennoi Dniam slavianskoi pis'mennosti i kul'tury 23 maia 2003 g.,* ed. Tamara Semilet, 236–44. Barnaul: Altai State University Press.

Mamilov, Sulambek. 2000. Fil'my o Chechne ne nuzhny gosudarstvu. *Iskusstvo kino* 7: 11–12.

Manakov, Artem. 2001. S liubov'iu i bol'iu o Rodine. Bitva za Rossiiu. *Pokolenie,* no. 5.

MANPO (Mezhdunarodnaia Akademiia Nauk Pedagogicheskogo Obrazovaniia). n.d. http://www.manpo.ru/manpo/about/index.shtml.

Marcus, George E. 1999. "Introduction to the Volume: The Paranoid Style Now." In *Paranoia within Reason: A Casebook on Conspiracy as Explanation,* ed. George E. Marcus, 1–12. Chicago: University of Chicago Press.

Marin, Dalia, Daniel Kaufmann, and Bogdan Gorochowskij. 2000. "Barter in Transitional Economies: Competing Explanations Confront Ukranian Data." In Seabright 2000, 207–36.

Martin, Emily. 1994. *Flexible Bodies: The Role of Immunity in American Culture from the Days of Polio to the Age of AIDS.* Boston: Beacon Press.

——. 1990. "Toward an Anthropology of Immunology: The Body as Nation State." *Medical Anthropology Quarterly* 4 (4): 410–26.

Martin, Terry. 2001. *The Affirmative Action Empire: Nations and Nationalism in the Soviet Union, 1923–1939.* Ithaca: Cornell University Press.

Marx, Karl. 1972. "The Power of Money in Bourgeois Society." In *The Marx-Engels Reader,* ed. Robert C. Tucker, 79–83. New York: Norton.

Mason, Fran. 2002. "A Poor Person's Cognitive Mapping." In Knight, 2000, 40–56.

Mathyl, Markus. 2002. "The National-Bolshevik Party and *Arctogaia:* Two Neo-fascist Groupuscules in the Post-Soviet Political Space." *Patterns of Prejudice* 36 (3): 62–76.

Maurer, Bill. 2006. "The Anthropology of Money." *Annual Review of Anthropology* 35: 15–36.

McClintick, David. 2006. "How Harvard Lost Russia." *Institutional Investor Magazine.* http://www.dailyii.com/article.

Medvedev, Roy. 2000. "Dvadtsat' let spustia. Aleksandr Solzhenitsyn: Odinochestvo posle vozvrashcheniia." *Nezavisimaia gazeta,* November 16.

Melley, Timothy. 2000. *Empire of Conspiracy: The Culture of Paranoia in Postwar America.* Ithaca: Cornell University Press.

Mel'nikova, Valentina. 2004. "Interview with Radio Ekho Moskvy." October 20. http://www.echo.msk.ru/guests/556/.

Mera za mery. 2003. "Govoriashchii karp iz 'Lebedinogo ozera' SShA." No. 13: 3.

———. 2002a. "Chtoby ne byt' travoi na pole boia." No. 40: 1

———. 2002b. "Chto i kak delat'. I delaetsia uzhe." No. 36: 3

———. 2002c. "Vne politiki—vne zhizni." 2002c. No. 34: 1

Mereu, Francesca. 2004. "Altai's Schwarzenegger Has the Last Laugh." *Moscow Times,* April 6.

Merridale, Catherine. 2006. *Ivan's War: Life and Death in the Red Army, 1939–1945.* New York: Picador.

———. 2000. *Night of Stone: Death and Memory in Twentieth-Century Russia.* New York: Penguin Books.

Mikhailova, Julia. 1995. "Snachala zabyli o mertvykh, teper'—o zhivykh." *Izvestiia,* November 17.

Miliukov, Pavel. 1993. *Ocherki po istorii russkoi kul'tury.* Vol. 1. Moscow: Progress.

Miller, Nancy. 2003. "'Portraits of Grief': Telling Details and the Testimony of Trauma." *Differences* 14 (5): 112–35.

Mil'shtein, Il'ia. 2003. "Gody i liudi. Messiia, kotorogo my poteriali." *Novoe vremia* 50: 32–35.

Minaev, Sergei. 2007. "Obrashchenie k chitateliu." In *Litprom.ru 2007,* 5–8. Moscow: Astrel.

Mironov, Viacheslav. 2003. "Ia byl na etoi voine." In Gordin and Grigor'ev 2003, 120–47.

Mirowski, Philip. 1994. "The Realms of the Natural." In *Natural Images in Economic Thought: "Markets Read in Tooth and Claw,"* ed. Philip Mirowski, 451–83. Cambridge: Cambridge University Press.

Mitrokhin, Nikolai. 2003. *Russkaia partiia: Dvizhenie russkikh natsionalistov v SSSR 1953–1985.* Moscow: NLO.

Mohkansing-den Boer, Elisabeth, and Hetty Zock. 2004. "Dreams of Passage: An Object-Relational Perspective on a Case of a Hindu Death Ritual." *Religion* 34: 1–14.

Mokhov, Vladimir. 2005. "Realii. V sud vyzyvaetsia…Basaev." *Krasnaia Zvezda,* January 15.

Moroz, Evgenii. 2005. *Istoriia "Mertvoi vody"—Ot strashnoi skazki k bol'shoi politike. Politicheskoe neoiazychestvo v postsovetskoi Rossii.* Stuttgart: Ibidem.

Morozov, Sergei. 1999. *Zagovor protiv narodov Rossii segodnia.* Moskva: Algoritm.

Morskaia gazeta. 2002. "Petrovskaia Akademia b"iet v nabat." December 7.

Moscow News. 2004. "Over 200,000 Killed in Chechnya since 1994." November 24.

Moshkin, Mikhail, and Gennadii Savchenko. 2006. "Veterany raznogo sorta." *Gazeta,* May 17.

Mosse, George L. 1990. *Fallen Soldiers: Reshaping the Memory of the World Wars.* New York: Oxford University Press.

Mukhin, Vladimir. 2007. "Propavshie i zabytye." *Nezavisimoe voennoe obozrenie,* March 23, 8.

Mukhin, Vladimir, and Aleksandr Iavorskii. 2000. "Voinu proigrala ne armiia, a politiki." *Nezavisimaia gazeta,* February 29.

Musemwa, Muchaparara. 1995. "The Ambiguities of Democracy: The Demobilization of the Zimbabwean Ex-combatants and the Ordeal of Rehabilitation." In *Dismissed:*

Demobilisation and Reintegration of Former Combatants in Africa, ed. Jakkie Cilliers, 44–57. Halfway House: Institute for Defence Policy, 1995. http://www.iss.co.za/pubs/Books/Dismissed.html.

My zhdali vas, synov'ia… 1999. Barnaul: Altaiskaia pravda.

Nadkarni, Maya, and Olga Shevchenko. 2004. "The Politics of Nostalgia: A Case for Comparative Analysis of Post-socialist Practices." *Ab Imperio* 2: 487–519.

Namedni. 2001. "Peredaite tem, kto poedet v Chechniu." *Altaiskaia pravda,* January 31.

Na strazhe Rodiny. 2002. "Demografiia. Russkii krest." September 28.

———. 1997. "Syn pogib v Chechne, a chto zhe gosudarstvo?" September 9.

"Na toi voine, neznamenitoi…" 2000. *Iskusstvo kino* 7: 5.

Nedomerova, E. 1995. "Kuda tekut 'afganskie' milliardy?" *Segodnia,* May 4.

Negreev, Dmitrii. 2000. "Barnaulu groziat tiazheolye vremena." *Svobodnyi kurs,* November 23.

———. 2004. "Delo uchitelei." *Svobodnyi kurs,* January 29.

Nemirovskii, V. G., and D. D. Nevirko. 2002. "Regional'nye sotsiologicheskie shkoly na poroge XXI veka." *Sotsiologicheskie issledovaniia* 9: 135–36.

Nevskoe vremia. 2006. "Bezuslovnyi zapret na uslovnye edinitsy." April 25.

Nezavisimaia gazeta. 2001. "Chechnia: Khronika konflikta." February 10.

———. 1999. "Rossiia prodolzhaet nastupat' na grabli." August 10.

Nikulina, N. 1997. "Pokushenie na blagotvoritelnost'." *Vek,* May 30.

Nikulkov, Vladimir. 2004. "Politik ushel, dela ostalis'." *Ekspert—Sibir'* 7: 21.

Norka, Sergei. 2004. *Zagovor protiv Rossii.* Moskva: Vargius.

Noskov, Vitalii. 2001. *"Liubite nas, poka my zhivy."* Novosibirsk: RIF-Novosibirsk.

Novosti. 2004. "Ekho Moskvy." July 7. http://echo.msk.ru/news/197186.phtml.

NTV. 2004. "Chechnya: 11 dekabria 1994—…" Broadcast on December 11.

Nurmatova, Margarita. 2002. "Ne vse zoloto, chto blestit. No lutshee zoloto—nasha Rossiia." *Pokolenie,* no. 10.

"Ob Ukase Prezidenta RSFSR ot 7 noyabria 1991 g. 'O vvedenii chrezvychainogo polozheniia v Checheno-Ingushskoi Respublike.'" 1997. In Eremenko and Novikov 1997, 33.

"O deiatel'nosti Soiuza veteranov Afganistana (k postanovleniiu ot 9 avgusta 1988 goda, no. 989)." 1992. Ukaz Prezidenta RF ot 4 aprelia 1992 g., no. 362.

Odnokolenko, Oleg. 1992. "Dokumenty iz 'Osoboi papki.' Kto tebia vydumal, Afgan?" *Krasnaia zvezda,* October 17.

Olcott, Anthony. 2001. *Russian Pulp: The Detektiv and the Way of Russian Crime.* Lanham, MD: Rowman and Littlefield.

Oleinik, Aleksandr. 1996. "U prestupleniia na Kotliakovskom kladbishche ne dolzhno byt' sroka davnosti." *Krasnaia zvezda,* November 27.

Oliker, Olga. 2001. *Russia's Chechen Wars 1994–2000: Lessons from Urban Combat.* Santa Monica: Rand.

O'Loughlin, John, Gearoid O' Tuathail, and Vladimir Kolossov. 2004. "Russian Geopolitical Storylines and Public Opinion in the Wake Of 9–11: A Critical Geopolitical Analysis and National Survey." *Communist and Post-Communist Studies* 37: 281–318.

"O merakh gosudarstvennoi podderzhki deiatel'nosti obshchestvennykh ob"edinenii invalidov." 1992. Ukaz Prezidenta RF ot 22 dekabria 1993 g., no. 2254.

"O prave grazhdan Chechenskoi respubliki na priobretenie i khranenie lichnogo ognestrel'nogo oruzhiia i ogranichenie prava na ego noshenie." 1997. In Eremenko and Novikov 1997, 36.

Orlov, O. P., and A. V. Cherkasov, eds. 1998. *Rossiia—Chechnia: Tsep' oshibok.* Moscow: Zven'a.

"O Rossiiskom fonde invalidov voiny v Afganistane." 1991. Ukaz Prezidenta RSFSR ot 30 noiabria 1991 g., no. 248.

Ostroushko, Valentina. 2005. "Basaev gotov platit'." *Novye Izvestia,* January 18.

Ostrovskii, Andrei. 2004. "Vozvrashchenie na krugi svoia." *Vladivostok,* May 28.

"Otchet o deiatelnosti fonda "Pravo Materi" za 2004 god." 2004. http://www.hro.org/ngo/mright/2004/.

Oushakine, Serguei. 2007. "'We Are Nostalgic but We Are Not Crazy': Retrofitting the Past in Russia." *Russian Review* 66 (3): 451–82.

———. 2004a. "The Flexible and the Pliant: Disturbed Organisms of Soviet Modernity." *Cultural Anthropology* 19 (3): 392–428.

———. 2004b. "Mesto-imeni-ia: sem'ia kak sposob organizatsii zhizni." In *Semeinye uzy: modeli dlia sborki,* ed. Serguei Oushakine. Vol. 1., 55–89. Moscow: Novoe literaturnoe obozrenie.

———. 2003. "Crimes of Substitution: Detection in Late Soviet Society." *Public Culture* 15 (3): 426–52.

———. 2001a. "The Fatal Splitting: Symbolizing Anxiety in Post/Soviet Russia." *Ethnos: Journal of Anthropology* 66 (3): 1–30.

———. 2001b. "The Terrifying Mimicry of Samizdat." *Public Culture* 13 (2): 191–214.

———. 2000a. "The Quantity of Style: Imaginary Consumption in the New Russia." *Theory, Culture, and Society* 17 (5): 97–120.

———. 2000b. "In the State of Post-Soviet Aphasia: Symbolic Development in Contemporary Russia," *Europe-Asia Studies* 52 (6): 991–1016.

"O veterankh." 1994. Federal'nyi zakon RF ot 12 ianvaria 1994 g., no. 5-FZ.

Pain E. L. 2003. "Etnopoliticheskii maiatnik: Tsiklichnost' etnopoliticheskikh protsessov v postsovetskoi Rossii." *Obshchestvennye nauki i sovremennost'* 5: 122–30.

Panarin, A. S. 1998. *Rossiiskaia intelligentsiia v mirovykh voinakh i revolutsiiakh XX veka.* Moscow: Editorial URSS.

Paperno, Irina. 2001. "Exhuming the Bodies of Soviet Terror." *Representations* 75: 89–119.

Papernyi, Vladimir. 2004. *Mos-Angeles.* Moscow: NLO.

Paradowski, Ryszard. 1999. "The Eurasian Idea and Leo Gumilev's Scientific Ideology." *Canadian Slavonic Papers* 41 (1): 19–32.

Parry, Jonathan, and Maurice Bloch. 1989. "Introduction: Money and the Morality of Exchange." In *Money and the Morality of Exchange,* ed. J. Parry and M. Bloch, 1–32. Cambridge: Cambridge University Press.

Parshev, Andrei. 2003. "Andrei Parshev v priiamom efire." *Ekho Moskvy,* September 8. http://www.echo.msk.ru/guests/3622/.

———. 2001a. "Ia vzyvau k instinktu samosohraneniia." *EKO* 6: 102–4.

———. 2001b. "Ia vzyvaiu k instinktu samosokhraneniia. Materialy vstrechi." http://gladkeeh.boom.ru/Interviews/Parshev.htm.

———. 2001c. *Pochemu Rossiia ne Amerika. Kniga dlia tekh, kto ostaetsiia zdes'.* Moscow: Krymskii Forum-2.

Pelevin, Viktor. 1999. *Homo Zapiens.* Trans. Andrew Bromfield. New York: Viking.

Pesmen, Dale. 2000. *Russia and Soul: An Exploration.* Ithaca: Cornell University Press.

Petryna, Adriana. 2002. *Life Exposed: Biological Citizenship after Chernobyl.* Princeton: Princeton University Press.

Pikhoia, R. G. 2002. "Konstitutsionno-politicheskii krizis v Rossii 1993 goda: Khronika sobytii i kommentarii istorika." *Otechestvennaia istoriia*, 4–5.

Pine, Frances. 2002. "Dealing with Money in the Polish Highlands." In *Markets and Moralities: Ethnographies of Postsocialism*, ed. Ruth Mandel and Caroline Humphrey, 75–100. Oxford: Berg.

Pokolenie. 2002."Malen'kii prazdnik pokoleniia," no. 6.

Pokrovskii, Boris. 2004. "Tri dorogi 'Russkogo kresta.' V rossiiskoi demografii bez peremen: Narod vymiraet i kontsa etomu ne vidno." *Nezavisimaia gazeta*, November 24.

Pokrovskii, V., ed. 2006. *On vybral krest.* Moscow: Pokrov.

Polian, Pavel. 2007. "Operatsiia 'Chechevitsa.'" *Zvezda* 3: 167–74.

——. 2003. *Against Their Will: The History and Geography of Forced Migrations in the USSR.* Budapest: Central European University Press.

Politkovskaya, Anna. 2001. *A Dirty War: A Russian Reporter in Chechnya.* Trans. John Crowfoot. London: Harvill Press.

Politov, Iurii. 2005. "Krivoi stvol—eto dlia zritelia. Vladimir Putin i veterany-afgantsy posmotreli '9 rotu.'" *Izvestiia*, November 9, 3.

Pol'shchikova, Olga. 2002. "S chego natinaetsia Rodina?" *Altaiskaia pravda*, February 4.

Popkova, Ludmila. 2004. "Women's Political Activism in Russia: The Case of Samara." In *Post-Soviet Women Encountering Transition: Nation Building, Economic Survival, and Civic Activism*, ed. K. Kuehnast and C. Nechemias. Baltimore: Johns Hopkins University Press.

Popov, Egor. 2007. "Sborshchikov tsvetnogo metalloloma priravniaiut k terroristam. *Moskovskie novosti*, July 13–19.

Popov, Evgenii. 1998. "Podlinnaia istoriia *Zelenykh muzykantov.*" *Znamia* 6. http://magazines.russ.ru/znamia/1998/6/popov-pr.html.

Popov, Gavriil. 2000a. "Beregite russkikh. Razgovory o 'Rossiiaianakh'—popytka uiti ot problemy." *Nezavisimaia gazeta*, May 4.

——. 2000b. "Russkii kholokost." *Nezavisimaia gazeta*, April 26.

Popov, Sergei. 1995. "Materinskie naezdy. Vyigryvaet ili teriaet ot nikh armiia?" *Krasnaia zvezda*, July 4.

Popov, Sergei, and Anatolii Stasovskii. 1995. "Slezy soldatskikh materei beznravstvenno ispol'zovat' v korystnykh tseliakh." *Krasnaia zvezda*, February 4.

Popova, Galina. 2003a. "Russkii krest." *Altaiskaia pravda*, January 22.

——. 2003b. "Skol'ko nas? Gde my zhivem? Predvaritel'nye itogi perepisi." *Altaiskaia pravda*, July 17.

Portnova, Lubov. 2002. "Polku veteranov pribylo." *Parlamentskaia gazeta*, December 19.

Pratt, Ray. 2003. "Theorizing Conspiracy." *Theory and Society* 32: 255–71.

Prilepin, Zakhar. 2006. *Patologii.* Moscow: AdMarginem.

Prokhanov, Aleksandr. 2002. *Gospodin Geksogen.* Moscow: AdMarginem.

Prokhozhev, Aleksandr. 2002. *Tenevoi narod (k istorii evreev v Rossii).* Barnaul.

"Proshchai, oruzhie?" 2002. *Iskusstvo kino* 11: 5–21.

Punanov, Grigorii. 1998. "Vzryv na Kotliakovskom kladbishche: Delo v sude, no tochku stavit' rano." *Novye izvestiia*, December 29.

Punin, Nikolai. 2000. *Mir svetel liubov'iu: dnevniki, pis'ma.* Moskva: Izdatel'stvo Artist. Rezhisser. Teatr.

Putin, Vladimir. 2005. "Annual Address to the Federal Assembly of the Russian Federation." http://www.kremlin.ru/text/appears/2005/04/87049.shtml.

Pyasetskaya, Anna, and Heidi Brander. 1998. "The Lost Boys." *Granta,* 64: 113–18.

Raiskaia, Natal'ia, Yakov Sergienko, and Aleksandr Frenkel. 2001. *Infliatsionnye protsessy v Rossii (1992–1999): Tendentsii, faktory.* Moscow: Finstatinform.

Ram, Harsha. 2001. "Imagining Eurasia: The Poetics and Ideology of Olzhas Suleimenov's AZ i IA." *Slavic Review,* 60 (2): 289–311.

Rastov, Iu. E., S. I. Grigor'ev, L. G. Gusliakova, L. D. Demina, P. A. Trofimova, and A. Ia. Trotskovskii. 2000. *Altaiskaia sotsiologicheskaia shkola: Istoriia, sovremennost', perspektivy razvitiia.* Barnaul: AKOO Regional'nyi nauchnii tsentr, 118–24.

Rastov, Iurii. 2003. "Versii neovitalistskogo teoretizirovaniia v sovremennoi rossiiskoi sotsiologii." In Grigor'ev and Gusliakova 2003, 91–102.

Rastov, N. D. 2001. "Geopolitika i bezopasnost Rossii." In Semilet 2001, 37–46.

Regent, Tat'iana. 1998. "Rukovoditel' federal'noi migratsionnnoi sluzhby o sostoianii del s bezhentsami i vynuzhdennymi pereselentsami v Rossiiu." Interview. *Ekho Moskvy,* January 22.

Revunenkova, E. V., and A. M. Reshetov. 2003. "Portret uchenogo. Sergei Mikhailovich Shirokogorov." *Etnograficheskoe obozrenie* 3: 100–119.

Revzin, Grigorii. 2006. *Na puti v Boliviiu. Zametki o russkoi dukhovnosti.* Moscow: OGI.

Reznik, Iurii. 2000. "Sotsiologiia zhizni kak novoe napravlenie mezhdistsiplinarnykh issledovanii." *Sotsiologicheskie issledovaniia* 9: 3–12.

RIA Novosti. 2005. "Veshniakov: Sud'bu gibernatora Evdokimova reshit president." March 31. http://www.utro.ru/news/2005/03/31/423553.shtml.

Ries, Nancy. "2002 'Honest Bandits' and 'Warped People': Russian Narratives about Money, Corruption, and Moral Decay." In *Ethnography in Unstable Places: Everyday Lives in Context of Dramatic Political Change,* ed. C. Greenhouse, E. Mertz, and K. Warren, 276–315. Durham, NC: Duke University Press.

——. 1997. *Russian Talk: Culture and Conversation During Perestroika.* Ithaca: Cornell University Press.

Rigi, Jakob. 2007. "The War in Chechnya: The Chaotic Mode of Domination, Violence, and Bare Life in the Post-Soviet Context." *Critique of Anthropology* 27 (1): 37–62.

Rimskii, Vladimir. 2003. "Vybory bez strategicheskogo vybora." *Obshestvennye nauki i sovremennost'* 10: 49–59.

Robben, Antonius C. G. M. 2000. "The Assault on Basic Trust: Disappearance, Protest, and Reburial in Argentina." In *Cultures under Siege: Collective Violence and Trauma,* ed. Marcelo Suarez-Orozco and Antonius C. G. M. Robben, 70–101. Cambridge: Cambridge University Press.

——. 1995. "The Politics of Truth and Emotion among Victims and Perpetrators of Violence." In *Fieldwork under Fire: Contemporary Studies of Violence and Culture,* ed. Carolyn Nordstrom and Antonius C. G. M. Robben, 81–104. Berkeley: University of California Press.

Rock, Stella. 2001. "Russian Revisionism: Holocaust Denial and the New Nationalist Historiography." *Patterns of Prejudice* 35 (4): 64–76.

Rogers, Doug. 2005. "Moonshine, Money, and the Politics of Liquidity in Rural Russia." *American Ethnologist* 32 (1): 63–81.

Rorty, Richard. 1989. *Contingency, Irony, and Solidarity.* Cambridge: Cambridge University Press.

Rossiia i SSSR v voinakh XX veka: Statisticheskoe issledovanie. 2001. Moscow: OLMA-Press.

Rossiia, Rus'! Khrani sebia, khrani. 2001. Novosibirsk: BKZ.

Rossman, Vadim. 2002. *Russian Intellectual Antisemitism in the Post-Communist Era.* Lincoln: University of Nebraska Press.

Rowlands, Michael. 2004. "Cultural Rights and Wrongs: Uses of the Concept of Property." In *Property in Question: Value Transformation in the Global Economy,* ed. K. Verdery and C. Humphrey, 207–26. Oxford: Berg.

Ruble, Blair A. 1995. *Money Sings: The Changing Politics of Urban Space in Post-Soviet Yaroslavl.* Washington, DC: Woodrow Wilson Center Press.

Rudakov S., I. Kornfel'd, and V. Baranov. 2000. "Natsional'naia identichnost' kak faktor obshchestvennogo soznaniia." In *Problema natsional'noi identichnosti v kul'ture i obrazovanii Rossii i Zapada. Materialy nauchnoi konferentsii v 2-kh tt.* Vol.1, 7–19. Voronezh: TsChKI.

Rusakova, Alisa. 2002. "Osobennyi put' Rossii: Rossiia na puti globalizatsii." *Molodaia gvardiia* 1: 3–15.

Russell, John. 2005. "Terrorists, Bandits, Spooks and Thieves: Russian Demonisation of the Chechens before and since 9/11." *Third World Quarterly* 26 (1): 101–16.

Rybakov, S. E. 2001. "Sud'by teorii etnosa. Pamiati Iu. V. Bromleia." *Etnograficheskoe obozrenie* 1: 3–22.

Ryklin, Mikhail. 2003. *Vremia diagnoza.* Moscow: Logos.

——. 2002. *Prostranstva likovaniia: Totalitarism i razlichie.* Moscow: Logos.

Salanin, Vyacheslav. 2004. "Nakanune." *Kontinent-Sibir,* April 2.

Sanin, Grigorii. 1998. "Beznogii polkovnik nazvan organizatorim ubiistv." *Segodnia,* September 9.

Saunders, Rebecca, and Kamran Aghaie. 2005. "Introduction: Mourning and Memory." *Comparative Studies of South Asia, Africa, and the Middle East* 25 (1): 16–29.

Savel'ev, Georgii. 1996a. "Kriminal'nye khroniki 'afganskikh' voin." *Segodnia,* November 11.

——. 1996b. "Vzryv na kladbishche unes trinadtsat' zhiznei." *Segodnia.* November 11.

Savitskii, Petr. 1997. "Geograficheskii obzor Rossii-Evrazii." In *Kontinent Evraziia,* 279–94. Moscow: Agraf.

Savvateeva, Irina. 1995. "President pokonchil s privilegiiami." *Izvestia,* March 10.

Schattschneider, Ellen. 2000. "My Mother's Garden: Transitional Phenomena on a Japanese Sacred Mountain." *Ethos* 28 (2): 147–73.

Scheppele, Kim Lane. 2006. "Guardian of the Constitution: Constitutional Court Presidents and the Struggle for the Rule of Law in Post-Soviet Europe." *University of Pennsylvania Law Review* 154: 1757–851.

Schleifman, Nurit. 2001. "Moscow's Victory Park: A Monumental Change." *History and Theory* 13 (2): 5–34.

Schröder, Ingo W., and Bettina Schmidt. 2001. "Introduction: Violent Imaginaries and Violent Practices." In *Anthropology of Violence and Conflict,* ed. B. Schmidt and I. W. Schröder, 1–25. London: Routledge.

Seabright, Paul, ed. 2000. *The Vanishing Rouble: Barter, Networks and Non-Monetary Transactions in Post-Soviet Society.* Cambridge: Cambridge University Press.

Seale, Clive. 1998. *Constructing Death: The Sociology of Dying and Bereavement.* Cambridge: Cambridge University Press.

Sedov, Leonid. 2003. "Rossiiskii elektorat: Desiatiletniaia evolutsiia." *Obshchestvennye nauki i sovremennost'* 10: 60–69.

Segal, Hanna. 1974. *Introduction to the Work of Melanie Klein.* New York: BasicBooks.

Semilet, Tamara. 2004. Kul'turvitalism—kontseptsiia zhiznennykh sil kul'tury. Barnaul: Altai State University.

——. 2003a "Teoretiko-metodologicheskie osnovaniia kul'turvitalistskoi kontseptsii v sotsiologii. In Grigor'ev and Gusliakova 2003, 63–75.

Semilet, Tamara, ed. 2003b. *Zhiznennye sily russkoi kul'tury: Puti vozrozhdeniia v Rossii nachala XX veka.* Moscow: Magister-Press.

——. 2001. *Zhiznennye sily slavianstva na rubezhe vekov i mirovozzrenii. Materialy mezhdunarodnogo kongressa.* Part 1. Barnaul.

Semykin, Ivan. 2002. "Syndrom 'gologo korolia.'" *Altaiskaia pravda,* October 29.

Senjkovic, Reana. 1993. "In the Beginning There Were a Coat of Arms, a Flag and a Pleter." In *Fear, Death and Resistance: An Ethnography of War, Croatia: 1991–1992,* ed. L. Feldman, I. Prica, and R. Senjkovic, 24–44. Zagreb: Institute of Ethnology and Folklore Research.

Seremetakis, C. Nadia. 1993. "Durations of Pain: The Antiphony of Death and Women's Power in Southern Greece." In *Ritual, Power and the Body: Historical Perspectives on the Representation of Greek Women,* ed. C. Nadia Seremetakis. New York: Pella Publishing Company.

——. 1991. *The Last Word: Women, Death and Divination in Inner Mani.* Chicago: University of Chicago Press.

Severo, Richard, and Lewis Milford. 1989. *The Wages of War: When America's Soldiers Came Home—From Valley Forge to Vietnam.* New York: Simon and Shuster.

Sevriukov, Valerii. 2005. "Kadry. Priglashen na glavnyi rol'." *Trud,* August 26.

Shaburkin, Aleksandr. 1997. "'Afgantsy' oprovergaiut obvineniia v svoi adres." *Nezavisimaia gazeta,* October 8.

Shafarevich, Igor. 2003. *Russkii vopros.* Moscow: Algoritm.

Shapiro, Margaret. 1995a. "Chechen Guerrillas Free Final Captives, Flee to Mountains; Yeltsin Is Roundly Criticized Over Handling of Hostage Crisis." *Washington Post.* June 21, A14.

Shaul'skaia, Marina. 1999. "I togda sozdalos' 'Bratstvo.'" In *My zhdali* vas, synov'ia...1999, 95 96.

Shchekochikhin, Iurii. 2003. *Zabytaia voina: Stranitsy iz voennykh bloknotov.* Moscow: Olimp.

Sherbak-Zhukov, Andrei. 2003. "Samye pokupaemye knigi ianvaria." *Argumenty i fakty,* no. 6: 21.

Shestopal, Elena. 2004. "Avtoritarnyi zapros na demokratiu." *Polis* 2: 25–28.

Shevchenko, Iu. 2002. "Iz vospominanii o L've Nikolaeviche Gumileve." In *Lev Nikolaevich Gumilev. Teoriia etnogeneza i istoricheskie sud'by Evrazii. Materialy konferentsii,* 1: 27–33. St. Petersburg: Evropeiskii Dom.

Shilling, Chris, and Phillip A. Mellor. 1998. "Durkheim, Morality and Modernity: Collective Effervescence, *Homo Duplex* and the Source of Moral Action." *British Journal of Sociology* 49 (2): 193–209.

Shirokogorov, Sergei. 1924. *Ethnical Unit and Milieu: A Summary of the Ethnos.* Shanghai: E. Evans and Sons.

——. 1923. *Etnos: Issledovanie osnovnykh printsipov izmeneniia etnicheskikh i etnograficheskikh iavlenii.* Shanghai.

Shishkov, Iu. 2001. "Smertnyi prigovor reformiruiusheisia Rossii." *Mirovaia ekonomika i mezhdunarodnye otnosheniia* 12: 115–20.

Shklovsky, Viktor. 2004. *A Sentimental Journey: Memoirs, 1917–1922.* Trans. Richard Sheldon. Ithaca: Cornell University Press.

Shlapentokh, Dmitry. 2007. "Dugin, Eurasianism, and Central Asia." *Communist and Post-Communist Studies* 40: 143–56.

Shnirelman, Viktor. 2006a. *Byt' alanom: Intellektualy i politiki na Severnom Kavkaze v XX veke.* Moscow: NLO.

——. 2006b. "Lev Gumilev: ot 'passionarnogo napriazheniia' do 'nesovmestimosti kul'tur.'" *Etnograficheskoe obozrenie* 3: 8–21.

——. 2006c. "Rossiiskaia shkola i natsional'naia ideia." *Neprikosnovennyi zapas* 6: 232–49.

Shpakova, Rimma. 2003. "Zavtra bylo vchera." *Sotsiologicheskoe obozrenie* 3 (3): 83–89.

Shumiatskaia, Ol'ga. 2005. "Apokalipsis vchera, segodnia, vsegda." *Moskovskie novosti,* September 30.

Simmel, Georg. 1978. *The Philosophy of Money.* Trans. Tom Bottomore and David Frisby. New York: Routledge.

Skidmore, Monique. 2003. "Darker Than Midnight: Fear, Vulnerability, and Terror Making in Urban Burma (Myanmar)." *American Ethnologist* 30 (1): 5–21.

Small, Christopher. 2001. "Why Doesn't the Whole World Love Chamber Music?" *American Music* 19: 340–59.

Smetanin, Dmitrii. 2005. "Neob"avlennaia voina." *Severnyi Kavkaz,* January 26.

Smirnov, O., ed. 1990. *Nikto ne sozdan dlia voiny.* Moscow: Molodaia Gvardia.

Soboleva, Svetlana, ed. 2000. *Faktory ustoichivosti malykh natsional'nykh grupp. Teoretiko-metodologicheskie i prikladnye voprosy issledovanii.* Novosibirsk: IEiOPP SO RAN.

Soldatov, Andrei, and Irina Borogan. 2004. "Razliv 'Mertvoi vody.'" *Moskovskie novosti,* March 19.

Solnik, Steven L. 1996. "The Political Economy of Russian Federalism. A Framework for Analysis." *Problems of Post-Communism,* November—December, 13–25.

Solovei, T. D. 2003. "Russkie mify v sovremennom kontekste." In *Bazovye tsennosti Rossiian: Sotsial'nye ustanovki. Zhiznennye strategii, Simvoly. Mify,* ed. O. Riabov and Kurbangaleeva E., 97–112. Moscow: Dom intellektual'noi knigi.

Solov'ev, Aleksandr. 2004. "Institutsional'nyi dizain rossiiskoi vlasti: Istoricheskii remeik ili matritsa razvitiia?" *Obshestvennye nauki i sovremennost'* 2: 64–76.

Solov'ev, Sergei. 1963. *Istoriia Rossii s drevneishikh vremen. V piatnadstati knigakh.* Vol. 2. Moscow: Izdatel'stvo sotsial'no-ekonomicheskoi literatury.

Solzhenitsyn, Aleksandr. 2003. "Potemshchiki sveta ne ishchut." *Literaturnaia gazeta,* no. 43: 3.

——. 2002. *Dvesti let vmeste. (1795–1995). Chast' II.* Moscow: Russkii put'.

——. 2001a. *Dvesti let vmeste. (1795–1995). Chast' 1.* Moscow: Russkii put'.

——. 2001b. "Nash dukh sil'nee gnetushchego bytia." *Argumenty i fakty,* January 24.

———. 1998a. "My perezhivaem tret'iu smutu." In *Tverskoi Solzhenitsynskii sbornik: K 80-letiu klassika russkoi literatury,* ed. V. Kuzmi and V. Yudin, 5–18. Tver: Tverskoi Gosuniversitet.

———. 1998b. *Rossiia v obvale.* Moscow: Russkii put'.

Solzhenitsyn, Aleksandr. 1995. *The Russian Question at the End of the Twentieth Century.* Trans. Yermolai Solzhenitsyn. New York: Farrar, Straus and Giroux.

Somov, Konstantin. 2001. "Dmitrii Kappes: Boi po pravilam." *Altaiskaia pravda,* April 28.

Sontag, Susan. 2003. *Regarding the Pain of Others.* New York: Picador.

Sovetskaia Rossiia. 2005. "Russkii krest kosnulsia detstva." May 31.

Spelman, Elisabeth. 1999. *Fruits of Sorrow: Framing Our Attention to Suffering.* Boston: Beacon Press.

Sperling, Valerie. 2003. "The Last Refuge of a Scoundrel: Patriotism, Militarism and the Russian National Idea." *Nations and Nationalism* 9 (2): 234–53.

Spivak, Gayatri Chakravorty. 1993. "An Interview with Sara Danius, Stefan Jonsson." *Boundary* 2 (2): 24–50.

Stacewicz, Richard. 1995. *Winter Soldiers: An Oral History of the Vetnam Veterans Against the War.* New York: Twayne Publishers.

Stewart, Kathleen. 1999. "Conspiracy Theory's Worlds." In *Paranoia within Reason: A Casebook on Conspiracy as Explanation,* ed. George E. Marcus, 12–21. Chicago: University of Chicago Press.

Subetto, Aleksandr. 2001. "Ideia kommunizma v XXI veke." In Semilet 2001, 63–66.

———. 1999. "Patrioticheskoe soznanie nachinaetsia s ponimaniia istorii svoei strany, svoego naroda." In Grigor'ev and Semilet 1999b, 10–17.

Sunlianskaia, Valentina. 2005. "Otpravliat' postradavshikh v Chechne za kompensatsiei k Basaevu—obychnaia praktika v Rossii." IA REGNUM News Agency. http://www.regnum.ru/news/389145.html.

Suny, Ronald Grigor. 1993. *The Revenge of the Past: Nationalism, Revolution, and the Collapse of the Soviet Union.* Stanford: Stanford University Press.

Svobodnyi kurs. 2004a. "Dannye po vyboram na Altae." March 15.

———. 2004b. "Vybory gubernatora Altaiskogo kraia hotiat sorvat'." April 3.

———. 2004c. "Vtorzhenie nachalos'?" April 3.

———. 2002a. "Prepodavatel' BGPU prizyvaet k vsenarodnomu tribunalu." October 17.

———. 2002b. "Primaia liniia: Gotov'sia v dal'niuiu dorogu, prizyvnik." November 7.

———. 2001. "Kak lechat 'chechenskii sindrom.'" January 18.

Tamarov, Vladislav. 1992. *Afghanistan: Soviet Vietnam.* San Francisco: Mercury House.

Tatum, James. 2004. *The Mourner's Song: War and Remembrance from the Iliad to Vietnam.* Chicago: University of Chicago Press.

Taussig, Michael T. 1980. *The Devil and Commodity Fetishism in South America.* Chapel Hill: University of North Carolina Press.

Theweleit, Klaus. 1989. *Male Fantasies.* Vol. 2, *Male Bodies: Psychoanalyzing the White Terror.* Minneapolis: University of Minnesota Press.

Thompson, James. 1996. *Models of Value: Eighteen-Century Political Economy and the Novel.* Durham, NC: Duke University Press.

Tishkov, Valerii. 2007. "Chto est' Rossiia i rossiiskii narod." *Pro et Contra* 11 (3): 21–41.

———. 2003. *Rekviem po etnosu: Issledovaniia po sotsial'no-kul'turnoi antropologii.* Moscow: Nauka.

———. 2001. *Obshchestvo v vooruzhennom konflikte (etnografiia chechenskoi voiny)*. Moscow: Nauka.

———. 1998. "U.S. and Russian Anthropology: Unequal Dialogue in a Time of Transition." *Current Anthropology* 39 (1): 1–7.

Tokmakov, Vladimir. 2002. "Za vernost' natsional'nym traditsiiam." *Altaiskaia pravda*, June 1.

Tolstaya, Tatiana. 2003. *Pushkin's Children: Writing on Russia and Russians*. Trans. Jamey Gambrell. Boston: Houghton Mifflin.

Toshenko, Zhan. 2002. "O poniatiinom apparate sotsiologii." *Sotsiologicheskie issledovaniia* 9: 3–16.

Trenin, Dmitry, and Aleksei Malashenko. 2004. *Russia's Restless Frontier: The Chechen Factor in Post-Soviet Russia*. Washington, DC: Carnegie Endowment for International Peace.

Tretiakova, Liubov'. 1999. "Chetyre raza gorel v tanke." In *My zhdali vas, synov'ia...* 1999, 24–26.

Troitskii, E., ed. 1997. *Natsional'nye interesy russkogo naroda i demograficheskaia situatsiia v Rossii*. Moscow: Shtrihkton.

Troshev, Gennadii. 2001. *Moia voina: Chechenskii dnevnik okopnogo generala*. Moscow: Vagrius.

Trotsky, Leo. 2004. *The Revolution Betrayed*. New York: Dover.

Tsintjilonis, Dimitri. 2004. "Words of Intimacy: Re-membering the Dead in Buntao." *Journal of Royal Anthropological Institute* 10: 375–93.

Tsirel', Sergei. 2003. "O mnimoi defektnosti russkoi prirody." *Novyi mir* 7: 182–87.

Tuchkova, Alla. 2000. "Ofitserskie zheny protiv soldatskikh materei." *Nezavisimoe voennoe obozrenie*, March 31.

Tumarkin, Nina. 1994. *The Living and the Dead: The Rise and Fall of the Cult of the World War II in Russia*. New York: Basic Books.

Turner, Victor. 1969. *The Ritual Process: Structure and Anti-Structure*. New York: Aldine.

"Ukaz Prezidenta Chechenskoi respubliki ot 9 dekabria 1991 g." 1997. In Eremenko and Novikov 1997, 34.

Umland, Andreas. 2003. "Formirovanie fashistskogo 'neoevraziiskogo' dvizheniia v Rossii. Put' Aleksandra Dugina ot marginal'nogo esktremista do vdokhnovitelia postsovetskoi akademicheskoi i politicheskoi elity." *Ab Imperio* 3: 289–304.

van der Kolk, Bessel, and Onno van der Hart. 1995. "The Intrusive Past: The Flexibility of Memory and the Engraving of Trauma." In Caruth 1995, 158–82.

Verdery, Katherine. 2000. "Privatization as Transforming Persons." In *Between Past and Future: The Revolutions of 1989 and Their Aftermath*, ed. Sorin Antohi and Vladimir Tismaneanu, 175–97. Budapest: Central European University Press.

———. 1999. *The Political Lives of Dead Bodies: Reburial and Postsocialist Change*. New York: Columbia University Press.

———. 1996. *What Was Socialism and What Comes Next?* Princeton: Princeton University Press.

Vernadskii, Vladimir. 1998. *The Biosphere*. Trans. David B. Langmuir. New York: Copernicus.

Veselov, Iurii, ed. 2004. *Ekonomika i sotsiologiia doveria*. St. Petersburg: Sotsiologicheskoe obshchestvo im. M. M. Kovalevskogo.

Viktor. 2004. "Kapitalizm—der'mo! Oni i My." *Pokolenie,* no. 17.

Vines, Alex.1998. "Disarmament in Mozambique." *Journal of Southern African Studies* 24 (1): 191–205.

Voinovich, Vladimir. 2002. *Portret na fone mifa.* Moscow: EKSMO.

Volkov, Vadim. 2002. *Violent Entrepreneurs: The Use of Force in the Making of Russian Capitalism.* Ithaca: Cornell University Press.

Voloshinov, Valentin. [1929] 1998. *Marxism and the Philosophy of Language.* Trans. L. Matejka and I. R. Titunik. Cambridge, MA: Harvard University Press.

von Hagen, Mark. 2004. "Empires, Borderlands, and Diasporas: Eurasia as Anti-Paradigm for the Post-Soviet Era." *American Historical Review* 109 (2): 445–68.

———. 1990. *Soldiers in the Proletarian Dictatorship: The Red Army and the Soviet Socialist State, 1917–1930.* Ithaca: Cornell University Press.

Voronkov, Viktor, Oksana Karpenko, and Aleksandr Osipov, eds. 2002. *Rasizm v iazyke sotsial'nykh nauk.* St. Petersburg: Aleteiia.

Vremia Novostei. 2004. "Ekho 'afganskikh' vzryvov." April 7.

Vtorzhenie v Rossiiu. 2003. Moscow: Eksprint.

Vygotsky, Lev, and Alexander Luria. [1934] 1994. "Tool and Symbol in Child Development." In *The Vygostky Reader,* ed. Rene van der Veer and Jaan Valsiner, 99–174. Oxford: Blackwell.

Wagner, Philip. 1991. "Geographical Reviews." *Geographical Review* 81(2): 323–24.

Walicki, Andrzej. 1979. *A History of Russian Thought from the Enlightenment to Marxism.* Trans. Hilda Andrews-Rusiecka. Stanford: Stanford University Press.

Walter, Tony. 1994. *The Revival of Death.* London: Routledge.

Waters, Anita. 1997. "Conspiracy Theories as Ethnosociologies: Explanation and Intention in African American Political Culture." *Journal of Black Studies* 28 (1): 112–25.

Wedel, Janine R. 2003. "Mafia without Malfeasance, Clans without Crime: The Criminality Conundrum in Post-Communist Europe." In *Crime's Power: Anthropologists and the Ethnography of Crime,* ed. P. Parnell and S. C. Kane. New York: Palgrave.

———. 1998a. *Collision and Collusion: The Strange Case of Western Aid to Eastern Europe 1989–1998.* New York: St. Martin's.

———. 1998b. "The Harvard Boys Do Russia." *Nation,* June 1.

Wegren, Stephen K. 2004. "The Communist Party of Russia: Rural Support and Implication for the Party System." *Party Politics* 10 (5): 565–82.

Weiner, Annette B. 1985. "Inalienable Wealth." *American Ethnologist* 12 (2): 210–27.

Welsh, Peter. 1997. "The Power of Possession: The Case Against Property." *Museum Anthropology* 21 (3): 12–18.

West, Harry G., and Todd Sanders, eds. 2003. *Transparency and Conspiracy: Ethnographies of Suspicion in the New World Order.* Durham, NC: Duke University Press.

Weston, Kath. 2001." Kinship, Controversy and the Sharing of Substance: The Race/Class Politics of Blood Transfusion." In *Relative Value: Reconfiguring Kinship Studies,* ed. Sarah Franklin and Susan McKinnon, 147–74. Durham, NC: Duke University Press.

Wheeler, L. Richmond. 1939. *Vitalism: Its History and Validity.* London: H.F. and G. Witherby Ltd.

White, James Boyd. 1985. *Herakles' Bow: Essays on the Rhetoric and Poetics of the Law.* Madison: University of Wisconsin Press.

White, Hayden. 1973. *Metahistory: The Historical Imagination in Nineteenth-Century Europe.* Baltimore: Johns Hopkins University Press.

Winnicott, D. W. 2000. "A Child Psychiatry Case Illustrating Delayed Reaction to Loss." In *Psychoanalytic Explorations,* ed. Clare Winnicott, Ray Shepherd, and Madeleine Davis, 341–68. Cambridge, MA: Harvard University Press.

——. 1971. *Playing and Reality.* New York: Routledge.

Winter, Jay. 1995. *Sites of Memory, Sites of Mourning: The Great War in European Cultural History.* Cambridge: Cambridge University Press.

Wittgenstein, Ludwig. 1958. *Philosophical Investigations.* Trans. G.E.M. Anscombe. New York: Macmillan.

Wong, Leonard, Thomas A. Kolditz, Raymond A. Millen, and Terence M. Potter. 2003. *Why They Fight: Combat Motivation in the Iraq War.* Carlisle Barracks, PA: Strategic Studies Institute, U.S. Army War College.

Wood, Tony. 2007. *Chechnya: The Case for Independence.* London: Verso.

Woodruff, David. 1999. *Money Unmade: Barter and the Fate of Russian Capitalism.* Ithaca: Cornell University Press.

"Yale Connection to Harvard Russian Fraud Case." 2000. *Yale Insider.* http://www.yaleinsider.org/article. Archived by *Johnson's Russia List,* 22 September 2002, #6450, http://www.cdi.org/russia/johnson/6450.cfm.

Yanov, Aleksandr. 2003. "Bor'ba s apatiei kak platforma liberalov." *Nezavisimaia gazeta,* January 14.

Young, Allan. 1997. "Suffering and the Origin of Traumatic Memory." In Kleinman, Das, and Lock 1997, 245–60.

Yurchak, Alexei. 2006. *Everything Was Forever, Until It Was No More: The Last Soviet Generation.* Princeton: Princeton University Press.

——. 2000. "Privatize Your Name: Symbolic Work in a Post-Soviet Linguistic Market." *Journal of Socioloinguistics* 4 (3): 406–34.

Zakharov, Aleksei. 2000. "Voennaia sluzhba: Napravlen v Chechniu—poluchi kompensatsiu." *Parlamentskaia gazeta,* September 20.

Zarinov I. Iu. 2003. "Issledovanie fenomenov 'etnosa' i 'etnichnosti': Nekotorye itogi i soobrazheniia." In Kozlov 2003, 18–36.

——. 2000. "Vremia iskat' obshchii iazyk (problema integratsii razlichnykh etnicheskikh teorii i kontseptsii)." *Etnograficheskoe obozrenie* 2: 3–18.

Zdravomyslov, Andrei. 1999. *Sotsiologiia rossiiskogo krizisa.* Moscow: Nauka.

Zhdakaev, Sergei. 2005. "Veteran chechenskoi voiny pytaetsia vzyskat' ushcherb s Basaeva i Maskhadova." *Izvestiia,* January 13.

Zhembrovskii, Aleksandr. 2003. "Iz boevogo zhurnala." In Gordin and Grigor'ev 2003, 235–44.

Zhurzhenko, Tat'iana. 2004. "Staraia ideologiia novoi sem'i: Demograficheskii natsionalism Rossii i Ukrainy." In *Semeinye uzi: Modeli dlia sborki,* ed. Serguei Oushakine, 1: 268–96. Moscow: NLO Press.

Zinoviev, Aleksandr. 2002. *Russkaia tragediia (gibel' utopii).* Moscow: Algoritm.

——. 1985. *Homo Sovieticus.* Trans. Charles Janson. New York: Atlantic Monthly Press.

——. 1979. *The Yawning Heights.* Trans. Gordon Clough. New York: Random House.

Ziuzin, Sergei. 2000. "Posle Chechni nashi parni b'iutsia za svoi 'boevye.'" *Svobodnyi kurs,* November 23.

Žižek, Slavoj. 2001. Did Somebody Say Totalitarianism?: Four Interventions in the (Mis)use of a Notion. London: Verso.

Zorin, Iaroslav. 2005. "Veterany Chechenskoi voiny posovetovali sudit'sia s Basaevym i Maskhadovym." *Gazeta,* January 12.

Zubtsov, Iurii. 1994. "Ne v svoi sani? Solzhenytsin kak telezveda." *Argumenti i fakty,* October 19.

Zvereva, Galina. 2002. "'Rabota dlia muzhchin'? Chechenskaia voina v massovom kino Rossii." *Neprikosnovennyi zapas* 26. http://magazines.russ.ru/nz/2002/6/zver.html.

Index

ethnovitalism, 85, 115–29, 139
etnos, 81, 118, 119, 127. *See* Shirokogorov
etnosphere, 92, 127
etnos theory in the USSR, 81–95; and its
    post-Soviet interpretations, 82–83, 85,
    106–9, 111–13, 124, 126. *See* Bromley;
    Gumilev
Eurasianism, 90, 92–93; and Eurasian civili-
    zation, 127–28. *See* Savitskii
Evangelista, Matthew, 139n7
Evdokimov, Mikhail, 63–67, 121
Ewing, Katherine Pratt, 13
exceptionality, 60, 62; 117n48, 183–84, 187,
    252. *See* inconvertibility
exchange of sacrifices, 138, 165, 174, 184,
    185–86, 192, 236
exclusion, 12, 186, 250, 257

Faubion, James, 128
Feitlowitz, Marguerite, 251n28
Feldman, Allen, 208,
Ferme, Mariane, 244
Filippov, Vasilii, 48, 84, 109–15, 117, 124
Flatley, Jonathan, 224, 232n20
foreign currency, 24, 25, 60–61
"foreign influence", 13, 15–19, 47, 49, 99,
    255–56; and NGOs, 112, 154, 213–14
Foucault, Michel, 38, 45, 83
fragging, as a controlling device, 160, 193
fragmentation, 68, 76, 207; of public space,
    19–21; and symbolization, 69, 75–76, 81,
    156, 195–96, 236; of transactional system,
    25–26. *See* splitting
Freud, Sigmund, 226
funeral customs, 11, 209, 227–29, 231, 243–
    44, 246–47. *See* graves
funeral letters (*pokhoronki*), 133, 153, 240, 245

Gaddy, Clifford G., 59, 61
Gaidar, Yegor, 15, 24–25, 33, 47n35, 60n44,
    91n44, 131. *See* kamikaze team
Gal, Susan, 246
Gaudilliere, Jean-Max, 225n14
Gazmanov, Oleg, 36n24, 199
Geertz, Clifford, 162
geographical determinism, 58–59, 78, 93,
    128; and collectivity, 61–62; and ethnic
    development, 89–96; 127; and Russian
    economy, 59–62. *See* Parshev
geopolitics: and cold war, 71; and the collapse
    of the USSR, 79–80. *See* Eurasianism
Giard, Luce, 244

good death, 228
Gorbachev, Mikhail, 31, 123, 141–42, 259
Goux, Jean-Joseph, 49, 50, 51, 236
Graeber, David, 174
Grant, Bruce, 232n20
graves: cultural importance of, 48, 57,
    209–10, 227–34, 246. *See* reburials
Great Patriotic War, 36n25, 179n49; decon-
    textualization of, 191, 194–96; and post-
    Soviet identity, 36, 52–53, 62, 193, 243; as a
    tool of mediation, 54–55, 196
Green, André, 5, 79, 207, 234. *See* work of the
    negative
grief, 7, 119, 213, 250, 251n27, 253; univer-
    sality of, 219, 253. *See* memorialization
Grigor'ev, Sviatoslav, 118–28
Grozny: the New Year's Eve storming of, 33,
    144–45
Gudkov, Lev, 84, 114n46, 138, 179n49
Gumilev, Lev, 86, 89–94, 100, 107, 111,
    125–26, 127
Guriev, Sergei, 26, 27

Hallam, Elisabeth, 237
Harding, Susan, 15, 74
Harrison, Simon, 21, 50, 51n39
Heidegger, Martin, 207n5
Hemment, Julie, 209n6, 212
Hesford, Wendy, 253n29
Hesmondhalgh, David, 250
Hidalgo, Stephen, 160
"hidden forces", 5, 7, 21, 43, 47, 67, 98
Hill, Fiona, 59, 61
Hirsch, Francine, 10, 31n3, 82n6, 86
history: alternative versions of, 35, 41, 53,
    194, 197, 207, 231; ethnohistories, 81–83,
    89, 94, 96–98, 108, 256–57; national, 5, 55,
    57, 90
Hockey, Jenny, 237
holocaust: moral, 23, 76; Russian, 89, 103
Hosking, Geoffrey, 97
Humphrey, Caroline, 8, 27, 51, 114, 184n54,
    245
Hynes, Samuel, 131n3, 164, 187n57, 195

Ickes, Barry W., 26, 27
identity, Russian, 7, 10–11, 120, 138, 179n49,
    249
ideology and state, 2, 45, 47, 103, 132, 158,
    191; ideological hailing (interpellation),
    162–63, 172, 191, 220, 243
inalienable property, 21–22, 50–51, 126